Echoes
from Lane Field

A History of the San Diego Padres 1936-1957

This book is dedicated to the men who played baseball at Lane Field and their families and fans who loved them...

by
Bill Swank

TURNER PUBLISHING COMPANY
Paducah, Kentucky

TURNER PUBLISHING COMPANY

Publishers of America's History

412 Broadway•P.O. Box 3101

Paducah, Kentucky 42002-3101

(502) 443-0121

Publisher's Editor: Bill Schiller

Author: Bill Swank

Designer: David Hurst

Cover Design: Herbert C. Banks II

Publishing Rights: Turner Publishing Company

Library of Congress Catalog No. 98-89788

ISBN: 1-56311-497-6

LIMITED EDITION

Printed in the U.S.A.

ECHOES FROM LANE FIELD

A History of the San Diego Padres (1936-1957)

TABLE OF CONTENTS

PUBLISHER'S MESSAGE

Dave Turner, President

Turner Publishing takes great pride in presenting this book to the people of San Diego as well as baseball fans across the nation. In today's reality, Baseball is more than just a game-it is an institution which factors heavily in the political, industrial, and socio-economic concerns of our community. The game, like the players, has changed over the years, but one thing has remained constant . . . baseball's power to unite people from different backgrounds and various stations in life for a common cause . . . to cheer for the home team.

Our work began early in the 1998 baseball season, well before anyone predicted that the present San Diego team would win the National League Championship or play in the World Series. We followed their season closely, paid extra attention to Padres outfielder Steve Finley, one of our local boys from Paducah, Kentucky. We cheered the wins, lamented the losses and took some comfort in the knowledge that there are no losers in the World Series. It is the pinnacle of the game, solely for winners.

San Diego established a reputation for producing winners over sixty years ago, with the dawn of Lane Field and rise of the Pacific Coast League. Time and nature often collide in pragmatic fashion, however. The ball park and the League each had their day but the sun set too soon. Only a few may recall that one of Baseball's greatest sluggers, Ted Williams, once wore a Padres uniform. Fewer yet may recall Saturnino Orestes Armas-Arrieta . . . known to thousands of fans as Minnie Minoso. And there are more examples . . . players like Max West, Jack Graham, Al Rosen and Baseball Hall of Famer Bobby Doerr, all were considered as Padres at various stages in their careers. Read between the lines of their stories and you will hear the love for a sport and the level of sportsmanship which tends to get obscured in today's world of contract negotiations and commercial endorsements. This book is an account of those men who helped set a standard that future players could meet, and maybe, even beat.

Though it has been a team effort to produce this book, the MVP award goes to Bill Swank. Motivated only by his personal admiration for the game, history, the players and the fans in San Diego, Bill spent unmeasurable time and energy in finding, interviewing and recording the tales of those Lane Field Padres who appear in the following pages. Having been familiar with our work on the Louisville Diamonds and SABR (Society for American Baseball Research), Bill recognized that we shared some of the same interests. We recognized his work as a homerun. Nothing left, but to round the bases and on that note, it is only fitting to remember that the original echoes from Lane Field were essentially the sound of cheers .... for the players and for that most American of past-times . . . Baseball.

Dave Turner, President
Turner Publishing Company

A History of the San Diego Padres (1936-1957)

Author's Notes

*I*n 1993, Bill Kinsella and his wife, Ann Knight, told me about their rotisserie baseball team, the "Memo Lunatics." They were surprised I knew that Memo Luna played for the St. Louis Cardinals... and the PCL Padres. With the help of Bill Deane at the Baseball Hall of Fame, I found Memo living in Mexico. To commemorate the quest, Ann wrote the following poem.

Opening Day

"Batter up!" *Dónde está Memo Luna?*
Where is Billy Moon, least heat pitcher
of the '54 Cardinals? (In two-thirds
of an inning, Memo racked up a lifetime
earned run average of twenty-seven.)
They printed his baseball card before
his hour upon the stage: "No major league
experience," it proclaims. Prob'ly better.

Finding him, could parallel J.D.'s search
for Moonlight Graham (whose baseball record
was perfected on a Field of Dreams.)
Memo is the reincarnation of that diurnal
quest, a longing to recall the notes
of a song no one's heard in fifty years:
"Happy landings to you, Amelia Earhart,
farewell, first lady of the air.

"Strike three." Our research concludes quickly. *Luna*
está en Los Mochis (an industrial seaport town one
unpredictably-scheduled ferry ride across from Baja
to the mainland.) We can make the trip next winter,
collect Memo's signature, smile. No mystery is left
to us. We know. But as spring training ends, I relish
having cared enough to learn where one Mexican
baseball legend lays his head, *this* opening day.
reprinted with permission

I had no idea that finding Memo Luna would evolve into the search for every Padre who ever played at old Lane Field. In October of 1994, Frank Kern, the curator at the San Diego Hall of Champions, told me about the Pacific Coast League exhibition that was coming to the San Diego Historical Society Museum in Balboa Park. They wanted someone to do an accompanying article about the PCL Padres for their journal.

Frank introduced me to James D. Smith III. Jim had interviewed several great ballplayers from the Lane Field era, including Ted Williams and Bobby Doerr. In the meantime, I located several players. We incorporated their oral histories into an article entitled, "This was Paradise." In April of 1995, the Historical Society hosted a wonderful reunion for the players in conjunction with the opening of their exhibit, "Runs, Hits and an Era."

Former Padre second baseman Pete Coscarart had introduced me to Ray Brandes, who was then occupied in writing a history of the PCL Padres. Ray invited me to work with him and encouraged me to track down the players from the Lane Field years. Our combined efforts became a two-volume set published by the San Diego Padres Baseball Club in 1997. Since the set is not readily available to the general public, I resolved to produce this additional book to share the history, memories, interviews, photographs and statistics with those who loved the original Padres.

The average fan will be surprised by how many of the ballplayers he recognizes. For several players, San Diego was a rail stop on a journey up to the major leagues. For others, it was a haven on their way back down. The experience was also the zenith for many ballplayers whose stories are seldom heard. They all remember San Diego as a good place to play ball, because of the good weather, lifestyle and fans. The Coast League was unique and the 22 years the Padres played at cozy Lane Field spanned a dynamic period in San Diego history.

The players I talked to were pleased to be remembered and willingly shared their love for the game. Although their salaries become pale when compared with those demanded by today's players, none of them would relinquish the fun and camaraderie he had with old teammates. Lane Field was a friendly and intimate ballpark. The players and fans interacted with one another. These were men who understood that they were heroes to the kids. They made themselves accessible and signed autographs gladly. Nothing makes an old-timer more angry than the thought that modern ballplayers charge kids for autographs.

Many of the Lane Field Padres have passed away, but baseball remains important to their families. Wives, children and grandchildren were delighted to provide stories about their husbands, fathers and grandfathers. As a result of this project, old friends are again in contact with one other. There have been subsequent get-togethers, but the largest and best was the Lane Field Reunion hosted by Padres owner John Moores in September 1997. I finally got to meet Memo and many other out-of-town friends who had been interviewed by telephone.

Interestingly, many players did not even have pictures of themselves. Photographs have been graciously provided by many people and copies of these were sent to the players and their families. Special thanks for help with pictures is given to Al Hogan, Dick Dobbins, John Spalding, Bob Dreher, Rich Faber, Jim Smith, Paul Madigan, Mel Zeddies, Jim Fuller, Bud Relyea, Bob Shumake, Frank Kern and Don King at the San Diego Hall of Champions.

The players and their family members who generously shared photographs include Jack Graham, Charlene Mesner, Gene Leek, Bill Glynn, Tony Criscola, Pete Coscarart, Opal Seats, Jan Rice, Mel Mazzera, Donna Saucedo, Ruth Clay, Dick Faber, Whitey Wietelmann, Mary Olsen, Mel Skelley, Bill Skelley, Ed Stewart, Ed Erautt, Bob Kerrigan, Autumn Keltner, Lou Vezilich, John Henry Williams, George Zuverink, Eleanor Doerr, Larry and Tina Hernandez. Many others contributed their individual pictures to the project.

Numerous others assisted in a variety of ways: Wade Cline, Seymour Prell, Paul Maracin, Bill Capps, Rich Nelson, Bill Dunne, Chuck Primeau, Pete Grijalva, Ed Olson, Norm Syler, Jeff Frank, Kevin Kernan, Todd Tobias, Jose Rodriguez, Bud Maloney, Bob Ottilie, Sue Jensen, Ray Crawford, Norm & Al Lubke, Ruby Caldwell, Pete Tapia, Shawn Harp, Jennifer McIntyre, Skip Wills, Bill Ohler, George Bergmeister, Mary Edwina Dluhy, Dick Beverage, Joseph Schaeffer III, Roger Pena, Joe Moore, Earl Keller and my son, Billy Swank. Thank you all...

Think of this book as a reunion and imagine the players are speaking directly to you. Do you have any questions you would like to ask them? I have attempted to make this book as accurate as possible. If you find any mistakes, they belong in the box score as E - Swank. Please send questions, comments and errors to:

Bill Swank
3474 Via Beltran
San Diego, CA 92117

INTRODUCTION

The breeze that once carried baseballs from Lane Field onto Pacific Highway still blows in from San Diego Harbor. Today, it teases a discarded paper-cup that rolls aimlessly between silent cars in a parking lot. This nondescript property located at the corner of Broadway and Pacific Highway was the birthplace of the San Diego Padres.

This book contains the golden memories of the men who played at Lane Field from 1936 through 1957. The origins of the Padres began far from San Diego with H.W. "Hardrock" Bill Lane, who made his fortune in the gold fields of Alaska and the Yukon. A former semi-pro ballplayer, he also scouted and managed baseball teams at the various mining sites. In 1911, Lane and his fellow investors created the Salt Lake City ball club in the newly formed Union Association. This league folded three years later, but Lane's organization rescued the original San Francisco Mission franchise of the Pacific Coast League and moved it to the Utah capital for the 1915 season.

Renamed the Bees, Salt Lake enjoyed modest success on the ballfield, but Lane could only survive by selling his top players to the big leagues. Earl Sheely, who would average .300 in "those Eastern Leagues," was his first star. San Diego's first major league ballplayer, Gavy Cravath, who set the modern major league season (24) and career (119) home run records which were later broken by Babe Ruth, managed the Bees in 1921. The baseball season was a long one in the PCL and remarkable records could be made. In 1923, Paul Strand established an all-time record for organized baseball with 325 base hits in the course of a 200 game schedule. In 1925, Tony Lazzeri, aided by the thin desert air, obliterated the Coast League home run

record with 60 circuit blows and was promptly dispatched to the New York Yankees. "Hardrock" recognized the limited growth potential of Salt Lake City and was aware of the complaints of the other franchise owners about the cost of transportation to that distant destination. The prospector began to look elsewhere.

When the Vernon Tigers abandoned the Los Angeles area in 1926 and reappeared as the new San Francisco Mission ball club, Lane pulled up stakes and headed for the Golden State. The Bees became the Hollywood Stars and, capitalizing on the popular Rudolph Valentino silent film character of the era, they were dubbed the Sheiks. Without a ballpark of their own, the Hollywood team was forced to share newly constructed Wrigley Field with the long ensconced Los Angeles Angels.

In 1928, as the result of a mix-up, the Stars unexpectedly became the first baseball club to travel by air. The

1913 Salt Lake City Club.

Opening Day Lane Field, March 31, 1936.

ECHOES FROM LANE FIELD

franchise soon developed into a perennial pennant contender and won the league championship in 1930. The ace of the Hollywood mound staff was Frank Shellenback, who surely would have been a big leaguer but for his spitball, which was an illegal pitch in the major leagues. The Sheiks also featured Coast League legends Cleo Carlyle, Emil Yde, Smead Jolley and Johnny Bassler. Except for Carlyle, all of these players would leave their mark in the big leagues.

As the economic depression continued, the Stars struggled and plummeted into the cellar during the second half of the 1935 season. Attendance was dropping while Wrigley Field management wanted to double the rent to $10,000 a year. Facing decreased revenue and increased expenses, the old miner resumed his search for a new claim.

In January of 1936, while others scoffed at his interest in a small border city, Bill Lane reached a tentative agreement with city and harbor officials to relocate his ball club to San Diego. His only condition was a suitable ballpark at a reasonable rent. The season opener was set for March 31, 1936. Could a ballpark be built in two short months?

Since San Diego's venerable Balboa Stadium could not be reconfigured with adequate dimensions for a Class AA diamond, Sports Field at the foot of Broadway was selected as the site for the new ball yard. The right field line at Sports Field, which ran parallel to Harbor Street, would become the left field line at Lane Field. Home plate was moved from the northwest corner of the location to the southwest corner adjacent to the Harbor Department building at the intersection of Broadway and Harbor Drive. The land for the new ballpark, dredged from San Diego Bay, was the property of the Harbor Department.

Lane signed an agreement with the Harbor Commission on January 28, 1936 to pay rent of $3,000 in each of the first three years, $3,500 in the fourth year and $4,000 for the final year of the lease. Construction costs were estimated at $25,000. An application was made to the Works Progress Administration for federal assistance to finance the project. In a fine example of cooperation between different government agencies, construction on the 8,000 seat stadium began immediately.

A contest was held to rename the team. Dons, Flyers, Gobs, Blues, Balboas, Friars, Tars, Skippers, Gaels, Tunas, Gorillas, Vaqueros, Pilots, Aviators, Twilers, Giants, Don Juans and Sandies were all suggested. Eight people submitted the name "Padres," which was an immediate hit with the fans and sportswriters who appreciated the tribute to San Diego's early history.

Ironically, Lane's team opened the 1936 season at Wrigley Field and lost the game to their former landlord. On March 31st, they came home to engage the Seattle Indians in the inaugural contest by the bay. Although the backstop and grandstand roof had not yet been installed, 8,178 paying customers roared approval as Herm "Old Folks" Pillette and the Padres registered a 6-2 victory. The new San Diego Padres finished their first season in a tie for

Vince DiMaggio

Sports Field, pre-1936.

second place with Oakland, a game and a half behind the Portland Beavers. The enthusiasm and loyalty of their fans was the surprise of the Pacific Coast League, since the year's attendance was an astounding 178,075 in a city of only 165,000 inhabitants. At the end of the season, future Hall of Famer Bobby Doerr (who hit .342) and Gene Desautels (.319) were sold to the Boston Red Sox. Vince DiMaggio (.293, 19 home runs) went to the Boston Braves and a skinny young outfield prospect named Ted Williams returned to Herbert Hoover High School to complete his senior year.

216,870 tickets were purchased by cheering fans as the Padres claimed their first league playoff championship in 1937. George Detore won the league batting title with a .3341 average and Ted Williams led the team with 23 home runs. Rupert Thompson smacked five playoff home runs as each of four pitchers (Manuel Salvo, Wally Hebert, Jim Chaplin and Dick Ward) hurled a pair of complete games and the Padres swept Sacramento and Portland in the Shaughnessey playoffs. San Diego made more money than any other team in the circuit. Lane had finally struck pay dirt. "The Kid" (Ted Williams) was sold to the Red Sox and George Myatt went to the New York Giants.

Although the Padres fell to fifth place the next year, both Manny Salvo and Jim Chaplin became 20 game winners while Byron Humphreys led the PCL with a 2.33 ERA. On August 30th, Dick Ward threw 12-2/3 innings of no-hit ball in a 1-0 victory over Los Angeles, a game which lasted 16 innings. This was to be Bill Lane's final game. He suffered a stroke that night and died on October 9, 1938.

In 1939, veteran Cedric Durst replaced Frank Shellenback as manager of the scrappy Padres, but San Diego remained in fifth place, 19 games behind Seattle. Two factors contributed to the second division finish: Pitching ace Jim Chaplin was killed in an automobile accident in National City just prior to the start of spring training and the executors of Lane's estate were unable to obtain new talent to challenge the league's top teams. On the positive side, Dominic Dallessandro led the Coast League in batting with a .368 mark. Wally Hebert won 20 games while George Detore and Mickey Haslin hit .355 and .345, respectively. Local high school products Al Olsen and Johnny "Swede" Jensen joined the ball club and both would become popular, long-term Padres.

San Diego was dismissed as a contender for the 1940 season, but their newly acquired shortstop, Steve Mesner, ignited the locals to a respectable fourth place finish. Heber Newsome went 23-11 and Mesner batted .341 to be selected as the team's MVP. The turnstiles clicked to the highest level since 1937, but 60,000 of the Padres' best fans were "somewhere in the Pacific." The fleet was out of port with the threat of war on the horizon. Throughout

L-R: Hal Patchett, Howard Craghead, Frank Shellenback, George Myatt, Ted Williams, unk., Bill Lane, 1937.

War time billboard, Lane Field.

Lane Field with new roof, 1937

the Lane Field years, the Navy would always provide boisterous support for their neighbors on Lower Broadway.

Behind the brilliant pitching of Yank Terry (26-8) and Wally Hebert (22-10), the Padres vaulted to third place in 1941, 4-1/2 games behind Seattle. Terry's 2.31 earned run average was also the league's lowest, earning him most valuable player honors for the PCL. September 19th was Wally Hebert Night. Teammates gave "Preacher" $104 for each Padre victory he had recorded since 1936. Fans presented him with a live chicken and a Louisiana catfish, as Mrs. Hebert's Southern cooking and hospitality were widely known and appreciated.

Although the country was at war in 1942, President Franklin D. Roosevelt decreed that baseball should continue because of its function as a morale booster for servicemen and defense workers. On August 4th, with two outs in the 4th inning of a game against Sacramento, eight consecutive Padres: Jack Calvey, Hal Patchett, John Hill, Mel Mazzera, George Detore, Bill Salkeld, John Jensen and Mel Skelley, hit safely to produce a PCL record for consecutive hits and a team record of 13 runs in a single inning. Mel Mazzera Day was celebrated on August 30th to honor the popular outfielder. The Padres finished the year in fourth place, four games above .500, but 14 games behind the Sacramento Solons.

In 1943, an abbreviated 155 game schedule saw San Diego drop to seventh place. Larry Powell had become the first Padre to be drafted the previous year and several players were now in military service. The Lane estate remained unsettled and the front office was in disarray. Former PCL pitching standout and trusted Lane confidant Charles "Spider" Baum was ousted as club secretary. On August 10th, with the club struggling some thirty games out of first place, Ced Durst resigned as manager and was replaced by George Detore, who also functioned as player/manager. George McDonald batted .330 for the season and established the team's all-time fielding average (.996) for first basemen. Detore hit .321 and Eddie Wheeler had a .304 average to go with only 3 home runs which tied John Jensen for the team lead. (Swede had departed for the Army Air Forces after 49 games.)

San Diego was bursting with service personnel and defense workers in 1944. A new season attendance record was set as 246,150 fans doubled the club's 1943 total in spite of the fact that the Padres had descended into the league's basement. Management was challenged to find players to fill a roster depleted by the requirements of military duty and the major leagues. 16 year-old Hank Sciarra signed with San Diego and found it necessary to sleep on tables and desks in the Lane Field office. Rex Cecil struck out 16 Rainers in a losing effort on April 18th, but four days later, hit a home run in the 12th inning to beat Seattle, 1-0. Fireballing Frankie Dasso won 20 games. A savior was found when former Padre catcher Bill Starr formed a syndicate that purchased the club from the Lane estate at the end of the season. Expectations were high that new ownership would translate into success on the playing field.

Starr's first move for 1945 was to hire former St. Louis Cardinal "Gashouse Gang" member Pepper Martin to manage the club. In a major shuffle, original Padre George McDonald was traded to Seattle. Lou Vezilich led the Pacific Coast League with 110 RBIs while pitchers Carl Dumler and Vallie Eaves each won 21 games. Starr had rescued Eaves from the drunk tank after the owner learned the big, likable Indian threw "smoke." Dick Gyselman hit .321 and Tony Criscola swiped 40 bases to complement his .311 batting average. San Diego improved to sixth place in the PCL as the war ended and season attendance registered another huge increase to 346,057. Manuel Hernandez, the youthful starting left fielder on Opening Day of 1944, tragically became the only Padre killed in action while engaging the enemy in Germany on March 22, 1945.

Padres snap L.A.'s 19 game win streak, April 22, 1939.

1946 saw the Pacific Coast League granted a new AAA designation. Returning military veterans, including baseball players, were promised re-instatement to their pre-war jobs. With an over abundance of talent in the game, players now passed through San Diego even faster than during the war years. Johnny Jensen led the team with a .300 batting average. Aged Vern Kennedy, who tossed a no-hitter for the White Sox in 1935, won 18 games and Lefty Al Olsen added 17 victories. Former Dodger All-Star second baseman Pete Coscarart of Escondido came home to join the club. Jack Lohrke was called up to the Padres from Spokane at mid-season. Shortly after he stepped off the Spokane team bus, the bus was caught in a rainstorm and went off a mountain road. Nine young ballplayers were killed in the worst accident in the history of organized baseball.

"Rip" Collins, a "Gashouse Gang" teammate of Pepper Martin, took over the Padre helm in 1947. San Diego had a good hitting club (Dain Clay .313, John Jensen .307, Max West .306 and Frank Kerr .300) with weak pitching. The top mound performance was delivered by Tom Seats (17-17). Although West led the league with 43 home runs and 124 runs batted in, the Padres were back in the cellar. During one stretch, San Diego lost 13 straight games. Attendance increased to 353,951, but fans were grumbling about the team's fifth consecutive finish in the lower division. Undaunted, Bill Starr spearheaded an effort to have the PCL recognized as a third major league. He viewed Balboa Park as a potential site for his new ballpark. Rumors abounded that San Diego would enter a working agreement with the New York Yankees. Speculation was that Yankee owner Del Webb would be awarded a contract to build the new Padre stadium.

John Ritchey, a local high school, American Legion and San Diego State College star, led the Negro American League with a .381 batting average in 1947. When Bill Starr signed Ritchey to a Padre contract for 1948 the "color barrier" was broken in the Pacific Coast League. Johnny responded with a .323 batting average. The most exciting newcomer was Jack Graham, who had already hit 46 home runs by July 25th. On that date the big slugger was unintentionally hit in the head by a pitch from Angel hurler Red Adams when Graham lost the ball in the late afternoon shadows of Wrigley Field. The Padres' challenge for first place took a nose dive to seventh place without Graham's productive bat in the lineup. Courageously, Jack returned to the club late in the season and was selected as the league's MVP. The Padres leading hurler was Xavier Rescigno (18-12), who conversed with God while working on the mound. John Barrett led the club with a .339 batting average. In December, Bill Starr and the Padres entered a working agreement with Bill Veeck and the World Champion Cleveland Indians.

![Lefty O'Doul congratulates Jack Graham after another home run.]

Lefty O'Doul congratulates Jack Graham after another home run.

Future Hall of Fame manager Bucky Harris guided the fence bustin' Padres during the '49 campaign. 192 home runs were hit in the course of the season. In 80 games, before being called up by the Tribe, a very large 34-year old rookie named Luke Easter knocked in 92 runs while blasting 25 home runs and hitting for a .363 average. Jack Graham had been sold to the St. Louis Browns, but Max West returned for his signal career season by leading the loop with 48 home runs, 166 RBIs and a PCL record 201 free passes to first base. Minnie Minoso added 22 circuit blows and was followed by Buster Adams (21), Harvey Storey (17) and Al Rosen (14). A fourth place finish was the Padres first winning season since 1942. Jesse Flores topped the pitching staff with a 21-10 record and 3.03

Dan Clay, Max West, John Barrett, Jess Flores, Gene Thompson.

ECHOES FROM LANE FIELD

earned run average. 493,780 patrons came to watch baseballs fly out of Lane Field.

Del Baker became manager for the 1950 campaign as San Diego continued to play long ball. Jack Graham was back. He and newcomer Harry "Suitcase" Simpson each hit 33 home runs. Simpson also drove in 156 runs, tops for the league. Max West pounded out 30 four-baggers and Minnie "The Cuban Comet" Minoso added 20 round-trippers along with his team high .339 batting average. Both Al Olsen and George Zuverink notched 20 pitching victories. Roy Welmaker's 16-10 record was the club's best winning percentage (.615) and "Red" Embree had the lowest ERA (3.32). This balance of pitching and hitting lifted the team into a second place finish with a record of 114-86, and for the third consecutive season attendance figures exceeded 400,000. The fans clearly loved their powerhitting Padres, but like breezes off the bay, the winds of change were blowing.

Baker spoke optimistically about the Padres' chances in 1951, but most of his young talent had moved up to the majors and San Diego sank to sixth place. West was dispatched to Los Angeles and Graham went to San Francisco. After 44 games with the Seals, Jack returned to San Diego to hit 30 home runs and finish the year with 105 RBIs. Bobby Wilson's modest .268 was the highest batting average on the club for a regular, although Clarence Maddern hit a respectable .311 in limited action (99 games) following the ill-advised West trade. En route to a 16-13 season, "Toothpick Sam" Jones registered a 2.76 ERA with a league leading 246 strikeouts. Season attendance tumbled to 217,102.

The Pacific Coast League achieved significant recognition for potential major league status with the new designation of "open" classification in 1952. The American Association

and the International League retained their AAA classification. After 17 seasons with the San Francisco Seals, colorful Frank "Lefty" O'Doul became the new San Diego skipper. Unsuccessful as a pitcher, he returned to the major leagues as an outfielder during the Twenties and compiled a lifetime .349 batting average. Lefty was one of the game's great ambassadors and annually toured Japan with big league stars during the off-season. Years later, when asked to name the best manager in baseball, Casey Stengel replied, "That feller out there in Frisco." Southpaw Memo Luna led the team with 15 victories while surrendering only 2.94 earned runs per game. Bennett Flowers went 11-10. In his final season with the Padres, Jack Graham led the club in most offensive categories including home runs (22). San Diego closed the season in fifth place and could attract only 168,617 fans to Lane Field.

The 1953 Padres duplicated their 88-92 record of the previous year, but slipped to sixth place in the final league standings. Outfielder Earl "Buddy" Rapp led the team

Bob Kerrigan is carried off the field after Padres win championship game, 7-2.

Lefty O'Doul

with 24 home runs and a .311 batting average with support from first baseman Tom Alston who hit .297 and poked 23 home runs. Crafty Memo Luna (17-12) posted the lowest earned run average (2.67) in the Coast League. Shortstop Buddy Peterson and second baseman Al Federoff formed one of the best keystone combinations in Padre history.

1954 proved to be a year of destiny for the Padres. Lefty Bill Wight (17-5) led the league and set the all-time team record with a stingy 1.93 earned run average. Bob Kerrigan (17-11), Ed Erautt (16-12) and Lloyd Dickey (14-11) rounded out a fine pitching staff. The team batting average (.276) was best in the PCL. Harry Elliott's .350 average topped the league and Earl Rapp was second with .337 and 24 home runs. Dick Sisler (.318), Milt Smith (.294), Buddy Peterson (.289), Walt Pocekay (.281), Al Federoff (.279) and Luke Easter (.278) all wielded potent lumber. Dramatically, the outcome of the season hinged on a single playoff game at Lane Field against the Hollywood Stars. This would decide the championship. A gutsy pitching performance by Bob Kerrigan and a pair of key home runs from third-sacker Bob Elliott highlighted a 7-2 San Diego victory over Tinseltown. After 17 years, the Padres were once again the Pacific Coast League champions.

Lefty returned to the Bay Area for the next season and was replaced as manager by Bob Elliott, the hero of the

'54 playoff game. The Padres started fast in 1955. In May, the team captured ten straight games before dropping a 5-2 decision to Hollywood. A victory the next day heralded the start of a record setting 15 game winning streak. Milt Smith hit .338 for the year, followed by Buddy Peterson (.306) and Eddie Kazak (.302). Earl Rapp had 30 home runs, a .302 batting average and his 133 RBIs were the best in the Pacific Coast League. Eddie Erautt (18-10) and Cal McLish (17-12) dominated on the mound. Julio Becquer (.291) and Ed Bailey (.282) passed through San Diego on their way to the big leagues. The headlines in the *San Diego Union* on August 25th proclaimed "Tuna Company Buys Padres." Jim Lane, (no relation to Bill Lane) president of Westgate-California Tuna Packing, announced that the sole intent was to keep the Padres in San Diego. In reality, C. Arnholt Smith now owned the Padres. San Diego finished the year in second place, three games behind the Seattle Rainers and one game ahead of Hollywood.

Bob Usher was a member of the San Diego Post 6 American Legion National Championship team in 1941. As a member of the 1956 San Diego Padres, he hit .350, second only to the .360 posted by Triple Crown winner Steve Bilko of the Los Angeles Angels. Ralph Kiner, the great National League home run king, was hired as general manager. A youthful Rocky Colavito hit 12 home runs and batted .368 before being called up by the Cleveland Indians after only 33 games. Dick Sisler

Lane Field. The last years.

ECHOES FROM LANE FIELD

slugged .329 and Ed Kazak again broke three hundred (.305). Pete Mesa (13-12) and Vic Lombardi (9-10) were the top hurlers. Despite their powerful offense (.283 team batting average), the Padres pitching was thin and the team dropped to seventh place in the standings. Attendance fell to 152,734, the lowest total since 1943. Lane Field was in disrepair and rumblings persisted to the effect that the city might lose the team unless the fans supported it. In New York, attendance was also a problem for the Giants and their cross-town rivals, the Brooklyn Dodgers. Would these teams heed the advice of Horace Greeley?

San Diego added talent during the off-season and improvement was expected in 1957. 35 games into the schedule, with the team but a game below .500, Ralph Kiner fired manager Bob Elliott. He was replaced by Kiner's former teammate and friend, George Metkovich, who had no previous managerial experience. Outraged, popular sportswriter Jack Murphy blistered the general manager in his column, but the team responded with a fourth place (89-79) finish. Significantly, attendance increased by almost 50,000. This team included many fine players: Dave Pope (.313), Rudy Regalado (.306), Floyd Robinson (.279), Earl Averill (.273) and pitcher Jim "Mudcat" Grant (18-7). Ex-major leaguers Bill Glynn, Bill Werle and Bob DiPietro contributed stability while future big league pitchers Bud Daley and Gary Bell, like the Padre team, showed promise for 1958.

Massive player turnover had now become commonplace in the minor leagues and the days were gone when people could identify with long time favorite hometown players. Fans even missed the well known rivals on opposing teams. Baseball and the entertainment tastes of the nation had changed during the Fifties and televised major league games were hurting minor league attendance across the country. Entire leagues were disappearing.

Numbers have always been important to baseball, but now the numbers appearing on the sports pages all seemed to have dollar signs in front of them. West Coast baseball was about to change forever and the PCL would not

become a third major league. The Dodgers and Giants announced their move to Los Angeles and San Francisco for the 1958 season. Concern now grew that the Pacific Coast League and the Padres might fold.

The only thing to fear was "fear itself" and the only thing to disappear was Lane Field. The termites lost their home when the ballpark was disassembled in March of 1958 and on April 29, 1958, on the present site of the Fashion Valley Shopping Center, the San Diego Padres opened the season by taking a doubleheader from the Phoenix Giants at newly built Westgate Park. This modern facility served the Padres until their final year in the PCL at San Diego Stadium in 1968. The following season, the National League Padres were created and the beloved Coast League team faded into oblivion. Yet the memories from the quiet bayfront parking lot persist for old ballplayers and fans alike. Listen to the . . .

left:
Bob Elliott

below:
Westgate Park

Echoes From Lane Field . . .

*These vignettes and interviews
are arranged chronologically.*

1936 Padres. Back: Jimmy Kerr, George Hockette, George McDonald, Ray Jacobs, Cedric Durst, Fred Vaughn, Eddie Mulligan, George Myatt, Wally Hebert, Bud Tuttle, Ernie Holman. Middle: Ed Wells, Bobby Doerr, Gene Desautels, Vince DiMaggio, Bill Lane, Frank Shellenback, Herm Pillette, Ashley Joerndt, Archie Campbell. Front: Vance Wirthman, Jack Hile, Ken Iverson, Berlyn Horne, unk. batbay, Joe Berkowitz. Manny Salvo, Dick Ward, Ivey Shiver, Howard Craghead, Ted Williams and Hal Doerr all joined this club after this photo.

The players' names do not appear on the original 1936 Padres team picture. Some men are even wearing old Hollywood uniforms. Sixty-years later, Bob Doerr studied every face and read several articles from his scrapbook until he was able to identify all but four of his teammates. The remaining names were provided by veteran Padres infielder and coach Whitey Wietelmann.

BOBBY DOERR, second base.
BORN: 4-7-18   PADRES: 1936

Bobby Doerr was born in Los Angeles and began his professional career while a high school athlete in 1934. Following his season in San Diego, Doerr played from 1937 through 1951 with the Boston Red Sox, where he drove in one hundred runs six times and at second base set an AL fielding record for consecutive chances without an error. A Yankee opponent once called him "one of the very few men who played the game hard and retired with no enemies." He was elected to the San Diego Padres' Hall of Fame in 1966 and Baseball's Hall of Fame in 1986.

"I joined the Hollywood Sheiks in the Coast League in 1934, when I was sixteen. I left school with George McDonald, who is five days younger than me. Mr. Lane owned the team. He was a front office man. Very seldom would you see him. He had kind of a crippled right hand, had a brace. As I understand it, it was something from mining. To us, being young like that, you thought he was quite old.

Frank Shellenback managed the team in 1935, the last year in Hollywood. He was a legal spitballer, pitching back in 1919, but he couldn't go back up to the major leagues because it was outlawed. He pitched the rest of his career in the Coast League. There were slippery elm tablets he'd suck on. He would spit on a spot on the ball and it was real slick - and once in a while in the infield, you'd grab the ball where that was and throw a 'spitter' to the first baseman. Shellenback was one of the real class guys you'd run into in baseball or anyplace else. He was Catholic and had a big family. He didn't discipline too much, but he didn't have to. He had that makeup you respected.

Wrigley Field in Los Angeles was a class ballpark, like a major league park, but I never thought it was a letdown to come to Lane Field. The fans were always so great. We were a first year team and it was really a fun place to play ball. The fans were so close.

My contract had been bought with an option to be exercised in the summer of '36. Of course my goal was to get taken by the Red Sox. I was having a good year and then Eddie Collins came out, I think in July, and I had a bad day... I think I made three errors. He called me

Bobby Doerr

between games on Sunday and said, 'Bobby, we're gonna buy your contract. Don't be nervous.' That was real nice...

I had a six-for-six day against the San Francisco Seals. Things just went good for me that year (.342). I don't think we had lights until the middle of the season. And it was a nice place to play - never overly hot like Sacramento. I saw Ted Williams come in for a tryout in June. Shellenback was pitching batting practice and he said, 'Let the kid get in and hit a few.' The older players around the cage didn't like this too well, as he would take up their time. Ted hit about seven or eight balls and I think about two or three were out of the park. So everyone started to say, 'Who is this kid?' One of 'em said, 'This kid will be signed before the week is out.' And he was. It was really something to

Frank Shellenback

know I was there when some kid you never knew got his start and became the greatest hitter ever.

It was fast company, but the thing is in those days you played so much baseball against those kinds of players in the winter time that you were exposed to pretty good baseball. In Southern California we had the weather... You learned the fundamentals of the game. Those fellows would stand around and talk about different things. You listened and absorbed what they passed on.

And Shellenback - a nice guy and still a lot of man. I remember he'd throw a 'spitter' and the best chance you had of hitting it was to hit it to the opposite field. When he saw a guy doing that, he had a sign. He'd pull down on the bill of his cap twice and that meant he was going to knock the guy down.

My dad kept a scrapbook of every ball game I played in - in fact, every box score I played in San Diego."
INTERVIEW BY JAMES D. SMITH III

WALLY "PREACHER" HEBERT, pitcher.
BORN: 8-21-07   PADRES: 1936-42

Sandwiched between stints with the St. Louis Browns and Pittsburgh Pirates, Wally Hebert set a team career record with 126 victories during his seven seasons in San Diego. He was a 20-game winner three times for the Padres and led the mound staff in wins and ERA in 1936, 1939 and 1942. Preacher also established the club record for complete games (33) in 1942 while logging 319 innings of work. He baffled opposing batters with his "nothin" ball. They could gets hits off the lanky Cajun, but it was never easy to score runs against him.

"In '31, '32 and '33, I was with the Browns. I didn't do much there, but I did get to pitch against Babe Ruth. He was strictly a fast ball hitter and I threw him a lot of what he called 'shit stuff.' He told me to stick it up my butt! I had good success with him. The first time I pitched against the Yankees, the first hitter was Jimmie Reese and he got a single. Then I got Babe to hit into a double play. He was sure mad. I was just a rookie.

Me and Jimmy Levey were traded to Hollywood for Alan Strange in '34. Somethin' happened that first year or maybe it was the second. Ed Wells just came down from the Yankees and he had a one run lead in the ninth. He had one out and (manager) Oscar Vitt put me in. I made one pitch and we lost the game. You don't forget those games. But, another time against Seattle, the bases were loaded with no outs and I went in. A fly went to Jimmy Levey and he caught it at second. He could have walked to first, but he threw it. Otherwise he could have made an unassisted triple play. So, I had one throw and got three outs!

I remember a catcher got to arguin' with an umpire about a pitch and they were goin' nose to nose. Well, time wasn't called and the runner at third just nonchalantly walked home and the catcher said, 'Can you imagine that dumb son-of-a-bitch doin' that to me?' He was callin' the runner dumb. To me, he was the dumb one.

I remember George Myatt. He kicked a few now and then, but he could really run. But, when he'd kick one, they'd go all the way to the outfield. I never said anything to a boy when he'd make an error, 'cause I knew he was tryin'. Old (Lefty) Grove used to get real mad at 'em and shake his finger. Old Connie Mack put up with a lot from him that he wouldn't take off other pitchers, but I wasn't like that.

I've got a good story for Ted (Williams). Oakland had a stiff breeze that would blow against the hitter. It was like in Chicago, but it was all the time. Well, Ted was battin' and a big, old strong pitcher was firin' real hard. Ted hit a line drive over the fence, but it was foul. Of course, we all thought it was fair. But, the very next pitch, he hit another line drive over the fence, but this time it was fair. I remember him as a kid sittin' in the dugout seein' other guys hit long home runs and he'd say, 'Boy, I wish I could hit like that.' Well, he was better than they were, but he just didn't know it yet. He was a natural hitter.

Wally "Preacher" Hebert

Preacher and Byron Humphreys relax during spring training.

I went dove huntin' with him in San Diego on the edge of the desert. The doves would come to this water hole for a drink and you'd shoot 'em. I told Ted it was dirty pool; they died for water. They'd keep goin' back and I didn't think it was right to kill 'em just 'cause they were thirsty. I still hunt duck.

Another thing about Ted. He loved to go to the movies and he was always tryin' to get somebody to go with him, but he'd holler and laugh and you wanted to get away from him. You could always spot old Ted in a movie house, 'cause he'd be alone...

I remember the series with Sacramento in '37. Pepper Martin was their player-manager. They were about seven games ahead of us and we beat 'em seven straight. Even Pepper Martin was throwin' balls away. We got 'em so shook up and then we beat 'em four straight in the playoffs, too.

I'd always pitch twice in Seattle. I pitched better when I pitched on every fourth day. I had better control. If I had too much rest, I felt like I could be over powerin' and I was best when I had my control. We had a lot of fun in the Pacific Coast League. My last year, we played Los Angeles in the playoffs. The first game was in Los Angeles and I pitched against Ray Prim. He beat me, 1-0, but they came down here and I beat him, 1-0 in the sixth game. That had to be in '42. 'cause I went to the Pirates in '43. Well, the Angels won the seventh game.

Durin' the war, the town (San Diego) got real crowded, but you could get gas. Those Navy and Marine guys would come to the games from basic trainin' and cheer for us. Those old boys from Louisiana would call me 'Preacher,' 'cause that's what everybody in Lake Charles called me. That's how y'all knew I was 'Preacher.' When I was in 'bout the second grade in Fourth Ward School, one little old boy said we wore funny hats, my brothers and me. They were in the fourth and first grade. He said they looked like preacher hats, but I didn't think they did. Anyhow, that's what everybody started callin' us: the 'Preacher Brothers.' Everybody in Lake Charles calls me 'Preacher' and it don't have nothin' to do with church. Bein' a left-hander, they'd also call me crooked arm or Lefty, but it's Preacher to everybody 'round here.

I've got an older brother who is 89 (in 1995) and my younger brother who is a year younger than me. Then there are all my sisters who are in their eighties. Yes, all eight of us are all alive. My mother was 95 when she died and my dad was 92. We live pretty long. I'm supposed to be the oldest living athlete in Louisiana."

GEORGE MYATT, shortstop.
BORN: 6-14-14   PADRES: 1936-37

A smooth middle infielder, "Mercury" enjoyed seven major league seasons, batting .296 and stealing thirty bases for Washington in 1945. On his way up, "Foghorn" was the first lead off batter in PCL Padre history, starting at shortstop in their 6-2 victory on Opening Day at Lane Field. He led the team with thirty-three stolen bases each season in San Diego while batting .276 and .281 in addition to scoring 117 runs in 1936. He managed the Philadelphia Phillies in 1968 and 1969.

"In 1936, we trained in Riverside, California. I made $125 a month in '35. Mr. Lane sent me a contract for $200 a month in '36. I held out for $275. 'Spider' Baum, the secretary [who pitched in the inaugural 1903 PCL season - Ed.] talked me into signing a dollar contract for spring training. He said if I wasn't in camp, Mr. Lane would fine me. So I did, had a good camp, and when we went to San Diego to start the season, opening day I had to sign my contract. Mr. Lane was very rough, giving me hell. I got mad and told him I had to have $325. He really raved and said I was robbing him - but he wrote the contract. I had a good year for the Padres, really loved

San Diego and the fans...

Bobby Doerr and I were close, good friends, roomed together, and he was my best man. I met my wife in National City. She played softball real good. Mr. Lane gave us a week in 'Frisco for our honeymoon if we got married at home plate. We had a quartet on the club - Vince DiMaggio, Red Campbell, Berlyn Horne and another player - and they sang 'Those Wedding Bells are Breaking Up that Old Gang of Mine.' Mr. Lane was a harsh man, but I liked him a lot; he gave me good advice.

One thing I remember about San Diego was Mr. and Mrs. W.C. Tuttle (President of the PCL), her in her big hat and him in his cap, at the games.

George Myatt

George Myatt's wedding.

INTERVIEW BY JAMES D. SMITH III

HERMAN PILLETTE, pitcher.
BORN: 12-26-95   DIED: 4-30-60   PADRES: 1936-42

Herm "Old Folks" Pillette is the all-time Pacific Coast League leader for games pitched with 708 mound appearances. The previous record of 621 games was held by Padres secretary and president, Spider Baum. In the late Teens and early Twenties, Herman posted a lifetime 34-32 record in the major leagues and enjoyed his best year with Detroit in 1922 when he finished the season with a 19-12 record. Pillette's 23-year career in the Coast League is also a league record. He threw a no-hitter for the San Francisco Mission Reds on October 5, 1929 against Seattle. Herm was the winning pitcher when the Padres defeated Seattle in the first game played at Lane Field. Over the next seven seasons, used primarily in relief, Pillette went 34-26 for San Diego. As his fiftieth birthday approached, "Old Folks" threw his final pitch for the Sacramento Solons in 1945. The

Herm "Old Folks" Pillette

following interview was conducted with his son, Duane, who played for San Diego's American Legion Post #6 National Championship team in 1938 and later pitched eight years in the major leagues. The younger Pillette won the Orioles' first game after the franchise moved from St. Louis to Baltimore in 1954. His dad did his best to keep young Duane away from "a bum's game."

"My father took me to a couple of ball games, but I wanted to see more, so I got a job selling peanuts at Lane Field. There were night games and he didn't want me staying up late. I'd sell my peanuts, watch them play and he didn't know I was there. I'd cash in about the seventh inning and go home. My mom never told him. He was a hard-nosed Catholic and didn't think it was good for a sixteen-year old boy to stay up until eleven at night.

He was one of the few pitchers to lose thirty games in one year (Portland, 1921), but the next year, he won 19 for Detroit. My uncle, Ted (Pillette), also played with the Mission Reds. He played for about fifteen years in the late Twenties and Thirties. They were the first brother combination to pitch on the same team. I've got both Zee-Nut cards. I used to save Zee-Nut cards when I was a kid and we'd play a game by flipping them against the door. We traveled around a lot, because my father was in baseball. The cards and my souvenirs got left at another player's home, but he moved, too. We never found that

old chest with all my treasures. That's when I decided not to save things.

In the old days, they'd have metal belt buckles on their pants. The pitchers would file grooves into the buckles and if they got two strikes on a hitter, they'd scrape the ball against their buckle. It would be like a file. It made the ball act like a spitball. He said he never threw a spitter and he didn't lie, but he did own up to scraping the ball.

He was in San Diego one time and he relieved. Frenchy Uhalt was on first and he was a good base runner. My father picked him off and Frenchy yelled, 'He balked! He balked! Dammit, he balked!' The umpire told him, 'He's been in the league for twenty-some years. He can't balk.' The thing is that he did balk and good base runners could pick up on it. My father would give a little flick with his knee to the good base runners. After he'd been in the league for a while and realized the umpires didn't pick up on it, he'd use the move on the good base runners. He'd pick them off every time, because they'd commit to run."

GEORGE McDONALD, first base.
BORN: 4-12-18   PADRES: 1936-44, 46

Stylish George was one of the best defensive first baseman in all of organized baseball. His .996 fielding average in 1943 established the Padres team record for first sackers and he led the club with .330 and .310 batting averages in 1943 and 1944 respectively. Mac averaged .291 during his ten seasons in local flannels, but he was known as a "clubhouse lawyer" who was often at odds with management over issues that affected the players' wallets. A colorful character, few things (throws in the dirt, poker games, parties or practical jokes) got past George McDonald.

"Bobby Doerr and I quit school in the eleventh grade. We both turned down scholarships to USC. We were sixteen years old and playing in the Pacific Coast League for the Hollywood Stars. There were two teams in San Francisco: the Seals and the Missions. The Missions came to Hollywood and our club went to San Diego. We were the first Padres.

I almost lived at his (Bobby Doerr's) home when we were kids. The best man I have known in my life is Bobby. He is the only person I've ever known in my life who never said anything bad about anyone. We had one of the best American Legion clubs that was ever assembled. We were fifteen years old. Mickey Owen, catcher (Cardinals, Dodgers, Cubs, Red Sox); Dick Conger, pitcher (Tigers, Pirates, Phillies); me on first; Bobby on second (Red Sox); Steve Mesner on third (Cubs, Cardinals, Reds); Al Lyons (Yankees, Pirates, Braves) in center field and the best hitter was a kid named Ripsinipki who didn't want to keep playing ball, so he became a doctor. We beat Ted Williams' team for Southern California to go to the State Championship. We played San Francisco on Catalina. They won the first game, 16-1, but we won the next two, 3-2 and 2-1. They had Eddie Joost (Reds, Braves, Athletics and Red Sox) and Walt Judnich (Browns, Indians, Pirates).

I was sixteen and making $150 a month playing baseball in '34. I paid $650 for a Chevy coupe. My mother, who was Norwegian and spoke broken English, said that I bought a 'stingy' car. She meant it only had one seat.

[Talking about Ted Williams] He had the prettiest swing of anybody I ever saw! When I saw him later, when he was hitting .400, his swing wasn't as pretty as when he was young. Ted Williams would always eat too fast and our pitcher, Dick Ward, would tell him to slow down. He wasn't cocky at all. He just had a drive. When he said, 'Some day, I'll walk down the street and people will say there goes the greatest hitter who ever lived,' he wasn't bragging or being cocky. He just had that kind of confidence and it made me angry when the Eastern writers didn't understand that. That first year, I was leading the league in hitting for about the first month. Then Tommy (Rupert) Thompson was leading it and then Ted hit about 17 home runs in that last month. The thing I remember most about all those years with the Padres was getting knocked down all the time. I hit behind Ted and Tommy and, in those days, the pitchers would always take it out on the next guy and that was me!

The owners have cheated ballplayers for so long that I'm glad to see them get whatever they can. Old Bill Lane... We never did get along. There were four teams that wanted me. He told me that. Ernie Johnson came out to scout me, and Bobby will tell you this, they took him instead. He went to the Red Sox and I stayed in San Diego. We (McDonald and Bill Lane) had our biggest squabble in '37, because he said he could sell me to the Giants, but he wouldn't do it.

I was called the clubhouse lawyer and it hurt my career. If the guys didn't get enough meal money, I'd be the one to go talk about it. It was like that with Lane. Then there was Major Lott. He was a major (while in the military), a nice guy, but he didn't know anything. Then Rip Collins. I used to get on him when he was with the Angels, because he thought he was a big shot from the Cardinals. Then he's our manager. Bill Starr told me, 'I know Collins dislikes you' and he gave me free agency. Probably my best shot was when I hit .350 in spring training with the Browns in '47, but I was offered more money in the Coast League, so I didn't go.

Herman 'Old Folks' Pillette... What a nice, nice guy. Easy going. I roomed with him for a year. Every morning, he'd

George McDonald

take a shower, brush his teeth and fill a water glass half full of 100 proof whiskey. He called it mouth wash, but I never saw him drunk.

Shanty Hogan caught for us. He weighed about 280 and was always half drunk. (New York Giants manager John) McGraw was always on him to lose weight, but he never dropped a ball and he was never sober. I saw him drink a lot, but he could catch Manny Salvo fast balls and never drop one. We were all beer drinkers, but Shanty would have a boy bring a pitcher full of ice to his room. He'd pour in a pint of whiskey and fill the rest with water. That was his highball glass.

Another time, up in Portland, we were out with some young ladies. I won't tell you who was with me. They gave us a lot of sweet gin drinks and I was never so sick in my life as the next morning. I said, 'You've gotta tell Shellenback I've got the flu.' My roommate said, 'You've gotta be kidding.' It was about 2:30 in the afternoon. I tried to eat, but couldn't. About 4:30, I got a hamburger sandwich to stay down. I told Les (Cook) that I felt bad and he gave me a couple of aspirin. I could hardly hit the ball during batting practice. That night, Ad Liska, an underarm pitcher was on the mound. I got a single, a double and a triple. I thought my heart was coming out of my shirt on the double and I almost fainted on the triple. What a time!

Bill "Hardrock" Lane

Cedric Durst

We had camaraderie. We did every thing together. We'd put a blanket on the table in our room and play poker all night. You couldn't hear the money when it landed on the blanket. Shellenback would check the halls, but we'd be inside playing cards. We'd stay up 'till morning.

Did you know that I played Wally Pipp in *"Pride of the Yankees"* with Gary Cooper? I even got to talk. You ought to see it on video or on TV. Lefty O'Doul got me the job. Babe Ruth played himself. The director told the other ball player extras to look over the fence when the great Bambino swung regardless of how he hit the ball. He hit grounders which they fielded by instinct. The director was losing his patience. They just wanted Ruth swinging and guys looking toward the fence. The magic of Hollywood would make it appear a home run had been hit. They finally got the scene done.

I hit the longest home run in history. I hit a home run and

Professor Durst and his honor students, Anton Jeli, Pete Charowhas, Jack Millard, and Bus Devolder.

it bounced on Coast Highway (Pacific Highway) and it went into a freight car headed to L.A. I'm the one who did it. Now, they tell the story that Ted hit it, but it was me. Ask Steve Mesner's wife! It was in *"Ripley's Believe It or Not."* [Charlene Mesner confirms George's version of this story.]

CEDRIC DURST, outfield, manager.
BORN: 8-23-96   DIED:2-16-71   PADRES:36-43

From 1922 through 1930, Ced Durst played for the Browns, Yankees and Red Sox. He was a member of the legendary '27 Yankees with Babe Ruth and Lou Gehrig. In the final game of the 1928 World Series, the Babe hit three home runs while Gehrig and Durst each hit one out as New York swept the St. Louis Cardinals. Five home runs in a game is a World Series record. Ced was San Diego's first centerfielder and became the team's player/manager when he took over the reins from Frank Shellenback in 1939. Although he turned 40 during his first season with the Padres, he hit .306 and averaged .297 through the remainder of his playing career. He is the winningest manager in Padres history with a 417-407 record. Durst was the first president of the San Diego Hot Stove League and an active supporter of youth baseball. The following memories are from his daughter and devoted fan, Autumn Keltner.

"We used to go to spring training in El Centro. As kids, we'd go down during spring vacation. My brother and I got baby rabbits and kept them in the bath tub. George McDonald and Jimmie Reese wrote a letter on hotel stationery that they were going to kick us out for keeping rabbits in the tub. We were real scared. I was eleven or twelve. George and Jimmie were real good to me. They'd buy ice cream cones or take me to the movies on their days off.

I was only ten when Ted Williams joined the team, but remember Dad was assigned to watch over him. Ted was so young and Mrs. Williams was worried about him going off with the ball club. My dad went over to her home and made her understand everything was going to be OK. Ted was the youngest player and Dad was the oldest. He never used profanity and was good with young people. He roomed with Ted to watch over him.

When my dad talked about Ted, he said all he wanted to do was hit. Dad worked with him on his fielding skills. Of course if Ted was going to be successful, he'd have to do more than hit. Ted was a good kid. All of his coaches in high school and Legion ball had taken him in tow and watched over him.

There was a building contractor who entertained the ball club on Mondays. I was in junior high. My mother wrote a letter saying I was sick, but my picture appeared in the paper with the baseball players. I had one teacher who saw it and gave me a hard time.

We were devastated when my dad was traded to Hollywood in 1938, but it was apparently part of a deal that he would be coming back to manage the next year. My dad got along very well with Bill Lane. He later managed in Rochester, Omaha and another team in the Cardinal chain. He loved San Diego. He loved the people here and never thought of moving out of San Diego.

He used to scare the wits out of me when he was managing and he'd put himself in to pinch hit. He'd deliver, but sometimes he didn't. I so wanted him to do well. I lived at the ballpark. I would have given my eye teeth to sit on the bench. If I'd been a boy, I could have. My brother was four years younger and he had no desire to. My biggest desire was to be a sportswriter. I was sports editor for the Point Loma *"Pointer"* in high school for a little while.

This picture is of Earle Combs, Jr. and me with Babe Ruth. My dad respected Babe as a baseball player. Later, it was exciting to see the movie stars (in Hollywood) and get autographs. Bing Crosby would come to see the games down here and he would invite players to Del Mar. He was a very gracious host.

On December 7, 1941, I was at Lane Field, keeping score for the Junior Padres, for my dad. Frankie Stinson, Jack Lohrke and Earle Brucker, Jr. were on the team. As a teenager, I loved to keep score for those good looking young men. It wasn't difficult for my dad to talk me into it."

MANUEL SALVO, pitcher.
BORN: 6-30-13   DIED: 2-7-97   PADRES: 1936-38, 46-48

Starting his Coast League career with Sacramento in 1932, Manuel Salvo made it to the big leagues in 1936. Suddenly, he was back in the PCL. His disappointment was San Diego's good fortune as he was a consistent winner. He returned to the majors after winning 56 games for the Padres and twice leading the PCL in strikeouts. During his major league career, Manny hit just one home run. This came in 1939 when the Giants went on a binge of five home run in a single inning to establish a major league record. Salvo is remembered as being a good pitcher on weak Boston Braves teams during the early Forties. In 1940, he led National League pitchers with five shutouts. He came back to San Diego in 1946 and led the team with a .519 percentage (14-13) in 1947. Although the sportswriters referred to him as the "Big Portuguese" (6'4", 210 lbs.), he was very proud of his Sicilian heritage.

Cedric Durst, Autumn Durst, and Bing Crosby confer at the DelMar Racetrack.

Autumn Durst, Babe Ruth, and Earle Combs, Jr.

below: Cedric Durst and plate umpire discuss a call as Mickey Haslin listens.

"On opening day in 1936, I was sitting on the bench in Boston. They had made a deal with San Diego for Bobby Doerr and George Myatt. Mr. Cronin called me into his office and said (Padre owner Bill) Lane had called and told him, 'You either send me Salvo right away or I'm calling this deal off!' Cronin showed me the telegraph and asked how I'd like to go. I said I'd prefer to fly. They made arrangements. They held up the plane and it was raining like hell. I didn't feel the take off and the guy sitting next to me said we were in the air. It was my first flight in a plane. It was one of those old (Ford) Tri-Motors with motors on each wing and one in the middle. I met the team in Oakland.

In the playoffs, I think it was '37, Sacramento wanted to play us so bad, they could taste it. We knew we had the pitching to beat them and we beat them real bad. Portland was in the playoffs, too and we beat them three straight in San Diego. Then, we went all the way up there and beat 'em again. We had Howard Craghead, Wally Hebert, Tiny Chaplin, myself and Herman Pillette. We only had six pitchers (Dick Ward being the sixth) that year and in good tight games, we'd relieve each other. We'd warm up and pitch a few innings. We had a good staff.

Ted (Williams) joined our club in the middle of the year (1936) when his school got out. He had a good year. You could just see he was going to be something

Manuel Salvo

special. He could sure hit! He hit some balls with our club that I still remember. He hit one against the wind in San Francisco that went out of the park at 365 feet. It went over a street and that was 150 feet and into a park across the street. After the game, kids said it landed half way into the park. He hit 'em out in Oakland and Sacramento, too. He didn't hit for a big average at first, but he could sure hit some long balls. We had some good kids on that team. They (Ted Williams, Bobby Doerr, George McDonald) were teenagers and I was twenty-four-years-old.

In '44, I was working for my in-laws in their bakery in Sacramento. Oakland called and asked what I wanted. I told them and they said 'OK' and they bought me. It was half way though the season, but I led them in pitching (18-7, 2.14 ERA). Then the Army drafted me. When I got out, I went back to Oakland. They said, 'You don't belong to us. The Philadelphia Athletics drafted you.' I had to call Connie Mack. I said I was out of the service. He wanted to know how much I wanted and he wouldn't pay it, so he sold me to San Diego. I ended up my career in Sacramento and after playing, I became a marshal in Sacramento County. It was a good job, but they had mandatory retirement at 60 back then and here I am, still kickin'."

HOWARD CRAGHEAD, pitcher.
BORN: 5-25-08   DIED: 7-15-62   PADRES: 36-40

In June of 1936, the Padres traded pitcher Ed Wells for Seattle fastballer, Howard Craghead. During his thirteen years in the Coast League, Craghead posted a 182-179 record on the mound. His top year was 1929 when he went 21-12 with Oakland. He appeared briefly with Cleveland in 1931-32 after leading the PCL in 1930 with 199 strikeouts. Howard won 69 games for the Padres and his best season with San Diego was 1936 (16-12). He was nicknamed "The Professor" because he had a degree in philosophy from Fresno State College. The following interview was conducted with Tom Rinks. Tom's mother died when he was sixteen-years old and he moved in with the Cragheads.

"He was a perfect role model for a husband and a father, yet he and his wife never had any kids. He was the mentor for our American Legion team that won the World Series. He was our pitching coach and we had all those left-handers: Ronnie Wilkins, Larry Elliot and Joel Mogy. There are throwers and pitchers. He taught kids how to pitch- getting ahead of the batter - staying in the zone - when in doubt, throw the curve. The old adage in baseball is throw the pitch they can't hit. Until a batter proves he can hit a pitch, keep throwing it. It might be a curve or a high fast ball.

Howard was a fast ball pitcher. He didn't throw the

spitter. They don't need the spitball anymore with the split-finger fast ball. You've got better control. It was rare that the spitball was ever effective. It was too hard to control, but it used to scare the hitters.

Typically, they didn't get him a lot of runs. He said this would happen to certain pitchers. Look at (Andy) Benes. He'd just say it was something that happened in baseball. It's a mind-set, that's baseball. The team thinks, 'We've got our number one guy on the mound' and there's a complacency that sets in. You don't consciously do it, but you're not on that fine edge doing the things you need to do to win ball games. But he never complained about non-support. He was always positive. The thing that made him so different, he was so nurturing.

He never wanted center-stage. He'd never give advice unless asked. I was engaged about three times when I was playing ball and he said, 'Tom, you're gonna have a hard time beating that gal in Minnesota' and he was right. We've been married 34 years.

Howard had a very calm demeanor and he was such a perfectionist. Baseball took its toll, because he internalized everything. He died on the municipal golf course in San Diego, right across from where he used to live by Balboa Park. But he was doing something he loved and he'd had heart trouble.

Howard Craghead

When I was a kid, I idolized professional athletes and now I can hardly stand them. Now they make too much money. Howard put those fourteen years in baseball and never made any money. He worked his way up at SDG&E. He started as a furnace salesman and later became secretary for the whole company. He was only secretary for two or three years before his coronary.

He and Ced Durst were best of friends long after baseball. Howard did so much for others. He could talk on any subject. He was especially bright and donated his time to amateur sports. I remember he referred to Ted Williams as 'that kid.' He had so many stories about Williams. He used to compare Larry Elliot (Tom's teammate on Post 492, later a PCL Padre and a major leaguer) with Ted Williams. Larry was just a raw talent like Ted. He used to say that Larry hit the ball as hard as he ever saw one hit. He went with us all the way to the National Championship at his own expense. He compared Billy Capps (1954 American Legion Player of the Year) to many of the major league shortstops. He was such a positive influence on so many lives. He had a degree in philosophy from Fresno State and Howard's definition of a good manager is the one who does the least amount of harm. Think about it... He was absolutely right."

IVEY SHIVER, outfield.
BORN: 1-22-07   DIED: 8-31-72   PADRES: 36

Before he played professional baseball, Ivey "Chick" Shiver was a gridiron star at the University of Georgia. He was briefly with the Detroit Tigers in 1931 and later played for Cincinnati in 1934. During the Padres' inaugural season, the hard-hitting Shiver (.309, 7 home runs, 41 RBIs in 191 ABs) replaced a youngster named Vance Wirthman in left field. At the time, league rules specified that PCL rosters must include five rookies and twenty veterans. In August, Shiver unexpectedly jumped the team to take a football coaching position at his alma mater and Ted Williams, who had just turned eighteen, became the Padres' starring leftfielder. The following information was provided by Chick's grandson, Ivey M. Shiver IV.

"My Grandfather died when I was five. My Dad passed away in '81. I had just turned 15. I just really didn't know that much about my grandfather. I was at an age when I would have just been getting interested in knowing about the past. I've learned more from you in ten minutes than I ever knew about him. To think Ted Williams took his place, that is unbelievable! I do know he was an All-American end in '27 at the University of Georgia. He coached at Georgia and was head coach at Savannah High School in the late Thirties and Forties. Then he went into the insurance business.

Ivey "Chick" Shiver (right) left the team to coach football at his Georgia alma-mater. The departure created an opening for Ted Williams who went on to play left field and distinguish himself as one of the greatest sluggers in the history of baseball.

TED WILLIAMS, outfield.
BORN: 8-30-18   PADRES: 1936-37

San Diego's best known native, Ted Williams has been called baseball's greatest hitter. In his major league career with the Boston Red Sox (1939-60), punctuated by military service in World War II and Korea, he hit 521 home runs and batted .344. Baseball's last .400 hitter (.406 in 1941), "The Kid" was elected to the Baseball Hall of Fame in 1966, the same year he was inducted into the Padres' Hall of Fame. Ted's 23 home runs in 1937 stood as a team record until Max West hit 43 circuit blows in 1947. Williams is warmly remembered and well liked by his Padre teammates.

"Old Bill Lane was quite an old character, you know. He was one of the owners of the Hollywood Stars and when they went to San Diego, he went there. Earl Keller (the sportswriter) could tell you about him. He's a great guy.

Before the Padres came to town, I didn't have any ambition to play up the coast for the L.A. Angels or for a big league team. My only real concern was just becoming a good hitter. The big leagues were in the next world years ago. It was just the playgrounds. I grew up right by the water tower on Utah Street.

Three shots of the legendary Ted Williams.

" I was nervous - not because I was born there, but because it was a whole new experience playing before crowds, professional baseball. San Diego was the nicest little town in the world."
                                                                    —Ted Williams

I was always serious about baseball- not about my future, but about my love of the game. Have you read *"My Turn at Bat"*? It's all there. Anyway, I went to Hoover, because I thought my chances of making the baseball team were better than at San Diego High. I was on the border line. Hoover was a newer school and I wanted to play on the team. I was a pitcher.

Here's a funny thing. There's not one hitting picture of me until I signed my first professional contract. All of them in high school were pitching. So the first was in a Padre uniform.

I played my last year of high school ball in '36, then back to school and graduated in '37. So I was in my second year of pro baseball then, I probably needed at least that much seasoning. I didn't do much my first year (.271) and then I played enough (.291, 23 home runs, 98 runs batted in) so the Red Sox bought me and sent me to spring training (in 1938). They sent me to Minneapolis and I had a big year there (.366, 43 home runs, 142 RBIs) and things really started to come.

I remember my first at-bat for the Padres. The manager, Frank Shellenback, sent me in to pinch hit and I took three strikes right down the middle. Didn't even swing. Then he sent me in to pitch one night and I got hit like I was throwing batting practice. But that first time I pitched, I also hit - and I hit a double. I pitched two innings and the next time up, I hit a double. And then I was in the lineup. I went over to Lefty O'Doul one day and I said, 'What do I have to do to be a good hitter?' He said, 'Kid, don't ever let anybody change you.'

I neglected my fielding in the early years and always regretted it. That was the looseness of the organization. And the lights were lousy at Lane Field, in professional baseball. But we had some good outfielders and Vince DiMaggio was a great outfielder. He had a good arm, good power as a hitter, but a blind spot: high inside. What you've gotta do is adjust. Anticipate it and make sure it's not a ball.

That 1937 team was a good composite team: young, old, former major league players, good leadership under Frank Shellenback, the nicest man I ever met in baseball. Why we didn't win it, I don't know? There was no friction. Did we win the playoffs in '37? [Yes! -Ed.]

Lane Field was an old wooden ballpark, nice park for a left-handed hitter, and the ball carried pretty good. We played a lot of day games. I enjoyed guys like Herm Pillette, Howard Craghead, Jimmy Kerr, George Myatt, Bobby Doerr... Some of the best hitters I remember in the Coast League were Lou Vezilich, Steve Mesner, Johnny Frederick and Lefty O'Doul, who I first saw from about 450 feet away through a knot hole in the outfield in San Diego.

A History of the San Diego Padres (1936-1957)

There was no particular pressure on me playing in San Diego. I didn't know what pressure was. I was nervous - not because I was born there, but because it was a whole new experience playing before crowds, professional baseball. San Diego was the nicest little town in the world. How the hell was I to know it was the nicest town in the world? I'd never been anyplace."

INTERVIEW BY JAMES D. SMITH III

GENE "BUD" TUTTLE, pitcher.
BORN: 3-15-14   PADRES: 1936-37

"Bud" Tuttle played for Hollywood in 1935 and came south when the team relocated to San Diego. He was primarily a relief pitcher who doubled as a sportswriter which led to a 50 year career in the newspaper industry. The former Hollywood Star wrote an entertainment column, "Wheeling Around Las Vegas" for the Las Vegas Review-Journal and served as a publicity agent for Jayne Mansfield, Lionel Hampton and Eddie Fisher. Tuttle, an accomplished author, has published 25 books, written numerous screenplays and appeared in several movies. He has 70 books waiting for a publisher and continues to produce new manuscripts. His early work primarily consisted of Western novels, but as the market declined, he prepared such diverse titles as "Alien Agent," "Where God and Religion Differ," "Without Gun or Badge" and "Stars in My Life." Gene is a prolific man of letters who still dreams of riding with the cowboys and throwing strikes past batters in baggy uniforms.

"You hit the jackpot! W.C. Tuttle was my father and I played for the original Padres in '36 and '37. It was a wonderful experience. I don't feel like a son now at 84 and haven't played ball since 1958. I have the large photo of the '37 Padres on the wall next to my desk and I sit and look at it every day and think of some of the things that took place at that time.

My Dad really was some man. He died in 1969. He wrote over 250 books and close to 2,000 short stories. He wrote about the West. His father was a sheriff in Montana and Dad later served as a deputy. As you know, he was the president of the Coast League from 1936 through 1942.

My biggest thrill in

Bud Tuttle

baseball was pitching winter league at Wrigley Field when I faced Satchel Paige. He beat me, 1-0. That was when he was in his prime. I pitched, played outfield and first base. I remember hitting a home run for the Van Nuys Merchants. I played with Bobby Doerr. I played with Gene Lillard, too. My father got him signed up with the Los Angeles Angels. Last time I saw him was in Frisco when we were playing the Seals. That was over 60 years ago.

When I played for Hollywood, I wrote stories in my room after the games. In the winter, I'd sit at my desk and write stories. My only time off was when Dad would tell me to work out and we'd play catch. He wore the catcher's mitt and I'd throw 100 pitches. He kept me in shape.

My contract with the Padres in 1936 was only $75 a month. We got free meals in restaurants because they loved the Padres. The hotel was fifty cents a day, so I was able to make it on $75.

Ted Williams was my roommate the second year. He hit a home run in San Francisco and won two free dinners. He was going to take me but when he learned that he had to wear a tie, he turned it down. Ted never wore a necktie, not even for a free dinner.

I remember Ted in his pajamas swinging a rolled up newspaper in his hands in front of a full length mirror. He worried that his eyes were going bad and he was always going to the doctor. He had perfect vision, better than perfect vision, but he wanted to make sure.

We traveled north into Portland and Seattle by train and went through the small town of Dunsmuir where the train stopped for 15 minutes. There was a lady on the platform with a small wagon. She had home-made ice cream and everyone wanted some. As we pulled into the depot, Ted would climb out the window and drop to the platform and get ice cream for both of us. It sure was good on hot days as there was no air conditioning on the train at that time.

PCL President W.C. Tuttle, Jack Lelivelt, and Cedric Durst.

I also roomed with Vance Wirthman. He was a real decent fellow and we had a lot of fun together going to restaurants and shows and walking down the street to the ballpark each noon. Vance was always looking for things on the sidewalk, saying that this or that would help him get a hit — and it did!

The funniest guy on the team was Berlyn Horne, a pitcher, but he was able to be a good ventriloquist when he wanted to. He kept Pullman porters going here and there trying to figure out what was wrong. He never pulled it on umpires which he should have done.

I met Earl Keller in San Diego and we teamed up together to write about the Padres. We went to his office after the games and did batting averages for all the players. Then we'd go out to dinner.

Wally Hebert was on the Padres. Wally helped me in 1935 when we were the Hollywood Stars by teaching me many things about pitching as we were both left-handed. I didn't realize that he was that old. Gee, I'm seven years younger than he is! Yes, I'm getting up there, too.

I don't know what happened to Ernie Holman. He became very ill and needed blood. Wally Hebert and I had the same blood type. We each gave Ernie a pint. He pulled through and several years later, I ran into him in Hollywood and he hugged me.

The Padres were very serious. Frank Shellenback was serious and we knew how to behave. It was very different back then when a home run was hit. There weren't any demonstrations at home plate. It was serious.

When we won the playoffs in 1937, we had four pitchers and each one of them pitched two complete games. Imagine four pitchers throwing eight straight complete games today. That just doesn't happen now, but it was expected back then. Herman Pillette and I spent most of our time in the bullpen."

HAL DOERR, catcher.
BORN: 5-15-13   DIED: 3-2-83   PADRES: 1936

It was Harold A. Doerr's ambition that his sons would become professional baseball players. The boys fulfilled their father's dreams and provided him with many clippings for his extensive scrapbook collection. Hal was the oldest and began his professional career with the '33 Portland Beavers. He hit .256 for the Bevos in 1934. After the '36 season with the Padres, Hal immediately went to work for the phone company in San Diego. He continued to play several years of winter ball for Farley's Clothiers together with many other Padre players and was actively involved in youth baseball for the remainder of his life. The following information was provided by his wife, Eleanor, and his brother, Bob Doerr.

[Eleanor] "He only played (for the Padres) at the end of the season. Desautels hurt his hand, so they needed Hal to fill in. He'd just been released from Houston, but San Diego knew that he was a good catcher with a great arm. His parents would both come down to watch the games (with both of their sons playing for San Diego). That was his last team and he enjoyed it very much.

Vince DiMaggio lived with Mr. and Mrs. Doerr during the winter. Mr. Doerr bought Steve Mesner his first uniform. Anybody who came to their home was welcome for dinner. They fed the entire Portland team when they'd come to Los Angeles. It was the Depression, but that's the way they were. Everybody called him (Mr. Doerr), 'Pop.' Everybody loved him. Everybody that wanted to play baseball, he'd help them.

Hal was the captain of the baseball team at George Washington High School in Los Angeles. He was five years older than Bob. Bob went to Fremont (High School) with George (McDonald) and Steve (Mesner) and Dee Moore. They had that good American Legion team and went to Ogden, Utah in a tournament. I remember Hal playing at Wrigley Field in Los Angeles when those great Colored teams would come in. He was born left-handed, but he played baseball right-handed, so his eyes weren't as good as Bob or Ted's (Williams). He wrote left-handed, but batted and threw right-handed.

In 1933, Hal and his buddy went back to play ball in the Midwest. Hal with Omaha and his buddy, Jake Ratherton from L.A., with Springfield. Hal was catching when his buddy got hit in the head when he was batting. He fell right there and, in those days, there was no medical care. When he got up, he kept playing. He died. They said his skull was thinner than most. Hal had to buy him a suit and he accompanied him home on the train. They went there to have fun and his friend died. That always affected him."

[Bob] "He broke in before I did. He caught for Portland and Los Angeles. He was just with the Padres for a short period of time when Desautels was hurt. We were in a lot of 2-1 and 1-0 ball games and he did a fine job catching. One day, we were up in L.A. and we needed another pitcher. Ted said, 'I'm a pitcher' and Hal caught him. Ted didn't do too well and he never pitched again, but it was my brother who caught him in his only professional appearance.

That game was on July 3rd (1936). I've got it here in the scrapbook that my dad kept. It says Williams hit the ball right on the nose both times and the first hit was against

the bleacher screen. Ted went 2-for-2. [Ted Williams pitched 1-1/3 innings and allowed two hits and issued one walk. He also had two singles and scored twice. They were his first professional hits. The following day, he got his first double off Bob Joyce of Los Angeles and, on September 1, 1936, he collected his first triple off Forrest Porter of Sacramento. Ted did not connect for a home run until April 11, 1937 against Stew Bolen of the San Francisco Missions. When he became a regular on August 31, 1936, Williams batted eighth in the order. Young Teddy's inauspicious debut occurred June 27, 1936 while pinch hitting for pitcher Jack Hill. He fanned on three consecutive offerings by Sacramento hurler Henry 'Cotton' Pippen. -Ed.]

Wes Schulmerich hit a homer off Ted that day. Hal remembered that, so when I saw Wes years later up here in Oregon, I asked him if he remembered Ted. He didn't think Ted would make it as a big leaguer, because he was 'too wiggly at the plate.' Then he said, 'Of course, nobody ever offered me a scouting job.'

They (the Red Sox) bought George Myatt's and my contract. When Collins came out, he saw Ted taking batting practice and liked him so much, he wanted to buy him right there. Collins had the foresight to ask for first rights. He and Bill Lane shook hands and that is how Ted went to Boston. It was fun to see young Ted Williams break in."

Hal Doerr

George Detore   Luke Easter

Jimmie Reese

Jimmie Reese demonstrates his talent with the Fungo bat for young fans at Westgate Park.

GEORGE DETORE, catcher.
BORN: 11-11-06   DIED: 2-7-91   PADRES: 1937-44

Born in Utica, NY, George Detore played major league ball in 1930-31 as an infielder with Cleveland. Slowed by injuries, he switched to catcher and for the 1937 champion Padres, led the PCL with a .334 average. Consistently productive with the bat, George broke three-hundred four more times with averages of .355 in '39, .321 in '40, .320 in '41 and .321 in '43. He managed the team from August 10, 1943 through the 1944 season, closing the era in which Bill Lane's "estate," headed by Major Lott, owned the team.

"In 1935, I started catching in Milwaukee and in '36, we won the (American Association) pennant and Little World Series. We had a little tiff on the train coming back home. The treasurer of the club came in our car and started gettin' a little nasty about the money we were going to get. Rudy York [6'1", 210#] got up and I thought he was going to tear him apart. I jumped between them and pushed the treasurer out to the other car. He told the president I attacked him. Instead I saved his neck - which was a mistake. So I was sold to the Padres.

I was an Easterner and had never been out West. But I was willing to try it and had to make a living. I heard about the Coast League and nobody said anything good about it... But you know one thing about the guys we had in '37? Nobody ever made a mental mistake, a bonehead play. And Shellenback was a 'beaut' - an excellent baseball man and hell of a guy personally.

In 1938, we were in Seattle and Shelly wanted to pitch. He had 296 PCL wins and wanted four more to make three hundred. We had 'em beat in the last of the ninth, 2-1, and all he'd thrown was spitters. Two men out, one man on base... then he threw a sidearm curve and it disappeared over a schoolhouse in left field that was about 200 feet high. Shelly stood there and he came in and said, 'How dumb can a guy be?' I said I wouldn't know. He never forgot that and he wouldn't pitch again.

When I managed, Major Lott and I got along real well- but there wasn't a lot of talent."
INTERVIEW BY JAMES D. SMITH III

JIMMIE REESE, second base.
BORN: 10-1-01   DIED: 7-13-94   PADRES: 1937-38

Jimmie Reese was involved in professional baseball for 78 years. A major leaguer with the Yankees in 1930 and 1931, he roomed with Babe Ruth while the team was on the road. He played 90 games for the Cardinals in 1932 and posted a .265 batting average. Reese earned distinction as the second baseman on the all-time PCL team. He was a Padre player, coach (1948-60) and short-term manager (1948, 1960-61). As California Angels conditioning coach, renown for his fungo hitting and host of friends, he was honorary AL captain in San Diego's 1992 All Star Game. There was a hand lettered sign above the doorway in his home: "How rapidly doth fame fleeeth" (sic). This humble spirit made a lasting impression on the legion of players and fans whose lives were touched by this dedicated man of baseball.

"I was a bat boy with the Angels in 1917. Frank Chance [Tinkers to Evers to Chance] was the manager - of the Cubs prior to that, but he came out here for his health. I broke in with Oakland in 1924 and stayed until 1930. Lyn Lary and I were sold to the Yankees in 1927 and we were to report in 1929, but I had a bad year so I stayed and he went on ahead. I had my best year in 1929 and hit .337. That was with Oakland and then I went to the Yankees

I came to the Padres from Los Angeles in 1937. Coming to San Diego was fine. There was a lot of ...not animosity, but a lot of rivalry. The '37 team...Ted Williams, Tommy Thompson, 'Tiny' Chaplin. Listen, you're bringing back names I'd almost forgotten about. Frank Shellenback was the manager. Tiny Chaplin was one of the finest young pitchers I've ever seen. And no doubt was going to eventually go to the big leagues. He had an accident coming from Tijuana. Somebody hit him from the rear and he died right there. A very fine, a really good friend of mine. It really broke me up.

There was George McDonald, a fellow named Hal Patchett, George Detore, George Myatt. Bobby Doerr already went to Boston. I played second and Myatt was the shortstop. I was Bobby's replacement.

Ted Williams used to stand in front of a mirror in the clubhouse and take different poses with the bat. He went to take those poses and everybody said, "Look at what that busher's doing." But it turned out he wasn't crazy. Probably one of the premier hitters of all baseball in any time. He had a great year...and then was sold to Boston for the big sum of $35,000. I think they got a bargain. Williams believed in himself, didn't think anybody could get him out, and Babe (Ruth) felt exactly the same way.

There was a lot of excitement in San Diego when I played there. I played with a fellow named Bill Starr. He was a good friend of mine, a catcher at the time. We were going to San Francisco, somewhere, to play in the Coast League, sat down on the train and he said, 'Jimmie, I've got to give up this game. I don't make enough money. I want to get married. I want to raise a family.' He went into the real estate business and did an unbelievable job. To make a long story short, he became the owner of the ball club in 1944 and is one of the finest men I ever met in the game. And knew more about the game than anybody.

Many people from the Coast League wanted him to become president, but he turned it down.

I came back to the Padres in 1948 when Bill Starr was the owner. When I first came back, a fellow named Bucky Harris managed the ball club. I consider Bucky Harris one of the finest managers of all time. I coached third base for a year and he wanted me to go back with him to Washington the following year. I asked Bill about that and he said, ' Jimmie why don't you stay here. You might be here a lot longer than Bucky will be there,' which no doubt became true as I was with him (Starr) for fourteen years.

That 1949 team: Max West and, ah, Luke Easter! He drew more people to the Coast League than any individual in the entire (history of) baseball in the Coast League. He was the greatest drawing card you ever saw. He hit home runs wherever he went. He was a left-handed hitter and hit balls as hard to left field as he did to right. People from all over the league used to call Bill Starr and want to know if Luke Easter was going to play and, if he was, they'd want to make reservations.

Jack Graham was great there. In one period he had forty-eight [actually forty-six-Ed.] by July of 1948 and he got hit in the head. In Wrigley Field one time, an afternoon game, there's the sun and shadows and he lost sight of the ball and it hit him right in the head.

Bill Starr brought in John Ritchey and some of the early black players. It was hard to adjust to it right away. The same situation occurred when Rickey brought Robinson in. People like Minoso, Simpson and Easter helped speed the acceptance of black players- no doubt about it. You know in one period you had to be twice as good. They were handicapped to start with and now its accepted without t any problem. They're part of baseball and have played a big part, I'll tell you that.

Now in '54, I was a coach and Lefty O'Doul was the manager. He had been in San Francisco and was a great hitter, you know. Right up until his late years, he used to hit in batting practice to kind of show the boys how it should be done. I was sorry to see Lane Field go. It was like old home week all the time. Of course, we later went to one in Mission Valley (Westgate Park) and that was one of the finest little ballparks I ever played in. Lane Field was right near the railroad tracks, near the ocean. There were a lot of navy ships and many sailors used to attend the games. It was only a stone's throw from the ocean. The fans were real close. When we won the pennant, I never saw such enthusiasm and excitement in my whole life. That was in 1937.

You know I miss the Coast League. I started here. I was a coach and player for years. The Coast League, in the period when I played there, when they had DiMaggio, Williams and Oscar Eckhardt and those fellas, it was the finest minor league in the country... very close to the major leagues. The only thing missing was the majors had a good pitcher out there every days. It was a good league, an eight club league. There were a lot of guys who made a career in the PCL. By 1950, it was more of a farm system.

Now, of course, it's a different sort of league. The [expanded] major leagues are taking all the top players, the cream of the crop. I miss the old Coast League."
INTERVIEWED BY JAMES D. SMITH III

EARL KELLER, sportswriter.
BORN: 3-30-15   **DIED**: 11-13-95

Earl Keller was a Tribune sportswriter for 46 years. He covered the PCL Padres from Opening Day (March 31, 1936) through the 1964 season. "Earl the Pearl" became the recognized expert of the Lane Field era. He was president of both the National and PCL Baseball Writers Association in 1962. A stickler for accuracy, Keller prepared Records of San Diego Padres, 1936-1965. Earl is remembered for his energy and generosity. Over the years, he maintained lasting friendships with the Padre players.

"We were just a little hamburger town. Things really picked up when the Padres got here. They were named at the old San Diego Athletic Club. We had a couple of meetings and they decided on the Padres because of the missions. It was kind of a contest and a committee picked it.

I was in high school and I learned at the old *San Diego Sun*. Mike Morrow taught me how to keep score. Old Mike, 'Turkey Neck', what a good guy. The *Sun* called me up and asked if I wanted the job [covering the Padres] at $100 a month and I said, 'Boy, do I!' Then I went to the *Tribune*. Twenty-five bucks a week was like a million then. I was getting five bucks a week writing golf news. I learned in the old Scripps-Howard days and, boy, they worked.

Bobby Doerr came down from Hollywood with George Myatt and George McDonald. He was steady. I remember one Saturday in San Francisco and he went six for six. Even O'Doul pitched one inning. Doerr was a quiet, soft-spoken, steady player.

Shellenback was a good pitcher. He was an awful nice man. On a Sunday, he pitched against Freddie Hutchinson on his debut and beat him, 2-1 in Seattle in a seven inning game.

Do you remember Tommy Thompson? I'm talking about thrills. This guy, tenth or eleventh inning, he'd hit a home run. I'll never forget in right, the fence was about four feet high and he ran for a ball, caught it and went over the fence. I remember Cole, the umpire...they argued about it half an hour or so and finally said, 'No.' He was off the playing field and didn't allow it. Swede Jensen, in left field, that fence was about four feet, would go back and fall over it. They put up another fence on top of it.

We got Chaplin and Dallessandro for Vince DiMaggio. DiMaggio was a nice guy with a great arm, but he would swing at balls two feet outside. Chaplin won 23 in '37. We were in spring training (1939) and I was going to come back. I brought him [Chaplin]. He had to talk to [Padres President] Lott about the contract for that year. I dropped him off at Lane Field. The next morning, I had to go to work at 5:30 in the morning and was told so-and-so is trying to get a hold of you. Jim Chaplin was just killed in an auto accident. We rang the police. This woman was a good friend of he and his wife in Florida. They went down (to Mexico) on Friday night and they were coming back. A car was stalled in the road and she didn't see it and hit it. He went through the windshield and his jugular vein was cut and he died on the steps of the hospital. He was a fine person and what a pitcher.

Dallessandro came here in '38. He was built like a little fire plug. He hit .368 and 50 doubles in 1939. He hit'em everywhere. Just a damn good hitter. The major leagues were just a little too fast for him.

Shanty Hogan and Jimmie Reese lived at the Southern Hotel. He'd (Hogan) drink a whole bottle. They didn't have any room service. If he wanted another, he'd just shout, 'Heeeeeeeyyyy' and shake the whole place. They knew what he wanted. He stole second base one time. Oh-oh was his number. He tore up half the dirt sliding into second.

Bill Thomas, he was a nut... bad news, divorces, wives. All I know he was always in some kind of trouble, di-

Lane Field action, 1940s.

vorce, beating up his wife. I remember he threw hard. [Thomas holds the minor league record with 383 pitching victories. He was also suspended for 2-1/2 years for 'conduct detrimental to baseball'] Yank Terry was a fastballer... a fast pitcher. He went to the Yankees. He was a fine gentleman.

Mel Mazzera, do you remember him? Right fielder in '42. We sold him to the White Sox and he wouldn't go. *There* was one of the most spectacular players. Left-handed thrower and hitter. He threw out so many guys trying to go from first to third. He only hit about .270, but he drove in over a hundred runs and always when it counted. The

Mel Mazzera Day.

next year, he did the same. I always liked those money players. He always came through and he had a great throwing arm.

Players are so different now. All they care about is the money. Norman Brown was here in '42 and he used to open a can of Campbell's Soup and *gulp* it went right down. The players used to have picnics and their wives and everybody would get together. Nowadays they don't give a damn. There was more spirit then.

Bill Starr said fans don't like seeing them [players] too friendly with the other team. They want to see 'em strike 'em out. I remember Jack Calvey, he was the shortstop in '42, '43, '44, he had a bottle right underneath the dugout and he'd go in there and between innings, he'd have a snort. He was something.

[Dick] Gyselman was a great fielder. He was one of Bill Starr's favorites. He could hit. On the train, he'd take his kids along and was going up and down those cars chasing those little bastards.

Bill Wight was a fine person. Great curve ball. Never saw such a curve ball. God, how that would drop.

Somebody phoned Greenberg and said, 'I've got a helluva right-handed hitter for you.' Later they found out he [Luke Easter] was left-handed. Old Bill Veeck

Spring training, 1946.

found out and wanted him back, but Bill Starr said, 'No, you've got an agreement for him to stay here for half the season.'

Up in Ontario, in spring training, his first time up, he lined one over the right field fence. When Luke Easter hit, the ball would rise just like a golf ball. Luke had a bum knee. One night, the third baseman was playing way back and Old Luke laid down a bunt and he hobbled down to first base and he beat it out for a hit. I'll never forget that.

In '66 or '65, I was in Rochester, New York for a baseball meeting. I went out to take a walk and went down a couple of blocks and here was Luke Easter. He picked me up and squeezed me. He was so big and powerful. He was a fine man. It was terrible how he was killed by robbers. He wouldn't give them the money."
INTERVIEW BY JAMES D. SMITH III AND BILL OHLER

BILL SKELLEY, infield.
BORN: 1-7-19   PADRES: 1937

Hoover High School had Ted Williams; San Diego High had Bill Skelley. When local high school talent was discussed, Ted Williams and Bill Skelley were mentioned in the same breath. They grew up playing baseball together at University Heights playground. Bill's tenure with the Padres was brief, but he played well in the 1937 Shaughnessey playoffs when San Diego won the PCL Championship in an eight game sweep. He was the most valuable player of the Western International League in 1939 when his 208 hits produced a .366 batting average for Wenatchee, Washington.

"I graduated from high school in February of 1937. I think the Padres were just looking for another young man from San Diego, so I sat on the bench. Wally Hebert and Cedric Durst were two real nice guys. Whether you were a vet or rookie, it didn't matter. The thing that impressed me as much as anything was riding in taxi cabs, riding on trains and staying in hotels. And, we won the playoffs that year, too and I got to play. George Myatt and Jimmie Reese were out for some reason, so I got to play in the Sacramento games. Our team won eight straight! I remember the first two times up, Ted hit the wall in center field, which was almost 400 feet and got doubles. The next time, he almost decapitated the first baseman and then he singles up the middle. Four for four! He was a pleasure to watch. Ted was exuberant, but he had a lot of common sense and he sure knew pitchers. He would tell us how a pitcher would pitch in a certain situation to a certain kind of hitter and what we could do and he was almost always right.

As kids, we lived on the stub of Olive Street at the north end of the bridge on 30th Street. Ted lived up on Utah (Street). My friends and I would go up to University Heights playground and play ball as soon as it was open. It was well supervised and fenced. They were great places for kids to play and we used to play Over-the-Line. Ted was the best of us all. He could dunk and he could hit it out there. If there was a game, Ted was in it. We also played a game called Big League. There were two guys on a team and we'd hit into the backstop. There were many rules and ways to get hits by hitting certain spots on the backstop. They had caged handball courts there. They were about 20 feet by 40 feet by 20 feet high. We'd play in there and you didn't have to chase the ball. Ted loved 'pepper' and he had the bat a lot of the time. Sometimes, he just couldn't hold back and the baseball

Bill Skelley

Brother Mel Skelley slides back to first base during an exhibition game with the Chicago White Sox at Lane Field.

Out at home?

Ed Stewart

would ricochet and it was dangerous sometimes with him batting. I never got hurt. We were just kids playing and having fun.

There was a 20/30 tournament up in Pomona. San Diego High and Hoover went up there. There were a lot of fields without fences. The ball kept rolling into our field and every time I looked, it was Ted rounding the bases. If the other teams knew him, he went 0-for-0, because they'd just walk him. If they didn't know him, he went 4-for-4.

When Ted and I were with the Padres in '37, I had a '29 roadster. I'd pick up Ted at his home on Utah and he'd ride to the games with me. I remember his mother saying, 'Teddy, have you got a handkerchief?'"

ED STEWART, outfield.
BORN: 6-15-16   PADRES: 1937-40

Eddie Stewart, Bobby Doerr, Steve Mesner, George McDonald and Rod Dedeaux were all Lane Field Padres who learned to play baseball at Manchester Playground in Los Angeles. Ed attended UCLA where he was on the all-conference baseball team for three years. After languishing on the Padre bench, Stewart was sent to Bellingham (Western International League) in 1939. He hit .320 in 74 games and led all third basemen in fielding. He once knocked himself out when he swung so hard at a pitch that the bat came around and hit him in the head. Stewart also played 61 games for San Diego that season and hit .306. A good year with the Padres in 1940, earned promotion to Pittsburgh. In a nine year major league career with the Pirates, Yankees, Senators and White Sox, Ed complied a lifetime .268 BA and twice led the American League in pinch hits.

"Bobby Doerr recommended me to San Diego when I was playing at UCLA. As soon as the semester was over, I went right to San Diego. They wouldn't let me take road trips, because Lane was trying to save money. I'd get so mad. I didn't play that much in '37 and played more in '38 (.270 BA). Then I got sent to Bellingham and started to hit. They had me at third, but I wanted to get back in the outfield. In '40, I had a great season (with San Diego) and hit .320. I played right field all year and led the PCL outfielders in assists. I think it was 27. I had a good arm then.

We were playing Oakland in my first year in '37. Joe Abreu was the shortstop for the Oaks. A ground ball went to him and he missed it. He went to pick it up and missed it again. Then he kicked it. I yelled out, 'Hey, Joe! Get a stick and kill it.' He looked over and smiled. He didn't know who said it. You couldn't see in or out of the dugouts at Lane Field. They were really dugouts. They were below the field. When we won in '37, they voted me a third share. I told Ced (Durst) I didn't deserve any, because I didn't play. He said to take it and I did. It was $60.

They had him (Steve Mesner) chewing tobacco in San Diego. He had a tough play and swallowed his chew. They had to take him out of the game. Oh, did he get sick! He never chewed again after that as far as I know.

Howard Craghead was a gentleman and he had a good curve. Jack Salveson was a strike pitcher. He was always around the plate. He didn't waste a pitch. I loved to hit against him. His games went about an hour and thirty minutes.

I got married on a Monday in 1940. That was our day off. Seattle came in Tuesday. 'Kewpie' Barrett was pitching and he hit me right on the handle. It was a dying swan that the shortstop couldn't catch and the left fielder couldn't get in on. Someone in the Seattle dugout called out, 'Honeymoon line-drive.' The whole ballpark heard it and everybody laughed.

Look at this picture. Like a damn fool, I took it to the umpires' room to show it to them. I had all three umpires converge on me. 'What are you doing here? Get the hell out of here!' They knew they blew it. That was in 1940. The press box was way up over home plate and they took the picture for the paper. It was early instant replay.

Stan (Sperry, Padres second baseman) got on me one day. People were getting base hits and I'd kind of lob the ball in. He'd yell, 'Throw the ball! Throw the ball!' So I did and he was happy.

When I went up to Pittsburgh in 1941, it was the first time I had ever been in New York. I asked Rip Collins to show me the town. I thought I could see all of New York in one night. This is a picture (a photograph of Stewart in a New York uniform) that I really like. It is really something to wear the Yankee pinstripes.

The best ball club I ever played on was Kansas City in '47. Billy Meyer was the manager. He was the best I ever played for. Half the team went up to the majors the next year: Hank Bauer, Gus Niarhos, Jerry Coleman, Bill Wight, Harry Craft, Cliff Mapes. I remember the first time we went up to Minneapolis. They had Nicolett Park. You could reach out and touch the right field wall. That's the only ballpark I ever tried to hit home runs in. I got one my first time up and it would have been a home run in any ballpark, but that right field fence was so short. Bill Wight took a look at that wall and hid his face in his hands.

Minnie Minoso was a great guy. We had a doubleheader in Philadelphia and Minnie just owned them. He'd get three or four hits every time he faced their pitchers. Well, they'd keep knocking him down and finally they hit him. When the first game ended and we were in the clubhouse, he said, 'I'm going to make myself white.' He poured milk all over himself and we went out for the next game. Well, the milk soured and nobody would sit next to him, because he smelled so bad.

BILL STARR, catcher, owner.
BORN: 2-16-11 DIED: 8-12-91 PADRES: 1937-39

"Chick" Starr was born in Brooklyn, raised in Chicago and made his home and fortune in San Diego after joining the Padres in 1937. He began his professional baseball career in 1931 with Lincoln in the Nebraska State League. He worked his way up

through the minors to the Washington Senators where he was a reserve catcher in 1935-36 before coming to San Diego. He was also a back-up catcher for the Padres and liked to point out that he also once pinch hit for Ted Williams. He was the principal owner and operator of the Padres from 1944 to 1955 when he sold the team to C. Arnholt Smith. Starr worked diligently to gain major league status for the PCL and he was instrumental in getting an Open Classification for the league in 1952. He was a major developer in San Diego and generous with charitable organizations. In 1989, Starr wrote the fine "insider" book, Clearing the Bases.

"When I got here in 1937, the town had one interest and that was baseball. There was no horse racing to amount to anything or football or basketball. San Diego had a trolley going down Broadway. We played one night game a week, on Thursdays, and had seven game series. Many fans would just take the afternoon off. There were lots of bleacher seats - actually too many to make any money, because they charged fifty cents. In case we had an overflow crowd, they'd be in the outfield, roped off. Of course, no food peddled out there so we'd get benefit of that. We won the championship, the Shaughnessy Playoffs. We had a fellow in right field by the name of (Rupert "Tommy") Thompson who had the greatest year I've ever seen any player have.

We were playing in Oakland. It was a tie game. The bases were loaded in the bottom of the ninth with one out. A ball came out to right and Thompson knew it would fall in for a base hit. Instead of charging, Thompson began pounding his glove. The runner went halfway, then went back to tag up. Thompson caught the ball on one bounce and threw a perfect strike to throw the runner out. A perfect decoy and we won the game. Ted Williams wasn't that raw. Every player who ever saw him recognized that perfect swing and they would watch him take batting practice. His swing here was the same as you saw later in the major leagues. If you ever saw him, you knew he would be one of the best hitters there ever was.

Spencer Harris was a left handed hitter and thrower. He had a nice level swing. A pretty hard nosed guy. He'd finished his major league career and was probably in his thirties, but he was an excellent hitter. Not too good an outfielder, just there, not as good as Hal Patchett who was an exceptionally good outfielder, but he was a good hitter.

Owners are never popular, I don't care who he is, with the players. Almost like a line drawn. Bill Lane was the owner and had no heirs. A very wealthy man. He was a crabby old guy, but nice enough. One of the players on the club was the son of the President of the league. He was a writer. He used to tell me that Bill Lane asked him to also serve as his secretary, which he did. He said, 'You know that every month he gets checks and one check

Bill Starr

Vallie Eaves

Jim Lane signs contract to purchase Padres from Bill Starr (standing), 1955.

comes from mining stock and it is always about $10,000!' That's a lot of money, just one check.

One day he decided he wanted to distribute some money to some players, so he got ten or twenty dollar bills...brand new, crispy ones and put them in envelopes. When we sat down in our booths, there was this envelope with money in it. No note, nothing, just a gift. I remember one of the players opened it and said, 'How about that? A lousy ten dollars.' It stuck in my mind. A fella did something out of a sense of generosity and even though it was a small amount, it was just a nice gesture.

You have to remember that night baseball was new and the lighting was poor. Today's players have great lighting and they play most of their games under the lights. It was very difficult to play night baseball in the old days. During the Depression years, owners didn't have too many baseballs and they'd get very dirty. I remember the owners used to whitewash the balls. When a pitch would come at you, it would look like a cue ball. It was very scary for the hitter. You've got to see the seams. When you see the seam, you can see the rotation. You can follow it and see if its a breaking ball.

Dick Gyselman was tall, slim, could run like a deer, a great defensive player, hit well over.300 and he never got a look. It was right in the Depression and he never had a chance in the major leagues.

Between the end of my playing career and the time I purchased the Padres in 1944, I had no connection with the team. I was working in the off-season for a clothing store, Farley's. An official was a big fan and said, 'What are you doing at the end of the season?' I said, 'Going home to get married and get a job.' He said, 'Get married, come back to San Diego and work for me ... I'll make a salesman out if you.' I was given a job in the credit

department, did that for three years, retired from baseball and started my own credit collection business. We did that for five years, made a few dollars.

Well, Lane had died and the estate was just trying to get rid of the ball club. And I thought, 'Gee, I'd like to get back into baseball.' So I got a friend or two of mine to put up a little money. Actually, Arnholt Smith agreed to finance me. A wonderful man. That's how I got into ownership and stayed with it eleven years.

The situation was very bad when I came in. We purchased the club in competition with another group of people who were trying to manipulate the estate. They were just trying to drive the price down to get a bargain. The executor was a very honorable guy and said he'd never sell the club to that particular combine. When we came on the scene, we being Judge Luce, the father of Gordon Luce, and me, this guy said to the judge, 'I'm going to tell you what the price is. It's not negotiable. The way we do it, you hand me a check and I'll hand you a stock certificate for 100% of the stock. We want it clean and quick.'

There isn't a lawyer in the world who'd make a transaction like that. You don't know the condition of the corporation. We said can we look at the books and he said we'll give you three days and no more. We took a fast look at the books and he (Luce) said, 'As far as I can tell, nobody has been cooking the figures. You're taking the risk.'

Of course, the risk was also being taken by Arnholt Smith. Imagine a banker supporting a deal like that and he said, 'Well, sometimes you take a risk' and that's how we bought the ball club and when we bought it, it came as a complete shock to the other group. When I walked in to go to work, they'd cleaned out all the files. We had no records of any pending transaction. All I had was a list of the players and the payroll. It was really a bad situation. My test was to now find players.

The war was on. You never knew if you'd have a ball club. In 1945 I got a call from Pepper Martin, our manager, in Los Angeles: 'I haven't got anybody to play the infield. They're all gone.' I drove to Los Angeles, went to a playground, saw a kid who wouldn't get hurt too bad and said, 'Would you like to play for the Padres today?' I signed him. Baseball being a small industry, run by sixteen clubs, there were some wonderful men. They sent telegrams welcoming me to the lodge, so to speak. I said, 'I need players.' One said, 'I know one hell of a pitcher if you can get him out of jail: Vallie Eaves.' He was an Indian, but a drunkard. A judge got him out and he won a lot of games for us.

Pepper Martin was a real tough guy and he was a very religious guy. He never swore and didn't drink, didn't chase women, but he had a violent temper and he had the ball club intimidated. I said to him one day, "What can you do to keep this guy Vallie Eaves sober?" The next time he saw him drunk, he just punched him and knocked him cold. That's how he handled Vallie Eaves; he just flattened him.

The next year, he was pitching for us and I got a wire from Branch Rickey and it must have been a yard long. He wanted to buy Vallie Eaves, but typical Rickey, he was telling me all the bad things about Eaves. He was willing to take a chance about Eaves and set a fair price. He'd like him to pitch one more game before his offer was final, so I said, 'OK.' I called Vallie Eaves in and I said, 'Now Vallie, you've got a chance to go back to the major leagues. You're going to pitch tomorrow night. Get yourself a good night's rest. Stay away from the booze. This is your opportunity.' He said, 'I understand, Mr. Starr.'

Well that night, he want back to the hotel got himself a quart of liquor and several pints and got himself wholly drunk. He got up on top of the building of the hotel and began throwing bottles down on the people. Don't ask me to explain the rationale. Of course, the police came and got him and that ended that. I often wondered if I made a mistake by telling him? Did I put pressure on him and this was how he relieved the pressure?

When I became the operator, in the fall of '44, developing players and selling players was what kept us going. We were an independent league, as most were, and had loads of talent. We were sort of a professional hatchery. We didn't have any great ball clubs until we finally hooked up with Cleveland in 1948. The owner, Bill Veeck, said, 'I've got a manager for you: Bucky Harris.' Harris was with the Yankees. They won the pennant and lost the world series. That's the game when Bill Bevens lost the

no hitter and McPhail fired Harris! [The Yankees won the '47 World Series 4-3 over Brooklyn. Harris was fired for finishing 2-1/2 games behind Cleveland in 1948.-Ed.]I said, 'I don't think I can pay the salary he requires,' and he said, 'We'll take care of that and I also want you to take Red Corriden as his coach.' I said, 'I've already got a coach. I've got Jimmie Reese.' He said, 'Don't worry about it. I'll pay Corriden's salary' and I said, 'fine.' Ours was the only minor league club that had two salaried coaches and they got along fine.

But 1947 was the year Jackie Robinson came up. And I got to thinking, 'What would happen if I searched out and found some capable black player?' The Coast league was lily white and had some old timers who were very critical of Branch Rickey. I thought it was kinda stupid. That's how we got John Ritchey. Then we got Luke Easter. *INTERVIEW BY JAMES D. SMITH III and BILL OHLER*

AL NIEMIEC, infield.
BORN: 5-18-11   DIED: 10-29-95   PADRES: 1938-39

After playing college baseball at Holy Cross, Al Niemiec turned professional in 1933 with Reading in the New York-Pennsylvania League. Niemiec went to the Athletics in 1936, but he was back in the minors the following year. He hit .313 and was the top fielding second baseman in the Southern Association in 1937 for the pennant winning Little Rock Travelers. Al was sold to the Boston Red Sox and came to San Diego in 1938. He hit .304 that first year for the Padres and .279 in 1939 while leading the team with 26 sacrifice hits. In a landmark case after the war, a federal judge upheld Al Niemiec's suit against the Seattle Rainers and ruled that ballplayers returning from military service were entitled to one year's salary. Al got a full year of pay minus the $667 he had earned working as a beer salesman for team and Rainer Brewery owner, Emil Sick.

"We had a good ball club and had a lot of fun. We had a good bunch of guys and we'd all pull for each other. I was closest with Joe (Berkowitz) and George (McDonald). George was a comedian. Joe had a big nose. We were in the elevator and George said, 'Hey, Joe.' Joe says, 'What do you want?' And George said, 'Don't turn your head suddenly. You'll knock off everybody's hat!' George was always pulling gags on Joe and Joe was kind of serious.

One time, we were on the train. It was a hot, sunny day and the windows were down. They were playing cards and Les Cook was winning. Then the wind blew the money out the window. Les pulled a gun and said he was going to shoot. It sure was funny and George needled him.

Shanty Hogan was our catcher. He weighed about two-hundred-sixty pounds. He was on first and nobody paid much attention to him. He took off for second and slid in head first. He never got there and he dug a furrow in the sand. The players called time and they had to all pitch in to fill the hole he made. At night, he'd take a bottle of whiskey to bed and read wild west books.

My wife was expecting, so Shanty was going to go back to Connecticut with me. I told him I'd meet him the next morning at 7:00 outside the hotel. He wasn't there and about 7:30, Lt. (Mike) Shea (SDPD) drove up with Shanty. They'd been boozing it up all night. He was half asleep and he got in my car. I was going up a steep grade in the mountains east of San Diego. It was about six or ten feet to the edge and straight down. Shanty happened to wake up and he looked over that cliff and sobered right up real quick. He was sober the whole trip after that.

Lefty O'Doul was a great needler and he'd try to get your goat. He'd call me 'busher' and I'd just laugh at him. Then, one time, we picked off one of his men on second. O'Doul came running out and I says, 'Way to go, you bush league manager.' He swung at me and I ducked. I swung and hit him on the chin. They broke us up. It was a big fight and the police came. Mike Shea grabbed me, but nobody grabbed O'Doul and he hit me. We had a lot of fun and Lefty and I used to talk about that time.

Ted (Williams) went to Boston. (Dominic) Dallessandro and myself went to San Diego. They must have thrown in about a million bucks and a whole carload of jock straps, too. I was in officer training in Tucson and then Navy preflight at Corpus Christi. They needed a second baseman for a title game, but Ted squashed the deal. He said, 'Nothin' doin'. He can't play.' So I didn't get to go. One of the planes crashed. The game was in Pensacola, and half the team died, so Ted did me a favor.

Later, I applied to be the manager of Spokane (Western International League). Lucky for me I didn't get the job, because that was when Jack Lohrke wasn't on the bus that went over the cliff. I guess I've been pretty lucky in life, too. When I was in the Navy, we stopped in Boise. The plane wouldn't start, so we waited until the next day. A blizzard blew in and we heard that several planes had crashed, so I was lucky again.

In San Diego, Paul Gregory hit me right between the eyes with a pitch. I swung and couldn't get out of the way. I was staggering, but I didn't go down. Paul came running in to see if I was OK. I told him, 'If you're going to hit a Polack, don't hit him in the head!' He said, 'That was my very best fast ball. I must be losing my stuff. Maybe it's time for me to quit when I hit someone with my best pitch and he doesn't go down.' Paul is the one who got me into the Navy.

One time, in the ninth inning of a tight game, I told Jim Tobin (brother of Padre Jack Tobin), 'Brother, get on your shoes, throw the ball down the gut and no extra innings.'

Al Niemiec

Spencer Harris and Al Niemiec do a little fishing during Lane Field flood.

Shanty Hogan

A History of the San Diego Padres (1936-1957)

Joe Hauser

Spencer Harris

John "Swede" Jensen

Earl Keller used to kid me that I was the first Black player in the PCL, because my skin was so dark.

That picture of us fishing is a good one. Spencer Harris and I were just pulling a gag. We got a couple of rods and went out on the dugout. We had a lot of fun in those years.

I was playing for Seattle in '42 and Hal Turpin pitched a no-hitter against San Diego. The sun shown badly at second during the ball game. There was one out to go and (Bill) Salkeld was pinch hitting with two outs. He swung and the ball came my way, in the sun, but I caught it for the third out. Turpin walked to me and said, 'Thanks.' They are all good memories and it sure was a lot of fun."

SPENCER HARRIS, 1B, outfield.
BORN: 8-12-00   DIED: 7-3-82   PADRES: 1938

Spencer Harris is the all-time minor league career leader with 3,617 base hits, 2287 runs, 743 doubles and 4,104 total bases. He collected 164 hits with the Padres in 1938. That year, Harris batted .301 and led the team with 39 doubles and 92 RBIs. A minor league star who broke in with Tacoma in 1921, he also played four seasons in the major leagues with the White Sox, Senators and Athletics from 1925 to 1930. The following interview was conducted with his old teammate from the Minneapolis Millers, 98 year old Joe Hauser. "Unser Choe" was quite a hitter himself. Twice in the minors he hit over 60 home runs and in 1924, his 27 homers for the Athletics were second only to Babe Ruth's 46 home runs in the American League. He also managed Sheboygan for several years in the Wisconsin State League. Joe died in 1997.

"Spencer Harris is dead? I didn't know that. We played together for five years in Minneapolis. He was a little bit of a punch hitter if you know what I mean. Not a long ball hitter, but a good hitter. He could hit in the clutch and the clutch was every day. I think he hit third. Christ! That's 60-70 years ago and I can't remember a whole lot from back then. He was a nice guy, but I didn't do much with those guys away from the ballpark. I don't care what they did away from the ballpark.

I know we didn't make any money. I hit 69 home runs and drove in 182 runs for Minneapolis in '33 and I was cut to $400 (a month). If you got around twenty (home runs) in those days, you were a big man. I got $400 a month for all five years I was with Minneapolis. It was, 'Take that or you won't have a job!' The owner was a son-of-a-bitch and so was Ty Cobb!"

JOHN "SWEDE" JENSEN, outfield.
BORN: 3-2-17   PADRES: 1939-49

John Jensen came from the San Diego sandlots to play for the Padres in 1939. "Swede", a popular and consistent performer, hit over .300 four times. He led the team with a .305 average in 1941 and tied for club leadership in home runs two years later despite playing in only 49 games. Jensen and his good friend, Al Olsen, went into the Army Air Forces during the 1943 season. He returned from the service to hit .300 in 1946 and a personal high .307 in 1947. "Swede," who is actually of Danish descent, spent most of his professional baseball career in San Diego. He is the first of eight graduates from Hoover High School to have played for the Padres over the years.

"We all grew up in North Park. Ted (Williams) lived on Utah (Street) and we lived on Iowa (Street). We'd go up to the playground when it opened. All the kids played at the playground then. There was no Little League. I'm not a big fan of Little League. Those coaches put too much stress on the kids. I remember taking a bunch of kids to Little League and someone was always crying when we came home. Baseball should be fun.

I was working at Graybar Electric (on West Market Street) after high school. I hadn't picked up a bat and ball for a couple of years and one time, I stopped by North Park and they were a man short for winter league. I played 8, 10 or 12 games and I was going great. A nurse owned the Padres then and Major Lott (Padre president) called me. He said, 'I understand you're a young man who likes to play ball.' He opened his desk and started pulling out $100 bills. I hadn't seen quarters 'till then. When he got to $700, I signed. That was 1939.

I remember the first game I played for the Padres. It was against a left-hander whose name I don't recall. I got two hits in the ball game and I was so elated. I had a single and a double in my first three times at bat.

I played at home, but didn't get to travel with the team. I was left off the list for three trips and I got up the gumption to go to Major Lott and the next day, I was on the list. Dom Dallessandro played against right-handers and I played against left-handers. They sold him and I played regular in '40. I hit .305 or something like that. Dominic had hit .360 or .370. He was a good ballplayer. We finished in fourth place and each of us got three or four hundred dollars. That was good money.

It was just as well for me to have played in the Pacific Coast League as the major leagues. They almost made us (the PCL) a major league. We had a working agreement with major league teams and they'd send guys down. They couldn't break into our lineup. It was a good league with good pitching. Tony Frietas struck me out five times one night with his screwball.

George McDonald was the best first baseman anywhere. He held out one year, so when he came back, Al Olsen and I started singing, 'Somebody else is taking your place. Somebody else is playing first base.' Of course, as soon as George came back, he was on first.

One guy I really admired and who wasn't recognized enough was Lefty O'Doul. He should be in the Hall of Fame for all he did for baseball. I would have loved to have played for him. He had Ferris Fain up in 'Frisco. He took a rope and tied Ferris Fain into the batting cage so he couldn't pull out. He used to get on me at Lane Field. He'd really chide me, 'Pitch him outside. Pitch him

outside so he can hit those nice flies to deep center.' And, I'd hit them to Dom DiMaggio and Lefty would clap.

I was told I'd get a $500 bonus if I hit .300 and the last day of the season, I was .2996 and Dick Gyselman was the third baseman for Seattle. The outcome wouldn't change the standings. I told Dick that I needed one base hit to get my bonus. He said, 'I'll tell you what. I'll play so far back, if you lay one down, you'll beat it out by thirty feet.' I bunted and it was so hard it went through the pitcher's legs to center!

I remember when we stayed at the old Empire Hotel in San Francisco and they were having a big dance. The ballplayers were playing around in the hallways in their pajamas and riding the elevators with the guests who were all dressed up for the dance. Another time at a dime-a-dance place in Oakland, a bunch of us went and there was a real pretty girl, but she was deaf and dumb. We told Cookie (Trainer Les Cook) that she had seen him and really liked him. He bought a bunch of tickets and spent them all on her. When he came back, he said, 'You know, I told her all about myself, but she never said a word.

Del Ballinger could back into a pitcher's throw like nobody else. I've seen where he'd get hit on a strike by sticking his butt into it and the umpire wouldn't let him take first base. One day, we weren't playing and we got some of Cookie's black cord that he used to lace up gloves. We nailed it into a ball. The dugouts in San Francisco were three or four feet deep. I hid in the bottom and Del stood at the top. He rolled the ball out. Old Powell was the umpire. The pitcher was getting ready to pitch and Powell called, 'Time.' Ballinger said, 'Now' and I moved it about a foot. He came after it and I kept pulling it a little. Finally, he threw us both out.

One day, we were playing the Hollywood Stars. Babe Herman was playing for them. We had a pitcher named Pat Tobin. He was having one of his worst days. I was

Swede Jensen and Debs Garms

Al Olsen

The Olsen family in new car presented on Al Olsen Day, 1950.

playing center field. I must have chased four or five balls in left and right center that went for doubles and triples. I came in to the dugout and an old gentleman sitting there said, 'Son, why don't you learn to play the hitters better?' I said, 'Why don't you go home.'

At the end of the season, I got a call from Railway Express. The voice asked if I needed a job for the winter? I sure did! When I went in, the man asked if I remembered him. He had gotten on me when I was having a bad day and I had gotten smart with him. Well, he gave me the nicest job and he was the nicest man. I was embarrassed. We were good friends with the fans and the kids in those days. It was wonderful.

I always felt bad about the way John (Ritchey) was treated. He had to room alone. He was a helluva fine ballplayer. He was a helluva hitter and catcher. He was quiet and a good man. When I got sent to Atlanta, my teammates couldn't understand how I could play on the same field with colored ballplayers. I told them, 'One of these days, you're going to be shaking their hands when they cross home plate after hitting a home run.' They didn't like that and they ostracized me.

I liked to pitch batting practice, but the only guy I was leery of was Luke Easter. He was so strong it was scary out there on the mound. He was a great guy. I remember years later when I was at an all-star game. Now, I'm a big man, six foot one, but someone came up behind me, wrapped their arms around me and the next thing I knew, I was two feet off the ground! It was Luke. It was either Luke or Ted (Williams) who hit the longest home run on the train. I think it was Luke.

A lot of guys think that the game will last forever, but it doesn't. I had eleven glorious years in baseball in San Diego. Baseball came easy for me. A lot of ballplayers had to work at it. I never found it a hard job. It just came natural."

AL OLSEN, pitcher.
BORN: 3-30-21   DIED: 7-3-94   PADRES: 39-43,46-48,50-52

Lefty Al Olsen was a Lane Field Padre longer than anybody else. Over the course of eleven seasons, he won 114 games, with his best year in 1950 when he posted a 20-15 mark. After returning from the Army Air Forces in 1946, Al lead the Padres with a 2.91 earned run average. For years, The Baseball Encyclopedia credited him with a major league appearance in 1943. Research revealed that the player was someone else wearing the uniform assigned to Olsen by the Red Sox during spring training. Following baseball, Al Olsen went into coaching and later became athletic director at San Diego State College. He is remembered for hiring an unknown football coach named Don Coryell who led the Aztecs to national gridiron prominence. This interview was conducted with Al's wife and high school sweetheart, Mary Olsen.

"He was almost 18 when he signed with the Padres. His birthday was in March. We got married when we were both 20. We went to Las Vegas, but the man said, 'I'm sorry, son, but you're not old enough.' I was, because girls only needed to be 18. He told Al to call his folks, so he did that. We waited and waited. They knew we were going to get married. Finally, Al said, 'Let's try another clerk and I'll lie about my age.' And, that's what he did and we got married at The Hitching Post. Every time we'd go past it when we were in Las Vegas, we'd give it the raspberries.

Mel Skelley and Al were close buddies. They were in the same class at San Diego High School. Al was an only child and the Skelleys were a big family and they were a wonderful family.

Al wasn't real big. He was slight in build, but he threw hard. He blamed it on his youth. If he didn't like certain food, his parents wouldn't make him eat it. He played on the sandlots and tennis courts all the time. Tennis might have been his favorite sport. I'll tell you, Al couldn't dance a lick, but he was very graceful on the tennis courts or playing badminton.

Al and John Jensen went in the service together. They were the best of friends. They didn't know what to think when the other men were dismissed and they were told, 'You and you, stay!' They were sent to Special Forces. Al went to Guam, Saipan and Tinian. He was the athletic trainer for the pilots when they'd come back from a mission. They played baseball, too. It was so hot, they hardly wore any clothes. They liked to drink beer after playing ball. Don't all ball players do that?

Al was given this trophy the year he won 20 games (1950). He always said you can't eat trophies. They gave him the night and a car. He got all kinds of nice gifts and the fans received a picture of Al in his uniform. He autographed them. They made it into a baseball card. I was very shy, so I remember going down on the field. Thank goodness they didn't ask me to talk. It was a nice tribute to Al."
INTERVIEWED BY: RICH NELSON AND BILL SWANK

PAUL MADIGAN, photographer.
BORN: 8-28-16   DIED: 4-1-96

Paul Madigan's photos record the history of motorcycle and automotive racing in San Diego. He also loved to capture the artistry of professional wrestlers and strippers at the old coliseum and the infamous Hollywood Theater. Madigan collected cornets, trumpets and motorcycles. As a youngster, he marched with the Bonham Brothers Boys Band and later won numerous marksman awards with his pistol. He helped build the railroad layout at the San Diego Model Railroad Museum. Paul was a man of many diverse interests, but since he did not like baseball, he would dodge trips to Lane Field whenever possible. It is a shame there are not more exciting Madigan action shots of the Padres.

"I went down (to Lane Field) on assignment by (San Diego Union sports editor)Steiner . He'd tell me who he'd want pictures of. I remember names like Dallessandro, Minoso, West, Graham, Easter. They used to hit home runs and they'd bounce out on Pacific Highway. I did my own processing. I'd make the pictures and they'd use them (in the paper) the next morning.

In those days, they didn't have a box (for the photographer). You'd go on the field to take the pictures. I was about ten or fifteen feet away from the batter. I just composed the picture to fill up the negative. If you got hit in the head, that was your fault. I'd stay up there til I got what I wanted, then I'd beat it. I was never criticized for hanging around too long.

The press box was a unique vantage point, but it was isolated from the action. I preferred being down on the

"How to make a baseball disappear in two easy lessons by the Mighty Mite." - Headline which appeared in San Diego Union, August 8, 1939. Photos of Dom Dallessandro.

Steve Mesner

Steve and Charlene Mesner, with daughter Steffani.

Steve Mesner turning double play.

field to get the guy sliding home and getting tagged out. They were the most interesting shots. You always wanted action shots.

These pictures are of (Dom) Dallessandro. They were used in the paper. Do you see the caption says these pictures weren't posed? They were real action shots taken during the game from only about ten feet away.

◆◆◆

STEVE MESNER, shortstop, third base, second base.
BORN: 1-13-18   DIED: 4-6-81   PADRES: 1940, 48-49

Steve Mesner was a very valuable ballplayer. In 1937, young Stevie was selected as MVP for his hometown Los Angeles Angels. After batting .341 in 1940, he was named the Padres' Most Valuable Player. Mesner was voted the Most Valuable Player by the 1946 Sacramento Solons. Although at the end of his career, he still hit .343 for Ogden in 1952 to lead the Pioneer League. Despite a six-year major league career, Steve truly loved playing in the Pacific Coast League. He was inducted into the Padres Hall of Fame in 1966. His Baseball Guide collection was used extensively to research this project. At the time of his death, Steve was working on a baseball calendar. For years, he had cut small pictures from newspapers and wrote the players' names beside their birth dates. Steve was, himself, a true baseball fan. The following interview was conducted with his biggest fan, his wife, Charlene "Mom" Mesner.

"Steve's favorite story was that when he started in baseball, Bobby Doerr's father bought him his first uniform and his own father burned it. Steve's parents believed in work, work, work. They didn't believe in baseball. Well, the Angels had a tryout camp. Steve was only fifteen. Truck Hannah was the coach and Steve went up to bat. Hannah said, 'Hey, kid, get out of here! You're too little." He started to go, but his old American Legion manager told him to go back. He hit three over the fence! So they put him in at shortstop and he kept hitting them harder. He handled everything and they signed him to a

contract and sent him to Ponca City (Oklahoma where he hit .359 in 1934).

One time, Steve was spiked from his knee to his ankle. He had something that looked like a rain gutter strapped to his leg. He was sitting in his street clothes, but his team needed him to pinch hit. He went in the clubhouse, put on his uniform and hit a triple or home run to win the game. He was tough. He got beaned so many times. Once he was in the hospital and the next thing you knew, he was on the field. He told the manager the doctor had released him. He hit a double and passed out at second. He thought he was a sissy for passing out. Some of those pitchers were mean. I got a hold of Kewpie (Dick Barrett) one time and told him he'd better never do that again!

We were up in Hollywood, at Gilmore Field, about five rows back, and Betty Grable came over and rubbed Steve's head. He had a burr hair cut. Steffani, she was about three, went down and said, 'Don't rub my daddy's head.' When she came back to me, she said, 'That sure was a pretty lady, Mommy." It was fun to go to Hollywood. George Raft, Gary Cooper, Lucille Ball, Harry James, they'd all be right there. Steve was in some movies, too. He was in *The (Monty) Stratton Story* with Jimmy Stewart.

We'd be sitting in the lobby of a hotel waiting for breakfast. All the guys would be sitting there. Steve would take Steffi along and the guys would tell her to go up to another player and say, 'Tell him he's a son-of-a-bitch.' I had to carry one of those little hotel bars of soap and I broke her of that. The guys sure thought that was funny. She was about three then. She couldn't talk too well yet.

When the hotel lobby would be full, the players would light a teammate's newspaper on fire. He'd run outside with the burning paper and they'd take his seat. They were grown men, but they'd laugh and think it was so funny.

Sometimes we'd be in the bar of the hotel when we were on the road. A player would be talking to a woman and

I'd spot his wife looking for him. Steve would tell him that his wife was there and I'd go to delay the wife until they got rid of the woman.

Winters were always tough. There was no money. (George) McDonald was always at our house. He is the funniest man I ever knew. He got a new toupee once and said, 'This one's so real I've got to feed it a saucer of milk.' I remember once we were eating chili and beans out of little cups. We never thought we were poor. We were just young, having fun and Steve was always happy and he was playing ball.

Big, old Ernie Lombardi. We loved him. He had the biggest hands. Steffi could sit in his hand. And Lou Novikoff was our friend. He would sit there and drink beer. He'd bite the caps off with his teeth. He really was a Mad Russian, but that Sacramento team was the drinkinest bunch I ever saw. One night, they all piled into Steve's Cadillac and he backed into a fire hydrant. A geyser went up ninety feet in the air. The guys told Steve to take off. But he felt so bad, the next day he went to the police and told them he did it. It cost him a lot of money to fix it, but that's the way Steve was.

Satchel Paige, I just loved him. Steve barnstormed with him and the colored teams. I was scared at first, but they were so nice. I remember Rockin' Chair Bassett. They were showboats and they were good, too.

Steve would give the shirt off his back. More than once, he'd see somebody he knew on the other team and they'd say, 'I like your shirt.' He'd take it off and give it to them. He was very generous. The players were always off on Mondays (in the PCL) and if they saw kids playing ball, they'd play with them. That's just the way Steve was. He loved baseball and he was so humble."

DEL BALLINGER, catcher.
BORN: 3-17-19   DIED: 3-18-91   PADRES: 1941-46

Del Ballinger, a Hoover High School teammate of Ted Williams and Johnny Jensen, began his professional career by hitting .307 with Midland (Texas) in 1938. He came home in 1941 and played for San Diego until they traded him to Portland during the 1946 season. Ballinger had a respectable .277 career batting average with the Padres. He set a PCL record in 1945 when he was hit 30 times by pitched balls. On occasion Del was known to get hit by pitches in the strike zone. He was also a league leader in practical jokes. The following interview was conducted with his daughter, Donna Saucedo.

"My dad loved to read these old baseball record books. He knew everybody in them and he was always talking baseball. After he retired from baseball, he worked as a bartender in about seven different bars in San Diego. When he'd move, the customers would leave with him, so the owners liked to keep him. A lot of people came just to hear his old baseball stories, like about Ted Williams, who was his best friend. Baseball players would visit him at the bar and the customers just liked to listen to them tell sports stories.

My parents got divorced when I was ten and my dad had to give up baseball to get custody of me. The judge didn't want all the traveling around. It was unusual for a dad to get custody back then. He gave up something he loved for someone he loved. I always felt guilty about that. He was the only dad at the Girl Scout meetings and he was the only dad for school open houses. He'd never miss those, but he did get me a substitute for a couple of mother-daughter banquets. 'Lefty' Darnell's wife would go with me. 'Lefty' played ball, too. I was the bat girl for the Ryan Aircraft baseball team. I was a tomboy. All guys want sons. Especially sports guys want sons.

I'm sure you've heard about my dad and the cap pistol. Well, here's the letter that they sent to him. I thought it was mean, but he thought they were as 'weak-minded' as they thought he was. He did it (shoot a cap pistol), because the game was so ludicrous at the time. [San Diego was losing, 13-3. -Ed.] The president of the league didn't understand how much the fans enjoyed his antics. People would say, 'You sure do pick it up' or 'We're coming back to see what you do next.' He made baseball entertaining and he loved baseball. He'd never pull anything when the game was on the line, because the game always came first.

He got along well with some of the umpires and he'd let them in on it if he was going to trick the batter. He'd pretend like he'd thrown the ball back to the pitcher and the batter didn't know that it was still in his glove. The pitcher would wind-up and go through his throwing motion. Then my dad would hit his mitt. The umpire would call, 'Strike!' The poor batter wouldn't know how the ball got past him. He'd do that a couple of times a year and sometimes they'd catch on. I know he did it in regular games in the PCL

Dell Ballinger

and the strikes counted. He told me about it. Sometimes he'd have the pitchers throw behind the batters and the umpire would call 'Strike' and that would always get the hitters mad, because they could really see the ball then. They couldn't say much when they didn't even see it.

If he'd get mad at an umpire, he'd move his glove and let the pitch hit the umpire in the mask. They'd have their face right over his shoulder and he'd just let the ball smack 'em. One time, I think it was in New Orleans or Indianapolis, it rained so hard that the dugout was full of water. His relatives from Tennessee were there watching the game. He fell into the dugout chasing a foul ball. He caught it and disappeared in the water. Well, he dropped the ball, but he swum around under the water until he found it. He came up with the ball. The umpire called the batter out. He said, 'He went in with it and he came out with it, so he's out.

He told me, 'I lost the doggone thing', well, probably he used a little stronger language, but in everyday talk, he didn't swear. But when he talked baseball, he used locker room talk. He tried not to swear around me. He was a good dad. I sure loved him."

DARWIN "GUS" HALLBOURG, pitcher.
BORN: 10-31-19   PADRES: 1941

Gus Hallbourg was 21-11 for Pampa of the West Texas-New Mexico League in 1940. After going 15-15 for Anaheim in 1941, he was recalled by San Diego. But Hallbourg's only mark in Padre history was a hitter and not a pitcher. After military service, Gus had a tryout with San Diego before being farmed to Spokane in the Western International League. There, he was one of seven to survive a fatal bus accident that claimed the lives of nine teammates on June 24, 1946.

Darwin "Gus" Hallbourg

"Rex Dilbeck and I were teammates in Pampa, Texas and we both made the All-Star team in 1940. Then we were both purchased by San Diego. I was never a regular, but I had a good year in Anaheim in '41 and I joined the Padres in Oakland. It was late in the season, after our season at Anaheim, in September. I got into a game in Oakland and I got a base hit and we tied the score. I guess they wanted to win the game, so they took me out and we ended up losing the game anyhow. It was the only time I got to hit in the Coast League. [1.000 lifetime batting average -Ed.] Then I got in the way of a line drive against Hollywood in San Diego and I was through for the year.

All the pitchers used to have contests about who would get the most hits. We had a big guy who was in the Cardinal organization and he would always win.

The War came and I was working in an airplane factory by Lindbergh Field and then I went in the service. I came back in '46 and '47 for spring training, but I didn't stay with the club (San Diego). I played with Bill Nettles at Anaheim. He and his brother, Wayne, were twins. They became cops in San Diego and Wayne's son is Graig Nettles who was the great third baseman for the Yankees. Pete Charowhas and I played together at Anaheim. He was a very nice guy. I also knew Jack Lohrke well. I was on the bus wreck in Spokane. Those of us who lived were very lucky. Jack was a fine player and he had just left for San Diego.

In those days, you'd never get released by a team. I ended up being owned by the Dodgers. I wanted to play for the Stockton Ports when they'd be in town, but the Dodgers wouldn't let me. That was in 1949 and I had a family. I had to go make a living then. When you start a family, you have to go to work!"

MEL MAZZERA, outfield.
BORN: 1-31-14   DIED: 12-17-97   PADRES: 1941-42, 44

After compiling a .268 lifetime batting average playing for the St. Louis Browns and Philadelphia Phillies, Mel Mazzera became a San Diego Padre. He led the team in home runs, triples, total bases and RBIs in both 1941 and 1942. Each season, he also topped the PCL in three-baggers. During 1942, Mel had the highest batting average (.308) on the ball club. His popularity with the fans resulted in "Mel Mazzera Day" on August 30, 1942. Mazzera subsequently became a Stockton police

Mel Mazzera

officer and retired as a sergeant after twenty-five years of service. In appreciation for his involvement in youth sports, Mel Mazzera Field was dedicated in his honor in Stockton on July 15, 1995.

"San Diego sold me to the Chicago White Sox in '42, but I turned it down because Chicago wouldn't give me what I was making in San Diego. I'd get a bonus from the Padres for hitting .300 or getting 100 RBIs and the White Sox wouldn't give me that much. San Diego was mad, because they had to return whatever they got for me, if anything, so I decided to fold it up. It wasn't worth it, so I became a policeman. San Diego told me later that if they knew I wanted to become a cop, I could have joined the San Diego PD and played for the Padres, too.

As things worked out, I rejoined the club in '44 when they would play in Sacramento, Oakland and San Francisco. I'd take vacation from the Stockton PD and go play ball for the Padres when they'd come up here.

I really enjoyed playing ball in San Diego. We sometimes wondered if we'd have been better off staying there. Eddie Pellagrini and I really enjoyed it in San Diego. They even had a special day for me. The fans were good. Jack Hatchett was a Padre, too. We both belonged to a baseball club consisting of former American Legion ballplayers. We played for Karl Ross Post in Stockton. We gave a $1,000 scholarship to the outstanding player each year and also helped out financially to the team. Jack passed away two years ago.

I would have enjoyed seeing George McDonald and Johnnie Jensen and the many friends we made while living in San Diego. From the photo, George hasn't changed much since I last saw him (in 1944). I visited with Jack Lohrke and some of the players I played against when they had the Coast League reunion at the Oakland Museum. Regarding the possibility of a get-together (in September 1997, San Diego), I hope, God willing, my wife and I can make it."

EDDIE PELLAGRINI, shortstop.
BORN: 3-13-18   PADRES: 1941

Eddie Pellagrini was San Diego's star shortstop in 1941 when the Padres placed third in the PCL. Batting .273, Pelly led the team in at-bats, runs and two-base hits. His baseball career was interrupted by the war, but after a four year layoff, he hit a home run in his first major league at-bat for the Boston Red Sox on April 22, 1946. Pellagrini played eight years in the big leagues with the Sox, Browns, Phillies, Reds and Pirates. He was baseball coach at Boston College for 31 years and their diamond was renamed Eddie Pellagrini Baseball Field in 1997. A very busy man, Pelly's social calendar is booked through 2003.

"I was only a kid when I played for San Diego and Mel Mazzera took care of me. He was a handsome guy and such a good guy. There were a lot of Italians on that team. Jack Divincenzi looked like Tony Martin, the singer. Of course, I was the best looking one of them all. Art Garibaldi had been Joe DiMaggio's roommate up in San Francisco. He said that everybody who roomed with him became a big league star. I was a very gullible kid. Very religious. Didn't swear or drink. I asked him, 'Do you need a roomy?' He was the first guy to tell me what a Dago was. I'd never heard of Italians being called Dagos. What a great bunch of guys!

This was our team: (Mickey) Haslin, third; Pellagrini, short; (Stan) Sperry, second, George McDonald on first. The outfield was (John) Jensen, (Hal) Patchett and Mel Mazzera. (George) Detore and (Bill) Salkeld and (Del) Ballinger were the catchers. Wally Hebert was a pitcher. I was talking with Ted (Williams) recently and when I was telling him about guys I played with on the Padres, he said, 'I grew up with most of those guys.'

That was a great league! (The PCL) That league could probably win the American League now. I loved San

Diego. They had the prettiest women and the nicest fans. I'd love to live there, but the best thing I ever did was coaching the (Boston College) Golden Eagles.

I started playing in 1938 with Danville, Virginia. Then I went to Canton, Ohio, then Scranton, Pennsylvania, then San Diego. I was always on a winning team. Then I joined the U.S. Navy in 1942 and we won the War. Then I joined the Red Sox and we won the pennant (1946). They sold me and it took 'em 21 years to win it again!

Zack Taylor was the manager at St. Louis (Browns). He could moan and I'll always remember Jack Graham coming into the dugout and telling Zack that he moaned too much. It was just the way Jack said it that was so funny. Look at Jack, he hit 25 [24 -Ed.] home runs with St. Louis and they released him the next year. He was one of the top home run hitters in the league! It didn't make any sense.

Rogers Hornsby was a tough guy. When he looked at you, it was like an animal looking at you. One time, I said, 'Well, Skip, I know a better hitter than you.' He looked at me and snarled, 'Who is it?' I told him, 'Ted Williams.' He'd didn't play me much after that. Look him up in the record book. For five years, he averaged over .400! [Playing for the St. Louis Cardinals from 1921 through 1925, Hornsby averaged .402 with 1,078 hits in 2,679 at bats. -Ed.]

Do you know what Pellagrini means? It's not even spelled right. It was probably some Irishman who changed it. It was my high school Spanish teacher, Spike Hennessey, who told me that I had a beautiful name. He said it should be spelled P-e-l-l-e-g-r-i-n-i. When the Pope goes out to greet the people, he says, 'A la Pellegrini' which means 'All you Pilgrims.' I'll always remember him telling me that.

Another thing I remember about playing in San Diego was that Bill Salkeld's brother worked in the movies up in Hollywood. I met this beautiful star and the guys were saying, 'Hey, Pelly, she likes you.' Kinda got talking to her and learned that she had broken her nose playing softball. I don't know why I did it, but I touched her nose and all her make-up came off. It was embarrassing. Then I walked in on Edgar Bergen doing a scene and screwed that up. Ced Durst was our manager. He'd tell us to keep your mind on baseball when we'd be playing in Hollywood with all those pretty stars watching us. Then I look over in the dugout and he's getting autographs!"

◆◆◆

FRED LANIFERO, second base.
BORN: 5-23-19   PADRES: 1941,46

Alfred Lanifero hit .279 for Cambridge in 1938 and earned honorable mention All-Eastern Shore League. Batting .302 for Springfield in 1939, Fred moved over to Western Association rival Topeka and registered a .328 batting average the next season. Military service would interrupt a promising career for the young Padre second sacker. After swatting an even three-hundred for San Diego during the '41 campaign, Fred's average slipped when he returned to the Padres following the war. But from 1947 through 1953, playing for Albany, Lanifero averaged a respectable .290 and his 169 base hits led the Eastern League in 1948. Later, he managed High Point, North Carolina in the Carolina League.

"I broke in with Cambridge, Maryland in '38, Class D. I played with Danny Murtaugh. Then I went to Springfield, Missouri, Class C and hit .300, but Branch Rickey released me. Next, I played with Bill Rigney at Topeka. Every year, I led the league in double-plays. I cheated a lot; I never touched the base.

Fred Lanifero

Yank Terry and son, Ronnie.

Larry Powell

San Diego bought me. I had a choice of playing in an all-star game in Salem, but the Padres were playing in Hollywood. I said, 'Hey, I'm going to Hollywood!' I remember the Ritz Brothers were in the stands, but I didn't really get to see any stars.

The army took it out of me. I was always a good stick man. Hitting was my forte. I was the guy who was supposed to take Jack Lohrke's place when he came from Spokane. I refused to go. I had told that to Les Cook. I didn't want to go before it (the accident) happened. Les stuck up for me and I didn't have to go.

I have that picture with the six Italians. They had great imagination in those days for taking pictures like that one of us getting haircuts. Eddie (Pellagrini) is a good friend. I went to his retirement party at Boston College and I would watch them when they'd come down to play Providence. We roomed together with the Padres. I stayed at the Southern Hotel. We were like family in those days. The fans recognized us and we were close. Money drives people apart. That's what killed baseball. It cuts down the camaraderie."

LARRY POWELL, pitcher.
BORN: 7-14-14   PADRES: 1941

Native Californian Larry Powell played most of his professional baseball career west of the Mississippi River in the San Joaquin Valley League, California League, Western International League and Pacific Coast League. He was 12-11 in '39 and 12-7 in '40 for the San Francisco Seals. Powell came to San Diego in 1941 and posted a 2-0 record before entering the army. He managed his hometown Visalia team in the California League during the 1954 season. Larry is a retired rancher.

"I was Seals property. Dominic DiMaggio and I were part of a deal with the Red Sox. He went up in '39 and I had to stay an extra year with the Seals. I was five-and-oh against San Diego in '39 and beat 'em twice in '40. But when I came to the Padres in '41, I was two-and-oh, so they never won when I played against them and they never lost when I played with 'em. That's a unique situation.

I was Boston Red Sox property and was optioned to Louisville, American Association, in the spring of '41. Louisville was loaded with pitchers and I was headed for military duty, 1A in the draft, so Boston sent me to San Diego where I played before I was drafted into the army.

Cedric Durst was the manager. George Detore was catcher. George McDonald was on first, Eddie Pellagrini was shortstop, Artie Garibaldi on third, Johnny Jensen in left, Hal Patchett in center and I can't remember right.

Del Ballinger was the other catcher. Wally Hebert was one of the pitchers and Al Olsen and Woody Rich. Del, Woody and I ran around together. Woody and I came from Louisville.

The first game I pitched was a seven inning one hitter, the second game of a Sunday double header, and I think Woody pitched a seven inning one hitter, too. Back in Louisville, they must have thought the PCL was pretty easy, because we did so well, but it was a good league.

How well I remember Wally 'Deacon' (sic) Hebert. I was drafted into the army and a night or two before I had to leave the Padres, Wally invited me to his home where his wife and mother-in-law fed me a southern fried chicken dinner. Delicious! That was the kind of fellow Wally was and a tough pitcher to face!

After the war, I was with L.A. and San Francisco and it was terribly frustrating, because I couldn't figure out what was wrong. I got myself messed up and I wasn't throwing the ball good. I figured I must be the dumbest player in the game, because I just couldn't get it right. It was so frustrating. It was later in Yakima that I got to know Pete Coscarart real well. He's a great guy and we still stay in touch at Christmas time. And Ted Williams - What a delight to watch him hit."

YANK TERRY, pitcher.
BORN: 2-11-11   DIED: 11-4-79   PADRES: 1941

Yank Terry was in organized baseball for seven seasons before he joined the Padres in 1941. He had split the previous season with the Louisville Colonels of the American Association (7-9) and the Boston Red Sox (1-0). After being optioned to San Diego, Yank responded with the "Triple Crown" in pitching (victories: 26-8, 2.31 ERA and 172 strikeouts) and was selected as the PCL's most valuable player. His performance earned a return trip to the Red Sox where he posted a lifetime 20-28 record over five seasons. 1941 was the career year for the Hoosier hurler who almost single-handedly pitched the Padres to the Coast League championship. (San Diego finished 4-1/2 games out). The following interview was conducted with Mrs. Yank Terry.

"Yes, I remember 1941 in San Diego and Yank went 26 and 8. I went to nearly all of the ball games, but I didn't like being by myself alone when they were out of town. I don't remember too many of the games. I'm seventy-nine and that was a long time ago, but it was his best year ever.

I remember the picture of the Padre fathers with their children. It was in a diamond shape and here is the reason why. We didn't have a highchair and Ronnie, he's fifty-

three years old now, was sitting on his potty chair. By
making the picture in a diamond, they cut it so you can't
tell it's a potty chair, because they cut that part off.

Yank got a trophy about two feet high and about a foot of
writing saying how valuable he was. One time, I heard
something in the other room. One of the kids had turned
it over and was using it for a stool to get something and
he broke it. One of my other boys made a lamp out of it
when he was in high school.

My husband was born and raised in a little town south
of here named Huron. There were these two little, red-
headed, tongue-tied boys who couldn't say his name
which was Lancelot. They'd say 'Yankset' and that's what
everybody called him. He didn't like his name, so he took
'Yank' as his legal name.

FRANK DASSO, pitcher.
BORN: 8-31-17   PADRES: 1942-44

Frankie Dasso

*Fireballing Frankie Dasso led the league with 154 strikeouts
in 1943 and set a PCL record when he whiffed 253 batters
during a 169 game schedule in 1944. This was the most
strikeouts since 1928 when Oakland's George Boehler
fanned 278 batters in a 191 game season. Dasso's fast ball
also kept the batters loose at the plate. In addition to leading
the league in bases on ball during his three seasons with
the Padres, he also led the league in hit batsmen in '44.
During his 18 year career, Dasso was the league leader four
times in strikeouts and five times in walking batters. Frankie
went 20-19 for the last place Padres the year before going
up to Cincinnati in 1945. He is a member of the Italian-
American Athletic Hall of Fame.*

"I was lucky to play ball in what was probably the most
romantic period of the game. The Pacific Coast League
was well run, well attended and the crowds were fervent.
If people couldn't fit in the ballpark, they'd be outside
sitting up on a hill. The PCL was more exciting than the
big leagues. They were more political and you'd better
keep your mouth shut. In the Coast League, you could
spend your time as you liked and then go home. It was
really baseball and we were even making more money.

Boston wanted me when I was eighteen. Joe Cronin said
to go to White Sox Park. He asked what I wanted and I
told him. That's how I became a professional ballplayer.
Teddy (Williams) and I joined them (the Red Sox) at the
same time. Joe Cronin had a funny idea about young
players. He wanted guys like Lefty Grove and Jimmie
Foxx. We had a falling out and I was ticketed to go, but I
was happy to be in the PCL. I flew all night, got off the
plane and pitched a one-hitter for Hollywood. You went
where they sent you. There was glamour in Hollywood:

Barbara Stanwyck, Bing Crosby, George Raft. They'd be
sitting right there on the bench with you.

In 1944, we only had three or four pitchers. Chet Johnson
broke his arm and I had to pitch a double header. I'd beat
Seattle in nine innings, 5-2 and I was out running the
next day. (Manager George) Detore told me that Rex
Dilbeck had mono. He said, 'I'd like you to go out there
and go as far as you can.' After fourteen innings, we beat
them, 1-0. I pitched twenty-three innings in two days.
We used to do that and it never hurt anybody. Of course,
I'd get a bonus if I'd win twenty games and I'd pitch every
day to get that bonus! It's not like today when guys go
two innings and have to come out. Even though we were
in last place, or damn close to it, we drew so many people
(246,150) that (team president) Major Lott gave us all a
bonus. And, I went 20-19 to get my bonus. We tried hard,
but just had a little bad luck.

I hold the Coast League strikeout record and nobody has
ever broken it. The closest anybody came was Sam Jones
when he was with San Francisco and I think he came
within fifteen. ('Sad Sam' Jones struck out 246 while
playing for San Diego in 1951.) I set the record before
going to Cincinnati."

MEL SKELLEY, second base.
BORN: 12-2-20   PADRES: 1942, 46

*Mel Skelley followed in his brother Bill's footsteps from a
championship San Diego High School team to the San Diego*

Mel Skelley

Padres. Along the way, he played briefly in 1939 for Oswego of the Canadian-American League which included a contest against those bearded barnstormers from Benton Harbor, Michigan, the House of David. Skelley batted .274 his first full year of professional ball with Topeka in 1940. The following season at Salt Lake City, he was one of the top defensive infielders in the Pioneer League. Mel hit a respectable .252 as the Padres' second baseman in 1942 and was named to the All-Star team.

"My dad used to coach kids' teams. I don't know how he did it, because he worked all the time. The people across the street from our home didn't plant a lawn in between their driveway, because it was our pitching mound. My dad would fix the garage door about once a year. It was made out of slat-like wood and we'd hit holes in it.

I was twelve-years old when I made my first American Legion team. I was the 15th man. I wasn't good enough to make San Diego's, so I went to the Hoover team. Ted was the pitcher and star. I got a uniform and I can say I played with Ted Williams. I also got to play one game on a service all-star team with Joe DiMaggio. Bob Lemon played for the Naval Training Center and we won 56 straight.

I remember once we were swiping some peaches. We'd fill our pockets, but Ted (Williams) wanted more. So he was stuffing them down the front of his sweater. The fuzz all rubbed off and Ted was itching all over. My brother Bill's roadster was red with cream-colored wheels and a convertible top. They'd drive down Broadway (in 1937) with the top down and Ted would bang on the side.

I started playing with the men when I was twelve and we'd travel all around the county, but I really remember playing in Tijuana. We had to dress in a whorehouse. My eyes were big as saucers while the men were having fun with the ladies. After the game, they'd go to the bars. I couldn't go in, so they'd bring me a bottle of pop and I'd sit in the car. When I was 13, I wised-up and played for Mountain Meadow Dairy. After their games, we'd go to the dairy and eat ice cream. I loved ice cream.

I remember that Cramer Bakery used to sponsor girls softball teams and they were pretty good. They called them 'the Buttercup Girls'. We hated it when we'd play them and slide into a base. We were 12 or 13 and they would help us get up. They couldn't always find enough girl teams to play against, so they'd play boy teams. Cramer was the grandfather or great-grandfather of the people who operate the Karl Strauss Brewery downtown and they are now opening a bakery.

In 1940, I was playing for Topeka, Kansas. I came on the bus one night with a bottle of pop. The manager made me get a beer. He said, 'You can't sleep sober on a bus.' That's how I got started drinking beer. He was right. We had some long trips at night and you slept better after a few beers.

Bugs were really bad back in the Midwest. You'd chew tobacco and put it on the bill of your cap, on your uniform and on your shoes. It would keep the bugs away. I'd learned that watching a movie, *Northwest Passage*, and the old-timer would use chewin' tobacco to keep the bugs off him. Then, at night, I'd use peroxide as a mouthwash to get the terrible taste out of my mouth.

Tom Rebello was the manager up in Salt Lake City. His claim to fame was signing Johnny Bench. There was this group of umpires that he didn't like. When he knew they'd be working a game, he'd have his wife fix things with a lot of garlic. I remember him going nose-to-nose with this umpire and the umpire kept backing away and waving his hand to get rid of the smell. Tom would cut up rubber bands. Then he'd sneak into the umpires' room and put them in the umpires' chewing tobacco.

Salt Lake City was the only ballpark I've ever been in that had a urinal in the dugout. Tom Rebello used to tell us not to take a leak before you'd bat. 'It'll take the edge off,' he'd say. We'd have to hold it...

I think I was the first striker the Padres ever had. I jumped from Class C to the Padres in '42, but they were paying me my Class C salary. I'd replaced Stan Sperry when he was sold to Louisville or someplace. I wanted to get married, so I asked for more money. I was out about a week. They gave me a little more, but not much, so I came back. I think I started for about $150 a month. Wally

Hebert sure was a nice guy. I remember that he and some of the guys gave me a rolls razor when I got married. It sure worked well and I don't know whatever happened to it. I wish I had it today.

I had a roommate who was always out late with the ladies. He'd come in, turn on the light and stand in front of the mirror combing his hair. Why would you have to comb your hair before going to bed? Then he'd leave a wake-up call and that would wake me up early in the morning.

The best roommate I ever had was 'Boots' Poffenberger. He looked just like Lou Costello. He came down to us from Detroit and he was pretty boisterous. When we were on the road, he'd spend everything he had the first couple of nights and then he had nothing. Guys were always borrowing your stuff, but he would never touch anything of mine, not even my toothpaste. He'd never make any noise coming in at night or if he got up early in the morning. When Boots was with Detroit, they had a detective follow him. He told them that they should give him the money they were giving the detective and he'd tell them where to go. All they'd have to do is go to the beer joint closest to the ballpark.

We had an old black man, Old Pegleg, who was like a mascot. He was always sitting in the dugout. I think Cookie (Les Cook) would let him in and he was never in anybody's way. He had to prop his peg leg up when he sat down. (Del) Ballinger took some thread and made a lasso. He hooked it around the peg when Pegleg wasn't

Boots Poffenberger

looking and he walked down the dugout. Then he'd gig it and the leg would move. Looking back, it was kind of mean, but everybody thought it was funny at the time.

When we were home, we'd be off every Monday and we'd all go to the beach with our families. Every guy would bring a case of beer and we always had to go get more. One time, George (McDonald) and Joe (Berkowitz) got so sunburnt chasing girls and riding their bikes that they had to cut George's uniform off after the next game. Another time, they were on the driving range and, somehow, somebody hit Joe in the head with their back swing. George and Joe had a lot of fun and got into a lot of mischief.

I threw a ball past George up at Sick Stadium (Seattle). He slipped and broke his leg when he went for the ball. There was some gravel along the wall for drainage and he lost his footing. Well, we visited him in the hospital and there was George jumping from bed to bed! He'd gotten something to drink right there in the hospital. But George is the one who taught me to throw low. He said, 'Never throw high. When you miss, miss me low and I can scoop them.' It made sense.

The coaches didn't really teach you much as far as fielding and hitting. Herm (Pillette) was the pitching coach and he'd pitch batting practice and run the pitchers, but that was it. Tom Rebello, in Salt Lake City, would bring out the scouts and that was the only time I ever heard of anybody trying to teach anybody in the lower minors."

◆◆◆

ED VITALICH, pitcher.
BORN: 4-22-20   PADRES: 1942, 46-47

Ed Vitalich's vivid memories of baseball in San Diego go back to the early Thirties. He played for St. Augustine High School and the University of Southern California, but his boyhood dreams were not fully realized until he wore a Padre uniform. Vitalich went 11-16 and 7-15 for the lowly Padres in 1946 and 1947. Wishing to stay close to the game, he pitched Padres batting practice into the Fifties. Ed is a retired optometrist.

"Jackie Allbright and I were the ball boys the night Babe Ruth came to San Diego to play an exhibition game. Bill Dickey was on the team, but Lou Gehrig wasn't. They played the San Diegans at old Navy Field. I couldn't have been much more than nine or ten years old.

On Opening Day of 1936, San Diego was playing Seattle. 'Kewpie Dick' Barrett was pitching for Seattle and Herman Pillette was pitching for the Padres. A friend and I got in and we drug the infield. There was a door to the Padre dressing room. They'd pick two kids to drag the infield and that is how I got to see the first professional game in San Diego with Bob Menke.

There's an old saying that the older we get, the greater we used to be. I think it was in 1937 and the Padres were playing against L.A. at Lane Field. The pitcher was Dick Ward and that was the day he pitched 12-2/3 consecutive hitless, scoreless innings. Pitching for the Angels was Ray Prim who later pitched for the Cubs. At the time, I was in high school. I worked at my dad's fish market (Chesapeake Fish) and I'd snuck off to see the game. At the end of nine innings, I felt I had to report in. I told my dad the circumstances and he gave me permission to go back. The Padres won in 17 or 18 innings. [San Diego won, 1-0 in 16 innings on August 30, 1938. -Ed.]

Now, in 1946, the first game of a double header, the Padres are playing L.A. and on the mound for the Angels is Ray Prim. I was on the mound for the Padres. We both pitched eight innings of shutout ball. The first of the ninth, an outfielder for the Angels, Eddie Sauer, hit one off the scoreboard for a home run. In the last of the ninth, Max West hit one out on the highway for a home run. Then we went scoreless to the twelfth inning and in the last of the twelfth, with two outs, Pete Coscarart came up to hit one in the left field bleachers to win the game! Pete is possibly one of the nicest guys to ever play ball and one of the most popular.

I loved Pepper Martin. When Rip Collins came, I didn't get along too well. He was aloof and a real hot dog. It's funny how when you're growing up, you have dreams to play baseball. In 1931, I was eleven years old. The old Hollywood Stars would take spring training at old Navy

Ed Vitalich

Field which was just north of where they built Lane Field. Home (plate) would have been beyond left field as it was facing the opposite direction. Do you know that to this day, I can name the first and last names of the whole team. Johnny Bassler and Hank Severeid, they were the two catchers. The pitchers were Frank Shellenback who later became manager of the Padres, Jim Turner, who had many good years with the Yankees, Emil Yde, a left-hander. First base was Ray Jacobs, second was Otis Brannan, third was Mike Gazella, shortstop was Dudley Lee, left field was Jess Hill, who later became athletic director at USC, center field was Cleo Carlyle and right field was Smead Jolley.

Oscar (Ox) Eckhardt led the PCL in batting so many times, but he couldn't quite hit big league pitching. Luke Easter was the same way. Pitch him high and tight. The Mad Russian Lou Novikoff - he used to scream at me. He was a great fast ball hitter and I'd give him the knuckle ball. He'd hit those towering fly balls for outs. He'd go around the bases and call me everything. Broadway Bill - they used to call old Schuster that. One day down here, he ran across home and went halfway up the backstop. And we had Del Ballinger who was a real practical jokester. When they put a string on that ball, I think they did something like that with a wallet on the sidewalk downtown. There were a lot of characters in the old PCL.

The funniest story ever told about Lefty O'Doul was when he was with the Seals. A young reporter asked, 'Mr. O'Doul, what do you think (Ty) Cobb would hit today?' He thought a while and said, 'Oh, about .277.' The reporter was surprised and O'Doul said, 'You've got to remember he'd be seventy-four years old now.

In 1942, I'd just graduated from USC and I signed with the Padres. The next day, I showed up at the Santa Fe station to catch the train to Seattle. I've got two suitcases and a top coat. I immediately got the business for that, because in those days, you only took one suitcase. They started calling me, 'Joe College.' When we got to Seattle and checked into the hotel, my roommate was Mel Skelley. We went up to our room and I began to unpack. What would I pull out of my suitcase first but my USC letterman's sweater and I absolutely never heard the end of it from Mel.

In those days, they had cathouses in San Diego and Joe Berkowitz got a case of it. They didn't know how to tell the manager, so Joe held his finger down and Mac (George McDonald) hit it with a bat. They said he hurt it playing pepper and nobody knew any better.

In '42, we (the Padres) weren't bad, but in '46 and '47, we were terrible. We were up in Sacramento. I started the first game of the series on Tuesday night and pitched an eight hit shutout against Tony Frietas. We beat 'em, four to nothing. Then I came back on Saturday night and pitched another eight hit shutout in twelve innings against their other ace who was lefty Al Smith, 4-0. Lefty Al Smith was pitching for Cleveland on the day they stopped Joe DiMaggio's 56 game hit streak. I don't remember if he was the starter, but he did pitch that day and get Joe out.

This is kind of a funny story that didn't turn out too good for myself. The headlines of the San Diego paper was that Vitalich had pitched 21 consecutive scoreless innings and he was going for the PCL record. That evening, my dad had all his friends in the stands and at the end of the third inning, I was in the stands sitting next to him. I never saw so many frozen ropes in my life! I think the final score was 13-2.

In about 1943, I called Wally (Hebert) at his hotel in St. Louis. He was kind of a loner, because he didn't do the things the other players did. He lived straight and narrow. I remember Frankie Dasso. He could really smoke 'em! Dick Gyselman was our third baseman. When one of those big, strong right-handed home run hitters would come up, he'd come over to talk to me. He'd say, 'This guy's weakness is for low, outside pitches' and he'd go back to third.

You wouldn't believe the locker room at the Vaughn Street park in Portland. If somebody would have struck a match, it (the ballpark) would have been gone. It didn't exactly exude comfort and there was a foundry outside right field.

I used to go down to Lane Field and pitch batting practice after baseball and I pitched it in high school, too. They said, 'Kid, we'll let you pitch to the reserves and pitchers.' But when they saw I had good control, they said, 'You'll pitch to the regulars.' Well, I was at the meeting in the dugout they had to decide who would pitch in the championship in '54. Bob Kerrigan said he'd do it and he sure did. We were the same kind of pitchers. We didn't throw hard. (Pointing to his head) We found other ways to get them out.

AL CAILTEAUX, infield.
BORN: 7-30-16   DIED: 1-28-85   PADRES: 1943-44

"Frenchie" Cailteaux hit .261, .308 and .223 during his three years with Vancouver in the Western International League. Playing for Salem in '42, Al's .276 batting average earned him a ticket to San Diego. He was an enthusiastic competitor for the wartime Padres, but was known more for defensive skills. His son, Al Cailteaux, Jr., shared memories of his father and the significance the game has had on their lives.

Al Cailteaux

"My dad passed away ten years ago. I know he was with San Diego for a couple of years and then he went in the army and hurt his knee. The biggest disappointment of his life was hurting his knee, because he could never play baseball like he used to. I was very young, but people tell me he was always happy before the injury and he was unhappy after it happened. It was the turning point in his life.

He did tell me about facing Bob Feller in spring training. He also played in the South for Birmingham and he told me how it was playing in the South. They had special sections for the Blacks and he was from San Francisco, so he'd never seen anything like that. He told me about the great Seals outfielder, Smead Jolley, who was a powerful hitter, but not a great fielder. One time a ball went through Jolley's legs, hit the wall and bounced back through his legs. When he finally got it, he made a throwing error. That story sticks out.

My dad was an all-city player for three years while at Mission High in San Francisco. He also played for Vancouver, too and that's where I was born. My mom went up to visit him and had me. They tease me and say I'm an immigrant. When I was growing up, he was still involved in playing ball and he'd always take me along. That was my outing. But my dad started to drink and I think it was because he was so sad about baseball. All of his baseball things were in a trunk and we don't have it. He apparently owed a bar tab and the trunk was being held as collateral. He never got it back and now it's gone forever. He loved baseball and was always a Padre fan. I'm a Padre fan, too. It just meant so much to him..."

◆◆◆

LOU ESTES, third base.
BORN: 6-8-24   DIED: 12-31-95   PADRES: 1943-44,46

Lou Estes went from San Diego High School to the Padres in 1943. After spending parts of three seasons with the hometown team, he went to the Western International League where he put up consistent numbers: Vancouver .305 (1946), Vancouver-Wenatchee .285 (1947) and Wenatchee-Yakima .286 (1948).

"I was an eighteen-year-old rookie and I played quite a few game in '43. It was great playing in the PCL. I remember it well. George McDonald was a magician with that glove; he saved me several errors. As a rookie, I pretty much kept my mouth shut. One time I threw right into the god damn runner and there was nothing George could have done to catch the ball. But later, he apologized to me saying he could have caught it. My mouth just dropped.

I was up in Oakland and tried to score from first on a double. I slid under Billy Raimondi and he missed me by a foot, but Powell called me out. I got right in his face, but he didn't throw me out. Later he said he was out of position. Well, what goes around, comes around. Late in the season, Los Angeles was in San Diego and Red Adams was beating us about 7-0. Powell was behind the plate and he said to the catcher, Bill Holm, 'How 'bout letting

Lou Estes

the kid have a hit?' Billy said, 'OK, where do you want it?' I said, 'How about a fast ball, about cock high?' I got a hit! The next time up, I asked again and Billy told me what was coming. I got another hit. Billy told me afterwards that Adams was tearing up the clubhouse, because the god damn kid could hit him.

Les Cook was the trainer. He was a real nice guy. He was the trainer and the traveling secretary. (Joe) Berkowitz wanted to go home early before the season ended. His wife was pregnant or something like that and they wouldn't let him go. I think it was (Major) Lott who was the president. Cookie said, 'You wanna go home? I'll fix it so you can.' He hit his finger with a fungo bat and they let him go. That happened before I joined the team. That was the story I heard.

We had 'Smokey Joe' Martin. He'd played somewhere and broke both of his ankles, so we'd use him as a pinch hitter. He was deathly afraid of spiders, so, of course, when (Del) Ballinger and (Al) Olsen found out, they had to think up a trick to play on him. They fixed up some eyelets on the top of the dugout and ran a string through them. They bought a toy spider and tied it on one end. Ballinger got Martin to sit next to him and Olsen was working the string. He let the spider down and made the legs jiggle right in front of Joe. He shot up and hit his head on the overhead. It cold-cocked him. (Manager) Ced Durst decides he wants him to pinch hit and the son-of-a-bitch is out on the deck.

I got hit twice in baseball and both times it was the same guy- Hub Kittle. He hit me in Oakland and later in Vancouver. I never saw either one.

Did (Johnny) Jensen tell you the story of him and Patchett up in San Francisco? I'll bet he didn't. San Francisco was a weird place with the wind and fog. Well Jensen was in left and Patchett was in center. It was foggy. A high fly went to left center. I turned and looked and so did (Jack) Calvey the shortstop. They converged and stopped. Jensen says to Patchett, 'Can you see it?' Patchett said, 'No, but it's up there somewhere.' Patchett was a very taciturn ballplayer and I remember him saying it was up there somewhere.

I suspect it was a lot more fun playing ball back then than it is now. I never thought Ced Durst had much of a sense of humor, but I guess with Olsen and Ballinger on the team, it would try a person's patience.

In 1944, I was with them (the Padres) for a couple of games before I was drafted. I was with them for a couple of games in '46 when I got out and I went to Vancouver. Bobby Brown, the owner of Vancouver, was a good friend of Les Cook's. I think that's why I went there.

The last time I saw George McDonald was the first year the Los Angeles Angels played in the American League. Know what he said to me? 'Even we weren't that bad!'

Did anyone tell you about Jack Calvey spiking himself in the head? He was on first and had a pretty good lead. He had to dive back in and hit himself in the head with his cleats. His legs came back that far. Cook went out and when he came back, they asked what happened. He said, 'The dumb shit spiked himself in the head.' He was an under-rated shortstop. He made everything look so easy, but when I saw him go in the hole and fire, he had a helluva arm.

Eddie Wheeler was faster than Calvey, but Calvey could get a better jump. He was a better base runner. Once they had a match race between Wheeler and a guy on the other team. Eddie beat him.

'Broadway Billy' Schuster - he was on second base. A ground ball came to me and there was a tap on my arm. Schuster said, 'Tag! You're it.' He ran back to second. I still got the guy at first, but it sure surprised the shit out of me when he did that. We once made a trip north with Los Angeles on the same train. Schuster was holding forth and we were all listening. He believed in living for today. He said, 'This game is fun. That's the way it should be played.' He was a character. He'd climb the backstop and cuss.

I used to sneak in to watch the Padres when I was a kid. I would have been on that (American Legion) national championship team, but I didn't get in a birth certificate on time. I was born on a farm in Arkansas, so I didn't have a birth certificate. John Ritchey was on that team. Did he tell you how he and Nellie (Manuel) couldn't play in the South? He is a good man. We lived within a couple of blocks of each other in Logan Heights. We played together and against each other for years.

Something that really impressed me about John was that it didn't make any difference what bat he used. It could be a thirty-three or a thirty-six. You know how choosy hitters are about what bat they use. I said, 'John, why don't you use the same bat?' He said, 'It doesn't matter. You can hit with all of them.' He'd just walk up to the plate and get his hits. He was a good hitter. John's dad must have been in his eighties when we were playing sandlot ball. He'd come out and watch us. He was a nice, old guy.

Jack Harshman was on our team in the Police Athletic League. He was a lot younger, but I started playing sandlot when I was twelve, too. We played Over-the-Line from the time I was eight-years-old. I think I was in the Western International League the year he led the league in home runs (Jack hit 36 home runs in 1947). Of course,

he had a pretty good place to hit them in Victoria (British Columbia, Canada).

We stayed at the Alexandria Hotel in downtown Los Angeles. I didn't know how to get to the ballpark, so I asked someone. He said, 'See that door? Walk out that door, catch the streetcar and take it to the ballpark.' I took the streetcar, but it kept going and going, so I asked the conductor how long to the ballpark? He said, 'You're going the wrong way.' I went back to the hotel and discovered there were two doors. Until I played for the Padres, I had never been far from home. I didn't even know they had sleepers on trains. The traveling was a lot of fun.

George Detore was the catcher, but he'd played some third base, too, so he'd give me tips. He told me to play in on the left-handed hitters on the edge of the grass. Babe Herman was up and he hit a line drive that you wouldn't believe and it ticked the grass about six feet from me. I looked at George and he said, 'Everyone but him, kid.'

Another Babe Herman story... Al Olsen was pitching and Herman would eat him up. It was a night game at Lane Field. Olsen had a way to load up the spitter in a way that he couldn't get caught. I saw him doing it. Herman hit it over the light standard in right center field over 375 feet away. When we came in, I said, 'Didn't it work?' I thought he was going to kill me."

EARL CHAPPLE, pitcher.
BORN: 9-12-18   PADRES: 1943-46

Earl Chapple's professional baseball career began in 1940 with Salt Lake City in the Pioneer League where he played parts of two seasons. While stationed in San Diego during the Second World War, he signed with the Padres. Returning to the team after the war, Chapple was used primarily as a relief pitcher. In 1947, he posted an impressive 10-4 record for last place Modesto in the California League. Over the next 48 years, Earl officiated a wide variety of high school athletic events in Idaho including 27 straight state basketball championships. He is in the Idaho High School Hall of Fame.

"I played for the Padres when I was in the army. I knew Major Lott real well, because I was in the athletic department in the army. He signed me to a professional contract. I was at Ft. Rosecrans for three years. We had those one-point-five searchlights. The Padres paid me $50 a month and I made $21 a month in the army. They only put me in games they knew they were going to lose. One game, we were behind Portland by about seven runs and they pitched me. We came back and their manager said, 'Hey, what's he doing playing in this game?' I only pitched when they were behind and they were behind a lot.

I pitched two games against Joe DiMaggio in 1943 while we were in the service. The Army won one and lost in San Diego, 4-3, where DiMaggio was stationed.

When I played in '46 with them, I remember Lou Costello of Abbott and Costello. He was a friend of Martin's and he'd follow Pepper. He'd always be sitting behind the dugout. We had Boots Poffenberger who looked just like Lou Costello. Old Pepper Martin... we were on a road trip and he wore the same pair of shorts - underwear. They were torn down the middle on each side of his cheeks. The guys grabbed 'em and tore them off. He got pretty mad and then he knew it was a joke and laughed.

I remember Debs Garms and his delayed steal. I'd never seen anybody better than him and every time we'd go to someplace new, he'd do it. He'd do it once in a series. He'd wait and then just take off. They never caught him.

Del Ballinger used to catch me. We went bowling one night. Del threw the ball and it went in the gutter. He took off running (down the alley) and slid into all the pins. He was a funny guy. He liked that 'invisible' pitch. I never did it with Del, but when I was down in the Arizona-Texas League, I was pitching a game one night. I went into my windup, threw my leg up and put the ball in my pocket. The catcher hit is glove. It cost me $15. That (the fine) wasn't too funny at the time, but it's funny now.

I remember the big avocados that Pete (Coscarart) brought down from Escondido. We had some good times. The memories are good. I'd like to bring 'em all back."

JOE VALENZUELA, pitcher.
BORN: 1-26-24   PADRES: 1944-45

Joe Valenzuela was a hard throwing young pitcher from Arizona who joined the team during the War Years. The Padres traded him to the New York Yankees organization during the '45 season. Joe played in their farm system with Binghamton, Newark and Kansas City. In 1946, his 1.73 ERA was the second lowest in the Eastern League. During the winter, Valenzuela played for Hermosillo in the Mexican Pacific Coast League. He remains active in the sports community of his hometown, Tucson, where one of the diamonds at Hi Corbett Park, spring training site of the Colorado Rockies, is named after him.

"I went from Tucson High to the Padres. I was young and wild, strong and fast. It was the last game of the first half of the season. We were playing San Francisco and Lefty O'Doul was their manager. We were a half game out of first place. It was a Sunday doubleheader. There was a rule that no game could start after 6:00. Pepper Martin was our manager. Chet Johnson was pitching and San Francisco got way ahead. If we could delay the game, we wouldn't play the second one. Bill Salkeld was catching. Martin brought me in from the bullpen after I had thrown just a few warm-ups. He said, 'Listen, Joe, I don't want anybody to make an out!' I was supposed to

Earl Chapple

Joe Valenzuela

walk everybody. Lefty got wind of it and told his players to swing at anything. I'd throw high and they'd swing. I'd throw outside and they'd swing.

Pepper Martin came out and told me to throw under their chin or at their ankles. He said, 'Joe, if you throw another pitch they can swing at, I'll send you so far away, it will take more than a 3 cent stamp to get to you!' I'd never heard that before. Jimmy Adair came to bat and there's Pepper giving me the signal to brush off. Jimmy says, 'Joe, if you throw at me, I'm coming out there with this bat.' Well, Jim went down and then he came at me. That fracas lasted about a half hour. Del Ballinger got to me first and he covered me, so they couldn't hit me. It was a terrible riot and the sailors in the stands got into it, too. Oranges and bottles were thrown. It was awful and I'm not proud of it. We lost the game. We both had to catch the same train back to San Francisco and I was worried. Then I felt a hand on my arm and it was Lefty O'Doul. He said, 'Joe, don't be afraid. We are not after you.'

We had some good guys on that team. Good pitchers like Chet Johnson, Rex Cecil, Carl Dumler, Frankie Dasso. And, Vallie Eaves, he had a problem with his shins. He liked to go to the railroad tracks and drink wine with his buddies. He was a good guy and he helped me a lot. His front teeth were missing, but he didn't care how he looked. He'd smile all the time. He was a good man. Hank Sciarra was a tall, lanky shortstop with a good arm. He was a good looking kid. And, Manny Hernandez. He could run like a deer. He was an above average hitter. He went in the service. Of course, you remember all the sailors in San Diego during the War. They were very supportive of the Padres. And, another thing I remember about Lane Field was fly balls to third or left (field) that looked foul. You'd wait and the wind off the ocean would blow them to you. You could lose the ball in the fog, too.

Joe Valenzuela, left, and Carl Dummer residing at Seals Stadium.

Here is a picture of Carl Dumler and me at the ballpark in San Francisco. It was 1945 and all the hotel rooms were full, so we had to sleep at the ballpark. There was an important international meeting going on. Know what it was? They were forming the United Nations.

When I was with the Yankee organization, I ran into many Yankee people who would get to the big leagues. They kept climbing up the ladder, but I stayed behind. I feel I was given a fair chance. They were just loaded with good players who would ripen and die on the vine. Look at the good catchers they had in the minors, but how are you going to get a chance when there's Bill Dickey ahead of you and then along comes Yogi Berra? There are only nine positions on a ball club and there are 3,000 guys who want them! A lot of very good players never got a chance to get to the majors."

MANUEL HERNANDEZ, outfield.
BORN:10-12-19   DIED: 3-22-45   PADRES: 1944

Manuel "Nay" Hernandez starred for Mike Morrow's powerhouse teams at San Diego High School during the late Thirties. He was found playing ball in the local industrial leagues and so impressed manager George Detore with his hustle that he was the Padres starting left fielder when they opened the 1944 season. Later that year, Nay was drafted into the army and fought in the Battle of the Bulge under General George Patton. On March 22, 1945, Pvt. Manuel Hernandez was killed in action as the Allies were advancing in Germany. On May 7, 1945, less than two months later, the Germans surrendered unconditionally.

[Over fifty years later, Tara McCauley contacted the San Diego Padres Baseball Club. She hoped to find her father, but her only lead was the knowledge that her grandfather played for the Padres a long time ago. It is difficult to find baseball players from fifty and sixty years ago and even more difficult to locate their offspring. Initially, another player named Manuel Hernandez was located, but he had not played for the Padres. Eventually Manuel "Nay" Hernandez Jr. was found. He was very enthusiastic to talk about his father. When Tara's name was mentioned, he exclaimed, "She's my daughter! I held her once in my arms when she was a baby. Her grandmother didn't like me. She took her from my arms and I never saw Tara again. I tried to send things to her, but they were returned. I always wanted to find her and now she has found me. When I was a boy, I wished my father was alive to do things for me. Now, because of baseball, my father found my daughter for me!"]

The following interviews were conducted with Manuel Hernandez, Jr. and his aunt, Tina Hernandez.

Nay Hernandez

Pvt. Manuel Hernandez

The Hernandez Brothers: Larry, Manuel, Chapo, and Goyo.

[Manuel, Jr.] "I remember my Uncle Chapo would put me on his shoulders and jump over the seats to get down to the field (Lane Field). I was a little guy (three years old) and it scared me, but my Dad would come to the fence. He'd hand me over the fence. My Dad would hug me and hand me back to my uncle.

My last memory of my Dad was when he went in the army. We lived across the street then. I was at the gate and he told me to take good care of my mother. He was killed in the war.

My Dad was all-state in high school for three years. They were going to go to Japan (to play baseball), but they didn't go because they knew the war was coming. He played in the industrial leagues before he signed with the Padres. Here is his contract. They paid him $250 a month. That was the only year he played for the Padres. His brothers all went (to war) and he said if my brothers went, I should go, too.

I heard stories about my Dad being so poor he couldn't buy baseball bats. They used to use old axe handles. Their father used the axe to kill chickens to feed all the kids.

When I was growing up, my aunts worked at Lane Field. Maggie would give me free hot dogs and Tony sold beer. We used to go under the stands. You'd be surprised by all the money we'd find. Then we'd tell my aunts we could pay for our own hot dogs. I knew exactly what door we could go under without getting caught (sneaking into Lane Field). I knew every inch of that place.

After the war, people were putting their lives back together and there was always the baseball game to go to. You'd see people up on top of the boxcars looking over the fence. There used to be this sign on the outfield fence. If somebody hit it, they'd get a free meal or

something like that. It's funny the things you remember. They played the game because they loved it and the fans loved baseball."

[Tina] "I used to go to the ball games at Lane Field all the time. Two of my sisters worked at the concession stand. One was Nay's twin sister, Margaret. Nay started in left field, then he went to center field. He liked left field better. Then he was drafted, because the war was going bad. He was just a rookie. He had a murmur. They said if he's good enough to play baseball, he can be in the army. They put him in the infantry and he didn't last two months. He got killed in the Battle of the Bulge.

He was a good ballplayer. Our whole family played ball. There were ten sisters and five brothers. I played softball. We'd play against the men. There was an all-star game in 1942. It was played at Lane Field. The men against the women. The pitchers and catchers played on the opposite teams, so I was the catcher on the men's team. We had a helluva good time.

My brother, Nay, was one of the youngest. He was so dedicated to baseball. We'd play baseball in Logan Heights. We had our own Hernandez team and we'd play everybody. My sisters were good, too, but Nay was the best. My brother was a good player. I don't say that because he was my brother. I say it because he was that good. Every day after school, he'd go practice. My mother would ask where he was and Nay was always practicing baseball. Mike Morrow (San Diego High School baseball coach) picked the best players and Nay was one of them.

I remember him running for a long fly ball at Lane Field with the Padres. He was tall and lanky. He caught it leaping over the fence, but he hung on it. He caught the ball and went over the fence. He was so good to all of us. I miss him so much."

right: Lou Vezilich.

far right:Morrison Abbot and Lou Vezilich at the beach.

LOU VEZILICH, first base & outfield.
BORN: 5-30-14   PADRES: 1944-46

San Diego signed one of the Coast League's top hitters when they obtained Lou Vezilich in 1944. He batted close to .300 while playing for Sacramento during the Thirties and hit .317 for the Solon team swept by the Padres in the '37 playoffs. On April 22. 1945, Vezilich hit two grand slam home runs during a Sunday doubleheader in Los Angeles. Lou went on to lead the PCL with 110 RBIs that year while batting .307 for the Padres. If you need life insurance, Lou is still selling policies in Oakland.

"1945 was an exciting year for me. I'll never forget that year. Did manage to play every game, although I had only one week of spring training. The draft board had me go to work at the Rohr Aircraft at the beginning of the season. I was working the shipyards and the draft board let me go down to San Diego. It was only while the team was home getting to work at 7:00 a.m. in the morning and be ready for the night games. It wasn't too bad. Didn't last long as the war ended in about a month in Europe.

During the war years, being next door to Tijuana, a lot of us would go there for dinners, steak dinners I mean. They didn't have any rationing on deer meat. Joe Valenzuela was my roommate and he knew people and where to go. He had this friend who could get deer and lobster. That was what we had: deer steak!

Another happy thought in the 1944 season (was) hitting

a home run with a man on in the last game of the season in the final inning with two outs. Score: San Diego 2- San Francisco 0.

I remember when San Diego beat us four straight (in the Shaughnessy playoffs). We finished first. (Ted) Williams was on that team and hit everything. If I'm not mistaken, I think he played his first game against us in June of 1936 when he got out of school. I'm pretty sure the kid broke in against us.

In those days, you played every game. You played with sprained ankles and the flu. Today, guys get a headache and they want out. In '36 and '37 with Sacramento, I was never out of a single inning and didn't get much money. After I led the league in RBIs in '45, I got a $25 a month raise.

On Opening Day in Muskogee (Oklahoma) in 1934, my first hit in professional baseball was a home run in the ninth inning that won the game, 2-1. The second home run I hit was my first at-bat for Sioux City in the Western League. Muskogee sent me to the Sioux City Cowboys in July - that was July 4th - and I traveled all day in a bus from Bartlesville, Oklahoma to meet the team in Topeka, Kansas.

I had to find out where the park was and I finally arrived there by taking a streetcar. Got there when the first game of a doubleheader had already started. Dutch Zwilling, the manager, told one of his pitchers to take off his uniform and give it to me. He had me pinch hit in the second inning and I hit a home run. That was my debut in the Western League - the first hit - likewise with

Muskogee. Believe it or not, I ended up playing in both games. It must have been 100 (degrees). I didn't know anybody on the team.

After the doubleheader, the team took off for Sioux City and I arrived at 9:00 a.m. in the morning. I sure had a long bus ride that July 4th I shall never forget. Played a doubleheader between bus stops and saw three states that day: Oklahoma, Kansas and Iowa.

Incidentally, 1934 was a drought year with great sandstorms in Oklahoma. My salary with Muskogee was $90 a month for a 4 month season. It remained the same with Sioux City even though I got promoted to Class A. After the season ended, Hugh Luby and I took a night job at the Sioux City Stockyards penning hogs. By December, it got so cold I could hardly hold a pencil in my hand. Decided then to go home to Oakland and the stockyards gave me a pass on a cattle freight train. I rode the caboose with the trainmen. It took four days to get home.

A game I'll never forget was when I was with Sacramento. We had spring training in Riverside. We went to Anaheim and played against Seattle at La Palma Park. I hit a home run off Kewpie Dick Barrett. It was the first home run hit in the ballpark. Dan Doby was the master of ceremonies. He was the Hollywood fight announcer. Four of us had whiskers, because of the '39 World's Fair. They kidded me because I had an Abraham Lincoln beard. I shaved it off after a couple of weeks.

That Sunday doubleheader (April 22, 1945), both (home runs) were over the left field fence. I am a right-handed hitter. I think I knocked in ten runs and that helped a lot. That's about all I remember about it and we won both games.

After Hollywood let me go (1947), because (Jimmy) Dykes wouldn't give me a chance to play, I went to get a manager job in Fresno. I think I broke a record in doubles for Fresno. It was Class C ball then. I ended the season with the Seals in '47. The next year, I didn't get into managing, because Tampa paid me a Pacific Coast League salary to play. I led the (Florida International) league with a .356 batting average in '48. We played in Cuba. I hit .405 (.406 -Ed.) as manager at Vallejo (Far West) in '49 and led the league. I don't like to brag. I managed Eugene (Oregon) in the Far West League in 1950 and hit .348 in my last year.

Bob Joyce (San Francisco) was a tough pitcher. You know how it is. Some pitchers you can hit blindfolded and some you can't hit. You can't hit 'em all."

◆◆◆

HANK SCIARRA, shortstop.
BORN: 9-6-27   PADRES: 1944-45

It was difficult to find ballplayers during the Second World War. Fifteen year old Bill Sarni of the Los Angeles Angeles was the youngest member of the Pacific Coast League. Hank Sciarra was only sixteen when he came to play for San Diego in 1944. It was both a dream and a nightmare for the young Sciarra who had never been away from home. His memories of that experience are a unique entry in the history of the Padres and wartime San Diego.

"I was playing semi-pro ball in LA and a scout named Jack Talbert saw me. I was really conned into it. It was tough on a sixteen year old kid to be with those older players. Dick Gyselman and Del Ballinger, they were crazy! They did so many things to me, because I was a kid. Ballinger would walk past me in the dugout with his shoe in his mouth. He'd take it out and say, 'Hey, kid, hold this' and I'd do it. They'd put red-hot in my shoes and the armpits of my jersey. It wasn't anything real bad, but it was constant. I'd never played with ballplayers who were so nuts!

Do you know that we lived at Lane Field in one of the offices? I slept on a table or a bench until I could get into the Southern Hotel where the ballplayers lived. We'd walk to the park. I couldn't go on the road in '44 because I had to go to school. I went to San Diego High School. It was the law, so I was going to school and playing professional ball at the same time. The next year, (Baseball Commissioner) Landis said they couldn't sign any more

Hank Sciarra

kids. Later, I went back to school and he said I couldn't play baseball, because I'd been a professional player.

Some other things I remember is that we used nurse's stockings for sanitary hose because of the war. We didn't have sliding pads like today. We just had pieces of cloth. My first road trip was quite an experience. I'd never been in a sleeper in my life. They fixed my arm in a sling in the upper berth. It's a favorite trick to play when you're just a plain-ass rookie. Before, I was a kid shagging balls at Wrigley Field and now I was playing with these guys I idolized. Tony Criscola was always nice to me. And, Jack Calvey, the shortstop, was so loose, you thought he'd fall apart. There was Tony Filippo and myself. He was about 18. We'd never seen anything like this before.

I came back in '47 and they optioned me out. I played at Tacoma, Wenatchee and Salem in the Western International League. I was at spring training with Bucky Harris is '49 in Ontario. Luke Easter and Jack Graham, Max West and Dick Greco would have hitting contests. There was a shooting range beyond center field and they were just pounding that ball. Dick Greco could hit them farther than anybody! He was stronger than a bull. He put 'em over center field. You know how those other guys could hit home runs. I was just a skinny guy.

You learn a lot playing baseball. You travel 500 miles in a station wagon with nine guys and play a doubleheader. You didn't make any money, but you were playing the game. The fans were so nice. I've still got the very first fan letter that I ever got. I have the very first picture taken of me with a fan. Those are special memories!"

JOE WOOD, pitcher.
BORN: 5-20-16   PADRES: 1944

Joe Wood was 6 and 2 while limiting the opposition to 1.80 earned runs per game for Scranton (Eastern League) in 1941. Moving up to Louisville the following season, he went 10-19 over the next three years for the American Association team. During 1944, Joe pitched for the Red Sox, Colonels and Padres posting a combined 8-8 record. He finished his career with the Sacramento Solons in 1946. Joe is the son of "Smoky Joe" Wood who pitched for the Boston Red Sox from 1908 through 1915 (116-56) and switched to the outfield for the Cleveland Indians from 1917 through 1922 (lifetime batting average .283).

"I have fond memories of San Diego. The Red Sox sent Louis Lucier and myself to the Padres who were in absolute last place. Louie and I had just won a doubleheader for Louisville and they shipped us out to help San Diego. I remember one thing, Bill, and I probably shouldn't have done it, but we'd get a bonus if we'd win more games than we lost. We were only there for about a

month and it was at the end of the season and I'd won a game to get to four and four.

Well, with one day's rest, I pitched a shutout against Lefty O'Doul's San Francisco club and I got my bonus. It was a couple hundred bucks, but back then, it was like thousands. I remember that Frankie Dasso did the same thing to win twenty games and get his bonus. Back then, you'd rest the day after you pitched, but on the second day, you'd pitch batting practice. Then you'd rest again, but on the fourth day, you were ready to start again. I was always a starting pitcher. We were born fifty years too soon. Today, we'd be making millions!

Johnny Lazor is my good friend. We played together for four teams: Scranton, Louisville, San Diego and the Red Sox. And Tony Lupien was my friend, too. He's a former Harvard baseball captain and I was the Yale captain. My dad was the coach at Yale then, after he left the Cleveland Indians. He was at Yale for twenty years and he was their winningest coach. Dad finished up in '42 and George Bush played for Yale after the war. My dad was a real natural and he loved to play. We have rather strange physiques. My son has an extra vertebra. We all have long backs, long arms and strong fingers.

We played winter ball for Rohr Aircraft. It was Del Ballinger, Frankie Dasso and me. We had a very young and capable University of California player working out with us. We had a foot race and this young fella beat us. Do you know who he was? He was Bobby Brown who went to the Yankees and he became Dr. Bobby Brown and the president of the American League.

I finished up my career in Sacramento. I hurt my arm up there in San Francisco. It's damp and cold and I think it was a rotator cuff. They can fix them now, but they couldn't back then."

LOU LUCIER, pitcher.
BORN: 3-23-18   PADRES: 1944

In 1941, Lou Lucier started his professional career impressively by leading the Middle Atlantic League with 199 strikeouts, 23 victories (23-5) and a microscopic 1.51 ERA for Canton (Ohio). Lou played for the Boston Red Sox and Philadelphia Phillies during the War Years of 1943 through 1945, but most of his pitching was for the Louisville Colonels during that three year period (26-17). He was primarily used in relief for the Padres during the 1944 season. Although 1946 was Lou's last year in professional ball, he remained active in youth baseball as a coach, manager and umpire.

"Joe Wood and I were sent to San Diego when Rex Cecil went to Boston. We were playing for Louisville. We had

Joe Wood

Lou Lucier

John Lazor

a doubleheader in Minneapolis. Joe pitched the first game and I pitched the second one. We both won and were told we were going to San Diego. Joe and I drove in his car and our wives came later on the train. We loved San Diego and lived out past the marine base.

The person I remember best in San Diego was George Detore. I really admired that guy. He was a fine gentleman. It was a joy to play for him. My arm wasn't that good, but he always made me feel good. He'd been a catcher with Detroit. I relieved all the time.

I was pitching one night in San Diego and they stopped in the fourth inning. The fog was so bad that a ball almost hit the centerfielder in the head. He didn't even see it. Johnny Lazor was a very good hitter. We'd played together at Louisville. He was a terrific hitter.

I was 23-6 in Canton and made the jump from Class B to Triple A. I went 14-9 with Louisville and, at Christmas, I got a nice bonus and went up to Boston where I met Mr. Yawkey. That was a thrill. When I was through playing, I came home (Northbridge, MA) and I've been involved in baseball ever since: Little League, Intermediate League, high school and American Legion ball. I umpired high school and legion ball. This is a baseball house. We always have baseball on TV. We love the game."

JOHN LAZOR, outfield.
BORN: 9-9-12   PADRES: 1944

In 1935, Johnny Lazor came to San Diego from Hobart, Washington for a tryout with the Boston Red Sox at old Navy Field. Later, as a member of the Sox, he compiled a lifetime .263 batting average over four seasons from 1943 through 1946.

Johnny briefly patrolled the outfield for the Padres in 1944 and hit for a .301 average. The following season, he was back in Beantown and almost won the American League batting title with a .310 average for the Sox.

"I liked the city (San Diego) and remember going swimming at La Jolla. I wasn't with the club very long, but I know I hit over three-hundred. I do remember a games against Seattle. It was a ten inning game. I was on second base and a guy hit a slow roller to second base. I kept on going and scored. They didn't even throw to the plate. I caught 'em by surprise.

Another time, a guy hit a home run just over the infield. Nobody could find it. I don't think the batter even knew where it went. He just kept runnin' and I don't remember if it was our team or the other team. I think it was San Francisco. It was the first game of a double header and the second game was called off because of fog. It went for a home run and it was a pop fly that nobody saw. It was about twenty-feet in the outfield when they did find it.

In 1945, if I would have had 35 more at bats, I would have led the American League in batting." [George "Snuffy" Stirnweiss, New York Yankees, won the batting crown with a .309 average. John Lazor had 104 hits in 335 plate appearances for a .310 batting average. -Ed.]

JOE KATNICH, outfield.
BORN: 4-18-25   PADRES: 1945

Joe Katnich signed with the Padres following college in 1945 and he played in seven different leagues over the next three seasons. Although it was a frustrating experience at the time, he now reflects that they were the best years of his life. Joe is

Joe Katnich

First meeting of the Hot Stove League (1949). L-R: Tony Criscola, Kent Parker, Morrie Morrison, Buster Adams, and Jim Brillheart.

very proud to have been a member of the San Diego ball club. He is a cousin of former PCL and American League player, Walt Judnich. (As a footnote, following the 1937 season, New York Yankees scout Joe Devine recommended Judnich over Ted Williams.)

"I've still got a program from 1945 and it is very special to me. I got into five games and they optioned me out, but I pinch ran, I pinch hit and, officially, I came up twice and got one hit, so I'm a lifetime .500 hitter in the PCL!

I heard about a tryout camp in San Diego and they signed me out of Loyola. I still remember reporting to El Centro on February 5th. Swede Jensen was the home run hitter. Del Ballinger was the catcher and he was so funny. He led the PCL in getting hit by pitched balls. He used to show us how to do it. Tony Criscola was very nice to me. He played with my cousin Walt in St. Louis.

(Joe) Valenzuela threw the ball very hard. Other pitchers were Al Olsen, Frank Tincup, he was part Indian, and we had the wild Indian, Vallie Eaves! If he could have stayed sober the first week of spring training, he'd get a $1,000 bonus and if he could stay sober for the season, he would get an additional $5,000. Well, he broke the first week I was there. He could throw ninety miles per hour and he won twenty games (21 games. -Ed.), but what a wild man! I remember him throwing bottles off the roof in Sacramento. There was a palm tree in a pot in the lobby of the hotel. He took a leak in it.

The highest paid player on our team was Dick Gyselman. I liked our manager, Pepper Martin. We had another pitcher named Carl (Dumler) who also won twenty games (21 games. -Ed.), but he got released the next year (after compiling a 1-11 record. -Ed.)

In '46, everybody came back from the war and players were going everywhere. I was signed by Bill Starr (in 1945) for $250 and he sent me a contract for $250 again in '46. I'd been sent to Lockport, New York along with Hank Sciarra the year before. It was Class D, but I did hit .303, so when Starr sent the same contract back, I got in the car and drove down to see him. I told him that I hit .303 and he said, 'We expected you to hit .340.'"

◆◆◆

TONY CRISCOLA, outfield.
BORN: 7-19-15   PADRES: 1945-47

Tony was the starting centerfielder for the St. Louis Browns in 1943. He claims it was not until they got rid of him in a trade with Cincinnati in 1944, that the Browns won their only pennant. As a Padre, Criscola enjoyed his finest season in 1945 when he batted .311 and led the team in runs, hits, triples and stolen bases. He was a co-founder of the local Hot Stove League with Jim Fuller, Kent Parker and Morrie Morrison in 1949. For years, he operated Tony Criscola's Liquor Store, a landmark, in Pacific Beach.

"One of the funniest incidents that happened with the Padres was in 1945 up in Oakland. We were losing the ball game and somewhere around the seventh or eighth inning, Del Ballinger was told to go up and pinch hit for the pitcher. I didn't know what was happening, because I'd run in from the outfield and I was on deck. Well, Dick Gyselman, our third baseman, had his young son along with us. The boy was playing with a cap pistol on the bench. Ballinger was sent up. The first pitch was a ball, but the second was a strike right down the center of the plate. Ballinger complained like nobody's business. Then, he pulled out the cap pistol and shot the umpire! The umpire must have aged fifty years right then and he immediately threw him out of the game. When the fans realized what happened, they went crazy with laughter. I'm the next hitter and he searched me.

I remember another game that was up in Oakland, too. It was the ninth inning and a pinch hitter for the pitcher got on first with nobody out. The score was tied. I'm the next hitter and I get the bunt signal. I tried to bunt for a hit, but the ball went all the way to second and the runner was out. I was calling myself some names, but I made it to first. On the next pitch, I stole second. Now, I'm on second, taking my lead, and the pitcher doesn't even look at me, so I stole third. (Manager) Pepper Martin (who was coaching at third base) is mad at me and he calls, 'Time.' He takes his belt off and loops it around me. The umpire calls 'Time' and tells Pepper to take the belt off me. I score on a base hit. We win the game and go to the clubhouse. Martin says, 'You were fined $25 when you fouled up the bunt, but I took the $25 off when you made second. Then I fined you $50 for stealing third, but I took it off when you were safe at home. And, if you ever do that again, you'll be fined $100 if you make it or not!'

Pepper Martin loved to fish. When we went on the road, he always took his fishing gear. These pictures were taken at El Capitan. Del Ballinger and Jim Brillheart and I think this might be (Debs) Garms, but maybe not. Pepper got the keys to the gate from the warden and he had a duplicate made. He took the guys fishing. One time (Carl) Dumler was fishing the other side of the lake and Pepper was approached by an old man on a cane. The old man says, 'What are you doin', son?' Then he asked his name and Pepper said John or something. Pepper starts to walk and the old man says, 'Well, son, I'm gonna have to take you in.' Pepper starts to run and the old man couldn't keep up. He gets to the car and Dumler is on the other side of the lake. I think Pepper went and got him.

Jim Fuller came in the (liquor) store. He was living up the street. Morrie Morrison was there. He owned a restaurant and bar in La Jolla. Jim said, 'Why don't you start a Hot Stove League? I'll give you all the publicity you need.' We had a meeting with all the old ballplayers and a few personal friends. We met at Morrie's restaurant in La Jolla where Boll Weevil now is. Morrie's upstairs room could only hold 30 people, so we couldn't invite everybody. I furnished the liquor and Morrie furnished the food. We elected officers. Cedric Durst was the president. I was the vice president. Kent Parker was the secretary and Morrie was the treasurer. The next thing you know, Fuller was putting it in the paper every day and it was on the radio. We got a lot of publicity and that's how the Hot Stove League got started. It was always for the fans. The idea was to sit around the hot stove in the winter and chew the fat about baseball.

Baseball needs a strong commissioner and the owners don't want a strong commissioner. They told a story when I was in the big leagues about Judge (Kenesaw Mountain) Landis talking to the players. The owners didn't like that. He told his secretary to go to the safe and get the only thing in it. It was his contract and there were still a couple of years remaining on it. He said, 'Take this and shove it up your f-ing ass!' They gave him a new contract for five years. He was very foul mouthed, but he was a good commissioner.

Fred Haney told me about being called into his office. He and his wife were going to spring training and they were taking the train in those days. Big league ballplayers could only play four exhibition games at the end of the season. Well, Haney was in Los Angeles and he'd played about fifteen. Landis called him into his office and was really chewing him out using a lot of bad language. Fred told him that he wanted to close the door, because his wife was sitting outside and he didn't want her to hear it. Landis called her in and said he would like to take

Fishing with teammates: Tony Criscola, Del Ballinger, unk., Jim Brillheart.

Tony Criscola

them to lunch. They had a very nice lunch and had to catch a train at 4:00. It was about 2:30 and Judge Landis had his chauffeur drive them to the train station. Nothing more was said or done about the exhibition games.

It was wonderful playing in the Pacific Coast League. You were in a town for a whole week, so you weren't always packing and unpacking. Getting sold to San Diego was the best thing that ever happened to me."

◆◆◆

DICK GYSELMAN, third base.
BORN: 4-6-08 DIED: 9-20-90 PADRES: 1945-47

Paul Zingg, author of Runs, Hits and an Era, The Pacific Coast League, 1903-58, selected Dick Gyselman as a substitute on his All-Time PCL All-Star Team. On August 20, 1932, Dick tied a league record with seven hits in a single game while playing for the San Francisco Mission Reds. He was nearing the end of his illustrious career when he came to San Diego, but Gyselman was still able to lead the Padres in hitting with a .321 batting average in 1945. He also tied a PCL record for third basemen on August 15, 1946 with 13 assists in a nine inning game against the Los Angeles Angels. Dick was briefly with the Boston Nationals during the Thirties, but was one of the many players who preferred to remain on the Coast where they earned as much or more than their major league counterparts. The following interview was conducted with his

Dick Gyselman

son, Jim, who unwittingly provided the prop for Del Ballinger's most celebrated prank.

"I forget what year it was, about 1946. I was four or five and I traveled with the team a lot. I used to take my cap pistol around and all I remember was a lot of commotion going on. It was my cap pistol that Del Ballinger used (to shoot the umpire).

It was a treat for me to go with my dad on trips. My mother and sister would stay in San Diego. One time on the train, I cut my head on the window clip. There was a lot of blood and Pepper Martin called for the trainer. His name was 'Cookie.' I thought they were going to give me a cookie, but it was his name. He put some clamps on it and I was fine.

My dad played in the Pacific Coast League for about fifteen years and he went seven-for-seven when he was with the Missions. I think it was a record that was never broken. Another story he liked to tell was that he was playing in Joe DiMaggio's first game. He (DiMaggio) was shortstop for the Seals and he kept throwing the ball over first base, so they put him in center field. They both grew up in San Francisco and knew each other.

My dad loved San Diego, the area. The club would have a big shindig for the families on a ranch on Mondays. I remember playing and chicken dinner."

◆◆◆

JACK HARSHMAN, first base, pitcher.
BORN: 7-12-27   PADRES: 1945-46,61

Everybody knew young Jack Harshman was a slugger when he signed with the Padres, but it was as a pitcher that he made his mark in the major leagues. Yet twice in the minors, he led his league in home runs. Jack topped the Western International League with 36 round-trippers in 1947. He hit 47 circuit blows for Nashville in the Southern Association in 1951 and two years later led the league with 23 mound victories. From 1954 through 1958, Harshman was consistently among American League leaders in ERA and strikeouts. He has the highest all-time home run percentage (number of home runs per one hundred at bats: 4.9%) for pitchers with more than 350 times at bats.

"I started playing organized sandlot ball in San Diego when I was twelve. I was able to play with the sixteen-year olds and that was at first base, too. When I was a junior (in high school), I played in an exhibition game at Lane Field against Satchel Paige. At the time, I didn't realize how great he was. I remember trying to hit against him and that was just a joke.

San Diego High and Hoover played the championship

game at Lane. I hit a home run and almost hit another one out. That was unusual for a high school kid and Pepper Martin (Padre manager) was there. Brooklyn and St. Louis were scouting me. Both teams offered contracts. In those days, it was more an opportunity than money. My Dad and I decided that it might be to my benefit to sign with the Padres and wait for an organization that needed a first baseman. I might never gotten a chance to play behind Gil Hodges. Bill Starr was the owner of the Padres. We'd talked and never got to the bottom line and a figure. We decided that if he'd offer our figure, we'd take it. Then, Pepper Martin came into the office. Starr didn't really want him there. Pepper was very honest and up-front. He said, 'Mr. Starr, do you want this young man to play for the Padres?' That put him on the spot. He said, 'Yes.' Martin said, 'Then give him the money!' He gave me $3,000 to sign and I'd get an additional $4,000 if I got to the majors. Bill Starr made a lot of money when he sold me!

I signed in June of '45 when I was still seventeen and still in high school. I played a few games while still in school. You had to be careful what you said, because they (teammates) were much older. They didn't accept young players. If you're here, somebody they liked and knew wouldn't be. My first at bat was a ground ball to the pitcher and he beat me to first! It never happened to me again. That's how nervous I was. You can't hardly hit an easier ground ball than that.

I was in Victoria in '47 and didn't know the Giants were scouting me. They wanted me to play first base for the Padres in '48. They gave San Diego three triple-A players for the option and, if after '48, they still wanted me, they'd give four more. Rip Collins was the Padre manager then and Vince Shupe was their first baseman. They wanted me to play in the outfield, because they knew Shupe couldn't play there. They wanted both of us in the lineup and I was willing. Do you know how long that lasted? Two innings! A Giant scout was there and he said, 'You son-of-a-bitch! We didn't give you three players for Jack to play in the outfield!' Horace Stoneham (president of the Giants) called Bill Starr and angry words were spoken. He told him he didn't have four players and since triple-A players were worth $10,000 (each), he have Starr $40,000 and I went to the Giants spring training.

George McDonald was an excellent first baseman. He caught everything they threw. He was a good hitter, not for power, but a good hitter. I thought he was the best I'd ever seen, of course, I hadn't seen too much back then, but he was my hero.

I remember seeing Don Larsen several times in San Diego during the winter in '55. I told him to get in shape, because he was going to the World Champion Yankees. He had lost twenty games (3-21) the year before in Baltimore. He

reported nine days late to camp. Casey Stengel asked, 'Who's that big guy?' He was told, 'That's Don Larsen.' Casey added, 'of Denver' and he was promptly shipped down. The next year, Don started the second game of the '56 world series and lasted one and two-thirds of an inning when Casey pulled him. He figured he was through for the series and he didn't need much of an excuse to drink, so he was drunk every night. Three days later, badly hung-over, Casey advised Larsen that he was starting. Don Larsen went out and pitched the first and only perfect game in World Series history!

Comiskey Park had the same entry to the field for both teams, so the players could talk to each other under the stands without anybody seeing them and they wouldn't get in trouble. I was talking to some of the Red Sox players and Ted Williams came walking up. He said, 'I understand you have a young fella named Harshman.' They said, 'He's right here.' I was standing just a few feet away and it was a thrill. He was as nice as could be.

Years later, I was at the Padres office to get some season tickets for a friend and there was a commotion down the hall. I went to see what it was. It was Ted Williams sitting on a desk talking and the place was really packed. He was in town for a Hall of Champions dinner. He saw me and said, 'Hi, Lefty.' It sure made me feel good.

I was with Cleveland in '60. Ted and Herb Score left spring training and flew on the same plane. Of course, when

Jack Harshman

Back: George McDonald, Hal Patchett, Earle Brucker, Bob Elliott, Cedric Durst. Front: Buster Adams, Butch Wensloff.

Bob McNamara

you were with Ted, the conversation always got to the fine points of pitching. He was a frustrated pitcher and would have been a good one, too. I always had a lot of luck against Ted. He told Herb, 'If you want to know how to pitch well against the better hitters, talk to Harshman.' Because I pitched well against Ted, he figured I knew how to pitch well to all the good hitters."

BUTCH WENSLOFF, pitcher.
BORN: 12-3-15   PADRES: 1945

Playing for Joplin, Missouri, Butch Wensloff led the Western Association with 26 victories against 4 losses in 1939. His 21 victories for the Kansas City Blues set the American Association standard in 1942. He later pitched for the World Champion New York Yankees in 1943 and 1947, but the war brought Butch and his family to San Diego where he appeared briefly as a member of the Padres mound staff (3-4, 3.82 ERA). He actually played more industrial than professional ball in San Diego during the war years. Wensloff returned to Cleveland in 1948 and would have played on his third World Championship team, but he retired when his arm gave out before the series.

"I only played two or three games for the Padres. I had a pretty good little team at Consolidated (Convair) with Frankie Dasso, Joe Wood, Jr. and Del Ballinger and some Mexican boys who were good ballplayers. I was working swing shift as a guard at Consolidated, so I didn't get to always play. I was getting ready to be drafted, so I played for the Padres. I beat the Seals up there and they gave me hell for playing for San Diego. San Francisco was my hometown.

I was playing semi-pro for the Sausalito Fire Department team and we played the Seals. They had a great team, but they only beat us 2 to 1. That was about 1934. They signed six of us off that team. I went to El Paso in 1935 and Joplin, Missouri for the next two years. They were part of the Yankees farm system. Then it was on to Kansas City. What a team we had with (Phil) Rizzuto, (Jerry) Priddy, (Frenchy) Bordagaray and the Russian... Lou Novikoff! You meet so damn many kids in baseball, I can't remember them all, but they were some good boys.

Of course, playing for Joe McCarthy and the Yankees was really something. One time, I was pitching in Detroit and he took me out in the 4th inning. He said, 'I'll use you tomorrow.' I was tight and stiff the next day, but I went out and pitched nine innings to win. I didn't play in the '43 Series, because McCarthy didn't believe in pitching rookies.

I developed a pain in my shoulder. I had an 8" needle stuck in my back. It was saline/salt water and it cost $75 a shot, but it didn't do a bit of good. Hank Greenberg said, 'Where you goin'?' I told him and he said, 'How come?' I told him, 'I don't want to keep some young kid from making the team.' Back in those days, you played because you liked the ball game."

BOB McNAMARA, shortstop.
BORN: 9-19-16   PADRES: 1945

As a youngster growing up in the Los Angeles area, Bob McNamara played against future San Diego Padres Bobby

Doerr, Steve Mesner, George McDonald and Jack Graham in high school and American Legion baseball. McNamara was an infielder at the University of California and, later, with the Philadelphia Athletics. World War II and an injury cut his career short, but he did have a brief comeback with the Padres.

"The Padres convinced me to come play for them during the final year of the war. (Bill) Starr needed ballplayers and Marvin ('Who 'dat?') Gudat talked me into playing until they could find another shortstop. I started the season in '45. The money was good, so I gave it a try and, for three weeks, I was their shortstop.

I've always remembered that Pepper Martin hit a home run. Pepper played one of the games against the Angels up there. He hit a ball out of the park and I thought it was pretty amazing. I was still a pretty young guy and I thought he was an old man.

Something else I really remember was taking the boat over to Catalina and playing the Catalina Cubs. They were a rookie team for the Los Angeles Angels and the Chicago Cubs. They'd play semi-pro teams. We'd play the game and sleep in the sand. I was in college then, so it was in the summer. I was working as a house painter, so it was fun to go over during the week and stay there a little longer.

A thing I remember about Lane Field, down there on the water, was that the infield would get real wet and the ball would skip on the grass. It was a long time ago and they were so desperate to get somebody, they talked me into going. I reported the night before the season opened. I already had a good job, so when they got another shortstop, I went back to work."

LOU KUBIAK, short stop.
BORN: 6-10-21   DIED: 1-16-83   PADRES: 1945

Following his discharge from the Army, rookie Lou Kubiak appeared briefly at shortstop for the Padres at the end of the 1945 season. He had a workout with the San Francisco Seals prior to his military service, but San Diego was his first professional experience. Most of his time in organized baseball was spent in the Western International League with Salem, Spokane and Victoria during the late Forties. Kubiak hit .325 for the Salem Senators in 1947. Later, it was baseball that led to a 25-year career as a Los Angeles police officer. His wife, Alice, and son, Lou, provided the following information.

[Lou, Jr.] "My Pop played for the Spokane Indians and the Salem Senators. George Metkovich was his buddy. My Dad played for Pepper Martin. We went to a baseball camp when I was about ten. Pepper Martin was there and he must have been about 75 or 80. [Pepper Martin

died at age 61, so he must have appeared much older to a young boy. -Ed.]

Pop said, 'Pepper Martin, I used to play for you. Do you remember me?" He looked at him and said, 'Lou Kubiak, San Diego, 1945.' What a memory! It was really something. I'm a big fan and I played, but I didn't know who Pepper Martin was. My Dad told me about him then. I wasn't born when Dad played for San Diego. You should talk to my Mom. She would love to talk with you about my Dad and baseball...'"

[Alice] "Frank Gira got released and they (San Diego) signed Lou for the end of the '45 season, so he's not on the team picture. He had a tryout with the Seals before the War and I didn't get to see him play in San Diego, because I was in Los Angeles with our son who was a baby then. I'm looking at a press clipping and Lou played in a doubleheader. He went oh-for-three in both games. He had four assists and two put outs in the first game and five assists and three put outs in the second game. I did get to see him play the next year in Salem, Oregon. He loved the game and wanted to play in the majors.

My husband was an avid fisherman. They caught a big catfish and don't ask me why, but they put it in the bathtub. That night, when Lou went to bed, he knew something was wrong. He turned on the light and his roommate was laughing, because they'd put the catfish in his bed. They nicknamed him 'Catfish' after that.

Lou was with Salem when he got lent to Spokane following that terrible bus crash and those players died. I'm pretty sure he had the highest batting average for Spokane (43 hits in 103 at-bats for a .417 batting average) and it's on display up there. Salem had played in Spokane that night and both buses left. One went one way and the other went another way, but the Spokane bus never made it.

The Yankees bought his contract, but he didn't report. It was '48 and there was a big polio epidemic in L.A.. Our son had polio and Lou didn't think he should go. I told him it was his decision, because he loved baseball so much and I didn't want him to feel ten years later I had influenced him to give up his life's dream. Well, a friend

Lou Kubiak

told him to take a test with the LAPD and he passed with the second highest score. He went through the academy and they gave him a car and assigned him to Administrative Vice, but he also played for the LAPD baseball team and it would travel all over the state. I would get to go, too and they'd pick up the tab.

So, he got to keep playing ball, but when he didn't report for the Yankees, they sent him a letter saying he couldn't play for ten years. Ten years later, they sent him another letter saying he was free."

◆◆◆

PETE COSCARART, second base.
BORN: 6-16-13   PADRES: 1946-47

The Coscarart boys of Escondido were baseball players. Joe, the eldest, and Pete, the youngest, both played in the major leagues. Pete maintains that it was their middle brother, Steve, who was the best hitter in the family. They played together in Portland, but Steve got beaned before they could realize their dream of all three making it to the big leagues. From 1938 to 1946, Pete had a distinguished career with Brooklyn and Pittsburgh, twice being selected to the National League All Star team. He was considered by many as the best fielding second baseman in the major leagues. In 1946, Coscarart supported an attempt to form a major league players' union and found himself playing ball in San Diego instead of the National League. The following season, a pension plan was funded that excluded pre-1947 major league players. In 1996, in an effort to gain the pensions and royalties denied these players, Pete sued Major League Baseball on their behalf. Coscarat was inducted into the Brooklyn Dodgers Hall of Fame in 1996. He is one of the most popular and respected men to ever play baseball in San Diego.

"My family lived in what is now Rancho Bernardo. There were just three families: two Indian families and ours. We didn't play ball. We just worked. I was riding a horse when I was seven, rounding up horses and sheep. My father was Basque and we had sheep and goats. I remember a farmer let us gather lima beans that were left in his field after the crop had been picked. We got a big bag of them and they lasted all winter. I still like lima beans. It wasn't until we moved to town, when I was ten-years-old, that I played ball.

When we got older, Escondido had a good town team. Joe was playing for San Francisco and, after the season, he returned with his friend, Babe Dahlgren. Babe, you know, he took Lou Gehrig's place, was on first and we had a Coscarart infield. Joe was at shortstop, Steve was on third and I was at second. It was quite a good team.

I wasn't making much money (in baseball) and had to make ends meet, so I worked at a service station during the winter (1940). It was in Escondido. My job was to clean the windows, check the oil, check the battery. You remember how it used to be in the old days at a service station. I traded in my Dodger suit for a Texaco suit. Yeah, people today wouldn't believe it if they found out the guy washing their windshield was a major leaguer. Of course, they don't have service stations today.

I played in Johnny Vander Meer's second no-hit game. Early in that game, I hit a ball that Wally Berger caught at the wall. Just a little more and it would have been a home run. Looking back, I'm glad I didn't get a hit. Two no-hitters in a row was a tremendous accomplishment. [Johnny Vander Meer threw his second consecutive no-hit game on June 15, 1938 which was also the first night game played at Ebbets Field.]

Pete Coscarart in Brooklyn uniform.

Pete Coscarart wearing Texaco uniform.

Pete Coscarart in Padres uniform.

Pete Coscarart, Miss Padre Lorrie Lee, and Max West.

Escondido Town Team. Front, far right: Pete Coscarart.

[Speaking about the 1941 World Series] As soon as I saw the ball get past Mickey (Owen), I went to back up (Dolph) Camilli at first. I can still see that ball rolling toward the dugout. I was sure Mickey would get it, but it just kept rolling. I think it was a spitter (thrown by pitcher Hugh Casey). We had the game won and that was the turning point. [With two outs and the Dodgers leading 4-3 in the ninth inning, a third strike got past catcher Mickey Owen which allowed Tommy Henrich to reach first base. The Yankees rallied to take a 7-4 victory. A Brooklyn triumph would have evened the series at two game each, but New York claimed the World Championship the following day. -Ed.]

The Pacific Coast League... This was paradise. It was an old man's league. They requested that older players should come to the PCL, because they knew they'd last longer in the good climate. The older guys kind of took it easy and tried to make it last. San Diego always had good crowds. It wasn't a big park, but it drew well. I think the fans liked it, because the players were right close to the fans. Today I notice that at ballparks, the seats are way back. There isn't the closeness there was when I was playing. It sure was nice to drive home to Escondido after the game."

DON LUND, outfield.
BORN: 5-18-23   PADRES: 1946

After the war, former University of Michigan football, basketball and baseball player Don Lund was briefly a Padre during the 1946 season. He would later patrol the outfield for the Dodgers, Browns and Tigers during his seven-years in the big leagues. Although Don managed in the minor leagues, his biggest thrill in baseball was coaching the Michigan Wolverines to a 15-inning, 5-4 victory over the University of Santa Clara Broncos in the 1962 NCAA baseball championship game. Former Padre infielder/broadcaster Dave Campbell and Detroit catcher Bill Freehan were members of that Michigan team.

"1946 was really my first year of pro ball and I was in San Diego for about a month. I started in spring training with Brooklyn and went to St. Paul. Then I went to San Diego and I got caught in a train strike in Cheyenne, Wyoming. I had a short stay in San Diego when they realized I wasn't ready to play in that league. That (the PCL) was a darn good league!

The ballpark was close to the water and it was beautiful for us, because we were from the Midwest. When we got off the train at the depot, the cab driver told us he had a place for rent in a place called Crown Point. He took us there and we liked it, so we rented it. Yes, everybody in California is in real estate.

Don Lund

Pepper Martin was the manager. He was a really good guy, but just a little different. He'd still pinch hit and he was a real competitor. When we'd go on the road, he'd take his fishing tackle along. I really liked hitting in Wrigley Field in Los Angeles. Then I moved on to Mobile and there was even one day with Fort Worth, but I was told Branch Rickey wanted me to go on to Mobile. I played for several teams that year.

When I was coaching, there was a story I told to the players every year. In the final game of 1953, Al Rosen and Mickey Vernon were going for the batting title. If Rosen won it, he'd have won the Triple Crown. Vernon had bunted for his hit that last day and Gerry Priddy was filling in for us (Detroit) in the infield. He went out on the ball that Rosen hit, but couldn't get to it and Rosen beat it out. Priddy threw and the first baseman tagged the bag. Rosen had failed to tag it and he was called out. He just missed out on the batting title by one point. I always told my players that story. That's why the bag is there and you have to touch it. Rosen ran right over it and he was a real gamer."

TOM SEATS, pitcher.
BORN:9-24-10   DIED:5-10-92   PADRES:46-49

Tom Seats was the workhorse for several PCL mound staffs during the Thirties and Forties. He pitched for Sacramento, San Francisco, San Diego, Oakland and Hollywood. Seats won 25 games for the Seals in 1944 and posted the lowest ERA for the Padres in '47 and '48. Tom was in the majors with Detroit (1940) and Brooklyn (1945) where he recorded a 12-9 lifetime mark. The following interview was conducted with his wife, Opal.

"Tom died a few years ago and I miss him so. We were married for 62 years. He loved baseball so much. I still love the game. I watch a game every day on TV. I like (Barry) Bonds, the way he plays. The game has changed so much. When Tom would start a game, he always wanted to finish it. It's not like that anymore. Tom went in to pitch nine innings!

He started with Lincoln, Nebraska in 1934. We had two kids then. Tom wrote to Pug Griffin for a tryout and they accepted him. Prior to that, he was pitching Sunday games in Blythedale, Missouri and he made $15 a game. The town's gone now. My father had a grocery store and Tom worked there during the week. He made $60 a month at Lincoln and the next year, he made $75 a month for Springfield, Missouri. Tom liked to say that when he played for Detroit, he made as much money as Hank Greenberg. The Tigers went to the World Series in 1940 and he got the same share as Greenberg. I think it was about $3,400 which was pretty good money back then.

The book (*Baseball Encyclopedia*) says he was born in 1911, but he was really born in '10. He had to make himself younger to play. A lot of players used to do that.

His proudest accomplishment was when he won both games in a doubleheader. It was during the War and he was working the night shift at the shipyards in San Francisco. I picked him up at the ship yards and we drove over to Sacramento. He took a shower, dressed in his uniform, went out and won his game. I saw him warming up for the second game and I said to Lefty (O'Doul) that he'd worked all night. Lefty said Tom would be OK. 'We gave him a beer and iced him down.' Oh, Lord, it was hot in Sacramento that day, 103 degrees, and Tom perspired terrible when he was pitching. He won again and they were both shutouts! The phone rang off the hook for a week.

During the War, Tom took his turn every four days. He'd fly up to Seattle or Portland, pitch, fly back and go to work at 11:00 p.m. at the shipyards. There was a fellow with Western Airlines who would take care of him. Meet him, pick him up, make sure of everything. Tom thought the PCL was as good as the majors. He went back to the majors in '45 with Brooklyn and had a good year. Tom loved playing in the PCL, so he was happy to come to San Diego, but he didn't get a pension or insurance and that would have helped.

Tom Seats

The thing I remember the most about San Diego was living in Mission Beach. The kids just loved it. We'd have get-togethers with the other players and their families at the beach. Rip Collins was the manager and Bill Starr was the owner. I remember Mel Skelley and his wife, Leah. His father had a garage. They were such fine people. Tom was on the All-Star team once or twice when he was with San Diego. They are good memories.

As you know, Tom pitched left-handed. He wrote left-handed and he talked left-handed. He acted left-handed!"

◆◆◆

LEN RICE, catcher.
BORN: 9-2-18   DIED: 6-13-92   PADRES: 1946-48

Len Rice was a centerfielder when he started his professional baseball career in 1937. He earned MVP honors in the Texas-Arizona League while leading the Tucson Cowboys with a .358 batting average in 1940. An injury to a teammate pressed him into duty as a catcher and this proved to be his ticket to the major leagues. Rice appeared behind the plate briefly for the Reds in 1944, but his break came when he was sold to the Chicago Cubs in '45. He was their back-up receiver when Chicago went to the World Series. He came to the Padres for the next three seasons. Len loved living and playing in San Diego. The following interview was conducted with his wife, Jan.

"1937 was Len's first year in baseball. His mother said, 'If you go away, you'd better stay.' He was back in Tennessee and he did get home sick. He had no money, so he hopped a freight train. This old black man showed him the ropes and helped him all the way to Los Angeles. Then, Len took a train home to Oakland. Len never forgot this man.

The next year (1939), he went to Grand Island, Nebraska. One of the players had a car, so they pooled their money for gas to come home. Eddie Lake bought a bag of cookies and he wouldn't share. They never forgave him for that.

Then he played for the Tucson Cowboys in 1939 and 1940. He had two great years and was the best hitter on the team. He hit .358 in 1940 and received the most valuable player award. Unfortunately, he never went over about .290 after that. Len had been playing center field and one night their catcher was hurt. He's played catcher ever since. His salary was $68 a month plus room and board.

In '41 and '42, Len played for Columbia, South Carolina. He almost married a teacher from there, however he met me in the winter of '41 and he was caught! We married in February of '43. We both had gone to the same high school, but Len was five years ahead of me.

In 1943, Len played for Syracuse in the International League and had a good year. The following spring (1944), he was sent to Cincinnati and he caught behind Ray Meuller. That was a problem, as Ray was out to break a record of consecutive games caught, so the only time Len could play was to finish the last couple of innings of a game. He complained and asked to go back to Syracuse and he finished the year there.

He was sold to the Chicago Cubs and we went there in 1945. His salary was ($)275 and $450 a month in Syracuse and jumped to $750 a month in Chicago. We always had to come home and find winter jobs. We were still living with my folks in the off-season. We had some great times. Len and I, Stan Hack and Bill Nicholson would go to the Starlight Ballroom and dance and have a few beers. I remember after cinching the ball game (pennant) in Pittsburgh, the fellows were there and Charlie (Grimm, manager) told them to call their wives and anyone they wanted to and to charge it to the club. Charlie always had them wear suits and ties on the road. Mrs. Grimm was there and she cut off all their ties. All the wives lived at the Sheraton in Chicago. We went out and partied with a couple of the disabled players. We were all mighty ill the next morning.

We lost the Series to Detroit in the seventh game in the seventh inning. Our cut was $4,900 and I believe the winners was about $7,500 plus rings. The wives also received diamond rings, furniture, etc.

Len Rice

Len was hurt mid-season while playing for the Cubs. He was going for a pop fly and Billy Schuster was running in from shortstop. He collided with Len. Len went to the hospital with a bad brain concussion. It was several days before he came out of it and it left a deep scar on his eyebrow. It was an exhibition game in Brooklyn for the servicemen. When Len was retired, he got brain cancer. It could have been caused by all the times he got hit in the head. We wondered if it could have come from all those injuries? At fourteen, Len injured a kidney playing football and had it removed. The doctors told his parents he would never be able to play contact sports, but he never had any further trouble. He participated in several sports and ran the 100 yard dash in 9.9 (seconds).

Len was sold to San Diego. He played there in 1946-47-48. We had three great years which left us with a lot of fond memories. We lived at Mission Beach and several others did, also. Every Sunday, after the ball game, we would all go out to Morrie's (Morrison) restaurant in La Jolla. Morrie, being a great fan, would give us the upstairs room and serve us wonderful dinners. We would dance, play cards and party. Harry and Ruth Douglas were great fans and our dear friends. They never missed a ball game. They had box seats right by the dugout, so they knew all of the players. They used to go to Morrie's with us occasionally. One night, we were all dancing and they were playing a fast piece. Tom (Seats) insisted on Ruthie to get up and dance. Being a good sport, Ruth did and was trying to jitterbug. Tom was tossing Ruth all around. When the dance was over, Len told Tom that Ruth had a wooden leg! It really shook him up and he never asked Ruth to dance again. Ruth lost her leg when she was 18 in a boating accident. She was head of the USO during the war and helped to rehabilitate the amputee servicemen.

Monday was their day off and we would all go to the beach and relax. All the wives would bring potluck. We'd take beer and soda water and stay at the beach all day until it was dark. We had many small children of the players, so we played many games with them and enjoyed them.

Len and I were never able to have children and we wanted to adopt with no success. We went to the welfare department right there in San Diego. Len was turned down as he only had one kidney. We explained that this happened when he was 14 years old. They said we couldn't have a child. They said, 'You're just tourists!' I'll never forget that. Several players had adopted in other states with no problems

Tom and Opal Seats had three girls then and they shared them with us. We are still dear friends with them, however, Tom and Len are both gone now. Tom and Opal

had another daughter in 1949. I always said they should have named her Del Mar.

Len's salary was about $1,000 a month. Len always caught Tom's games and sometimes Len said when he went out to talk to Tom, his breath would knock you out! He kept a bottle stashed under the seats and he would take a shot between innings. Len liked catching Tom Seats, Vern Kennedy and Manny Salvo, in fact, he just liked catching.

Len liked Pepper Martin as a manager, although he got along with all of them. He said they would play cards sometimes on the train from Seattle to San Diego and not get much shut-eye.

Len, Tom and Jim Brillheart used to go out in the outfield and use fungo bats to kill frogs. We used to have some great frog leg dinners. Back in Columbia, South Carolina, Len was catching and the frogs were hopping all around. The umpire told him he was afraid of them. Later in the game, Len put one in his glove. When the umpire caught a ball, it spattered all over. I think he lost a friend that night.

I remember one night, and it was a foggy night, he played center field, which usually never happens, and someone, I don't recall who, hit a fly ball to center. Len came running in to catch it and they couldn't even see where it went.

Len was sent to Dallas in the spring of 1949. Len received $1,250 (a month) in Dallas. He had a good year. I had to leave in early summer due to an illness and couldn't take the heat, so I went home to Oakland. It was the first time in our married life that I didn't spend the season with him. We were both very unhappy and he told them he'd like to go back to the Coast League. They said he could go as a playing manager to Little Rock, Arkansas. They told Len if he went as a free agent, he would have to wait three years before he could sign up to play again. San Francisco tried to get him, but because of the free agency clause, they couldn't.

Len went to work for Lucky Lager, Howatt Beverage, and stayed with them for 14 years until he had a bad heart attack and could no longer handle the truck and sales route. Then he worked and managed Spring Valley Golf Course, restaurant and bar. He played semi-pro every winter until we moved to the mountains in 1961. We built a home and have been in Arnold (California) ever since. Len went to work for Claude C. Wood Company, paving contractors, and retired in 1981.

He started the Little League up here in Arnold. Being a Rotarian, he was able to have the Rotary sponsor and furnish uniforms for the teams. It's still going strong. He also started women's softball up here. He called them 'The Bouncing Boobs.'

Len was real active in the community, especially with the young people. They really admired him. Several of the young men that played for him, still come over to see if I'm all right. Many of the young men spoke at his memorial and praised him for helping the youth in our area. In fact, the children of those boys are now active in Little League.

This brings back so many memories of good times. I sure miss Len and I'm still a baseball fan. I could go on and on. I mention his name or think about the good times every day."

◆◆◆

BEN GUINTINI, outfield.
BORN: 1-13-20   PADRES: 1946

In addition to playing for the Padres in '46, Ben Guintini also made a brief appearance with the Pittsburgh Pirates that year. Most of his career in the Pacific Coast League was with the San Francisco Seals. Guintini was an acrobatic and entertaining player. His antics won admiration from the fans and his teammates, but management was not always amused by his clowning. Ben now suffers from Parkinson's disease and he is unable to communicate. The following interview was conducted with his wife, Helen.

"Ben cannot write his name nor participate in get-togethers anymore. He was such a big, strong, healthy, active man, but the disease has destroyed his mind and

Ben Guitini

body. It is so sad to see him shrivel up. I care for him and I have Lou Gehrig's disease. He would have loved to have attended the reunions and talk about baseball. They played for the love of the game is what Ben used to say. Everybody liked him. He was a cut-up and a clown.

His dad whittled his first bat for him when he was a little boy. His father didn't really know what baseball was. Ben didn't speak English until he went to school. His father was an acrobat from a prominent family in Northern Italy, but he was the black sheep of the family. He left home and married a girl from Southern Italy and they came to America and settled in Los Banos (California). When Ben was nine years old, he was playing with the men. They made him a little shirt and he played center field. He was discovered playing in this dinky little town. They sent him to the Salt Lake City Bees and he starved the first week. He was used to his grandfather breaking the bread and handing it out to the family. They would use it to eat from their bowls. Now he was seeing food he'd never eaten before and he had to learn how to eat it.

When he was playing for San Francisco, a lot of friends and family came up from Los Banos to see him play. He was so happy, he did hand-stands all the way out to center field and Lefty O'Doul benched him, so nobody got to see him play. A cousin of Ben's was a nun at a hospital in San Francisco. She was a baseball fan, but she had to stop going to the games in her habit, because she'd get so mad and yell 'Damn you.' Poor Sister Ann. Well, one day Lefty was at her hospital and she saw him. He had been drinking, so she told him, 'If you don't stop this, you'll never get to heaven.' He told her, 'I'm just trying to get to an elevator right now.

When Ben was up with Pittsburgh, he and his roommate worked out a routine. Ben was real agile. One guy would do a drum roll and Ben would come into the room doing flips and he'd land on the bed. Finally, he broke the bed and he had to pay for it. He loved to do things like that. He was just a clown and a performer. Joe E. Brown wanted him to come to Hollywood to get into pictures. I told him, 'You're better looking than old Chuck (Connors, The Rifleman and former first baseman with the Dodgers, Cubs and PCL Angels)".

◆◆◆

JACK LOHRKE, shortstop.
BORN: 2-25-24   PADRES: 1942-46

Jack Lohrke played briefly for the Padres in 1942 as an eighteen-year old shortstop before entering the military service. He was batting .345 for Spokane in the Western International League on June 24, 1946 when he was instructed to immediately report to San Diego. He got off the bus in Ellensburg, Washington and headed south while his team proceeded toward Spokane in a drizzling rain. Tragedy struck when the bus plunged 350 feet down a mountainside. Nine players were killed in the worst accident in the history of organized baseball. Although greatly disturbed by this event, he hit .303 in San Diego and led the Padres with eight home runs. By 1947 Jack was playing third base for the New York Giants. He complied a .242 lifetime batting average over a seven-year career in the major leagues.

"I haven't seen Pete (Coscarart) since 1946. I remember Johnny Jensen, Tony Criscola, Del Ballinger and Dick Gyselman. Del and Billy Schuster were some kind of nuts. Del was a good guy, but Billy really was nuts! Gyselman had idiosyncrasies, too. When I was recalled and went to the Padres, I went out to play third base. Dick Gyselman said, 'I don't know where you're goin', son, but I play there.' I went to shortstop. He was like an old man to me. I just observed these old pros like they were gods. It was a real thrill to play in the Coast League.

My father and mother were fruit-pickers and I had two brothers. We'd travel all over the state from Santa Paula to Escondido to Chula Vista to San Juan Capistrano to Santa Susana, that's up in the Simi Valley. We had a home in L.A. through the Depression, so we had a place to go. My parents sure worked hard and we worked, too. I started playing softball at night for Ward's Cafe when I was fourteen. Then I was playing semi-pro and a guy who was a semi-scout for San Diego signed me to a contract.

The Padres optioned me to Twin Falls, Idaho and then I went to Spokane in the Western International League. That was when there was the terrible bus accident and nine players were killed when the bus went off a cliff. I'd gotten off the bus, because the Padres recalled me. That's how they started calling me, 'Lucky.' I never used the name and the players don't call me that. Then there was a plane (Jack missed a military transport plane that crashed) and a train, too, but it was all about terrible things, so, in baseball, they give you a honker like that, but I never use it. You see why.

In those days, from the first day you signed a contract, they owned you. I was just glad to get a contract every year. That's the way they did it in those days. You just signed and you were happy. Remember how those guys went to Mexico? Sal Maglie and Vern Stephens. Stephens led the league in RBIs and they wanted to give him a pay cut! He belongs in the Hall of Fame. If that Mexican General hadn't been killed, I think that Mexican League could have made it.

When I was in San Diego, I was hittin' good. When you're hittin' good, your hamburgers taste better. When you're not hittin', everything goes bad. That's the way it is in baseball.

I remember the sailors walking down Broadway. I was staying in a dive for a dollar a night. It was just a two-

Jack Lohrke

Jack Lohrke

story walk-up. I can remember watching Manny Salvo playing three cushion billiards in those billiard parlors along Broadway. He was very good and that is a tough game. It was nice to travel in the Pacific Coast League, because you were gone for two weeks and you'd get to stay in each town for a whole week. It was a real good league, but it sure was a long time ago."

BRUNO KONOPKA, outfield.
BORN: 9-16-19   DIED: 9-27-96   PADRES: 1946

Bruno "Bruce" Konopka went to the University of Southern California on a basketball and baseball scholarship. In 1941 he was captain of former Padre Rod Dedeaux's first baseball team at USC. Bruno played two seasons (1942-43) with the Philadelphia Athletics and returned to the Mackmen following the war after a brief appearance in San Diego.

"I wasn't there long enough. Pepper Martin was the manager and Philadelphia wanted me to play regularly. They had a pretty good first baseman, George McDonald. I was sitting there, furious, because I wasn't playing. I finally told them if I'm going to sit, I'd just as soon sit in Philadelphia! But, I think I did hit one home run there. Philadelphia sent me to Atlanta. Kiki Cuyler was the manager and I sat there, too. Then I went to Little Rock.

Bruno Konopka

Bill Dickey was the manager and he still liked to take his swings at batting practice. I didn't learn to hit until I went to Little Rock. I just watched Dickey and learned a lot from that, but that was the end of my professional career. I played a lot of semi-pro ball here in Colorado and in Nebraska after that.

When I was at Philadelphia, I remember Connie Mack sitting by first base. Earle Mack came by and showed me how to hit. Then another coach came and showed me. Then another. I grabbed my glove and as I got by Connie Mack, he motioned me over. 'You listen to the coaches when they talk, but when you get back in the batter's box, you hit the way you do. We got you, because we like the way you hit.'

Al Simmons was one of the coaches. He was very selfish and second guessed everybody. Lena Blackburne was the other coach. He was a gentleman, a terrific guy. Yes, he is the one who went to a (New) Jersey lake and found the mud they all rub on the baseballs now. [In 1938, Blackburne discovered that mud from a mysterious location on the Delaware River removed the shine from new baseballs. His heirs continue to be the sole supplier of Lena Blackburne's Baseball Rubbing Mud which umpires rub on all major league baseballs prior to their use in the game. -Ed.] He'd always talk to me and try to help me. He wanted to help the team. Simmons was just the opposite.

My first year, the next to the last game of the season and I was going up to bat. This old-timer, I don't even remember his name, was a catcher for Washington. He looks at me and he says, 'Look what we've got, a rookie. He looks big and strong. I'm gonna let you know every pitch.' He was talking to the ump and I didn't know what to make of him. Washington and Philadelphia were in seventh and eighth place. He says, 'Fast ball down the middle.' I looked at it and it was right down the middle. Then he says, 'High and outside. Don't pay any attention to it.' I didn't know if he was telling the truth, but it was high and outside. Then he says, 'He's coming back with the first pitch.' I lined it over second for a single. The next time up, he says, 'No more! You do it on your own now.' I did get another hit and finished the year batting .300, three for ten.

When I was 17 years old, I played in a tournament for Holsum Bread. $10,000 for the winning team. We played the Kansas City Monarchs in our first game: Satchel Paige, Josh Gibson, Cool Papa Bell! I think I struck out twice against Satchel. They really beat us. I remember Satchel flew in for the game in his own plane.

The money they make today and the parks they play in - it makes me want to cry. Take away fifty years and I'd be out there gettin' rich!"

Dain Clay

Dain Clay with daughters and new car.

Dain Clay

◆◆◆

DAIN CLAY, outfield.
BORN: 7-10-19 DIED: 8-28-94 PADRES: 1947-50,52-53

Dain Clay hit .335 his first year (1938) in professional ball with Portsmouth in the Mid-Atlantic League. From 1943 through 1946, he averaged .258 for the Cincinnati Reds. Dain led the National League with 656 plate appearances in 1945 and finished third with 19 stolen bases. He became a Padre in 1947 and the fans selected him as their favorite player. Clay was named to the '47 PCL All-Star team while hitting .313 and swiping 40 bases. He averaged .291 during six-seasons with San Diego. The following interview was conducted with his first wife, Ruth Clay.

"We were high school sweetheart back in Cuyahoga Falls, Ohio. It's between Cleveland and Akron. Dain played football, basketball, baseball and track in high school. He was a wonderful athlete and he was named Ohio's greatest sandlotter in 1937 when he graduated from school. He and Johnny Single got to see the World Series that year in New York as their prize. Don't they look great in their hats and top coats?

He played baseball from the time he was a little boy and when he signed a professional contract, I remember him saying, 'They're going to pay me to play baseball!' There was a blackboard in the kitchen and he'd write how much he was making. I remember when he wrote $100 a month. He was so happy.

His biggest thrill was hitting a grand slam and then the game winning single in the 11th inning for a victory over Pittsburgh on Opening Day. It was in 1945 and the next day, it was the headline of the Cincinnati paper and down below, they wrote about the war. He couldn't believe he was bigger news than the war.

It was kind of an adventure to come this far (from Ohio) to play baseball. California was paradise. Dain didn't think major league baseball would come to the west coast because of the transportation. When he played, they didn't fly - it was all by trains. When we came to San Diego, we rented Bob Elliott's house. On our way out here, we saw somebody walking down the road. Dain said, 'That's Bob Elliott's wife. What's she doing out here?' It turned out that when Bob would get gas, his wife would take the girls and walk up the road for exercise. Then he would stop and pick them up. It was probably on Route 66, but what a coincidence to cross each other like that.

It was very exciting when Dain won the car for being the most popular Padre. Imagine how you'd feel winning a brand new car! There was a Navy guy that year who booed him all year, but later he found out that he'd put in about one hundred votes for him.

When you go to the games every day, you can't remember them all. We'd be glad when they won and sad when they lost. My mother and Charlene Mesner's mother both loved baseball, too. You learn to keep quiet at the games. I'd say, 'How would you like it if I came outside your home and started yelling how bad your husband is?' But that's the fans' right and I learned to keep my mouth shut. I was never very mouthy, but I'd feel so bad when someone's husband would strike out and a fan would say, 'Get rid of him.' I'd feel so bad for the other girls.

My daughter Danette's husband's parents met at Lane Field while Dain was playing for the Padres. They (Cecil and Virginia Starling) are a great baseball family. Her

Dain Clay and Johnny Single at 1937 World Series with Yankees manager Joe McCarthy.

Frank Kerr

father-in-law and Dain loved to talk baseball and go to Padre games together. They are very involved in Little League and sponsor teams.

We packed and unpacked seven times one day. We were in Rochester and heard that Dain had been sold to Pittsburgh, then to Philadelphia, then to St. Louis and, finally, to the Cincinnati Reds. They'd call and say you're going and then they'd call and say you weren't going. Like life, things change in baseball very quickly.

Dain and I always remained friends. Maybe we were even better friends after the divorce. Alice (his second wife) gave me a lot of these pictures after he died, because she knew they would mean more to us. He didn't even tell us how ill he was and he went so fast."

FRANK KERR, catcher.
BORN: 3-5-18   PADRES: 1947,50-52

Frank Kerr was an iron man in an iron mask. Like so many players of his era, he would do anything it took to stay in the lineup. There was always somebody eager to take your place. In 1939, he began playing organized baseball in the obscure Bi-State, Ohio State and Kitty Leagues. Promoted to Pocatello the next season, Frank hit .311 with 18 home runs. After serving in the armed forces and coming up through the minor league system, Kerr was able to play for his hometown Padres in 1947. He delivered 11 home runs and a .300 batting average. Frank returned to San Diego in 1950 and averaged .249 over the next three seasons. He later became a Coast League umpire.

"In Fremont, North Carolina, or was it South Carolina, we were ahead by four runs when our catcher got hurt.

There wasn't anybody else who could catch and we'd have to forfeit the game. I said I could do it and I never caught before. I was behind the plate and I noticed our third baseman hitting the dirt with his glove. I figured that was the signal and on the first pitch, with the bases loaded and no outs, I picked the guy off third. The next pitch, I caught the guy stealing third. Then the next one, I threw the guy out trying to steal second. Three pitches and three outs. We won! I never cared how I did it. All I wanted was for the team to win and I decided that I liked being a catcher.

There was once this play at home. I blocked the plate and his spikes came right up my shin guard and cut me. I told the umpire, 'Jack, I think I'm hurt.' Les (Cook) came out, looked at my knee and said, 'Oh my God!' The kid who spiked me felt real bad. He was a nice kid, too. Well, their manager called Les a quack, but he (Les) said I'd be playing in seven days. Les cleaned me out, put three clamps on it, put some black stuff on it and cleaned it every day. It was pretty bad. You could see the kneecap and it was three inches long, but Les was right. I was playing again in a week.

This was when the Coast League played a 200 game schedule (1947). That year, I caught 177 ball games. I was the starting catcher on the All-Star team. I think I hit two-ninety-nine point nine, around three hundred, but I hit behind Max West and he drove everybody in. The only one for me to drive in was Max if he hadn't already hit a home run.

Bobby Kerrigan, our little left-handed pitcher, he'd throw up a ball about 65 miles per hour. One batter caught it and threw it back and said to put something on it. One time, I went out with a fielder's glove. He refused to pitch, so I took it off and I was going to catch him bare-handed.

One time we were playing pinochle on the plane and the co-pilot came back and was watching us. We didn't pay any attention to him. But when the pilot came back and started watching, we said, 'Who is flying the plane?' He said Jack (Graham) was!

My uncle umpired for eighteen years in the PCL. His name was Bill Englen. The guys didn't know he was my uncle. They'd ask, 'How can you cuss him out? He only gives us ten seconds, but you keep it up.' Hell, he lived with us. If he threw me out of the game, I'd throw him out of the home! Actually, it was my mother's home and I knew just how far I could go with him.

I umpired in the PCL in '56 and '57. It was the worst job I ever had. I lost all of my friends."

◆◆◆

VINCE SHUPE, first base.
BORN:9-5-21   DIED:4-5-62   PADRES:47-49

Vince Shupe replaced longtime Padre George McDonald at first base in 1947. He set a club record with 117 assists for the position and lead the team with 42 doubles that year. Vince hit a respectable .269 for the '45 Boston Braves during his only season in the big leagues. When his playing days were over, Shupe returned to his native Ohio and became active in youth baseball. He coached Mike Hershberger, who played center field for San Diego in 1961. The following was provided by his daughter, Kathy Crowther, his good friend, Al Michaels, and his protege, Mike Hershberger.

[Kathy] "I was just a baby when my Dad played in San Diego. I was so small that I slept in a dresser drawer. My Dad just loved baseball. He lived on an apple orchard when he was growing up in East Canton and that was his thing to play baseball. All I remember about San Diego is going to night games. I also remember going from one car to the next on the train, because it was so loud. My Mom talked about the people who dressed in drag. Before he married Mom, I guess my Dad was quite a lady's man. He dated Jean Peters, the movie star who was married to Howard Hughes.

When he came back to Ohio, he still played baseball. He was a salesman for Pure Oil and he traveled a lot. He always brought me good stuff from the openings of stations. Mike Hershberger and Al Michaels could tell you more about his baseball."

[Mike] "Vince coached and helped manage us with Al Michaels when we played for Halters Contractors. We had a good team - five or six signed pro contracts. The whole infield signed. Vince played baseball in the leagues around here, too. A lot of ex-pro players played Canton Class A ball. I didn't realize that he (Vince) was a Padre. Those are some fond memories of San Diego. It was beautiful out there. We had Herb Score and 'Suitcase' Simpson. Jim Bolger was there. We had a good club."

Vince Shupe

Mike Hershberger

ECHOES FROM LANE FIELD

Max West

Max West in skivvies (far right) drinking beer with teammates after ballgame on Tiniian during the war.

[Al] "Vince was a great guy. He was a helluva ballplayer. He died in my arms of a massive heart attack at the bowling alley. His brothers died of heart attacks, too. One was 45 and the other was 44. Vince was the greatest guy you'd ever meet. A lot of jokes and a lot of fun. We played together until I went in the Navy in '43. He originally pitched with the Dodgers. He told so many stories, but he died so long ago, I hardly remember them. He was impressed with Vern Kennedy who pitched for San Diego. Kennedy threw a no-hitter for the White Sox in the Thirties.

I remember something Vince did here. He pointed to center field and hit a home run. I think Hershberger hit three that day. Mike had a good year in San Diego. He hit over .300 [.310 -Ed.] and went right to the White Sox. That team we coached together that had Mike on it won the National Championship. It was Connie Mack Ball."

MAX WEST, outfield and first base.
BORN: 11-28-16   PADRES: 1947, 49-50

Max West was one of the all-time great Pacific Coast League sluggers (218 career home runs in the PCL). He lead the league three times in home runs (1947, 1949 and 1952). In 1949, West smashed 48 circuit blows, scored 166 runs, drove in a like number and, incredibly, was walked 201 times (a league record). He was the star of the 1940 All Star game when his three-run, first inning home run was all the National League needed in their shutout victory over the American League by a 4-0 score. West played professional baseball from 1935 through 1953, missing three years while he was in the Army Air Forces in the Pacific during World War II. On August 22, 1965, Max was one of the five original inductees into the San Diego Padres Hall of Fame.

"I was doing well (with the San Francisco Mission team) and had a new Chevrolet. I was in the clubhouse at Wrigley Field (Los Angeles) and I was told, 'Don't put on your uniform.' I was sold to Boston. I cried. It was like going to Siberia! But Casey (Stengel) treated me like a son.

After the war, I was in Cincinnati. I wanted some money from (Reds owner) Giles and he sent me a telegram that said, 'You didn't like it here and you won't like it where you're goin'!' It was San Diego and I was treated like a king! Bill Starr was a great guy. That was the nicest time of my life. I lived in Coronado. My brother-in-law was in the Navy. I would take the ferry.

There wasn't any game I played (at Lane Field) that the place wasn't full. Those stands were full of sailors and Starr sold them a million beers. That Starr - he made me play every inning of every game. He made me earn every dollar. We'd play two hundred games. At that time, it was my opinion that the Coast League was better than the National League. Just a couple pitchers more and the PCL would have been better.

I remember a time when Oakland came to town and the writers asked Casey (Stengel) how they'd pitch me. He said, 'I know how to pitch to Max. He used to play for me.' They were in front by about eight runs, but we kept scoring a couple here and three there. Then it got to the bottom of the ninth and there two or three on base and I hit a home run. We won something like twelve to eleven or thirteen to twelve. They had this huge lead and we kept pecking away at it. It was a game that really sticks out in my memory. Afterwards, Casey didn't say anything. There wasn't much he could have said. He shouldn't have said anything in the first place.

I hit off my back a lot. The pitchers would test you: inside, outside and then they'd say, 'Put him on his ass.' Al Rosen told me that he was always on his ass, because I'd hit a home run and he was up after me. (While with Boston) Manuel Salvo put me on my back five times. I'll never forget old Salvo. He was pawing the dirt and snorting like a bull. I said, 'Don't hit him.' Son of a gun, he does. I'm drilled by (Brooklyn pitcher) Whitlow Wyatt in the back.

We were up in L.A. We had those juiced balls for batting practice. Easter and I were hitting them over the scoreboard. We had Harvey Storey and Buster Adams would hit home runs to lead off a game. That day, Red Adams refused to pitch against us. The whole lineup could hit 'em out!

I had to take a cut to go to Pittsburgh, but I needed it for my pension. Most of the guys who played out here wanted to stay. Playing a season in Pittsburgh is like dying. We've got the good climate here.

When we had Easter, Storey, Adams, (Al) Smith, (Minnie) Minoso, (Harry 'Suitcase') Simpson - it was a picnic. We'd be four or five runs behind and we'd just laugh at them. Minnie scored for me on a fly ball from second! I never left him on base. That's how I got so many RBIs: Minnie Minoso. When we got to the playoffs, he'd say, 'Let's get money. Get money. No speak English.' They'd hit him and he'd laugh, 'Me no get black and blue.' He always gave 100%, 110%. If there was money, Minnie wanted it!

(Catcher) Dee Moore was strong and mean. He liked his throws three feet up the line and it better not be four (feet). We were playing Hollywood and I threw one three feet up the line. Carlos Bernier was coming home. We didn't like him. The next thing I knew, he was layin' over by the bats and Dee had a big grin on his face. In the old days, catchers waited until you'd start your slide and jump on you. Gabby Hartnett... he weighed about five hundred pounds... he got me good.

There was a foundry beyond right field in Portland. You'd get covered with soot. It was worse for the fans.

I remember a time in San Diego when Billy Martin hit a short single to right. I came in and he rounded first. He liked to dance, so I threw right at him! I can still see him trying to get out of the way of that ball. He called me everything. I was just having a little fun with him. I understand he lost every fight he ever had.

The dew was so bad at Lane Field that you'd come in from the outfield, take off your shoes and pour water out of them. Our cars looked like somebody put a hose on them. I had my Cadillac ruined by parking it there."

AL HOGAN, concessions and advertising manager.
BORN: 4-20-14   PADRES:47-74

While pitching in the Civilian Conservation Corps during the Depression, young Al Hogan was awarded a baseball scholarship to attend Washington State College. His love of baseball and the financial needs of his family prompted him to take a second job selling hot dogs at Lane Field in 1947. Eventually Al left his supervisory position at Convair to work full time as concessions manager and advertising salesman for the ball club. Hogan was honored as Concessions Man of the Year for Organized Baseball in 1964. He should be considered as the Padres original archivist since he salvaged numerous items including boxes of photographs and programs from the Lane Field area. Al retired as the Padres advertising manager in 1974 and continues to work for the San Diego Building Industry Association.

"Del Meredith and I used to carry metal hot dog servers that held a hundred hot dogs, a hundred buns and a jar of mustard. There was a steam table on the inside that held the hot dogs and there was charcoal underneath it to keep them hot. We'd take the hot dogs out with a fork, put 'em on a bun, spread on the mustard and wrap them in a napkin before we'd hand them to the customer. I had the third base side and Del had the first base side. At the end of the year, we'd be within $5.00 of each other in sales. We'd make about eleven or twelve hundred dollars. It doesn't sound like much now, but in those days it helped a lot and we had all that fun. We got to know the fans and Lane Field was like a small town.

Al Hogan

Earl Keller was up in the press box during the games. We had a big cooler for their drinks. At the end of the game, poor old Earl would order 15 hot dogs. He had two paper bags. He'd take the hot dogs out of the buns and put them in one bag and the buns in the other. Bill Starr said it was OK, because they didn't pay him enough at the paper to feed his kids.

In '54, when we won the pennant, my wife and I took the family back to Illinois. We were down at the station and Bill Starr's secretary came running over with my check because Bill wanted me to have it for our vacation. He included me with the winner's share which I never expected. I have nothing but good things to say about Bill Starr.

You'll never know how much Les Cook did to help run that club. He'd been with it since Salt Lake City so he knew how things were done under Bill Lane. He was just one helluva guy. He was also the road secretary. He'd get so pie eyed, but let anybody touch that little bag with the money and he'd get sober right now. He is one of the finest men I ever met. He was very good hearted and would go out of his way to help others. He used to let kids into the ball a park and would say. 'There's lots of room.'

We had a cooler full of beer in the locker room for the players after the game. Then they'd stop to see me, because they always wanted more beer. One time, the beer delivery was five cases short. The brewery made up the difference the next day, but I knew the players took it. We kept the commissary locked...not from the public; it was to keep the ballplayers out! Max West would always stop to see me in the commissary, but he never wanted anything. He just stopped to talk. I liked Max.

We also kept the cooler full in the press box. It scared the daylights out of the venders who took the beer up there. There were just little slats on the roof and the railing was very flimsy. I used to worry about some of the sports writers drinking too much and falling off the roof. There was a small fence to keep the foul balls off the roof. Boys would pick them up after the game, but it was hard to get people to go up there.

Gary Ball was the manager of concessions. This guy from Coca Cola gave Gary Ball a lecture on how he couldn't operate without Coca Cola. They didn't know Gary Ball like I did. He got up, opened the door and said, 'Thank you gentlemen for coming and good bye.' He called Frank Alessio and said, 'We're selling nothing but Pepsi Cola.' He would show Coca Cola that he could operate without their drink so that was when Frank Alessio put in a loan for a bottling works, because it came from L.A. before that.

We were very proud of our hot dogs. I would go to the meat packing plants and sample their different recipes with different mixtures of meat and spices. The best was Wilson up in L.A. Women would complain to me that they'd buy Wilson hot dogs, but they weren't as good as ours. We had a special recipe. People would want to buy hot dogs from us, but a thing like that can snowball. People even wanted my wife to get hot dogs for them.

Les Cook

Earl Keller in Lane Field press box.

C. Arnholt Smith would get in his brown or tan Cadillac real early in the morning. He'd drive to his shipyards, cannery and Westgate Park. If he saw something was wrong, there'd be a note in my mailbox like somebody left something in the stands or people threw cigarette packages in the planters, please clean it up. He had an eye for details and he did all this before going to the bank.

I don't know whose idea the tunies (tuna hot dogs) was? You can't tell the boss, 'Your Tunies are no good!' They just didn't sell. I don't think I ever heard a real compliment about them. I think the best I ever heard was, 'Well they're OK, but I really don't care for them'. They tried putting a lot of spices in them, but it didn't work.

My wife's favorite player was Minnie Minoso. He'd get on base and steal second, then he'd steal third and then he'd steal home. He was an exciting player. She'd watch the games from the press box with Al Schuss and Al Coupee. One time my wife called me up and said the garage was full of beer. She knew I didn't order it. The Aztec Brewery beer truck came and they said, 'Its for Al'. They left 40 cases in the garage. I couldn't park the car. I gave it all away to friends and after that, they'd always ask me if I had some beer when they'd be having a party.

Lefty O'Doul taught me to play golf. Did you know he was one of the ten best left handed golfers in America? Tommy Bolt liked to play with him. When Lefty learned that I pitched against him in '35 in Klamath Falls, we became friends. He was with San Francisco and they were on their way to Portland. A lot of that went on in theThirties. They'd play games along the way to build up fan support. Joe DiMaggio was on the Seals then.

Well, when he asked if I played golf, I said, 'It's a sissy's game.' He went to my wife and I don't know how he got the money out of her, but he bought me a set of clubs. Lefty took me out on Lane Field and every day, at 2:00, a sailor he hired off Broadway would shag balls. Lefty would give me pointers and by the end of the season, I was ready to play. The first time I played was Caliente and I took hard cash from my vendors. They wanted a chance to win it back and that's how I got hooked on golf. I got down to a two handicap and I owe it all to Lefty O'Doul.

It was my job to set up team pictures and that wasn't as easy as it sounds. Baseball players are very independent and they didn't like to show up for pictures. The manager warned them they'd be fined. but they still wouldn't show up. Bo Belinsky had a movie star girlfriend and he did everything she told him to do. He didn't show up because this Hollywood dame was so special and the team picture had to be canceled. C. Arnholt Smith's daughter liked Bo, too. She liked a lot of the players and that could get a little complicated sometimes."

BOB KERRIGAN, pitcher.
BORN: 9-1-20 DIED: 11-20-98 PADRES: 1947-48,51,53-56

Bob Kerrigan will always be remembered as the winning pitcher in the final game of the 1954 season when the Padres bested the Hollywood Stars for the PCL pennant. After going 18-14 for

Bob Kerrigan

1954 parade

Herb Gorman

Padres on the set of "Two Guys From Texas."

Boise (Pioneer League) in his first year of professional ball, Bob became a San Diego Padre in 1947. He went to Tacoma in 1949 and, in his second season, set the Western International League record for victories (26-7). Back with San Diego in 1951, Kerrigan lead the team with a .636 winning percentage (14-8), but he was shipped off to Indianapolis for 1952. Bob returned to San Diego for good in 1953. His top year was 1954 when he registered a 2.77 ERA with 104 strikeouts to accompany his 17-11 record. That was also the year Kerrigan set the league record for the lowest batting average for players with more than 50 plate appearances (.027).

[Pointing at the 1954 championship parade photograph] "I won that suit! O'Doul was coaching third and he yelled, 'Bob, get a hit.' He'd told me before, 'Bob, you are absolutely the worst hitter I've ever seen.' I swung at the ball. It went out like a dying pigeon. The infielders went out and the outfielders came in and it just fell there. I remembered that you're supposed to run to first base and looked over at O'Doul and he was lying prostrate on the ground. I went to Leo Beck and ordered a tailor-made blue suit. It cost $150 and that was a lot of money in those days. The next day, O'Doul said, 'I meant it about the suit.' And I said I'd already bought it!

[A friend teased Bob and said, 'Tell him about going oh-for-seven.'] Yeah, I went oh-for-seven... oh-for-seven years!

It was the last game of the season (1954) and Eddie Erautt had blisters on his fingers. He was out of the rotation and we were in a tie with Hollywood. O'Doul called us together and asked the team's opinion on who should pitch? Eddie couldn't pitch and our other two starters had just pitched in the doubleheader. I had two days rest. I told O'Doul that my stomach didn't feel good, but my arm was OK. I don't remember much about the game, believe it or not. After the first, it was Hollywood, 1-0. Somehow we tied it up and Harry Elliott drove in the potential winning run. Bob Elliott then hit two home runs and we won, 7-2. That particular game, they roped off the outfield. Frank Kelleher singled in both of their runs after they got ground rule doubles on balls that went beyond the rope.

I think it was about '53 and Herb Gorman hadn't been playing. He was a good hitter. O'Doul decided to put him in left field. It was about the second or third inning. Somebody told O'Doul that Herb wasn't feeling good. The game was stopped immediately. They brought him in and put him on the training table. An ambulance was called. They didn't have 911 in those days, but he died right there on the table. They did an autopsy and said his organs were of an eighty-year-old man. He was about 35-36. It was very sad. If they hadn't brought him in, he'd have died right there in left field."

JIM FULLER, reporter.
San Diego Daily Journal

Jim Fuller was a reporter for the old San Diego Daily Journal during the late Forties. He briefly wrote a column while the newspaper searched for a new sports editor. Jim believed the purpose of a sports column was both to entertain and crusade. In addition to writing entertaining stories about the Padres, he used his column to promote the value of youth sports in San Diego.

"I was on the *San Diego Journal* which doesn't exist anymore. There were Hot Stove Leagues in a lot of places.

Bucky Harris and Max West

Jim Fuller and Padres Manager Rip Collins.

I asked Tony (Criscola) and four or five other guys if there was an interest in forming one in San Diego. They said, 'Yes.' I wrote a story and took a photographer upstairs at Morrie's (Morrison) restaurant in La Jolla. We set up a hot stove and painted Tony and Morrie's name on the chimney. Tony and Morrie, Buster Adams and Jim Brillheart and Kent Parker were in the picture. (*San Diego Journal*, January 27, 1949) The Hot Stove League was set up for the fans. That was the original thought. I was in a position to give them publicity.

When we went to play in Hollywood, I arranged to see *'Two Guys from Texas.'* I think it was being filmed at Warner Brothers. It was around 1947. It was starring Dennis Morgan and Jack Carson.

I think the most memorable thing about the Coast League were the managers: Lefty O'Doul and Casey Stengel. When things weren't going right, O'Doul would pull out a bandanna and wave it at the fans in a very uncomplimentary way. Sort of 'up-yours.' I wrote about having a 'Bandanna Night' for the next time the Seals came to town. The park was completely filled and everybody was waving a bandanna. O'Doul complained to the umpires that it was bothering his hitters seeing those bandannas in centerfield. The umpires said, 'That's none of our business.'

Casey Stengel had a bag of peanuts and threw them into the stands. He said, 'Eat 'em, you monkeys.' We had a Peanut Night. The Padre fans threw so many peanuts on the field, they had to stop the game to sweep them off. In those days, teams didn't have a lot of coaches, so the manager would coach at first or third. One day, Casey was upset and he started shaking. He fell to the ground and he was still shaking. They thought he was having a fit and came out to give medical attention. He just got up, brushed himself off and acted like nothing happened.

Big Jack Graham hit home runs! During a pregame news conference with the sports writers, Casey predicted, 'Your

Graham Cracker is not going to get a home run off me!' Jack batted four times, leading the Padres to a win. The first three times at bat, the ball left the park. The fourth time, Jack's ball hit the top of the fence and bounded crazily back into the park. However he was fast enough to slide home before the bungled relay throw reached the catcher. Stengel was reminded of his pregame prediction. Never at a loss for words, the irrepressible Casey said, 'He didn't get them runs off me; I wasn't pitchin'!

Bucky Harris was fired by the Yankees, because he didn't win the American League by a game. [In 1948, Cleveland won the pennant with a 97-58 record. Boston finished one game out at 96-59 and New York was 2-1/2 back with a 94-60 record.] I ran into Bill Starr at the baseball meetings and said, facetiously, 'Congratulations for getting Bucky Harris (to manage the Padres in 1949).' He said, 'Who the hell told you?' I called the paper and we had an exclusive even before the New York papers.

Vern Kennedy pitched a no-hit, no-run game in the big leagues. During a game between the Padres and Hollywood Stars, he had several confrontations with the plate umpire. About the sixth inning, he'd had it! When an obvious strike was called ball four with the bases loaded, Vern called 'Time.' He went to the dugout and grabbed a bat. He borrowed sunglasses from a nearby fan and... tapping... tapping... tapping, he called, 'Help the blind! Help the blind!' The hometown crowd loved it. The home plate umpire calmly watched with his arms folded. As Vern completed his circuit of home plate, the umpire raised to his full height and with a meaningful banishing gesture, in his loudest, foghorn voice that could be heard by the tuna boats in the harbor, declared emphatically, 'YOU'RE OUTA HERE!"

Del Ballinger felt the umpire was favoring the opposing team and narrowed the strike zone of the Padres' pitchers to half the size that he was calling for the opposition. Del went out to the mound and called for a fastball where he'd be holding his mitt. The pitch came in hard and fast and on target. Ballinger lowered his glove and let the baseball smack into the umpire, laying him out on the ground. Del rushed around yelling, 'Water! Water!' Someone handed him a big paper cup. He rushed back to the fallen official, turned up the cup and drank the whole thing.

In this picture, Rip Collins and I were smoking cigars in the dugout which was against the rules. Lane Field had many monikers, among them 'Foggy Bottom' for obvious reasons. One time the umpires refused to call the game as the white stuff rolled in. Rip, surreptitiously placed a baseball in the back pocket of each outfielder. The pitcher was instructed to throw 'fly balls.' Each batter hit high balls to the outfield; each outfielder emerged from the low-lying fog waving a ball. When the game was finally called, the outfielders received accolades for their remarkable fielding ability by sound, not sight.

I am very proud of a favor I did for a friend and a beloved city. A few years after leaving San Diego, a telephone call came through from the *San Diego Union*'s editor commenting that good sports writers seemed to come from the Southwest. As the newspaper needed to fill a position, he asked for a recommendation. I gave him four names. He came. He interviewed. He hired a young writer from the *Oklahoma City Times*. In San Diego, he quickly became a local favorite. Realizing that a major league stadium was necessary for San Diego to become a major sports center, he dared to dream and dedicated his persuasive power of the press to advocate, crusade, cajole, relentlessly promote the project. Cancer cut his career short. The rest is history. His name lives in Mission Valley atop Jack Murphy Stadium."

JIM GLEASON, pitcher.
BORN: 6-22-27   PADRES: 1947-48

Jim Gleason is another Hoover High School ballplayer who played for the Padres. He was a star pitcher on the powerful, post-war San Diego State teams of Charlie Smith. In '46 and '47 he posted an 18 and 2 record for the Aztecs. Used primarily in relief by the Padres, it was a thrill for Jim to play for his hometown team.

"Unlike other sports, baseball drew from a diverse variety of backgrounds and there were a lot of characters back then. George McDonald was the Padres' first baseman for years. I think he had a couple bum deals from some of the managers, so he skipped to the Mexican League. When the promises and money started running out, George figured it was time to get out of Mexico. He was one of the many well known U.S. professionals who jumped the Mexican League. The problem was that he'd

gotten some money up front and he was worried about his personal safety. So he went incognito and took the name of Uni Gagan to escape from the country. I don't know how he came up with that name. He just got out of Mexico as fast as he could. He told me about that when we roomed together. We were both with Dallas back in 1950.

After World War II, minor league base splurged when all that talent came home from the service. Minor league baseball was fantastic family entertainment. I remember playing in the south. There wasn't any air conditioning and going to a ball game was a way to get out of the house. There was no television in homes yet, so for a couple of bucks, you could take the entire family to see a baseball game. The players and fans were much closer back then.

I never saw a pitcher deliberately throw at anybody's head. You'd pitch tight and that was the way you played the game. Sometimes you'd put one behind their butt. I was a sidearmer. I'd always lead the league in hit batsmen. Now, they charge the mound on anything close. I was so wild, I'd be getting beat up all the time today. I've hit batters in the strike zone!

I had a short cup of coffee with the Padres. My record was one and one, but I still remember the first inning I pitched in relief at Lane Field. It was a dream for me. There were a couple of runners on and Lou Novikoff came to bat. I struck him out on a change-up curve. He went

Jim Gleason

John Ritchey

Jim Gleason and Bob Schulte

for the downs and I think he's still swinging. I got out of the inning unscathed. It was just a thrill being with those guys. It was unrivaled. It was really good baseball and the community was involved.

I was a rookie pitching against Billy Schuster. I was tight and nervous. He hit a one hopper back to me. I was being robot-like throwing to first. Just as I threw the ball, he screamed and slid right into me! I was on the mound. I almost had a heart attack! On other occasions, he'd round third, score and climb up the backstop like a monkey.

That '47 Padre team had a bunch of rounders. (Bob) Kerrigan and I were about the only single guys. We were up in Sacramento. Manny Salvo's family had a bakery up there and his wife lived there. After one game, she told him that there were a lot of young women in the visitors box. She wondered if he behaved like that on the road. Manny was about 6'4" and he weighed about 240. When he told those guys to knock it off, you could have heard a pin drop in the clubhouse.

People can't recite lineups today like kids could back then. We'd pretend we were the Padres playing the Los Angeles Angels or the Seattle Rainers or other teams in the league in fantasy variations of the game. We could name all of the players on every team in the league.

As a youth growing up in San Diego with an interest in baseball that developed into a passion, I had two idols: Ted Williams and John Ritchey. When (Legion) Post 6 won the national championship with John Ritchey, Al Olsen, Ed Sanclemente and Bob Usher, I was very impressed. They were a great bunch of guys and, being a little younger, I thought that was the epitome of baseball. Winning the national championship brought a lot of publicity to San Diego and the citizens were proud of the team.

Watching Ritchey when he was a teen age star was an inspiration. Johnny had a great talent for the game which he enhanced by his enthusiastic attitude. Johnny loved the game. He played with a big, happy smile on his face. His enthusiasm and spirit were contagious, not only to his fellow players, but to the people in the stands. Johnny put much more into the game than what you would read about in the box score the next day. He was 'Johnny Baseball!'

Playing with him at San Diego State was a constant thrill. We had good defense and good hitting. They made me look good and Johnny was the best player on the team. He was a phenomenal athlete, but he was also a student of the game. He was an absolutely forthright guy. Charlie Smith was a technician. I learned more from him than from anybody else in baseball. Johnny picked it up and he would help people. He'd never say, 'Do it this way.' He'd say, 'Charlie said to do it this way.' He really helped people. Teammates respected him, because he brought so much experience to San Diego State.

Johnny was with you all the time. He'd concentrate and make you concentrate. He was the first guy who taught me intensity. He'd say, 'We can work together.' He gave you confidence. John always wanted to get wood on the ball. He wasn't interested in hitting for power. He'd hit ground balls and line drives. For 64 straight times, he put the ball in play. 64 straight plate appearances and he always put the ball in play. That's unbelievable!

His first five appearances with the Padres were five base hits! The fifth one went out of the park! Hank Camelli was one of the other catchers. He said, 'I'm sick; I'm quitting this game.'

The pressure on Johnny was intense. Playing with him for a short while on the Padres and later against him in the Texas League, I saw a transition. He brought that same enthusiasm, sparkle and talent to the Padres. He also carried a tremendous burden being the first black player in the PCL and, later, the Texas League. I'm taking nothing away from Jackie Robinson who was tougher, less sensitive and more of a fighter. Johnny was a very sensitive guy, a real team player and when some of his teammates treated him differently, Johnny felt this intensely. I never observed hostility, but I did observe a coolness, a distancing that was very apparent to Johnny.

The smile on his face disappeared. Playing was not the fun it used to be for 'Johnny Baseball.' Now he was only contributing to his team and the game what you read in the box scores. Those statistics fell, because the game he loved and the team spirit that buoyed him to better performance had now become burdensome and diluted his exceptional talent.

At another time, John would have been a major leaguer. He was tremendous. A few years later, it would have been easier for him, but Johnny made it easier for others."

JOHN RITCHEY, catcher.
BORN: 1-5-23   PADRES: 1948-49

John Ritchey led the Negro American League with a .381 batting average in 1947. The following year, he broke the "color barrier" in the Pacific Coast League by signing a contract with his hometown Padres. Johnny responded to the challenge with a solid .323 batting average. As a youth he played for American Legion Post 6, which won national championships in 1938 and 1941. Ritchey was also the top hitter on very good San Diego State baseball teams before and after World War II. Playing for Vancouver, his .346 average led all Western International League hitters in 1951 and the following season, John's .343 was second only to Walt Pocekay's .352 for the loop batting title. Ritchey would post a career .282 batting average in seven Coast League seasons with San Diego, Portland, Sacramento and San Francisco.

"My earliest memories are of playing baseball, because there wasn't anything else to do. Most of my friends were white. Peanuts (Harry Savin) was a Mexican kid. The others were Nelson Manuel, Billy Williams, William Indalecio, Tom and Louis Ortiz. We played sandlot ball and the San Diego Police sponsored the league. We got around in cars. Nelson was easy going and one time he got a job selling ice cream. It only lasted for one day, because he ate too much of the ice cream he was supposed to sell. He didn't get to eat much at home. They were good times playing with my friends,

With Post 6, I was taking batting practice in Albemarle (North Carolina) and I hit a couple of line drives over the fence. They wouldn't let me play for the national championship game. [John and several teammates were not allowed to play in the final game of the 1940 American Legion tournament on the basis of their race. Their opponent, Albemarle, North Carolina, won the series. -Ed.]

When I was playing in the Negro Leagues, I was in awe of those players. They were that good. And the Southerners were fun to listen to because I hadn't heard them talk before. They felt the same about Californians. They were funny and good ballplayers. It was a thrill for me to play with such good players. Buck Leonard and Josh Gibson were my heroes when I was a boy. They were the best!

It was a thrill to play for the Padres. The fans cheered and my feeling was it was because I was a San Diego boy making good. It had nothing to do with race. A lot of friends and family members were in the stands at Lane Field. It felt good just to get a turn at bat, but I grounded out to the first baseman. [In his first eleven plate appearances, Johnny would collect seven hits. -Ed.]

(San Diego manager Rip) Collins treated me OK and Les Cook was always good to me. I knew him at San Diego State. (Aztec baseball coach) Charlie Smith felt bad when the scouts came and they signed my teammates, but not me. He said it wasn't fair.

John Ritchey

One time I was coming home and the catcher tried to spike me in the leg as I came sliding under him. And (Los Angeles Angel Billy) Schuster was a terrible guy! Brush back pitches were part of the game. They didn't throw at me more than they did at white players, but some pitchers did. There was an Angel who threw four balls at my head. I took first. My teammates said nothing and there was no retaliation. Another time against the Angels, I got a double. The pitcher came to second base. He was spitting and yelling all kinds of bad language in my face. Then he left the game. Nobody said or did anything and I was lonely. I had to room alone, but I was never refused accommodations while playing in the PCL.

In 1951, I was Player of the Year for Vancouver. We were happy there. The fans were good and there was acceptance. And it was very comfortable to play in South America. I always played my best when I was happy and all I ever wanted to do was just play baseball."

◆◆◆

HANK CAMELLI, catcher.
BORN: 12-9-14   DIED: 7-14-96   PADRES: 1948

Prior to joining the Padres, Hank Camelli caught for the Pittsburgh Pirates and Boston Braves from 1943 through 1947. He enjoyed his best season in 1944 when he hit .296 for the Pirates. Hank recalls that the '48 Padres started with promise, but finished the year near the bottom of the league standings. Following his playing career, Camelli coached and managed in the minor leagues.

"We had a good ball club until Jack Graham got hit. Everybody was doing good and we were in first place for quite a while. Injuries at the wrong time can really hurt you, but if you're not prepared, that's all part of baseball. We had some good players on that team. (Xavier)

Rescigno was quite a kid. He came to play. John Ritchey was a rookie and he looked like a good prospect. Rip Collins was the manager and they fired Rip. That's part of baseball. The team was losing.

I was with Pittsburgh and went over to Boston with Bob Elliott in the trade that brought Whitey Wietelmann to the Pirates. That was a good team at Boston with Spahn and Sain. Speaking of Sain, it's raining here right now. We should have won the pennant in '47, but there were injuries. They will always happen at the wrong time. Pete Coscarart was on our team in Pittsburgh. He's a good guy, no, he's a great guy! Pete is a great guy! He still writes to me once a year. Say 'Hi' to him the next time you see him.

I started in 1936 with Abbeyville, Louisiana, the end of the world, but they play good baseball down in the Evangeline League. I was making $165 a month which was pretty good pay. Today, they play for the money and look how it's hurt the game. But people still love baseball and it will come back."

◆◆◆

XAVIER RESCIGNO, pitcher.
BORN: 10-13-12   PADRES: 1948-49

"X" led the Canadian-American League with a 1.56 ERA for Smith Falls in 1937. Two years later, he recorded the Eastern League's lowest ERA (2.21) pitching for Elmira. In the majors with the Pittsburgh Pirates from 1943 through 1945, Rescigno posted a 19-22 career record. In 1944 he led the National League with eight victories in relief appearances. After two identical 11-9 seasons for the Hollywood Stars, he became the ace of the Padres staff in 1948 while notching an 18-14 mark during 221 innings of work. Xavier was a character. A self-described bad loser, "Terrible Tempered Mr. X" was known to act up on the

Hank Camelli

Mr. X

Xavier Rescigno

ECHOES FROM LANE FIELD

field when he was behind in a game, but he loved the game and his teammates.

"I recall one game in Oakland against Casey (Stengel). Billy Martin was playing second base for the Oaks and was always looking for a fight. About the third inning, Al Rosen singled and promptly stole second base. He slid into Martin pretty hard and knocked Billy down. Billy got up and pushed Al who was a pretty good boxer and he promptly decked Billy.

Two innings later, Minnie (Minoso) reached first base and stole second on the next pitch. Same situation happened. Billy pushed Minnie and Minnie decked Martin for the second time. Out of the dugout came Stengel who took Billy out of the game. Stengel told Billy he was doing it for his own good. I quote Stengel: 'Get into the clubhouse before you get killed!'

On another occasion, I recall Minnie, who couldn't speak English very well, reached first base. Our first base coach was 'Red' Corriden who was always a little tipsy. He liked to drink. Minnie called 'time' to talk to Red. They were jawing for about two minutes. Bucky (Harris, San Diego manager), who had a sense of humor, said, 'Look out there. One guy can't speak English and the other guy is half-loaded. What a combination.'

I enjoyed playing in the Pacific Coast League more than I did in the big leagues. The beaning of Jack Graham by 'Red' Adams at Wrigley Field in L.A. was really something. Incidentally, I was on second base at the time. The ball just took off and Jack never saw it. I'll never forget the horrible incident. Red Adams was really shook up. Jack Graham was never the same hitter after that and neither was Red Adams the same pitcher after that. Red was a fine gentleman and he never got over that day.

I pitched John Ritchey's first game. He was a fine player and a great hitter. Rip (Collins) asked me, 'Hey, X, do you mind if Ritchey catches you tonight?' We were playing Hollywood and the lights weren't that good and my eyesight wasn't that good, either. I couldn't see his fingers, so I told him I'd look left for the fast ball, right for the curve and down for the change. Johnny would give me the fist for the knockdown. After the game, I saw some of the Hollywood players at the bar and they couldn't figure out John's signs. I just told 'em it was our secret.

A sportswriter was getting on Mike in the paper about his pitching. When he saw the writer at the ballpark, he picked him up and shook him. You know Mike Budnick was a big, strong guy! He told the writer to stop writing about his sore arm and the guy stopped. He didn't know what Mike would do next if he didn't.

My years playing on the coast were wonderful. Two with Hollywood, two with San Diego and one with San Francisco. I played for some great managers: Jimmy Dykes, Rip Collins, Bucky Harris and the great Lefty O'Doul. I'll never forget our coach at San Diego, Jimmie Reese. What a wonderful guy. I used to drive Jimmie crazy. I would nail his glove and spikes to the clubhouse roof. If I lost a game, I would refuse to run the next day for Jimmie. He never got mad at me. I loved that guy.

Bucky Harris was great to play for. He, like Jimmy Dykes and Lefty O'Doul, never second-guessed you. You know how little things can lose a game. Well, I set a record at Albany when I won 4 games pitching only 5-1/3 innings in relief. I was really a R.A. - red ass. I just couldn't stand to lose, but at 83 years old now, I lose a lot in golf and don't get mad anymore."

RINALDO "RUGGER" ARDIZOIA, pitcher.
BORN: 11-20-19   Missions, Stars, Rainers

Rinaldo Ardizoia is one of only five major league ballplayers born in Italy. Most of his professional baseball career was spent in the PCL with the San Francisco Missions, Hollywood Stars and Seattle Rainers from 1937 to 1949. Traded to Newark in 1941, Ardizoia was stopped at the border when his team went to play Montreal because a state of war existed between Canada and Italy. Upon becoming a U.S. citizen, Rinaldo served 28 months in the Pacific. He was with the Yankees briefly in 1947. "Rugger" averaged 13 victories a season in the Coast League,

Rugger Ardizoia

but contends he would have had at least three or four more wins each year if he could have just beaten the Padres.

"I remember losing a game to Wally Hebert that took one hour and twenty-nine minutes by a one to nothing score. Another time, I lost one to nothing in an hour and forty-four minutes to Manny Salvo. I remember losing one to nothing on a late home run by Allie Clark. (Minnie) Minoso, (Max) West and (Al) Rosen were in that game. Johnny Jensen beat me a couple of times with hits late in the game, too. Both times, three to two, and one game went eleven innings. I had pretty good success against the rest of the teams, but coming down to San Diego was something! I lost seven games in 1946. Three were by the Padres. It wasn't easy to pitch in the fog, either.

When I broke in with the Missions, I was seventeen years old and we were playing at Lane Field. Manny Salvo was pitching for San Diego and (Missions manager Willie) Kamm told me to get on him. I was yelling at him from the dugout and a couple of innings later, I was in the game. I pitched five innings and only gave up one hit, but when I came up to bat, (Padre catcher George) Detore shook his head. All I remember is the pitch coming right at my head. I learned a lesson: never get on other players, especially the pitcher!

Xavier Rescigno was really funny. Billy Martin would get mad and want to fight. Resigno would get mad and start cussing while looking up into the sky. We'd be in the dugout and say, 'There goes Rescigno' and laugh."

MIKE BUDNICK, pitcher.
BORN: 9-15-19   PADRES: 1948

After pitching for two years for the Giants, Mike Budnick came to the Padres with Jack Graham as part of the deal Bill Starr worked out when he sold Jack Harshman to New York. Arm trouble caught up with Mike and it proved to be his last year in professional baseball. The '48 Padres were a bunch of characters who showed early promise, but, like Budnick's arm, they suffered injury and could not recover.

"San Diego was one of my favorite cities. I still remember where my wife, son and I lived in a house at 32nd and Adams. The park was great. I remember we had a night game called because of a heavy fog coming in from the ocean. We went through three managers starting with Rip Collins, the old Gas House Gang first baseman. He couldn't put up with us and left early. Then came the great one, Jimmie Reese. He lasted about three weeks. In came Jim Brillheart and he went along with us and lasted the rest of the year. We had a good club and probably could win the American League West today, although we are all over 70 years of age. Names like Graham, Mesner, (Buster) Adams, Jensen, Clay, (Leo) Wells, (Jess) Flores, Rescigno, (Al) Jurisich, Kerrigan, (Al) Olsen, Camelli, John Ritchey. He was the first Black in the PCL. Don't let anyone tell you differently, he was a good hitter and a great guy.

Resigno and Camelli were always agitating each other. Every time the umpire would make a bad call, he'd turn around, look in the sky and talk to God. One time, Camelli threw the ball back to the mound and it hit Resigno in the back of the head. He said, 'What else, Lord?'

The next year, when Bucky Harris released me, I didn't know what to do. We packed our bags and loaded up the car. I decided to stop in San Francisco to see my old friend Lefty O'Doul. I told him I got my pink slip and that I didn't know what the hell to do. He said unpack and you've got a job with us. He told me I could pitch once a week in the seven inning game (on Sunday). I knew I couldn't get anybody out. He said to go and talk it over with my wife, so I did. I just cried. I felt guilty, because I

Mike Budnick

Carl's Baseball Inn

knew I couldn't do it anymore, but Lefty was giving me another chance. That's the kind of man he was. I told him I couldn't do it and we went home to Seattle.

When we were in San Diego, I used to hang out at Carl's Baseball Inn, so I opened a place fashioned after Carl's. I tended bar in New York Giants uniforms... a home uniform and a road uniform. I'd jump over the bar, do a hook slide and fill the place up. I called it the Hit and Run Room. Then I became a deputy for the King County Sheriff's Department. I even ran for Sheriff, but lost to an old umpire.

(Fred) Hutchinson was a year ahead of me (in school.) We were throwers and he was a pitcher. I was signed by the Seattle Rainers. I asked Hal Turpin how I could throw better? He said, 'With your fast ball, just aim for the middle and hope it gets there.' My scrapbooks are comical. They're all wins! I only put wins in them. My first year with the Rainers, I got to pitch Opening Day. It was Sad Sam Gibson against Kewpie Dick Barrett. Kewpie Dick got knocked out and Les Webber couldn't get anybody out either. I was pacing around and Jack Lelivelt (Seattle Manager) said, 'What the hell do you want, Mike?' I told him I wanted to pitch. He knew I'd pitched 20 minutes of batting practice before the game. Well, he let me in and I held the Seals scoreless the rest of the way.

I went to Twin Falls in the Pioneer League. I had a perfect game going once and the other pitcher put a fast ball under my chin. I said, 'You're leading off, be ready' and I hit him in the neck. We got into it. I punched him and semi-fractured my index finger. Well, he got first base, came around to score and I ended up losing the game, 1-0!

Another time, we were playing Great Falls and I challenged them to both games (of a doubleheader). I won the first, 8-7, struck out 15 and walked 15, but lost the second game, 4-3. I pitched a double header against Salt Lake City, too. The balls would really fly in that desert air. Their manager was Eddie Mulligan. He didn't swear. The worst he'd say was 'dirty rat.' He didn't like me, because I swore.

During the war, I was with the ballplayers in Hawaii. They were all major leaguers except me. The guys would cheer when they would announce all the big leaguers, but when they'd hear my name, they'd say, 'Who the hell is Mike Budnick?'

I won my first game in the big leagues by hitting a home run. I relieved Bob Joyce who won over 30 games with the Seals. It was hard to win in the big leagues.

Red Adams is a funny guy. He's up here with the Rainers.

Sweeney's the manager and Red's getting hit pretty hard. He's backing up third on a play and by the time Sweeney got to the mound, Red's already in the shower.

Jackie Robinson came to town in 1960. He called me and we had a couple of drinks together. He asked me, 'Mike, why the hell did you throw at me all the time?' I told him that if I didn't knock him on his ass, they'd fine me 25 bucks. Walker Cooper was our catcher. He was from the South and didn't like Blacks, but he'd get it from the bench.

Baseball today stinks! Most players today should be in Class C, B or A Leagues just to learn how to dress: pants down to their shoe tops, earrings, neck chains, gloves, helmets... bunch of collegiate clowns! Don't throw too close to me; I'll start a fight."

GENE THOMPSON, pitcher.
DOB: 6-7-17   PADRES: 1948-49

Gene "Junior" Thompson led the Kitty League with 18 wins while playing for Paducah in 1936. As a rookie, he went 13-5 for the pennant winning Cincinnati Reds in 1939. The following season, the Reds returned to the World Series and Thompson posted a 16-9 record. His major league career was interrupted by the War and he returned with the New York Giants in 1946 and 1947. The next two years were spent in San Diego where Gene contributed 8 wins with only 3 losses and a 2.00 ERA in '48. Thompson is currently in his 64th year of baseball as an active scout for the San Diego Padres. Named Scout of the Year in 1989, he recently won his sixth Topps Scout of the Month award for drafting Jacob Cruz.

Gene Thompson

"I had arm trouble before I came to San Diego. I told Rip (Collins), 'I can help you, but don't let me go long.' I could pitch a couple of innings, but that was it. I couldn't start. When I won some games, Bill Starr wanted me to start. I said, 'Hey, I'll start. It may take longer than you think for me to come back.' I pitched a 7 inning game. I think it was the second game of a double-header and it took a long time to come back. I would have lasted longer, if I had stayed a reliever.

I enjoyed my time in San Diego. D. C. Moore and I go back to Syracuse. He played every position. He's a great guy. I ran into him up in Williston, North Dakota when I was scouting. It was a show to watch Xavier Rescigno and Hank Camelli fight. They argued and fought all the time, but they were the best of friends. We had a lot of fun and a lot of good players. We had better conditions than the big leagues: good schedule, good cities and we'd fly. Guys would stay in the Coast League rather than go back to the big leagues. We had more fun than players do today.

Then I went to Sacramento. I had arm problems, and in the middle of the season, I became the pitching coach and Joe Marty was the manager. Then Joe Gordon took over. He was a great friend of mine. There wasn't anything he couldn't do well. He used to fly. A lot of ballplayers could fly and they'd let them take the controls on the chartered flights. He could play the horn and dance. He was a great fisherman and a great hunter. Of course, he was a great baseball player, too.

Charlie Dressen signed me in 1934. He was the Cincinnati manager then. He lived in my home town (Latham, Illinois). I scouted for Cleveland. I was with the Giants for 39 years and 4 years with the Cubs. I went to work January 1st , 1996 for the Padres. I am in my 64th year in the game and still enjoying it."

LEO WELLS, shortstop.
BORN: 7-17-17   PADRES: 1948

Leo Wells began playing professional baseball with St. Paul in 1938. He won MVP honors for the Saints in 1941 and was sold the following year to the Chicago White Sox. After the war, Leo returned to limited action with the Pale Hose and was sold to Sacramento in 1947. He and his friend, Steve Mesner, were sold to the Padres during the 1948 season and he batted a respectable .268 for the year.

"They (San Diego) made a deal for Steve Mesner and me. I played shortstop, Steve played second and Jeep Handley was at third. Steve and I were good friends. We had a pretty good ball club. We could score a lot of runs, but after Red Adams hit Jack Graham, we started sliding. The

Leo Wells

thing I remember about San Diego was that it was a pleasure to go to the ballpark. There were great fans in San Diego and we had a great bunch of guys on the team. I thought Rip Collins was a helluva manager and Jimmie Reese was great. I used to see him all the time when the Angels would come to play the Twins.

I was playing for Sacramento when the paper said Whitey Wietelmann was coming to play shortstop. I thought, 'What about me? I'm the shortstop!' They got rid of Steve and me and Ernie Lombardi. Whitey came to San Diego after Steve and me. Is he still making chili for the team? I enjoyed Sacramento. One time, I ran back for a fly ball over my head. I ran into Joe Marty and broke my nose. He was a big, strong guy. Helluva nice guy. He could really hit; could really hit the bottle, too. We were playing Portland once. Jack Salveson was pitching for them. Jim Turner was their manager. Guy Fletcher was pitching for us. People used to waive white hankies for surrender when Guy pitched. Well, Salveson won the game, 1-0 in 21 innings. He pitched the whole game. Fletcher went 12 innings. I was batting lead off. Think I went oh-for-eight.

Johnny Barrett was on the Padres. He was a good hitter. Dain Clay was a character. Xavier Rescigno was, too. Pete Coscarart and John Ritchey were good guys. John was a good hitter. Gene Thompson was a great relief pitcher. It really was a good team. We'd stay at a motel out at 60th and El Cajon when the team was in town. When we were on the road, my wife and son, Jimmie, would stay with her family in Compton. I remember getting rides down to San Diego with Steve Mesner. He was such a good guy and Char was always with the team. Their daughter was cute as a button.

I used to play handball at the 'Y' on Broadway; I'd play with Dave Starr. He was Bill's brother. On the last day of the ('48) season, unbeknownst to me, Bill Starr put Lenny Rice, me and others on the waiver list. Nobody claimed us and he sold us to Dallas. We set a minor league attendance record that year. We had old guys including Ben Gunitini. '50 was my last year.

You know I just don't go to games anymore. I've only been to the dome twice to see the Twins play. Frank Quilici (former Twins infielder and manager) is a friend of mine. He said that he's in favor of today's players getting as much money as they can, but he added, and this is a great line, 'The problem is they *think* they deserve it!'

I love going to reunions and seeing the old players. I went to St. Petersburg and Ted Williams was there. Of course, all the players want to get his autograph and talk to him. He's so good to them. He was the greatest hitter I ever saw. I say Joe DiMaggio was the greatest player I ever saw, but Ted Williams was the best hitter! Vince DiMaggio was a friend of mine. He was very friendly, but Joe was quiet. I understand Vince got very religious. I know he was selling Fuller Brushes. I called him once and he wanted to get together. I told him I was calling from Minnesota. He couldn't believe I was calling long distance. I know Joe was kind of tight. He wouldn't buy a (news)paper.

I was active in the Hot Stove League when I lived in San Diego. Chet Pagni is a good friend of mine. We were having a Hot Stove League golf tournament and Cedric Durst had a heart attack. He'd died that day. [February 16, 1971 -Ed.]

I think I played amateur ball with Joe Hare in what they called the Ban Johnson League in Kansas City where I grew up. Chuck Workman, Morton and Walker Cooper were in the league, too. Joe Hare was with the Padres in 1939. I think he moved back to Kansas City."

◆◆◆

BILL LILLARD, shortstop.
BORN: 1-10-18   PADRES: 1948

The Lillard Brothers grew up playing sandlot ball in Santa Barbara, California. Gene, four years Bill's senior, twice led the PCL in home runs while playing for Los Angeles (43 in 1933 and 56 in 1935). Bill broke in with San Francisco in 1938 and hit .335 in his first season. He was with the Philadelphia

Athletics the following year, hitting .316 in limited duty. Bill Lillard spent most of the Forties in the American Association and International League before joining the Padres in 1948.

"This (the manicured diamonds at Santa Barbara City College) is where I started playing baseball, but back then they were all dirt. I went to Santa Barbara High School and played baseball my first year there, but the athletic director was the football coach and he didn't like baseball, so we didn't have a team after that.

I started playing Sunday baseball with the men and my brother went up to the Angels and up to the Cubs. They had Stan Hack who was the best third baseman in both leagues. Gene pitched batting practice and the players complained that he was too hard to hit, because his ball had too much movement. So they told Gene he'd have to be a pitcher. Detroit wanted him as a third baseman, but the Cubs wouldn't let him go. He'd have hit a lot of home runs in that ballpark in Detroit!

He went to spring training in San Francisco and I graduated from high school and I went with him. I was having a good year. The Cubs sent Gene to pitch for the LA Angels. I hit .333 off him. Funny thing about that is almost every hit was with men on base. I was hitting .336 or .337 when I got hurt. I was hitting behind Dominic DiMaggio. He was on first and I hit a ground ball. The coach told me to keep running, but when I got to second, Dominic was holding his hands up. I turned and twisted my left knee and was out for the rest of the season. Mr. Graham, the president of San Francisco, was a real gentleman. I had been sold to Philadelphia and he said the deal could be called off, but Mr. (Connie) Mack said he wanted me.

The biggest thrill I had in baseball was hitting a home run against Red Ruffing. Bill Dickey said, 'That's was a great home run, son. You hit Red Ruffing's best pitch.' I

Bill Lillard, left, and Gene Lillard.

was a line drive hitter. The best fast ball pitcher I hit against was Bob Feller and the best curve ball pitcher was Tommy Bridges of Detroit. Feller had a wonderful curve, too.

When I was with the Athletics, I played with and against great players. I think Joe DiMaggio was the best all-around player. He could hit, field and throw. You can't imagine how much ground that guy covered. He threw our best guy, Wally Moses, out. He was on third and DiMaggio caught the ball in deepest center and threw him out!

The best hitter was Ted Williams. We were playing in Shibe Park. We'd have the shift on and the first times, he'd tap them into left. We were all on the right side of the diamond except the third baseman. He was at shortstop. But he loved to hit line drives, so he'd just hit line drives and still get hits against all those fielders. Williams loved to hit line drives through that crowd. People don't realize how many line drives were taken away from him and he had a lot of hitting taken from him in the Korean War and the Second World War. Williams would have broken all kinds of records. He was liked by his own teammates and the opposition, but he had trouble with those writers up in Boston.

The pitching in the majors is so much better. They hit the corners. That is the big difference between the majors and the minors. When I played in 1938, very few major league teams would ship their young players out to the coast. They wanted to keep them close to see them and get them quickly. We (the PCL) had older ballplayers and young ones from California going up and, as you know, a lot of very good players come from California.

You know that I probably remember more things about my first year in Tucson - more than all the other years, because it was all new. We got stuck in a dip in the desert for two days. We just barely got into Albuquerque for a night game and we had to play two double headers in a row. We didn't even get any batting practice. We were just real loose. We got 56 runs in four games!

Oh, gosh, I played with a lot of different teams: Minneapolis in the American Association, Baltimore and Jersey City in the International. I played with Jack Graham in Jersey City. I always liked Jack. We roomed together. I remember playing at Nicollett Park (Minneapolis) and they had that short wall in right. I was a shortstop, but I played a few games at second. I was at second and a fly ball went up and I had it. Well, it hit the fence and I caught it on first bounce and threw the runner out at second.

My brother started out as a third baseman and they made him into a pitcher and he came back as a catcher. And he managed some, too. Oh, he could have hit so many home runs in Detroit. It was a shame he didn't get to go there and stay at third.

I wasn't with San Diego very long and I only played part-time. I do remember hitting a home run to win a game at Lane Field. I had put in some time with Hollywood and then I came to San Diego. Actually, I went to an eye doctor and he said I had so much astigmatism, he said it was a wonder I could even see at all. My career was about over, but I really liked San Diego. I didn't have a car, so I didn't get around very much. I remember having lunch with a great Olympic skater. Somebody knew her, but I can't think of her name now. I got along OK with Collins and I remember John Ritchey. He was small and a good little hitter. There were good guys on that team and that's about it for my memories of San Diego."

JACK GRAHAM, outfield, first base.
BORN: 12-24-16 DIED: 12-30-98 PADRES: 1948, 50-52

Tony Lazzeri hit sixty home runs for Salt Lake City in 1925 to establish the Pacific Coast League record. In 1948, Jack Graham, son of former big leaguer "Peaches" Graham, was on a pace to shatter that mark. Only July 25th, Jack had already hit forty-six round trippers, but he was beaned in a game in Los Angeles. He came back from injury and finished with forty-eight home runs for the year which earned him the league's most valuable player award. Graham finished third in the American League

Jack Graham

Jack Graham receives 1948 PCL MVP plaque from League President Pants Rowland.

Pilot Jack with teammates.

homer run race in 1949. He came back to San Diego and was again the team home run leader for the next three years. In seventeen years of professional baseball, Jack hit 422 home runs. He is an original member of the San Diego Padres Hall of Fame, inducted on August 22, 1965.

"When I was a kid, my dad would take me to ball games, but I preferred to watch the planes at a nearby airfield. I'd help around the planes and some of the pilots would take me up. I wanted to be an Army aviator. In '33, when I started high school, I got interested in baseball, but I learned to fly, too.

I came to San Diego as part of the Jack Harshman deal. You know when you're in the process of doing something, you don't even realize how important it might be. That was probably my greatest claim to fame. I had forty-six (home runs) in July and it was a Sunday in LA. It was the second game of the double header and the ball would go into the shade. The hitters were in the shade and the pitcher was in the sun. The pitcher knocked me down, but didn't knock me out. (Sportswriter) Earl Keller told me that I would be the MVP if I came back, but I had a hemorrhage in my middle ear. Every time I'd look at the ball, I'd get a little dizzy. He (Red Adams) didn't throw that hard. He pitched me high and inside to keep me off the plate.

The funny story behind that was that Rip (Collins) approached me, because I got hit twice earlier up in San Francisco. He said he noticed I was getting tired. He told me to take off and just visit my family in Long Beach. I could get some rest and I'd be OK. The reflexes weren't working and he noticed it, but I vetoed it. You wanted to play in LA. If you couldn't hit a home run at Wrigley, you couldn't hit 'em anywhere. Every player has his year and that was mine.

I got my glasses in 1950, because I was either landing (my plane) two or three feet above the ground or bouncing it. With glasses, everything was great. But when I put them on to play baseball, I had to change everything. The ball had been fuzzy, but now it became smaller. I just lost my stroke and couldn't get around on the inside pitch. But it was great for me to hit in San Diego. I was a dead pull hitter and the wind blew off the bay to right (field). They'd fly out.

Del Baker was the manager in 1950. His steal sign for left-handers was the left hand on his chest. For right-handers, it was the right hand. I stole eight straight bases at the beginning of the season. Nobody was expecting me to go. The catcher would be back on his haunches. I was thrown out on the ninth time. Baker says, 'What's the matter with you? Don't you know the signs?' As long as I was successful, he didn't tell me that I had them wrong. Those were the only bases I stole all year.

Bill Starr was a pretty astute guy. In '51 I think it was, he sent me a contract. I said I wasn't going to sign it. 'I need more money,' I said, 'Give me $25 a month more.' He said, 'Sign it or not!' He knew I couldn't do anything about it, so I just signed it. But in '48 when I came from the Giants, I had a $6,000 guaranteed major league contract. Because we played the longer schedule in the PCL and I won the MVP, I made more money than if I'd been in the majors. It really worked out good for me that time.

I think it was '51 and they traded me to 'Frisco for Hank Sauer's brother, Ed Sauer. Lefty O'Doul was the manager in 'Frisco and I started oh-for-twenty-eight and they traded us back. Frisco was a terrible place for left-handed hitters and San Diego was tough on the right-handers.

Max West, Del Baker, Jack Graham, 1950.

Lefty O'Doul

Baseball is a game of rules. There are times when the bunt is in order. There are times when you play hit-and-run. If something works 51% of the time, you do it. If it works forty-nine times out of a hundred, you don't do it. Lefty O'Doul played the game backwards.

In 1952, Jesse Flores was pitching and I was on third. O'Doul told me to steal home. I took off, Flores threw a wild pitch and we won by a run. The thing about Lefty was that if it didn't work, he wouldn't get upset. He was a good guy and the sportswriters loved him. He loved to play golf and wouldn't get to the park until about fifteen minutes before the game was supposed to start. We were supposed to go over the hitters. He'd get into the first couple of batters and start telling stories. I don't think we ever got through the whole lineup.

I was rooming with Max West in 1950. I liked to get up early and go for breakfast. I loved that crispy bacon, but I can't eat it now. Max said, 'What the hell you doin' that for? Call room service!' So I did and they wheeled it in. I said, 'This is great!' And that's what I did from then on..."

CHARLES DWIGHT "RED" ADAMS, pitcher.
BORN: 10-7-21   PADRES: 1949

Red Adams pitched 16 years in the Pacific Coast League. He

started with the Los Angeles Angels in 1942 and, after a brief stint with the Chicago Cubs in 1946, was traded to the Padres during the 1949 season. The following year, Adams joined the Portland Beavers where he later posted the league's lowest ERA (2.17) in 1952. Red returned to Los Angeles during the '56 season and finished his PCL career with Sacramento in 1958. Following his playing days, Adams spent 34 years with the Los Angeles Dodgers including a dozen as their pitching coach.

"The thing that comes to mind is what a great bunch of guys who were there (in San Diego) and playing for Bucky Harris. I was disappointed in my contribution. I pulled a muscle in my side up in Seattle. I was well rested and warmed up, but early in the game it just felt like I got jabbed with a sharp knife. I had high hopes of contributing there, but I pulled that muscle. I kept checking it too often and kept pulling it. I remember pitching a few good games, but I was disappointed in my contribution.

You wanted to do well for Bucky, because he was such a good man. He had such a laid-back attitude. He'd take something that someone else would give you hell for and turn it into something positive. I think we got beat something like six out of seven games up in Sacramento and we really had been hoping to do better than that. We were standing around at the airport and Bucky said, 'It's OK to lose some games like that and get them out of your system.' He could always say something positive. And we had Jimmie Reese and Red Corriden as coaches and they were great guys. It was pretty much an offensive team. That was probably one of the strongest offensive teams in minor league history.

I was fortunate to get into carpentry around '47. I'd drive nails all winter. I always had a job to go to, but it took a toll on me as a pitcher. Gene Thompson, who was a member of that San Diego team, became a lifelong friend. He was a player-coach for Sacramento and Joe Gordon was the manager. In '51, Gene asked me to go to Caracas, Venezuela where he would be managing winter ball and I told him to take somebody who'd had a good season. They're highly interested fans down there and they liked to watch players who were coming off good years. Gene talked me in to going. It was nice and instead of driving sixteen-penny nails, I was where it was hot and I pitched pretty good and I had a good year in 1952.

I got beat the first game, one to nothing. I'd taken a cut in pay that year which I had earned. I was pitching good and leading the league in ERA, but I was oh-and-five. We had Bill Milligan as general manager in Portland. We thought he was tighter than hell, but we felt that way about all of them. He called me in, gave me the money he'd cut and said he hoped it would change my luck. Well, I did end up leading the league in earned run average, but I think I lost more than I won. [15-16. -Ed.]

Hollis Thurston was a good hitting pitcher. One year in San Francisco, he had a bad arm, so he played at first base, I think. But the story I wanted to tell you is that the year after he won twenty games for the last place White Sox, he wanted a raise. They wouldn't give it to him and he pointed out that he'd won twenty games for them. He was told that they finished in last place with his twenty wins and they could finish in last place again without his twenty wins.

I didn't know Jack Graham before I hit him. I'd heard he was grumpy with his teammates, but I felt so damn bad about hitting him, I had to go to the hospital. I didn't know if he'd climb out of bed and take a punch at me. Well, he had this big, old grin on his face and he said he knew I wasn't throwing at him. He said, 'I know you wouldn't be throwing at me, because I haven't hit you very well all season.' He was having an unbelievable season and I felt I had messed it up.

I remember the whole scene. He was a dead pull hitter. He could miss a ball, but with that upper-cut swing, he could still put it out of any ballpark! That shadow between the mound and home plate made it difficult to hit and pitchers loved to pitch then. I think it was his second at bat and he popped up the first time. He crowded the plate and I thought he was crouched more than usual, but he might be trying to see the ball better

Red Adams

Beaning of Jack Graham.

that way. I remember thinking I'm going to stay tight, but the ball sailed and my ball would normally sink.

Left-handers liked to hit off me. I usually had good control and didn't hit people, but that ball sailed. It bounced so far that I thought it hit his bat. It was just one of those circumstances with the shadow and the ball. If he'd seen it, he'd have gotten out of the way. I know he would have. You love to see a guy having the kind of year like he was having.

Another thing that looked bad was that I generally had pretty good control. I got some letters. Some guy really reamed me out, but Jack was so good about it. We became good friends. When I went to the plate, I'd heard if a person was bleeding from the ear if he got hit in the head, it wasn't good. But Jack told me later that his ear got cut on the outside. Normally, blood from the ear means the eardrum was broken. The doctor told him that ear wax saved him and that's why we have ear wax. It absorbed the shock and Jack had just thought about cleaning it out. I have that in my mind. I think Jack told me that or I read it. He is such a good guy.

When I broke in with LA, I was a twenty-year old kid. We went to San Diego and I saw Frankie Dasso. I thought, if this is how you have to throw to pitch in this league, I can forget it. He was impressive! The Angels had a good pitching staff in '42. I was sent to the Texas League and I was six-and-three or six-and-four, but I'd been lucky. I ended pitching fourteen years in the PCL. I was a mediocre minor league pitcher. [The Pacific Coast League record book shows that Red Adams was a good pitcher going 153-138 with a lifetime 3.48 ERA in 16 seasons. - Ed.]

Back then, we'd complete a lot of games. I completed 31 games in '45 and was not the league leader. I started about 35 or 36. If you were winning and pitching a decent game, they'd leave you in. I was hitting about .340, an indication of how weak the league was that year, so I also got to stay in. Today, pitchers come out for pinch hitters more often as the bullpens are stronger.

Oh, I think of those guys on the Padres. Dee Moore, a tough guy and a sweet guy. Harvey Storey - he was one of the nicest guys in baseball. Artie Wilson was a heck of a nice guy with a great attitude. He could hit and run, too. Bucky Harris used to say Buster Adams was a lousy lead off hitter, because he'd hit home runs. I think he hit 18 in that spot. Getting back to members of that club, I'm aware that quite a number have passed on. I wonder about several others: Bobbie Wilson played second base, John Ritchey, catcher, pitchers Xavier Rescigno, Bob Savage, Al Jurisich, Tom Kipp. I hear where Jess Flores died. I was very surprised when I heard about Dain Clay dying as he looked great the last time I saw him. My

happiest memories are the guys. You're part of a team... a big family."

TOM KIPP, pitcher.
BORN: 8-9-22   DIED: 8-23-98   PADRES: 1949

Tom Kipp was a star pitcher for Rod Dedeaux and the USC Trojans when they won the NCAA baseball championship in 1948. The following year, he was pitching for the San Diego Padres and posted a 7 and 5 record. Kipp led the Western International League with a 2.76 ERA pitching for Tacoma in 1950. His professional baseball career was brief, because Tom spent several years in military service before graduation from college.

"There are good and bad memories. A funny one lingers on... Big Max West, my roommate, shuffled out to the mound one day and said, 'Tom, won't you please slow down and give the outfielders a chance to catch their breath.' He was a helluva ballplayer! He was a good roommate, because he was older and had better sense. Minnie (Minoso) was a very funny guy. When he broke in, he wasn't much of an outfielder, but he could hit and he was exciting. Minnie and Dee Moore, of course, you can't print what Dee used to do to Minnie. I can still remember hearing Minnie say, 'Don't you call me a nigger! I'm a Cuban!'

Al Rosen was our third baseman when I played. He was learning to field, too, but he was a big hitter. Pitching batting practice to Big Luke (Easter) was one of the tougher assignments. He'd rip the ball knee high back through the mound! I remember Bob Savage and Lyman Linde. Lyman was from Green Bay. They were great guys. They used to drink a case of beer a day. I guess my biggest memory was when I beat the Oaks once in ten innings. I was mostly a relief pitcher which I didn't like. I got into a fight with (manager) Del Baker and I went back into radio.

I was news editor for KHJ in LA. It was during the McCarthy era and Martin Berkeley did *Inside the Underground*. He was the Hollywood screenwriter who turned in the 'Hollywood Ten.' The lawyers at NBC didn't want to do it, because they said the Communists would want to have equal time. My Dad

Tom Kipp

Dee Moore

Dee Moore, Jack Dempsey, and Steve Mesner.

said, 'Why don't you go out and make an honest living?' That kind of ended my radio career and I went into the automotive supply business with Wynn. But, the baseball years were a lot of fun. We beat George Bush and Yale for the National Championship!"

◆◆◆

DEE MOORE, catcher.
BORN: 4-6-14   DIED: 7-2-97   PADRES: 1949-50

D.C. Moore attended the same Los Angeles high school that produced Steve Mesner, Bobby Doerr and George McDonald. Before joining San Diego, Dee had traveled extensively through the minors before stops in Cincinnati, Brooklyn and Philadelphia. A very versatile player, in addition to catching, playing infield and outfield, Moore even pitched two games for the 1936 Reds. He earned a save to go along with his lifetime 0.00 ERA. In 1947, while playing for the Sacramento Solons, Dee set a Pacific Coast League record by collecting six consecutive pinch hits. Although nearing the end of the road, D.C. hit .311 and .281 during his two seasons in San Diego... and he still loved to tag out those runners at home plate!

"Jesus Christ, I've got a lot of stuff in my head, but I can't get it out! [Dee was talking by phone from a nursing home in Williston, North Dakota. -Ed.] I'll be OK once I start talking about it. I enjoyed the Padres more than any other team I ever played for. San Diego was a beautiful time and we had a good hitting team. There was Max West, Steve (Mesner), of course, Minnie Minoso... Minnie Minoso, he had the longest ding and I used to grab it when he'd come out of the shower. He'd get down on his knees and beg for mercy. He'd promise anything for me just to let go. You tell Minnie about that when you talk to him. He's a great guy. Everybody liked Minnie. What a ballplayer!

["There were two ways to get in the showers at Lane Field and a wall you could look over. Minnie would finish his shower and look over the wall for Dee. He'd never see him and, no matter which way he came out, Dee was always there waiting for him."
-Max West]

And Al Rosen, too. We had a lot of power, but not much pitchin', but we made it to the playoffs. Oh, this brings back the memories. I hit 12 home runs both years I played for San Diego. I came from Sacramento and it was so good to be in San Diego!

I used to go down there in the off-season and see Steve and play winter ball. You could pick up some loot and there wasn't much travelin'. I gave Bobby Doerr his first baseball uniform. He and Steve and George, they were younger than me, but what a great American Legion team they had. When Steve had a little tough thing [translation: Dee determined that somebody was picking on him at school. -Ed.], I'd tell him to run to me. I'd look out for him. When he (Steve) went to the White Sox, they railroaded him. It was the players who did it. He didn't get a chance. We both went to Ponca City and then L.A. together. Steve was a good ballplayer. In San Diego, he and Charlene took good care of me. We had such good times together. It was so long ago.

When I was a young kid, I played for Portland. I was with Syracuse, Macon, Georgia and Cincinnati. I caught a no-hitter in Syracuse for Whitey Moore. It was a Moore and Moore battery. I played for Brooklyn and then Philadelphia. After I got out of the service, and there were lots of us, the teams had to take you back. Ben Chapman was the manager at Philadelphia and we didn't get along. He had me catching batting practice and I said, 'Hell, I don't need this; I can go out to the Coast League and make as much money!'

A History of the San Diego Padres (1936-1957)

I'm sorry, Doc. I'm on a long distance call. When you see Charlene (Mesner), give her a hug from me. She's my baby! And don't forget what I told you to tell Minnie."

◆◆◆

MINNIE MINOSO, outfield, infield.
BORN: 11-29-22   PADRES: 1949-50

One of the most exciting Lane Field Padres was Saturnino Orestes Armas-Arrieta. His two older brothers, born of a previous marriage and named "Minoso" were already respected ball players in Cuba by the time young Arrieta began to play. His nickname was "Little Minoso" and American fans shortened it to "Minnie." With a lifetime .298 batting average, Minnie has the distinction of playing five decades in the major leagues (1949-1980). He was prepared to add the sixth decade in 1990, but the commissioner determined that he was too old to make one last plate appearance. [Many former Negro League players changed their birth dates for the opportunity to play big league baseball.] His "American" career began in 1945 with the New York Cubans in the Negro League. Minnie went to Dayton (Ohio, Central League) in 1948 and hit .525! He appeared briefly with Cleveland in 1949 before coming to San Diego. That first season, Minoso hit .297 and 22 home runs, improving to .339 with 20 circuit blows in 1950. On paper, Minnie was a 28 year old rookie when he returned to the majors in 1951 and hit .326. Minoso was selected for the PCL Padres Hall of Fame in 1967.

Minnie Minoso

"I was in San Diego not too long. Please give everyone my love and my respect and I really appreciated San Diego, because it opened the door for me. They said, 'Minnie, you can do it in the big leagues. We'll miss you, but we want you to go.' I had a good time in San Diego and the people were so nice. I lived with some people named Brown on Imperial Avenue in a very distinguished house. An old lady used to cook for me. I was like part of the family and the old lady was very sweet. I would sure like to find those people again.

We had such a good team. They used to kill a lot of cars on the highway hitting home runs over right field fence. Graham and West hit the longest balls in the Pacifico. We had a second baseman who hustle like the devil. Whitey Wietelmann was our shortstop and Harvey Storey and Jess Flores. Dee Moore was the catcher. He was such a sincere guy. He is a good guy, but he like to tease. He make me get on my knees and beg. You ask him what part he grab? [When advised that Dee had already described the part in question, Minnie reacted with a long and hardy laugh, but no comment.]

Mr. Starr is a very good man. He call me in his office and say, 'You are a nice, young fellow. I don't want you hanging around with Luke Easter. I don't want you getting his bad habits.' We used to go to Hollywood and see Mr. Randolph Scott who was making a movie. We stay up all night and we play a double header the next day. Luke got four-for-five. I am begging God, but I only get one-for-five. I know Mr. Starr is right. I say to Luke, 'I love you. You are my friend, but I can't keep up with you.'

There was a coach about ninety years old. He is my buddy: Jimmie Reese. When I was coaching for the White Sox, he gave me one of his fungos (bats).

Floyd Robinson is a real gentleman and he is from San Diego. When he started to romance with his wife, I said, 'Floyd, Floyd, she's gonna get you' and finally they were married.

Johnny Ritchey is such a nice guy. He had blue eyes. He was very quiet and a good left-handed hitting catcher. The people I lived with, Irene was sister to the lady Johnny married. He was very distinguished and a fine man. I want to send him a White Sox cap.

Max West was a very distinguished guy, a gentleman guy. He had a personality like Ted Williams. Some guys were jealous. He didn't talk much. He let his bat talk!

One time, we were in Oakland and behind three-to-nothing and two men were on base. I swung on a three-oh count and hit a home run. The take sign was on. All were very happy. (Manager) Bucky (Harris) say, 'Hey, Minos, congratulations! Nice you hit home run, but in big leagues, you be fined $500!' He say, 'Remember this kid is going to be out of here soon and I want him to learn.' When guys say he shouldn't tell me that, I say, 'I'm sorry, Bucky.' But he say, 'No, it's OK.' He was very clean and decent guy. He looked like he came from Hollywood.

Al Rosen wanted to be the leader all the time. He was a rookie (with the Indians). Now, I used to play third base. It was my position. It was Al Rosen and myself. Rosen kept playing ahead of me all the time. So one day, I stayed in the dugout. (Cleveland manager Lou) Boudreau say, 'Minos, what happened?' I tell him and he never bawl me out. He say, 'Now you going to throw with Dale Mitchell in the outfield.' I go out there. There are many third basemen and shortstops and second basemen, so outfield OK with me. I can play everywhere. Then Rosen come out, but I go in front of him. We have words and I tell him I want my bread-and-butter, too. 'You block me at third base. You not block me here!' After that, we OK and are friends."

AL ROSEN, third base.
BORN: 2-29-24   PADRES: 1949

Al "Flip" Rosen would surely be in Baseball's Hall of Fame if injuries had not cut his career short. He began playing professional ball in 1942 with Thomasville in the North Carolina League. Al was in military service until his return to baseball with Pittsfield (Canadian-American League) in 1946 where he led the league with 15 home runs and 86 RBIs while hitting .323. The following season, Rosen led the Texas League with a .349 BA and 141 RBIs. He hit 25 home runs and batted .327 for Kansas City in 1948 and was part of the '49 Padre juggernaut that included sluggers Max West, Luke Easter and Minnie Minoso. In 83 games, Rosen hit .319 with 17 home runs. From 1950 through 1955, he averaged almost 30 home runs and 110 RBIs for Cleveland while twice leading the American League in each category. Al was selected as the league's MVP in 1953. His lifetime totals in the major leagues include 192 home runs and a .285 career batting average. After his playing days, he was the general manager of the San Francisco Giants.

"I met some lovely people in San Diego. The experience was a great one, because you were playing with a lot of ex-major leaguers. I was optioned out on July 3rd and probably didn't spend more than five weeks in San Diego as I joined the team when they were on the road and I was only with them a couple of months. But I remember being on my ass a lot, because I was hitting behind Max West. He hit fourth and I was fifth.

I do remember being up in Oakland and Lou Tost was pitching against us. I remember him from the '48 World Series. He was a left-handed pitcher for Boston (Braves). He deliberately stuck it in my ribs. Nobody ever saw me rub it. I'd never rub it! I went to first and said, 'For Chrissakes, Lou, he (West) hit it, not me.' Tost said something. He and I got into it on the mound and I flattened him. Someone threw a punch from behind and it was Martin. We played against each other a lot in the majors and never became friends. He was always looking for a fight.

I boxed a lot in Florida (as a young man). I boxed in the (Golden) Gloves, A.A.U., the University of Florida and in the military. And Minnie (Minoso) was tough. He was as hard as that concrete over there. Nobody messed with Minnie.

I was a navigator on an AKA in World War Two and we sailed the ship into San Diego. I thought, 'What a great place to live.' I thought San Francisco was, but San Diego was special. The fans were very supportive. It was Max West who introduced me to Alaskan King crab up in San Francisco. I knew people in L.A. and Hollywood, so it was great to play there. That six-day schedule was great.

I had a garage apartment in San Diego at the beach. It was upstairs over the garage. You know how those places are out back at the beach and there was no bathroom. I

Al Rosen

had to go in the back door of the landlady's home to use her bathroom. I lived right by the Mesners. They were wonderful. It was like an open house at their place. Charlene would cook for us and we'd go to the beach. I remember sitting at the beach and listening to the Cardinals on major league recreated broadcasts. The Wietelmanns lived out there, too.

I remember Jess Flores very well. He was a tremendous guy and a terrific pitcher. I loved Jimmie Reese. He worked a lot with me. The year before, I played the entire season in Kansas City. The American Association had a lot of young prospects and the PCL had a lot of guys with a lot of experience. It was great for me. I was there to get the rough edges off and I learned a lot from the major leaguers.

The learning process today is in the majors; it used to be in the minors. I'm not going to say that today's players are better than the old-timers, but consider this - the ballparks are about the same size, but the players and gloves aren't. With longer arms and bigger gloves, you cut down a lot of holes out there. Look at how high the batting averages used to be in the old days. A lot of those balls aren't getting through today.

And Blacks have certainly changed sports. They are great athletes. Look at how they have changed basketball. I'm from the South. I was born in South Carolina and lived in Florida. I never saw Black players. I remember that Branch Rickey brought some up in the minors. I didn't think about the color of the skin. I thought, 'These sons-a-bitches can play!' They were good! If Luke Easter would have gotten an earlier start, he'd have been a Hall of Famer.

And Minnie Minoso, you could see he was going to be a great major leaguer when he was in San Diego. The biggest mistake (Cleveland general manager Hank) Greenberg made, well, he made a few, was to get rid of Minoso and keep (another former Padre Harry 'Suitcase') Simpson. He was great for San Diego, but if we'd kept Minnie, we'd have won a few more pennants. Minoso changed a ball game. He wasn't just another guy. That's what you look for in a Hall of Famer and he's as good as a lot of guys in the Hall of Fame. If you were picking a ball team, he'd be on it. He made an impact and that's what is important. The other team had to change everything with him at bat or on the bases. He was a tough man to get out and he loved to play!

Minoso and I were both trying to make it at third (with Cleveland) and (Ken) Keltner wouldn't take grounders unless I was out there. He knew I was the heir apparent. There was just one ballpark and we'd have to hit grounders to each other. Ray Boone, we're good friends, was trying out for third, too. When Minnie went in the outfield and I went in the outfield. He got really pissed! But we worked it out. He's a unique guy and a unique ballplayer.

(Padres manager) Bucky Harris would show up about ten minutes before the game started. Jimmie Reese and Red Corriden ran the team. I asked Bucky Harris one time, 'Bucky, I'd like to ask you a question. Will I ever play in the major leagues?' He said, 'No... You might make it as a sub, because you hit pretty good.' The next year (1950), he was manager of the Washington Senators and the first time we played them, I hit two home runs. On the second one, I couldn't resist to say, 'Hello, Bucky. How are you?' when I rounded third." (Al Rosen led the league with 37 home runs that year.)

BOB SAVAGE, pitcher.
BORN: 12-1-21   PADRES: 1949-50

John Robert (Bob) Savage of Manchester, New Hampshire started his professional baseball career pitching for the Philadelphia Athletics in 1942 after attending Staunton Military Academy in Virginia. He was wounded three times during the Second World War, but was able to return to Philadelphia and resume his baseball career in 1946. 2,000 Manchester fans went to Fenway Park that year on "Bob Savage Day" to cheer as their hometown favorite dueled the Red Sox for ten innings. Boston rallied to win, 4-3, but it was the

Bob Savage

highlight of his season. He was sold to the Browns on December 16, 1948. Used sparingly in St. Louis, Savage came to the Padres in 1949 where he was a starter and reliever. His two year record in San Diego was 10-18.

"During the winter of 50-51, Jack Graham and I were traded to the Seals. I was going to lose my GI Bill if I didn't go back to college, so I left San Francisco in July of 1951 to return to finish college. I guess it was a good trade, because I got my degree, but I did enjoy my ball career.

When I was with San Diego, they had Max West and Whitey Wietelmann. Max was my idol when he was with Boston and I was growing up in New England. And Whitey was playing for Boston, too. Actually, they were just a little older than me, but they were good players.

And we had Minnie Minoso and Al Rosen, who couldn't really make our team. Look at the great year he had when he went to the big leagues after the Padres. He was a great player, but he really couldn't break our starting lineup. Also there was Johnny Ritchey who was a really fine ballplayer.

I remember that 'Schoolboy' Rowe joined us in San Diego and Xavier Rescigno. He blamed everything on God. He'd look up to the sky and say, 'For Chrissakes, why me?' I enjoyed the Pacific Coast as much as the big leagues. I'm glad I played out there, but in those days, you didn't have much choice in where you played."

ARTIE WILSON, shortstop.
BORN: 10-28-20   PADRES: 1949

Artie began his career with Birmingham of the Negro American League in 1943. He averaged over .350 during his five years with the Black Barons and led the league with a .402 batting average in 1948. On opening day of 1949, Wilson was the Padres starting shortstop, but he was awarded to Oakland in a contract dispute initiated by the Yankees. He led the PCL by hitting .348 that first season and stole 47 bases. "The Birmingham Gentleman" is widely regarded as one of the finest shortstops to ever play in the Pacific Coast League. In 1951, Wilson was briefly with the New York Giants until his spot on the roster was taken by a promising youngster named Willie Mays. Artie was a career .312 hitter in the minor leagues.

"I had a good time there (in San Diego). I always wanted to stay in San Diego. When I was with Birmingham, we used to barnstorm in San Diego in the winter, so I was glad when I went there to play. Bill Veeck signed me. That's how I got on the team. Johnny Ritchey was on the team. He was a good hitter. We had Minnie Minoso and Luke Easter. Me and Luke lived together and Mrs. Johnson fixed our meals. We were treated so nice.

Artie Wilson

Everybody was just super to us. Luke had a big Buick and he could drive, but he liked me to drive it, so he looked like a big shot. I'd rather drive, because Luke would drink. I'd like to leave, but Luke would tell me to stay so I could drive him. Luke could carry on at night and go four-for-four the next day.

I started with the Birmingham Black Barons in '43. We won in '44 and '45, Kansas City won in '46 and we won again in '47 and '48. That's pretty good to win four out of five years. We had Piper Davis. We got Mays in about '45 and you knew right away he'd be a great player. His dad was a good player, too. Buck O'Neill played first base for Kansas City. We would play ball all winter, too. I love to play baseball. I still enjoy playing the game when I go to old-timers games. I took up golf a few years ago and I love it, too.

Oakland bought my contract from Cleveland and they couldn't have treated me any better. They said I needed a roommate and Billy Martin said, 'I'll be his roommate.' One time, we went to a restaurant and the waitress wouldn't wait on us for 45 minutes. When she came, Billy had a fit. She knew we were ballplayers. Billy wanted to see the manager and it took 30-45 minutes for him to come. Cookie Lavagetto, Jackie Jensen and Mel Desabu were with us. My teammates were wonderful.

Just getting a chance to play meant a lot to me. If anything bad was said, I didn't pay no mind. It just bounced off like a rubber ball. I'd think it can't be true. They didn't understand. I love the game.

I loved to run and I'd do anything to get on base. I was free to go any time I got on base. I was on my own. I might steal second, but I never went if I thought the next man would hit a home run.

Whenever I was playing in San Diego, I used to go across the border every day. I had a good friend working at the Douglas Hotel (on Market Street) and he'd let me use his car to go to Tijuana. My teammates always wanted to go and I remember I could buy a big bottle of cologne for $7.50 and I would give it away for gifts. I remember I had cologne that would last me for years. Tabu cost a lot more in the states.

I loved the PCL. I made more money in the Coast League in 1950 than I did going up to the Giants. I didn't get to play there and I've got to play. I didn't want to sit on the bench, so I was glad to get back to the coast. I was with San Diego, Oakland, then the Giants, Seattle in '52 to '54, '55 and '56 with the (Portland) Beavers and '57-'58 at Sacramento just before they moved to Hawaii.

I always played with fine players. Wherever they played baseball, I played baseball. I was in the Caribbean in the winters. I just played all the time. I played for so many teams, but I never took a uniform from a single team. I was always treated so good."

HARVEY STOREY, third base.
BORN: 8-21-16   PADRES: 1949-52

Harvey Storey began his professional baseball career in 1937 batting .347 at Tacoma in the Western International League. He moved up to San Francisco and established himself as a consistent .300 hitter. In his best season (1939), Storey hit .351 for the Seals. After serving in the armed forces during the war, Harvey returned to baseball and led the Coast League with a .326 average in 1946. He starred for Portland in the late Forties and was traded to San Diego in 1949. That year, he hit .301 for the Padres.

"I had three pretty good years in San Diego. My average kind of dropped those last two years, but I hit some home runs and drove in some runs. With that short right field fence, the left-handed hitters should have paid to get in. It

Harvey Storey

was the most enjoyable place I played. People think Portland would have been the most enjoyable, because it's near my home, but San Diego and San Francisco were better.

I think I led the league up here (Portland) in '46. Nobody even came to the ballpark to take my picture. There were four newspapers in San Francisco and it wasn't unusual for my picture to appear in everyone of them on the same day. They had 'Forest Grove Night' up here when I was with the Padres. The guys were kidding me that they'd give me a car or something nice. They didn't give me anything and that made Bucky Harris mad. He didn't even put me in the lineup, because they didn't do anything for me. A lot of people went to the game from Forest Grove and they weren't happy either. Bucky was a pretty cagey guy. I never asked him why I didn't play and he didn't tell me, but I always figured it was because the Portland team didn't do anything for me.

One night Kewpie (Dick Barrett) was pitching in San Diego. Ad Liska was pitching for Portland and I told Kewpie to tell Bucky if he needs a run, let me hit. I can hit Liska with my eyes closed. Bobby Wilson came up and the bases were loaded. Harris called me and said, 'Go up and see if you can hit a fly ball.' I hit it in the left field stands and we won 4-0. Kewpie was a showboat. He said I'd never have to buy a drink for the rest of the year. He didn't keep that promise, but he liked to tell that story.

In '49, we were tied with Seattle and had a playoff. We won that game and Minnie (Minoso) was the hero. The bases were loaded and he got a single up the middle. He ended up on third base and 3 runs scored. He was really a hustler. Whenever I think of Minnie, I always think of Dee Moore. He was a big, strong guy. He'd give Minnie a bad time. It was a lot of fun.

WHITEY WIETELMANN, all positions.
BORN: 3-15-19   PADRES: 1949-52

Whitey Wietelmann has been synonymous with the San Diego Padres for almost fifty years. After eight seasons with the Boston Braves and one with the Pittsburgh Pirates, he went to Sacramento in 1948. The following year, Whitey was traded to the Padres and became a permanent fixture in San Diego. Wietelmann has been a player, coach, manager and chili cook for the team. His best year in the majors was 1945 when he batted .271 for the Braves. In 1952, Whitey hit .262 for San Diego. His hobby is maintaining Padre scrapbooks and he has all the team pictures back to 1936.

My first year, in '37, I made $70 a month to play for Beaver Falls, Pennsylvania, but before my dad would let me go, he made me promise I'd finish school. I said I'd be back for graduation. I had good marks and the principal said, 'OK.' The Greyhound Bus cost seventy-five cents back then. I jumped on it, went to graduation, got on the next one back and didn't miss a game. It was only 75 miles from Beaver Falls to Zanesville (Ohio).

Then I went to Evansville (Triple I League in 1938) and Hartford (Eastern League in 1939). (Tony) Cuccinello broke his shoulder and I went up to Boston. It was quite a thrill. (Whitey singled in his first plate appearance.) That was in '39. [Talking to my twelve-year-old son] I used to be called Billy, too - Billy Wietelmann. In spring training, in 1939, Casey (Stengel) was going down the roster and he got to my name and said, 'I don't like Billy; you're Whitey!' My hair was all white back then and I've been 'Whitey' ever since.

I was sitting out here (in his garage) one day. The phone rang and my wife answered it. She came out and said, 'Whitey, it's the Postmaster General of the United States.' 'It's another prowl,' I said, 'Just hang up, Mother.' He called back and said, 'I know you get a lot of calls, but we are going to make a stamp. I understand you have a picture of Jim Thorpe playing on your dad's team.' I said, 'Yes, I do.' They put it on the cover of the envelopes they used for the first day it was issued. Here it is.

He got three dollars a game from my dad and that is how he had his Olympic medals taken away. He stayed at our house for two or three weeks. He stayed upstairs in a screened-in porch. I know he was a mean, goddamn guy, but he was nice to me. He was like Ty Cobb. My dad's team wasn't a minor league team; it was semi-pro.

Back then, if a guy told you to play third base, even if you'd never played it before, you did it or your ass was back in the lower minors. I could field and I had a good arm. (Boston manager Billy) Southworth even made me a pitcher. I got traded from Sacramento to San Diego in '49 and

I haven't left here since. I can handle the heat. I pitched in Yuma when it was a hundred and fifteen degrees, but I can't handle the cold and I never went back to it.

The '49 team was best with (Luke) Easter, (Max) West, (Minnie) Minoso, (Harvey) Storey, (Al) Rosen, Bobby Wilson at second. West and Easter alternated at first.

I played all nine positions in one game and a guy from the other team played all nine, too. Was he from 'Frisco? He was an outfielder, I think, but I can't remember his name. It was down at Lane Field. I played one position an inning. When I was pitching, I walked the first hitter, but got the next three out.

Whitey Wietelmann

A History of the San Diego Padres (1936-1957)

I've got a picture of Rosen somewhere at one of our barbecues. Every time we'd have a wienie roast, it was right outside my home at the beach. We'd get pretty inebriated on Sunday night and get up Monday and hit the beach. We'd plan for that Monday off. Harvey Storey and Al Rosen liked to come. We had all the families and kids. The Mesners lived there, too.

I was on that flight (when Jack Graham was piloting the commercial airliner) and everybody got scared, but he had his own plane and he knew how to fly.

I've got three TVs there [pointing to three television sets stacked on his workbench]. One is color and two are black-and-white. I'll have three games going, but there's no baseball now [during the baseball strike of 1994]. I've got every box score from 1969 to today (for the Padres) in here (scrapbook). I watch three games at a time: three baseball games, three basketball, three football. I played every sport back in Zanesville, but baseball is the best sport. Yeah, they were the good old days. Now all the ballplayers are dyin'... all the old-timers. Jimmie (Reese) died, but he was ninety-two, but I hated to see him go."

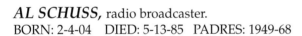

AL SCHUSS, radio broadcaster.
BORN: 2-4-04   DIED: 5-13-85   PADRES: 1949-68

"Therrre it goes" was the home run call of beloved Padres' radio announcer Al Schuss and "therrrrrre" was always added emphasis when the blows came off the Padre bats. Al first uttered what would become his trademark phrase to describe a Gabby Hartnett home run while broadcasting Cub games on CBS during the Thirties. He later teamed with Red Barber "in the catbird seat" to cover the Brooklyn Dodgers. Schuss used the professional name of "Alan Hale" while announcing baseball from 1934 through 1942. He returned to his native Pacific Northwest and worked in radio until he became the Voice of the Padres in 1949. As a young man, Al was a gifted athlete at the University of Washington. He excelled in basketball and was selected as an All-Coast performer, but baseball was his true love. The following information was provided by his long time Padres broadcast partner (1959-68) and friend, Al Coupee.

"Schuss was a helluva guy! He was all baseball. He was the only guy who enjoyed a baseball broadcast even when he wasn't watching the game. I remember those games in Hawaii and we didn't start our broadcast until 11:00 at night. We'd recreate them in the studio and they would drag on and on. We'd get an inning behind in case anything went wrong with the wire. When the game was over, I'd catch up on three strikes and you're out, but that Schuss would call every single pitch. He even added all the crowd sounds to make it sound real. I just wanted to go home and sleep.

Typical Monday on the beach.

Al Schuss

He'd gripe like hell when the Chargers would encroach on the Padres. When the football season started, he was grousing all the time. He was anti-football, but he loved baseball. He loved to talk about the Lane Field days, but I can't remember any of his stories. I think he lived at Lane Field. (Al's daughter, Valerie Foster, recalls as a child that she did not enjoy attending games at Lane Field, because her father would never leave. -Ed.)

When the Padres went in the National League, I went over to see Arnholt Smith about keeping Al. I wasn't anxious to travel, but Al really wanted to broadcast in the big leagues again, but he wouldn't blow his own horn. Buzzie Bavasi didn't want any resemblance to the PCL Padres and he hired Jerry Gross. Years later, Buzzie admitted it was a big mistake and he should have hired Al. He just didn't want any connection to the bush leagues.

Al really knew the players and he was a great bullshitter. He loved the game. It's too drawn out for me, but Al liked the pace. He could tell all those baseball stories and sometimes forget what was happening on the field. I liked the guy. He was straight-arrow all the way. Al was Mr. Baseball in San Diego."

◆◆◆

"RED" EMBREE, pitcher.
BORN: 8-30-17   DIED: 9-24-96   PADRES: 1950-51

"Red" Embree started pitching with Springfield (Ohio) in the Middle Atlantic League in 1939. He was with Cleveland in 1941 until 1943 when he voluntarily retired to work on his farm. Red twice led his league in victories, won-lost percentage and strikeouts (Wilkes-Barre 1941 Eastern League, 21-5, 213Ks, 1.69 ERA, and Baltimore 1944, 19-10, 225Ks). From 1944 through 1949, Embree played for the Indians, Yankees and Browns. He joined the Padres in 1950 and posted an 18-10 record with 113 strikeouts and a 3.32 earned run average. The following interview was conducted with his son, Jim Embree.

"My dad is in a nursing home now. He's confined to a wheelchair and his memory isn't what it used to be, but I'll tell him that you are going to be calling. He still loves to talk baseball and he loved giving autographs when people would write to him. He doesn't have that beautiful signature anymore and that bothers him. He had copies made of pictures of him in his uniforms and when people would write for an autograph, he'd surprise them with a picture. They would write back nice letters thanking him,

Charles "Red" Embree

because they wouldn't be expecting the autographed picture, too. That always made him feel good when they would respond.

I've watched my dad in pain all my life. He has great tolerance for pain. I remember him being at the chiropractor before and after every game he'd pitch. He's very tenacious. If something needed to be done, he'd do it, no matter how much pain it caused him. After baseball, he was a carnation grower and he'd work in the fields with the workers. He'd always be out there the next day, no matter how much pain he was in. He had other opportunities he didn't pursue, because that's what he wanted to do. During the Depression, they (ballplayers) were making very good money relative to what others were making and they had jobs.

An old umpire once told me that he recognized my name and asked if I was related to Charles Embree. I said he was my dad. He told me that my dad had the best curve ball he'd ever seen and he liked to be behind the plate when my dad was pitching. He had all the control on the world.

He is a Quaker. He didn't like the language and carousing around in baseball. The managers would give him the wildest players for roommates in hopes he'd be a good influence. They'd wake him up in the middle of the night with a floozy and he'd go sleep in another room. But if young players wanted help learning the game and came to him, he'd always help. He wouldn't push himself on them and he'd take the time to help them. He was good with the younger players.

To give you an idea of how my dad was, I remember once he tore the nail off his finger with a hammer and he said, 'Damn, that hurts.' I thought, 'My dad cussed!' And I was surprised.

[The following interview was conducted with "Red" who was in a nursing home.]

"You can't beat it when it comes to playing the game. I liked to work with the younger ones. I wish to the dickens my right arm didn't go wacky; I'd still be pitching."

◆◆◆

MILT NIELSEN, outfield.
BORN: 2-8-25   PADRES: 1950-51

In 1949, muscular Milt Nielsen led the Texas League by scoring 139 runs. He was called up by the Cleveland Indians that year and again in 1951. Between those trips to the majors, Nielsen was a hard hitting outfielder for the San Diego Padres, batting .298 during the 200 game schedule in 1950. Milt returned to his native Minnesota after baseball and has operated his own auto dealership, Nielsen Chevrolet-Oldsmobile-Geo, in St. Peter since 1967. He now claims to be a Minnesota Twins fan.

"I hurt my arm between '49 and '50, but I had two very enjoyable years in San Diego. We lived at the beach near Bobby Wilson and I remember eating albacore out there. Whitey Wietelmann bought our son his first swimsuit when he was about 18 months old. Whitey was so good with kids and he'd take him for rides on his bicycle. They were a good bunch of guys and be had a good team in 1950.

Del Baker was the manager and Jimmie Reese was the coach. Max West was in right field and Jack Graham was on first. Jack was my roommate and he used to tell me not to talk to him until he had his first cup of coffee in the morning. Harvey Storey was at third base and Dee Moore was the catcher. Dee had been with Del in Sacramento and he told him he was down to 12 beers a day. Harry Simpson was a heck of a centerfielder. He was long and lean. He could hit to right center and left center. He was a good man. We'd played together at Indianapolis. We had Minnie Minoso who could hardly talk English, but he could make change for a five dollar bill. We had Al Smith. He and Jim Busby raced a horse before a game up in Sacramento. I don't remember who won. Our pitchers were George Zuverink, Red Embree and Al Olsen. I saw Al knock down three guys in a row once. We had Bob Kerrigan, a little left-hander, Bob Savage, Al Jurisich and Harold Saltzman. The next year, we had Sad Sam Jones, but that '50 team was a very good team!

Milt Nielsen

Another guy I remember was our trainer: Les Cook. They don't have guys like him in baseball any more. He was a real old-timer and he had those old ways for fixing ballplayers and they worked. He did everything for the club. He'd get our hotels and transportation and gear. He'd always put Mennen aftershave on his lips to take away the smell of alcohol. This is just great talking about the Padres."

GEORGE ZUVERINK, pitcher.
BORN: 8-20-24   PADRES: 1950

The Baseball Encyclopedia includes every major leaguer from Hank Aaron to George Zuverink, so Rich Marazzi and Len Fiorito wrote a book entitled Aaron to Zuverink which provides biographical sketches on every major league player during the Fifties. The Lane Field Padre roster starts with Morrison Abbott and ends with George Zuverink. Ending ball games would become George's specialty as he developed into one of the top relievers of the Fifties. In 1956, he led the American League with 16 saves. From 1951 through 1959, Zuve pitched for Cleveland, Cincinnati, Detroit and Baltimore. He began playing pro-ball with Fresno in 1946 and was part of an excellent Padre staff in 1950 when he compiled a 20-14 record as the locals finished second in the PCL.

"I have a lot of happy memories of that year (1950) with the Padres. I still have the stub from our bonus for finishing second. We got $769.23! I was making about $400 a month and having a good year. I went to Bill Starr and he gave me $50 a month more, so I got $150 more for those last three months. A hundred and fifty meant a lot back then. When I went to Cleveland, I wasn't getting paid that much, so I asked (Hank) Greenberg for a raise. He said, 'You signed a contract.'

Del Baker was our manager at San Diego. Jimmie Reese was the coach and he was such a nice guy. Al Olsen used to pick me up and drive me to Lane Field. He won 20 games that year, too. Red Embree won 18 and Roy Welmaker won 16. We also had Al Jurisich, Hal Saltzman and Bob Savage. Even Bill Bevens, who almost threw a no-hit game for the Yankees in the '47 World Series, and my boyhood hero, 'Schoolboy' Rowe, were on the team. Getting to know him (Rowe) in 1950, helped me get over to the Detroit Tigers in 1954 when they picked me up on waivers from Cincinnati. Rowe was a pitching coach with the Tigers on Fred Hutchinson's staff. We had some good pitching! Our team led the PCL in earned run average that season.

We had good hitting, too. Harry Simpson and Minnie Minoso had good years. They hit over three hundred. Max West and Jack Graham were hitting home runs. We had Milt Nielsen, Buster Adams, Al Smith and Dee

Moore. Bobby Wilson was second baseman and Merrill Combs was at short. We had old timers like Whitey Wietelmann and Mike Tresh. It was a good team - the PCL was a good league. I gained a lot of confidence pitching for San Diego against guys who were former major leaguers. It was a thrill rubbing shoulders with old timers who had been up in the big leagues while I was on my way up.

I grew up in Holland, Michigan. When I pitched baseball in high school, I didn't win a single game, but I always dreamed of growing up and pitching for the Detroit Tigers. I did get to play with them for a little over a year, but everything started fitting together when I went to Baltimore and Paul Richards (manager) put me in the bullpen. He used to say I was a perfectionist and didn't think the other fellow was ever supposed to get a hit. Whenever he wanted somebody hit, he'd call me in. Once, I was trying to hit Dick Donovan and the umpire called it a strike! I got him with the next pitch. Richards even had me hit Ted Williams. My mother was at the game and she told me to quit baseball and come home. That's the way mothers are. I wouldn't throw at a batter's head. He wanted me to hit a Chicago pitcher when we were behind and I finally refused. He got mad and said, 'When am I going to get a pitcher with guts?'

A game that sticks out for me involved Jack Harshman. I'd come in early to relieve Connie Johnson when he got injured. We threw a one hitter, but so did Jack! The White Sox won, 1-0. You don't see a double one hitter that often.

I love to see old teammates and attend reunions. Rudy Regalado was my teammate at Indianapolis. They're all great memories including the glory days of the PCL!

◆◆◆

JOHN BERARDINO, infield.
BORN: 5-1-17   DIED: 5-19-96   PADRES: 1950

In 1937, Johnny Berardino hit .334 as a rookie for Johnstown (PA) in the Mid-Atlantic League and two years later, he embarked on an eleven year major league career with the St. Louis Browns, Cleveland Indians and Pittsburgh Pirates. A colorful performer, John entertained his Brownie teammates with skits and Shakespearean dramas while embarrassing the team ownership when it was revealed he collected $15 a week in relief checks during the off-season. Today, he is best known for his long time starring television role as Dr. Steve Hardy in the daytime soap opera, General Hospital. But, he is also remembered in San Diego for his role as a short time Padre shortstop.

"I was only there (in San Diego) for a month and a half. I had pleurisy and (Cleveland general manager Hank) Greenberg did me a favor sending me out to a better climate. I didn't make a contribution. Then I went up to Sacramento, but it didn't help, so I went back to Pittsburgh.

The St. Louis Browns do this, too. They cling to their memories. I want to forget them..."

George Zuverink

John Bernardino

Walt Dropo

◆◆◆

WALT DROPO, first base.
BORN: 1-30-24   PADRES: 1951

Walter "Moose" Dropo, All-American lineman from Moosup, Connecticut, tied for the American League lead with 144 RBIs in 1950. The big Red Sox first baseman also batted .322 and hit 34 home runs, which earned him Rookie of the Year honors that season. Walt was briefly with the Padres in 1951 for rehabilitation. He had 5 home runs and batted .286 in 33 games. Dropo returned to the major leagues where he averaged .270 over a thirteen-year career with the Red Sox, Tigers, White Sox, Reds and Orioles. He tied the major league consecutive hits record on July 15, 1952 with twelve straight safeties.

"San Diego! The San Diego Padres and the Pacific Coast League! It was a great league and I enjoyed playing in San Diego. I remember the ballpark was unique. It was like the reverse of Fenway (Park in Boston). That's where Jack Graham hit all those home runs, but it was very difficult for right-handed power hitters to get home runs in San Diego.

I played for the Sacramento Solons and Del Baker in '49 (.287, 17 HR). There was a fellow from San Diego with me in Sacramento. It was Pete Coscarart. And Tony Freitas and Joe Marty. We had a good team. I thought the PCL was about the major league level. There was a nice mixture of vets and rookies. Guys who were just a year away from going up and guys who had just come down. It was a good balance and they played good ball on the West Coast. Rogers Hornsby was the Seattle manager and he was a rough and tumble guy.

I was drafted by the Chicago Bears and George Halas, but Mr. (Tom) Yawkey (Boston owner) gave me a bigger bonus, so it was an easy decision.

I had a good year in '50, but I got hurt that spring (1951) and my wrist was broken. That's no excuse, but I went to San Diego for rehabilitation as I was having trouble at the plate. Del Baker was my manager at Sacramento and he was a friend of Joe Cronin's (Boston president), so I went out and they felt Del could help me. It was more of a rehabilitation than anything and that's why I was sent down there. I was only there a few months, but I remember going grunion fishing and all the sailors and the docks by the ballpark."

STU LOCKLIN, outfield.
BORN: 7-22-28   PADRES: 1951, 57-59

Stu Locklin was a "frequent friar" during the Fifties. Playing for the Wisconsin Badgers baseball team, Stu once collected 4 hits in five plate appearances against Michigan State and future Hall of Fame pitcher, Robin Roberts. While playing for Dayton in 1949, his 169 hits led the Central League. The following year he batted .298 with ten home runs and led the Texas League in doubles at Oklahoma City before promotion to San Diego in 1951. He hit .267 for the Padres and then enlisted in the Air Force during the Korean War. Stu was with Cleveland during '55 and '56 before returning to Lane Field where he registered a .310 batting average in 1957.

Ed Kazak checks Stu Locklin's blisters during spring training.

"I enjoyed playing with the Padres. The problem was I never completed a full season with them. In 1949, I went to spring training with them. Red Corriden was one of the coaches and he knew I went to the University of Wisconsin. When I'd go up to bat, he'd sing, 'On, Wisconsin.'

My first year, Walt Dropo, Charlie Sipple and I lived at the Mission Bay Motel. I played half a season with them from June until September (1951) and then, on the advice of Hank Greenberg who was in the Air Force, I enlisted and spent four years in the U.S.A.F. until 1955. I played a little in Cleveland in '55 and '56. In 1957, I played half a season until the 4th of July when I joined the Miami Marlins. In 1958, I was back in San Diego with Rudy Regalado, Rod Graber and Hank Aguirre. We lived in the Clairemont Apartments (Buena Vista) together. Earl Averill also stayed with us in the Clairemont Apartments and was the property of the Cleveland Indians at the time. My son was born in San Diego in 1958.

In 1959, I played with San Diego until the first of July when I joined Minneapolis under Gene Mauch. I can't complain, because I had a chance to win two Little World Series with Minneapolis. I did enjoy the company of some good ballplayers over my seven baseball years.

I remember going down to Tijuana to watch jai alai with some of the guys. A guy approached me and wanted to make me a jai alai player. I had played a lot of handball, but I never got to try jai alai. I also played a lot of winter ball in Mexico for Hermosillo, Sonora. My daughter was born there in a little hospital a doctor made. He lived upstairs. In our country, a baby goes home after it's born, but my wife would take the baby back to the hospital so she could watch the games and they'd watch the baby. It was a very nice set-up.

Then my daughter won a contest at Western Auto in Ocean Beach. People would turn in pictures of their kids and we turned in a picture of her answering the telephone. She was picked as the cutest and the prize was our choice of an appliance. We had been in Mexico where there weren't any washing machines, so that is what my wife wanted.

We had a lot of characters on our team in San Diego. There was the toothpick kid: Sad Sam Jones. He was quite a character... always had a toothpick. It seems like some of the Black players were afraid of flying and they'd take the train all the way up to Seattle and they'd show up a day later.

I remember having a good spring and I was hitting about .475. I maintained it for about the first month, but they were always looking for long ball hitters in San Diego. I was a line drive hitter and in San Diego, if you put the ball up in the air and you were a left-handed hitter like I was, the ball would just sail out over the rightfield fence. Did they have a high fence? No, it was just a wall. I didn't pull the ball and I do not remember really ripping it for that first month, but the players came down after the majors made their cuts. The pressure was really on and I kind of tailed off. I had good managers in San Diego: Bucky Harris, Del Baker, Bob Elliott, George Metkovich. There were some good guys and good times in San Diego. I still remember driving down Narragansett Street and looking out at the water. It was beautiful."

BOB MALLOY, pitcher.
BORN: 5-28-18   PADRES: 1951-53

Bob Malloy was a football star at the University of Pittsburgh who broke into organized baseball with Birmingham in 1941. He joined the Reds two years later and remained with Cincinnati through 1947. Malloy led the American Association with 21 victories at Indianapolis in 1948. This earned him return passage to the majors with the St. Louis Browns in 1949. After a disappointing season, Bob thought his playing days were over until Lefty O'Doul coaxed him into becoming a San Diego Padre. Used in relief, Malloy had 8 wins and 8 losses during his tenure at Lane Field.

Bob Malloy

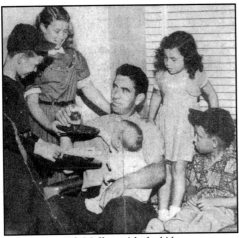

Bob Malloy with the kids.

Sam "Toothpick" Jones

Lefty O'Doul and "Joe Dokes"

"Why anyone who ever played in the old Coast League ever went to the majors always amazed me. That was the end of my playing career, but it was as near to what baseball was all about as anything could be. It had a variety of parks, weather and all the travel one could ask for in baseball.

Sam Jones was the reason I went to the coast. I had decided it was time to get a steady job to support my family. I'd pitched for Dallas the year before and couldn't break a pane of glass. I went to my first day of work at a General Motors plant here in Cincy at noon. When I got home that evening, my wife, Dorothy, said I was to call Al Lopez in San Diego. Al was managing Cleveland and he was interested in getting Jones. Bill Starr would give him first crack, if he got him a pitcher. I told Al that I could hardly lift my arm. He said, 'Hell, this is an old man's league.' They'd give me the same salary I got at Indy for a three month trial. I could bring my family, but I had to be on the plane that night. My wife agreed and that was the start of three wonderful Pacific Coast League years and some wonderful people and wonderful memories.

The first day I walked in, they gave me a locker next to Lonnie Summers. He said, 'You must be Bob. Let me tell you something. The San Diego Chamber of Commerce is going to be madder than hell at you! You'd better rub against me; you're too white!' Lonnie was Black and that was my greeting to sunny San Diego. Del Baker was manager and the world's nicest guy, Jimmie Reese, was his coach. Jimmie took me under his wing and found a big Swede chiropractor. Before I knew what happened, I was able to throw a little bit, but he almost broke my arm! They can say Ruth, Cobb, Aaron, Williams, etc. are to remembered for their records and rightly so, but I'll bet there is not one baseball player who will be remembered and respected as much as Jimmie. He affected the lives of many, many players just by his great concern for their well-being as well as honing their skills. San Diego sports should make a shrine for the man.

Things started going better for Sam, too. He wasn't doing to well. The other teams got on him about his race. He was red-headed and had freckles and always had a toothpick in his mouth. He even swallowed it a couple of times. The taunting bothered him and old Theolic Smith tried to talk to Sam. Theolic played in Mexico and in the Negro Leagues. He said, 'What the hell difference does it make?' Finally, the Jewish guys on the team set up a little ritual for him in the dugout. They had candles and called him over. They were going through some rites and said, 'Go out there and pitch! We officially made you a Jew.' He went out and had a good year after that.

I was playing football at the University of Pittsburgh and I joined the baseball team. We'd play Army, Navy, Penn State. Edgar Jones and I would go over and pitch batting practice for the Pirates. They had Pie Traynor, Arky Vaughan, the Waner brothers. They'd leave ten bucks by our locker every now and then. My brother pitched, too and he'd play for semi-pro teams. They'd give him five or ten bucks a game, but he'd make more money by betting on himself. He won a lot of games! Our Dad was killed working in the mines. When I was in college, I worked in the mines and then I got a job washing windows. That's going from one extreme to the other. I was five miles into the earth and eighteen stories up on those skyscrapers!

When I was playing with Indianapolis, my roommate had a double cleft and it was hard to understand him. We were playing Kansas City and (Jack) Cassini goes sliding into home. It's a close play and all hell breaks loose. Al (Lopez) goes out; (Tony) Cuccinello goes out. My roomie and I are sitting in the dugout. He starts yelling at the ump, 'You blind son of a bitch!' He goes on and on and the ump slowly walks over and says, 'Get the hell out of here.' My roommate asks why? The umpire says, 'You called me every rotten name there is!' Roomie tells him, 'My wife sits across from me at the breakfast table and she can't understand me. You're 200 feet away! How the hell can you understand me?' I'm laughing so hard, I got tossed, too. It was the only time I ever got thrown out of a game.

My brother and I used to play in exhibition games against the old Pittsburgh Crawfords. We got $50 a game traveling to play the Jackie Robinson All-Stars. We got to Chicago and the promoters offered us $1,500 to go out to the coast to play ten more games. That was good money in the off-season and we wanted it. We had to get permission and it was denied. We were told that if you're playing with them like that, they'd have to let them play in the big leagues.

It was unfair to Al Campanis when they kicked him out of baseball for making racial comments. His job was scouting the Negro Leagues back in the Forties and he was a friend to those players. Branch Rickey got treated like he was so religious and he wouldn't go to games on Sundays. He just drove past the ballpark to see how much money was in the till! It's never changed. There is too much hypocrisy in baseball. But there is hypocrisy everywhere. Preacher Rowe told me a story about Rickey. He had had a good year and went to see Rickey the following spring expecting a sizable raise. He said we talked for hours and I came out with two coon dogs.

I became an umpire in the Southern Association after San Diego. The best advice I got was from an old time umpire who said, 'You were a ballplayer. You will learn that they're nothing but rat bastards! No matter what you do, you're only going to be right 50% of the time. Be stern!' The way players behave today is terrible. They make five million and if they could fine 'em about $600,000, that would stop 'em!

Bob Burns was an umpire in the Southern Association. He thought (General Douglas) MacArthur was God. Every time you'd see him, he'd be talking about how wonderful MacArthur was and Truman was terrible. Burns was even a Democrat. We'd hear this day after day. He got real upset when Truman fired MacArthur and called him a son of a bitch. When MacArthur landed in San Francisco, the reporters asked him what he was going to do? He said, 'We're flying back to New York. We are going to the Polo Grounds. We are going to cheer the Giants and boo the umpires.' Burns said, 'They should have shot the SOB!'

Yes, I know the *Baseball Encyclopedia* says I died in 1976, but I've never been to Sandusky [which is listed as the place of death]. My autograph went up in value from $1.00 to $3.00 because I was dead! I prefer the $1.00 price.

I've got one more story to tell you. I was lucky enough to play for Lefty O'Doul. He was an institution on the Coast. He came to manage us in Dago after twenty years of managing the San Francisco Seals. He had been a great left-handed pull hitter. He loved teaching players to pull the ball. His theory about hitting was based on the fact that if you could pull a fast ball foul, you could be a good hitter.

He was loved by the greats of Hollywood. Many nights when we played at Dago, Harry James the bandleader, Joe DiMaggio or some other Hollywood celebrity would be in the dugout talking to Lefty. Or, Betty Grable or Marilyn Monroe would be on the outside sitting in their big white Cadillac convertibles with more people gaping over the back wall than were watching the game.

He had an import-export business in Japan and was one of the first people to take teams to play there. He loved to play golf and played 27 holes every day he could. He would come to the park just in time to make out the line-up card. We all loved to play for him.

As it happened, we had two lousy weeks on the road and we lost our Monday-off day. The pitchers were running in the outfield and the hitters were taking their swings. Everyone was dressed in shorts and sweatshirts and enjoying the warm old sun. There was a loud pounding on the gate in center field. We went to investigate. It was a friend of Lefty's and he wanted to bring his horse and trailer in off the highway. Pacific Highway ran outside Lane Field and Del Mar was a race track north of the park and Agua Caliente was south in Mexico. Del Mar ran Monday through Saturday and there were 12 races in Tijuana on Sunday. The driver traveled this road frequently with his horse who was named Joe Dokes.

Lefty said to let him in, so we did. As we gathered around gawking, the guy asked Lefty if he could let his horse run around on the field? Lefty let him know that we were having batting practice and the horse could get hit. The guy laughed and said the horse loved baseball, so Lefty said it was OK. You know, that horse ran around picking up the balls, flicking his head and firing the balls into the infield. Lefty laughed and commented that the horse got the ball back to the infield better than some of his outfielders. The owner then boasted that the horse could hit!

That was all Lefty had to hear. The next thing, the horse was up at the plate with a bat in his mouth and he was swinging his head back and forth. The first pitch came in and the horse pulled it over the right field wall and onto the highway. The horse proceeded to smash one right after the other against or over the wall. That is when Lefty said he wanted to use the horse the next night against Hollywood.

The next night, we're in the last of the ninth, losing, 2-1, with a man on first and two outs. Lefty calls time and the horse is brought up to the plate. It's wearing a 'Dago' cap and a blanket made out of a Dago uniform. Lefty tells the umpire that the horse, Joe Dokes, is hitting for Jones. The ump looks at Lefty and says, 'No way. Get this animal out of here or the game will be forfeited!' Lefty tells the ump to look up in the press box. There is Pants Rowland, the league president, and he is nodding his head, 'Yes.' Meanwhile, Bobby Bragan, the Hollywood manager, is talking to the horse's rear end, making believe that he is talking to the umpire. This gets Bobby tossed, but not before he tells the umpire to let the horse hit to get the game over.

The Hollywood pitcher can't believe it when the umpire gets behind the catcher and says, 'Play ball!' He takes a big windup and fires the ball to the plate. The horse, swinging his head back and forth, vigorously connects and pulls the ball over the right field wall! The man on first goes to second and on to third. All the while, Lefty is screaming his lungs out at Joe Dokes. 'Run! Run! Run you dumbbell!' He's in a frenzy and the horse is just standing there with the bat in his mouth, swinging his head back and forth. The trainer is sitting next to the dugout. He leans over and yells to Lefty, 'If the dumb thing could run, I'd have him up at Del Mar or down at Caliente and not here playing baseball!' That was Lefty's favorite story.

Tell everyone in San Diego, 'Hi', from the biggest BSer in Cincy!"

◆◆◆

NEILL SHERIDAN, outfield.
BORN: 11-20-21   PADRES: 1951

Neill "Wild Horse" Sheridan played for five teams in the Pacific Coast League. He led the San Francisco Seals with 4 home runs in 1944 when the scarcity of raw materials required to produce baseballs resulted in a brief return to "the dead ball" era. After the war, Sheridan hit .269 and .286 for the Seals in 1946-47 respectively. After a good spring training in 1948, Neill had a "cup of coffee" with the Red Sox, but it was difficult to break into an outfield that included Ted Williams, Dom DiMaggio, Wally Moses, Stan Spence and Sam Mele. He returned to the Coast and batted .312 for the Seattle Rainers that season. Then it was back to San Francisco in 1950 where he hit .288 and south to San Diego for 1951. Although his average slipped to .204, it rebounded two years later when he hit .293 for Oakland and Sacramento. On July 8, 1953, Sheridan hit a home run for the Solons that broke a car window 620 feet from home plate!

"My wife and I had an apartment that was a block and a half from the ocean in San Diego. We just loved it, but I was only there for a month and a half. Willie Mays was called up (to the New York Giants) and they needed an outfielder in Minneapolis, so that's how I left San Diego. Minneapolis was great, too and Hoyt Wilhelm was on that team. Nicolett was a great park for left-handed hitters, but I'm right-handed.

I played in the Coast League for about ten years. I made about all the stops, but missed playing for L.A. or Hollywood and Portland. I remember that Portland's groundskeeper was named Rocky and we called their ballpark 'Rocky's Rockpile.' It was pretty bad. The lights at Lane Field were terrible. It was like playing in your home at night with the lights on. San Diego had a pitcher named Vallie Eaves and he was very wild and hard to see at night. He'd throw behind you.

One night, we were playing Sacramento and they had those bleachers in left field at Lane Field. I hit a home run and it knocked the seat right off! I think the termites had already eaten it.

I played in the '47 All-Star game with Max West and Frank Kerr, the catcher from San Diego. I was with San Francisco. I remember it, because I think I drove in about five runs in that game.

When I was with San Diego in '51, Sam Jones was on the ball club. Segregation was still in effect then. My wife would sit with his wife at the games, but the other wives

Neill Sheridan

would sit apart from them. That's just the way it was back then.

I played with Jack Graham when he came to the Seals. He was a great guy. He was so unpretentious and he looked like a librarian, but he was a great hitter, too. Part of my memory of baseball is that there were very few guys that weren't great guys. They played for the love of the game and not the money."

BILL JENNINGS, shortstop.
BORN: 9-28-25   PADRES: 1951

After his discharge from the Navy in 1946, Bill Jennings worked out with the New York Giants. He signed a contract and hit .310 for Trenton that season. After a year with Jersey City, he was the top shortstop in the American Association for the Minneapolis Millers where he hit .285 in both 1949 and 1950. Bill began 1951 with the Oakland Oaks and came to San Diego for seven games before being sold to his hometown St. Louis Browns. His most memorable game was as the Brownie's shortstop in 1951.

"I was only a Padre for a short time, but I was at Oakland before coming to San Diego. I was on option from the then New York Giants. After being in San Diego a week or so, the Giants sold me to the St. Louis Browns. My small contribution to the Browns was that I was the Browns shortstop in the game Eddie Gaedel, the midget, was inserted by Bill Veeck, as in wreck.

I don't think anybody knew that was going to happen and I don't even remember him getting out of the cake. He didn't want to hit. I heard Veeck told him that he'd shoot him if he even swung. Bob Cain (Detroit pitcher) didn't want to hit him and, of course, he had a very small strike zone. I just saw Jim Delsing a few weeks ago up in Quincy (Illinois) where we went for a Major League Alumni golf outing. We got rained out and that was the beginning of the flooding here in the Midwest. Well, Jim ran for the midget after Bob walked him. I heard it said that he (Gaedel) was a feisty little bugger. He was drinking and got in a fight up in Chicago. When they went to his place the next day, he was dead. But, back to his appearance in the game, it happened so fast, it was over before we really knew what was happening. They didn't put him in the record book at first.

A lot happened to me in 1951. I got off to a good start with Oakland. I hit three home runs in one game against L.A.. My daughter was born and I'd never seen her, so my wife flew out to Oakland. But then I went to San Diego, but I was only there for about a week and the Browns bought me. We moved in with my parents (in St. Louis) and there wasn't much room. Rogers Hornsby was

Earl Rapp (left) and Bill Jennings.

the manager of the Browns and they sold me to Toronto. You weren't making any money back then. (Toronto owner) Jack Kent Cook wouldn't give me what I was asking. I wanted $6,000 and he'd only give $5,000. I finished up with Charleston and my second daughter came along, so with a family to support, I had to get out of baseball.

Mel Ott was our manager at Oakland. I remember seeing Mel and Lefty O'Doul have a home run hitting contest one night before a game with San Francisco. Lefty was San Francisco's manager. Augie Galan was on the Oaks at the time with Jim Marshall, Piper Davis, Ray Lamanno, Lloyd Christopher, Wes Bailey, Ken Burkhart and others I can't remember right now, Oh yeah, Bill Ayers and Lloyd Hittle. Here is a picture of me and Earl Rapp taken in Oakland in 1951. That's me on the right and Earl on the left. He was a really nice guy. He was a good hitter and a good ballplayer. Those were the times. We didn't make much money, but they were good times.

Jack Graham was with the Giants when I traveled with the team before I signed. He and all the Giants, as I remember, were all a good bunch of guys and didn't give a youngster a hard time. Come to think of it, Jack and the guys were youngsters themselves. It might be a little different today. Just look at the way they dress to go to a ball game now compared to how they used to get dressed up. Now they wear their baseball caps backwards! It's all changed so much. When I was with the Giants, it was pretty heady stuff for me to be eating across the table with Ernie Lombardi. They were great guys - great times.

I was with Minneapolis in '49 and '50. Tommy Heath was the manager. I think he was from Ventura (California). We had Hoyt Wilhelm, Jack Harshman and Ray Dandridge (elected to the Baseball Hall of Fame in 1987 on the basis of his outstanding career in the Negro Leagues). He was, physically, the worse looking player you'd ever seen. He must have had polio when he was young, but he was all shoulders. His glove was like a pancake without a pocket, but he could catch anything and he'd just float the ball. He was a real ballplayer and he never got a chance to play in the majors."

DICK FABER, outfield.
BORN: 7-13-28   PADRES: 1952-55

Dick Faber is the nephew of Hall of Famer, "Red" Faber, but he had to convince his father to let him play baseball in his senior year at Orange High School. Given the opportunity to play, he was chosen for the All-Southern California Interscholastic Prep Team. In 1948, Dick hit a home run in his first professional game and went on to bat .303 for San Bernardino in the Sunset League. Faber averaged .293 over the next three seasons in the Western International League and became the first player in the PCL to sign an Open Classification contract with San Diego in January 1952. That year his 21 sacrifice hits led the team. He made a catch in 1953 that was described by Lefty O'Doul as, "the greatest thing I've seen in forty years of baseball. I've seen 'em all, the best, and not even DiMaggio could have done it better." Faber hit .254 with 19 home runs and 92 RBIs in 1953.

"Winning the pennant was great! Bob Kerrigan won that game and we all got rings. I still wear mine all the time. Years later, I was at Knott's Berry Farm and a man asked if I was Dick Faber. He was from San Diego and he recognized me. We talked baseball and it was wonderful. But another memory with San Diego was helping Herb Gorman off the field when he died. That was a shock!

The first time I went to spring training with Lefty O'Doul in Ontario, he called a meeting. He said, 'Sit down, boys. I want to talk to you. Managers are all pricks, but (holding his index finger close to his thumb) I'm gonna be a little one.' He said, 'You guys can do whatever you want after the ball games, but you'd better give it all you've got in the games!'

Dick Faber

Jimmie Reese was quite a man. I've got a picture frame that he made for me. He was a magician with the fungo bat. I remember one day - we were at Lane Field - I was out there fielding grass. Jimmie was hitting fungos to the pitchers. He could lead them perfect. They'd run and just get to the ball, but they had to run. Theolic Smith was catching for Jimmie and he wanted to hit. He took one swing and broke Jimmie's fungo. Jimmie chased him and I thought he'd kill him. He was like a father. He was always so concerned about the ballplayers.

Dick Aylward was our catcher and he could really throw. Lloyd Dickey was a left-handed pitcher. I'd tell him he'd better get out of the way when Aylward was throwing to second.

I had great respect for Bill Starr. He treated me fine. I was the first player to sign when the PCL became an Open Classification. That meant the big leagues couldn't draft me; they'd have to buy me. I got a two year contract and a percentage of my contract when they'd sell me.

I originally was owned by Sacramento. I went to spring training with the L.A. Angels in Fullerton. My dad knew an umpire in the PCL and he contacted somebody with the Sacramento Solons. They offered me a contract before L.A. did and it was a better contract, too. I'm from Orange and they sent me to Anaheim. The team was only there for a month when it moved to San Bernardino.

Then I went to the Western International League with Wenatchee and Tri-Cities up in Washington. They sold me to the New York Yankees who wanted me to play in Norfolk (Virginia) which was clear across the country. The scouts all said the Western International was a better league, but the Yankees wanted me closer so they could watch me. Within two weeks, I got a call from Hugh Luby who was the manager of Salem (Oregon). We negotiated a contract on the phone and I got a third of the sales price when I was sold to San Diego. Hugh put together two all-star teams and we'd barnstorm after the season and split the gate. I made fifty bucks a game - that was a pile of money - but we sure had fun.

When (general manager Ralph) Kiner moved the Padre spring training to Palm Springs, the players were sent a letter - it was in March 1956 - that if their families came along, they should stay with the team at the Pueblo Hotel where it cost $8.50 for two people, otherwise it'll be $10 at other places, as you see, the living conditions are rather high. It was suggested that players leave their families in San Diego.

One thing about the old Pacific Coast League, you didn't live out of a suitcase. You could unpack, because you were in a town for a week. Jack Graham was my roommate that first year. He's a very nice guy and he took me under his wing, because he was an older player and I was a young one.

RAY PERRY, outfield.
BORN: 12-23-20   DIED: 5-4-73   PADRES: 1952

Ray Perry was the consummate minor league ballplayer who dominated the statistics of the Pioneer, Western International, Far West, Cotton States, California and Three-I Leagues from the late Thirties until the middle Fifties. In 1948 and 1949, in addition to hitting over four-hundred and leading the Far West League in home runs, he was also the league's vice president and the president, general manager, field manager and third baseman for the Redding Browns! Perry hit 348 home runs during 17 years in the minor leagues. In 1951 he was the only minor league player Lefty O'Doul selected to tour Japan with his all-star team. Ray had played for O'Doul in San Francisco briefly before and after the war. Lefty gave the aging slugger a tryout with the Padres, but he could not stick with the team. Regardless, he went on to win three more home run titles for other teams. This interview was conducted with his daughter, Christine Perry.

"They really idolized my dad here in Redding (California). They called him 'The Little Buffalo.' (5-7", 175#) They came out to watch him hit home runs. The old-timers still talk about him. My dad was a manager and a coach for years.

Bill James, the author (*The Bill James Historical Baseball Abstract*), says my dad is his favorite minor league player, because he did everything so well. He hit a lot of home runs. He hit a good average. He could steal bases. He was a good fielder. He hit over four-hundred twice and he was always hitting over thirty home runs. Bill James says that Dad led his leagues in home runs for seven years in a row and that is a minor league record.

[1948	Redding	Far West League	36 home runs	.411]
[1949	Redding	Far West League	45 home runs	.404]
[1950	Redding	Far West League	44 home runs	.366]
[1951	Redding	Far West League	18 home runs	.349]
[1952	El Dorado	Cotton States League	15 home runs	.308]
[1953	Bakersfield	California League	36 home runs	.337]
[1954	Bakersfield	California League	37 home runs	.341]

Redding has become a real baseball town because of him. In the World Ladies Softball League, the Redding team has won the championship two years in a row in Australia. There are a lot of baseball and softball fields here. My dad was a true small town baseball hero. The town and the fans could really identify with him. That's the way baseball should be. It should be fun."

LEN OKRIE, catcher.
BORN: 7-16-23   PADRES: 1952

Len Okrie caught four years with the Washington Senators and Boston Red Sox. He came to the Padres as his playing career was winding down, but went on to

Ray Perry

Len Okrie

manage and coach for 25 years in the minors. He was later in the major leagues with the Red Sox and the Tigers. In the early Twenties, his father, Frank Okrie, pitched for Detroit. Following baseball, Len went into law enforcement and retired as a desk sergeant with the Cumberland County (North Carolina) Sheriff's Department.

"It was many years ago that I played in San Diego. That was a pretty good league and I enjoyed my stay there. I was sent by the Red Sox, because Lefty O'Doul was the manager and they thought he could help me with my hitting. He never tied the rope on me, but he'd have the rope going through the batting cage on some of the guys. I didn't learn that much from him. Teddy (Williams) helped me more. He is a good guy and he would help everybody. He'd tell you to hit the top of the ball or hit the bottom of the ball. The rest of us were just glad to hit the ball, but he had such good eyes, he knew what part of the ball he was hitting. The sportswriters didn't like Ted, but the ballplayers did. When he'd hit, everything in the stadium would stop and even the peanut vendors would watch Ted Williams!

I signed with the Washington Senators for $5,000 a year in 1948. I was making $100 a month the year before in the Tri-State League, so I was in high cotton. Mr. (Tom) Yawkey gave me $18,000 a year with the Red Sox and that was the most I ever made, but even at that, it's tough to maintain two homes and I had to work in the winters.

I started managing with Blue Field, West Virginia and we won the playoffs. They said that I handled the kids well and I went up to the Red Sox and helped develop Carl Yaztremski with Pinky Higgins. The next year, (Dick) Williams came in. I went over to Detroit and was a coach for Mayo Smith. After baseball, I wanted to be a juvenile officer, but they made me a desk sergeant, because of my ability to deal with the public. I've been retired for six years, but they want me to come back as a bailiff. I'm thinking about it. I like to keep busy."

BEN FLOWERS, pitcher.
BORN: 6-15-27   PADRES: 1952

Bennett Flowers began playing professional baseball when he was 17 years old. The Red Sox sent Flowers to San Diego in 1952 and he responded with an 11-10 record for Lefty O'Doul's fifth place Padres. Ben returned to Boston the following season and later pitched for the Tigers, Cardinals and Phillies in 1955 and 1956. The Denver Bears won the 1957 Junior World Series over the Buffalo Bisons. Flowers was the winning pitcher in the series opener and again in the championship game.

"It (playing in San Diego) was probably one of the best years we had. We lived in Mission Beach. Back then, the salaries weren't high. We were looking for an apartment at the beach, but they were expensive. Finally we saw this one place. It was beautiful. It had a huge garage with brand new apartments above it. I went in and the woman said it was $350 a month. I told her, 'I'm here playing baseball.' She called her husband and said, 'How does $150 sound?' Her husband was Fred Neyenesch. He owned a printing company. They were sure good to us. They had a box and took us to Del Mar (race track). They took us to that hotel with the bar on the top (El Cortez). Their daughters played with our daughter. My wife liked the sunbathing. It was wonderful.

I was in Birmingham before I went to San Diego. I didn't care for the manager. He was always telling me how to pitch: over the top, sidearm, over the top. When I heard I was going to San Diego, honestly, I called Joe Cronin. I said, 'That's a long way from North Carolina.' He said, 'I'd rather see you go up than go down.' Well, I went to San Diego and won four straight games.

We were up in Portland. I had a couple brothers who lived in Grand Coulee, Washington. They came to watch. I had a no-hitter going for 6 innings and 3-2 on the batter. Lefty yelled, 'Don't walk him. Make him hit it!' The guy got a single. That was the only hit. That was one time I wish Lefty hadn't said anything."

We had the oldest pitching staff in the world (at San Diego with Al Benton who was 41, Jack Salveson 38 and Bob Malloy 34)). Theolic Smith was a nice guy. Memo Luna was a nice guy, too. He didn't have real command of English, but we could talk.

We were up in Sacramento and Jack Graham rented a plane. I'd just got my license and he said, 'Don't you want to take it yourself?'

One big memory I have was the first time I went in to pitch (in the major leagues.) It was in 1951 at Yankee Stadium. It was Joe

Bennett Flowers

DiMaggio's last year and Mickey Mantle was just getting started. Rizzuto was at short and Johnny Mize was on first. Old country boy comin' in. You don't think I was nervous? I shut 'em out for 3 innings!

I came back to the Coast League and a couple years later, they brought Hawaii into the league. I wish they'd done that when I was there."

◆◆◆

ALLEN RICHTER, shortstop.
BORN: 2-7-27   PADRES: 1952

Former "Gashouse Gang" utility man, "Specs" Toporcer, signed Allen Richter to his first professional contract with the Boston Red Sox organization in 1946. He was the top fielding shortstop for the Eastern League in 1948 and 1949. Al's best year with the bat came in 1951 when he hit .321 for the Louisville Colonels of the American Association. This performance earned him a late season promotion to the Sox. The following year, Richter was turning double plays in San Diego before he returned to Boston in 1953.

"I refused to go back to Louisville, so they sent me out to the Coast. You were like a slave back then. It's not like that today, but we did have fun. I was there (San Diego) in '52 with Lefty O'Doul and Jimmie Reese. Lefty O'Doul

Allen Richter

- what a colorful guy! A fun guy! He introduced Joe DiMaggio to Marilyn Monroe. When we'd play in Hollywood or L.A., Harry James, the trumpet player, or the guy who played Jackie Gleason's neighbor in *The Honeymooners* would always be in the clubhouse. Lefty knew 'em all.

Chuck Connors was the first baseman for the Angels. Another character! They'd have him do *Casey at the Bat* wherever he went. A casting director heard him one day and gave him a tryout. That's how he got to be *The Rifleman*.

We had a good team and I liked the Coast League. The cities were excellent and the schedule was terrific. You'd play one team for a week and have a doubleheader on Sunday with Mondays off.

We had a second baseman named Lou Klein. After every night game, he'd go out on those fishing boats. He'd sleep and they'd wake him up when they got to the fish. Lou would get 18 or 20 pound yellowtail and albacore and have 'em smoked. Between games in the doubleheader, he'd bring out his smoked fish and we'd have crackers to go with it. Normally you don't like to play doubleheaders, but we looked forward to it just for Lou's fish. I learned to fish in San Diego. That was the only time I ever fished.

There were a lot of characters on that team: Bob Malloy, Jack Graham, good guys. We were flying from San Diego to San Francisco. Jack Tobin was obstinate and enjoyed giving people a hard time in jest. The stewardess said, 'You'll have to button your seat belt.' Jack said, 'I've flown 10,000 hours and I don't have to use a seat belt!' She got somebody to come back and talk to him. Finally, he latched his seat belt. He was just giving her a hard time. I remember him claiming to have flown 10,000 hours. What difference would that make? We had a good team and a lot of fun."

◆◆◆

MEMO LUNA, pitcher.
BORN: 6-25-30   PADRES: 1952-53

Memo Luna was a brilliant young prospect from Mexico. In 1950, he won fourteen games for Ciudad Juarez in the Arizona-Texas League. The following season, he was the top pitcher for Tijuana in the Southwestern International League while posting a 26-13 record, a league leading 318 strikeouts and a 2.52 ERA. Luna fulfilled his promise by winning 32 games during his two years with the Padres. His 2.67 ERA in 1953 was the lowest in the Pacific Coast League. Based on this performance, Bill Starr sold him to St. Louis in 1954. Denied the opportunity to pitch in the major leagues, he returned to his homeland to finish his career. Memo is one of four PCL Padres enshrined in the

Guillermo LUNA
PADRE PITCHER

Memo Luna

"Salon de la Fama del Beisbol" (Baseball Hall of Fame) in Mexico. Other Lane Field Padres so honored are Claudio Solano, Jose Bache and Jesse Flores.

"You searched for Memo Luna. Now you have found him. I have lived in Los Mochis, Sinaloa (Mexico) for many years. It is very pretty like San Diego where I had my best years as a pitcher in my life. My job here is training many boys in baseball. I have a school for all ages. I am no longer the young man who played some time with San Diego and with St. Louis, but I still get on the mound and I pitch a few games with the young guys and the veterans.

The seasons that I spent with the Padres were my best. Lefty O'Doul was a great guy to me. He gave me a lot of advice and thus was a great manger to me. We never had any problems even though he spoke no Spanish. My catcher was Lonnie Summers. He was Black and spoke Spanish, because he played in Mexico for a long time as did Theolic Smith and Quincy Trouppe. [During the Second World War, Mexico "traded" 80, 000 workers to the United States for Negro League stars Theolic Smith and Quincy Trouppe to play in Mexico. Smith was later a Padre pitcher. -Ed] Theolic, John Davis and Tom Alston were very good friends of mine.

I remember Lonnie was giving the signals and I was pitching a good game. Then he wanted a curve ball, but

I shook my head. He kept showing a curve and I kept shaking my head. Lonnie called 'Time' and came out to the mound. I said, 'I want to throw a fast ball', but he said it was Lefty who wanted the curve. I told him, 'I'm on the mound.' I threw a fast ball and stuck him out. When I went to the dugout, Lefty said, 'I won't call your pitches any more.' Lefty was great.

Lonnie and I were in the bullpen and we saw something was wrong with Herb (Gorman). We called to the dugout and went out on the field just as Herb fell into our arms. I think he died before he got to the dugout.

In San Diego, I lived in the Hotel San Diego, but first I lived in Tijuana. Then Immigration would not let me go to Tijuana anymore and I was permitted to stay in San Diego.

When I arrived with the St. Louis Cardinals, my arm was hurt. That is why I couldn't play in more games. Also, I had the bad luck that the manager of the St. Louis Cardinals was Eddie Stanky. He didn't like Mexicans. That is why he didn't want me on the team and he only let me have 2/3 of an inning. Racist!

Today, we Mexicans have more opportunities and make more money, but before the major leagues were stronger and better. There were only eight teams in each league. Now it is more like Double A even though there are some good players, but very few."

LOU STRINGER, 2b, 3b, outfield.
BORN: 5-13-17   PADRES: 1952-53

While playing second base for the Los Angeles Angels in 1947, Lou Stringer set a Pacific Coast League record by handling 353 consecutive chances without an error. The streak spanned 64 straight games. Previously, Lou was a member of the Chicago Cubs from 1941 through 1946 with the middle years served in the Army Air Forces. As the Opening Day rookie shortstop for the Cubs in 1941, the smooth fielding Stringer established a major league record with 4 errors in his first game. That same year, he also led National League second sackers in assists. Hitting .333 in 1948, he was appointed manager of the seventh place Hollywood Stars and the team responded by playing .500 ball for the remaining thirty games of the season. Stringer returned to the majors with Boston at the end of the season and remained with the Sox through 1950. He came to San Diego from the Stars in 1952 and went to San Francisco in 1953.

"Let's see, I was with 'Frisco in '54 and L.A. in '51, so I was with San Diego and Frank (Lefty O'Doul) in '52 and '53. I went to Japan with O'Doul and we had quite a team: Ferris Fain was on first, Billy Martin on second, Alan Strange was shortstop and I was third. (Joe) Tipton was behind the plate and the outfield was all the DiMaggio Boys (Joe, Dom and Vince). (Mel) Parnell and (Bobby) Shantz, oh hell, I can't remember all the pitchers. Chuck Stevens and Al Lyons went, because they were West Coast guys and Lefty knew them.

We played to over a million people and we only lost one game and that was because some of the guys had gotten drunk. I think it was about 1950 and the next year he took Joe DiMaggio's wife (Marilyn Monroe), too. It was a lot of fun and they treated us real well in Japan.

My record for consecutive chances got some write-ups. I imagine it's been broken by now. I had a little glove back then. In fact, I've still got it somewhere. I thought about having it bronzed or something. Jigger Statz cut the pocket out of his glove and I had mine cut out, too. He was my manager my first year in L.A. back in '39 and '40.

I remember when Dee Moore was with Hollywood. He got me good coming home. He was big and strong and mean, but he was a good guy. Well, a couple innings later, he was on first and I was turning a double play at second. I got the ball and I was looking for Dee. I was going to stick it in his ear, but he was out in right field giving me the finger.

I never made any money in baseball, but they treated me

good in San Diego with Lefty. It was a good league and I played in all the parks. I liked Lane Field, but I was a right-handed hitter. San Diego had some good ballplayers. Tom Alston was good and Jack Graham was sure good. He's a good guy, too."

CARL "BUDDY" PETERSON, shortstop.
BORN: 4-23-25   PADRES: 1952-55

Carl "Buddy" Peterson and Al Federoff formed one of the all-time best double play combinations in Pacific Coast League history. After serving in the U.S. Navy, Buddy began playing professional baseball in 1947 with Salem (Oregon). He batted over .300 for three consecutive years in the Western International League and came to the Padres where he averaged .289 over the next four seasons. Pete went to the White Sox and later the Orioles, but San Diego was always his favorite venue. He managed in the minors and recently retired as a scout after almost fifty years in baseball. Buddy should work for the San Diego Chamber of Commerce and Tourist Bureau.

"It was a thrill for me to be in San Diego. I always consider it to be the best place I ever played. I was lucky to be there when Lefty O'Doul and Jimmie Reese were there... Jimmie Reese and his legendary fungos. He'd hit me a hundred balls a day to make me into a major leaguer. I'd go out in the outfield with the pitchers and he'd hit

Lou Stringer

Buddy Peterson

fungos. He could hit them just beyond where you could catch them. I loved to run and I'd go after them. He could do anything with a fungo bat like hitting batting practice. He'd make a circle in center field and he could hit six out of ten in it. That's hard to do. Nobody disliked Jimmie.

We had a good team in '54: Bob Elliott, Milt Smith, Dick Faber and Al Federoff. He was an exceptionally good second baseman both as a player and a person. He never gave me a bad throw on a double play. Dick Aylward was a fine catcher with a great arm. He's gone now and so is Buster Mathis. Bob (Kerrigan) had one of the best moves to second base I ever saw. We picked off a lot of people together. He won the championship game. We had a heck of a ball club!

It was a fun time. I loved the beach and the weather. When I was sold to the big leagues to the White Sox, I was kind of let down. It (San Diego) was paradise to me and I really had second thoughts about going to the big leagues. I lived at the beach. Back then we played ball and never made a lot of money. We had fun. The whole scenario down there was wonderful! If I could have stayed in San Diego, that was good enough for me. The (major league) pension fund wasn't in effect and I'd have loved to have stayed there for all my playing days.

O'Doul should have been a major league manager. He was before his time. He didn't put pressure on the players. If you drink too much or fool around too much, you wouldn't be here very long anyhow. That was his philosophy. He never really had a curfew. He said to make your own curfew.

He and Jimmie Reese sent me to the big leagues and it really broke my heart. If I was optioned out, I was supposed to come back to San Diego. Luis Aparicio was ten years younger than me and, by God, they wouldn't let me go back to San Diego. I went to Memphis and it broke my heart. I said to (White Sox manager Marty) Marion, 'I don't want to go to Memphis.' Jesus, hell, Christ! I really wanted to go back to San Diego! I almost got suspended, but I really wanted to go back, but in those days, you pretty much had to go where they sent you. Oh my god, I knew I'd never get back. Every player dreams of going to the big leagues and I wanted to stay in San Diego. I loved the beach. I loved to sail on the bay. We'd sleep until ten or eleven and go to the game. I loved that place!"

AL FEDEROFF, second base.
BORN: 7-11-24   PADRES: 1953-57

The saying went, "You're better off with Federoff batting lead off." Al Federoff was the Padres Most Valuable Player in 1956

and a PCL All-Star in both 1954 and 1955. He established team records for second basemen with 480 putouts and 124 double plays during the '54 championship season. His 110 runs also led the PCL. Al is mentioned frequently as one of the premier pivot men in baseball during that era. Several seasons, he was the Padre leader in stolen bases and runs scored. Prior to coming to San Diego, Federoff played two years for the Detroit Tigers in 1951 and 1952. When his playing days were over, he continued to coach and manage in a baseball career that covered four decades. Al was Carolina League Manager of the Year at Rocky Mountain, North Carolina in 1969.

"We had a great year in '54. Bob Elliott hit those home runs and Bob Kerrigan pitched that championship game against Hollywood. That was one of the biggest moments for me in the Pacific Coast League. I'd much rather have stayed playing here in my home town (Detroit), but I enjoyed my stay in San Diego very much. We lived out in Mission Beach.

A lot of players were hoping to get sent out to the Coast, because there were many players making more money there than in the big leagues. We had some pretty good ballplayers at San Diego like Earl Rapp, Buddy Peterson... (Dick) Sisler and (Luke) Easter, but they

Al Federoff

Al Federoff and Ed Erautt

were at the end of their careers. Did you find Harry Elliott? He was a great competitor and a great hitter. Dick Faber was the best there was at the delayed steal of second base. And, Bill Wight, he had the best move in baseball that I ever saw. It was kind of a half-balk, but he picked off a lot of guys.

It's great just hearing the names of old teammates. I'd sure like to see my friends again. Lefty O'Doul was the manager and, of course, old Jimmie Reese was the coach. We were buddies. Everybody loved Jimmie. When I was managing at Portland in 1970, Jimmie was one of my coaches. Gene Lamont and Jim Leyland [Both became major league managers. -Ed.] played for me in the Tiger system. I played with Don Lund at Toledo in the American Association. I think he was a four-sport letterman at (University of) Michigan. I also played three winters in Cuba. That helped us a lot (financially).

There's nothing like baseball, but not everybody can be a big leaguer. I'm concerned about the game today. The fans should stay away for a year to let the owners and the players know, hey, you need us! What do you think? It's so different now."

EARL BRUCKER, Jr., catcher.
BORN: 8-29-25   PADRES: 1953

From the time he was a little boy, baseball was very important to Earle Brucker, Jr.. His father, Earle Brucker, a star athlete at San Diego High School, caught for Connie Mack's Athletics and later managed in the minor and major leagues. Young Earle was always at the ballpark and eventually, in 1948, like his father, caught for Mr. Mack's Athletics. Prior to that, he played for the Padre Juniors, Point Loma High School and San Diego State College baseball teams. Brucker retired after a thirty-year teaching career at Dana Junior High School in Point Loma.

"I went to spring training with the Padres in 1953. (Walt) Pocekay was the catcher. I got in a couple of games and think I'm a lifetime five-hundred hitter in the PCL. I knew I was leavin' when O'Doul used me to bunt and I went to Beaumont in the Texas League. They owned Pocekay's contract and they'd have to buy me, so I went instead.

I knew Bill Starr from back in St. Joe (St. Joseph, Missouri) in the Western Association in '34. He was back-up catcher to my dad. He'd catch batting practice with his hand behind his back. In those days, you kept your hand in front and when the ball hit your fingers, you'd just rub them in the dirt. I remember Starr because of that.

I was the Portland bat boy in '35 when they won the PCL Championship. Years later, we were in the middle of Oregon and I was paying for my gas with a credit card.

The old guy recognized my name and he told me all about his memories of that season.

I've got quite a memory of Lane Field. I was standing on second base for the Padre Juniors when they turned on the PA system and said the War had just started. It took away a double, so it was a bad war. Then I remember four P-38s broke through and they were already here from the Army Defense Command in Burbank to protect the Bay. We didn't see two-tailers down here, because we were used to seeing Navy planes. I think it took them about four minutes to get down here.

When I was fourteen, fifteen, sixteen, I would catch batting practice for the Philadelphia Athletics. They could also use me to warm-up pitchers and that saved a spot on the roster. The pitchers were nice and they'd let me take batting practice, too. I was always careful not to say too much or act like I was there because of my dad, so everybody was very nice to me. I caught batting practice

Earle Brucker

for the Yankees one time and Joe DiMaggio said, 'Hi ya, kid.' He knew my dad. (Charlie "King Kong") Keller was up next and said, 'I got the locker next to him and he's talked to you more today than he has to me since he got here.' Joe was probably saying it because he knew who my dad was. Joe was very shy.

I spent seven years in baseball. I would play in the Padre old-timers games, because they could always use a catcher. I think I was in about four of them and I think I batted five-hundred in them, too. Yes, I was one of their all-time great hitters. I probably played more games as a Padre Old-Timer than I did as a Padre!"

HELEN BINGHAM and OPHIE PERCY
"THE BASEBALL GIRLS"

"The Baseball Girls." Ophie Percy (center) and Helen Bingham. Phil Collier in background in Lane Field press box.

Helen Bingham and Ophie Percy were called the "Baseball Girls," because they sent and received the play-by-play accounts of Padre games for Western Union during the Fifties. At that time, the radio broadcasters only traveled with the team as far north as Los Angeles. They remained in the studio for the other road games and expanded on cryptic Western Union teletypes to recreate the action. With the sounds of cracking bats and cheering crowds, many fans did not realize the announcers were actually broadcasting from San Diego while the team was in a distant ballpark. Ronald Reagan got his start in broadcasting by recreating Chicago Cub games for the fans in Iowa.

(Helen) "I was working for Western Union. My boss came up and asked if I would do the play-by-play (for the Padres). I didn't know a strike from a ball. This guy I was dating took me to a softball game. The umpire called the batter out and I said, 'Out! He didn't even strike at it!' It was a pitch down the middle of the plate, but I didn't even know he had to swing. I went in dumb, but I learned about baseball.

The men didn't want us in the press box. They said, 'We're not having any girls up here! We want to talk like we want to.' I said, 'You guys are men. If you guys want to cuss, go ahead and cuss. If you want to tell dirty jokes, tell 'em and we'll listen to them.' We'd even have a beer or two with them and we fit in. When we left, they didn't want us to go. They were very nice guys. I enjoyed working up there.

I did the play-by-play and Ophie operated the printer. What I'd tell her, she'd print. I gave the basics and the announcers would fill in the rest. We provided the information to the announcers in the other cities. If somebody got hurt, the announcers would ask questions, because the wives would wonder how they were.

One time, there was a fire out by the scoreboard. A telephone pole caught on fire and the lights on the scoreboard went out. The fire department had to come and they had to put the fire out before the game started.

When the team (Padres) was on the road, I'd go to the radio station. Sometimes, there were problems on the telegraph lines and I'd have to talk on the phone to the operators in the other cities. I'd have to repeat everything for the announcers and they'd ad lib while I was getting the information for them.

Al Schuss was a very nice guy. One time, I thought there was a mistake and I changed it. Al just gave me a look. He had a bat and he'd hit a piece of wood. It sounded like a baseball being hit. The thing I remember about him was I'd go out for a hamburger between games in a doubleheader and I'd ask him if he wanted anything. He'd say, 'No,' but every time he'd share my hamburger and french fries!"

(Ophie) "We really had a good time (doing the Padre games). At first, the men didn't want us there, because we were female and they wouldn't feel free to talk and swear like all men do. But we didn't pay attention to them and once they got to know us, they were great.

The man who did it before us was going to retire and there weren't any other men at Western Union to go. We said, 'We can't do it!' But our boss told us we should try and I'm glad we did. It was a nice experience.

Earl Keller really opposed our being there, but finally accepted us. Years later, I ran into him at the super market and discovered we lived a block from each other in Point Loma. We became good friends. He was a super, great person and I will miss him. My husband and I saw him and his wife in October 1995 about three weeks before he died. He was a caring person and I am fortunate to have known him.

When the team was out of town, we'd go down to the radio station. We never met the operators or announcers in the other cities, but we became friends. Just before a game started in Los Angeles, the announcer on KTLA said, 'I'm going to dedicate a song to one of the 'Baseball Girls' in San Diego.' He played a song called 'Ophelia.' I didn't even know there was a song named Ophelia. I don't remember who named us the 'Baseball Girls', but that's what everybody called us.

I would type everything Helen said on the telex machine. I would be typing away. If there was a fight, we'd tell who was in it and the announcers could really make the fights very exciting. All I'd type was so-and-so was in a fight and the umpire came in. I have fond memories of our working days at Lane Field."

WALT POCEKAY, outfield, catcher.
BORN: 6-4-29   PADRES: 1953-54

Walt Pocekay was primarily an outfielder, but he is credited with playing an important role in the 1954 Padres' championship drive by filling in admirably behind the plate during the pennant stretch. Walt starred for Ty Cobb's West team in the 1946 Esquire All-America Boys' Game when he collected four hits in a 10-4 victory. He set a league record by going 7-for-7 with Wenatchee on June 21, 1951. The following year, Pocekay led the Western International League with a .352 batting average. Remarkably consistent, he batted .279 and .281 during his two seasons in San Diego.

It was a lot of fun to play in San Diego and Lefty O'Doul was great. He would let you hit on a three-oh count if you got a good pitch and you took a good swing. It wouldn't matter, even if you made an out, because he wanted you up there hitting. If you swung at a bad pitch, he'd flip! Lefty used to say, 'There's no curfew, but if you can't get a gal by midnight or one o'clock, forget it, you ain't gonna get her.'

Tom Alston was a real nice guy. One time, Lloyd Dickey and I were watching Lefty work with him in batting practice. Lefty was trying to get Tom to lay back and he tied a rope on him. Jimmie Reese was feeding Iron Mike (the pitching machine) and he missed getting a ball in. Tom took a complete swing, but there was no ball. Lefty started yelling! 'What are you swinging at? What are you swinging at? That's what I'm talking about!' Poor Tom couldn't say anything. Lloyd and I just laughed.

I remember one night in Sacramento. Harry Elliott got mad at O'Doul. I don't know what it was about. Harry hit a home run the next day. You know how Lefty would greet you and slap you on the back around third. Harry ran right past him and Lefty really flipped!

I did hit a home run with the bases loaded in '54 to beat Hollywood, so I guess I did do something to help the team. O'Doul used me mostly for utility and pinch hitting. I did pinch hit a lot in '54. I only caught one year in Wenatchee in '52 and thought it might be a way I could move up. I've still got a ball from Lloyd Dickey that I caught for the final strike in a game he pitched that year.

Earl Rapp was a helluva hitter. You can't tell me there were many guys in the big leagues who could hit better than him. You can't believe how good he was with an one-oh or two-one (count). I remember that day when Ted Beard hit four home runs in one game at Lane Field. He wasn't very big and, of course, he was a left-handed hitter.

Luke Easter wasn't playing that much in '54 and we were up at Seals Stadium. There was an exhibition before the game and he was hitting 'em out of the ballpark. I don't care how big he was, that was not an easy park to hit a ball out of. And I remember Bob Elliott hitting those two home runs in the final game against Hollywood. He joined us in the middle of the year and he went up to the plate to hit. He didn't fool around. I can see why he was the MVP in the National League in '47.

I caught Memo Luna and he was a good pitcher. He had a knuckle ball that I hated to catch. When it was sinking,

Walt Pocekay

nobody could hit it and I mean DiMaggio or Williams. It was just unhitable. Well, he was ahead with an oh-two and I signaled for it. I never even got a glove on it. I don't remember if I got to the ball before the runner got to first. You couldn't hit it... or catch it!

Another time, it was against Portland, and I was hitting. It was one of their left-handers. I had two strikes and it broke. I couldn't have hit it with a paddle. How the hell are you going to hit a pitch like that?"

◆◆◆

LLOYD DICKEY, pitcher.
BORN: 9-18-29   DIED: 1-17-98   PADRES: 1953-56

Lloyd Dickey went 8-10 for the last place San Francisco Seals in 1951. The following year, the rangy left-hander hit .282 for the Indianapolis Indians, but his pitching record was 5-9. In three seasons with San Diego, Dickey was a dependable pitcher (28-31) whose best season was 1954 when he won 14, lost 11 and posted a 2.69 ERA. Lloyd was traded to Seattle early in 1956.

"I didn't come to San Diego until '53. Bob (Kerrigan) and I were together with Cleveland. When they released me, I quit and went home until Lefty (O'Doul) bought me. I'd played for Lefty with the San Francisco Seals. When I came to San Diego, they had Tom Alston and Memo Luna. They were sold to St. Louis for $100,000. Memo Luna was

Lloyd Dickey

the star of the staff. He had excellent control and led the PCL in earned run average that year (1953). Alston was a good hitter and, of course, we had Earl Rapp, too.

Lefty used to have fungo hitting contests. He'd give $50 to the guy who could put the most out of the park. He loved to give his money away. When we were on the road, he always stayed in a different place than the players, like in Hollywood. He was famous - a celebrity. He was a nice guy.

Harry Elliott was a different kind of guy. He wasn't afraid of anybody. He'd push Luke Easter out of the batting cage when he wanted to hit. You know how big Luke was!

I tell Bob (Kerrigan) that he won the (championship) ring for us. We thought we'd get a few bucks out of it (winning the regular season), but I don't think we got $350 and we lost in the playoffs. It was a letdown after the Hollywood game. We knew we had to win that one game. We had a slow team, but our pitching was good. At the end of the season, Cliff Fannin and Ed Erautt had sore arms. Al Lyons, who came from San Francisco, was an outfielder and a reliever. He did a lot of relief and saved us a few.

Bill Wight was a helluva pitcher. I think he was something like eighteen and four that year. [17-5 -Ed.] I pitched the short game of the double header we won to set up the game with Hollywood. And then Bob came in and won it! I told him, 'You pitch hard enough to pitch every day.' There weren't many guys left to pitch and Lefty liked to use left-handers at Lane Field."

◆◆◆

JOHN MERSON, infielder.
BORN: 1-17-22   PADRES: 1953-56

John was a versatile player for manager Lefty O'Doul, because he could be used for all of the infield positions. Merson enjoyed his best season with the bat for the Padres when he hit .282 in 1955. After John's graduation from high school in 1940, Joe Cambria signed the youngster to a professional contract with the Washington Senators and he was sent to Newport (KY) in the Appalachian League. After military service, Jack's impressive numbers with Uniontown (PA), York (PA), New Orleans and Indianapolis earned promotion to the major leagues. His final years in organized baseball were with the San Diego Padres.

"I had some good times out there in San Diego and I made the same money as in the majors. I wanted to play regularly, but when I got my chances I always did my best. My family had a great time. We lived at Mission Beach and had three kids at the time. They would get brown from playing at the beach all summer. Mrs. Robinson would call us to see if we were coming and she'd go live with her daughter. We lived at her place for four years.

Jimmie Reese was a wonderful friend. We'd go out to eat together after a road game. We'd go to their room and Old Cookie (Les Cook) always had a bottle of ET... Early Times. Jimmie used to say, 'Always drink it with water; you'll last longer.' He was right. He lived to be over 90 years old. It was good to experience life with him.

Jimmie had a place in Hollywood and he lived in the granny flat behind it. The people in the front had a little girl named Bonnie. She was about four and my wife was having our fourth child. It was at the end of the '56 season and we'd come home. One day, a big package came and it was a stroller, a crib and a high chair. It was Bonnie's and Jimmie sent it clear across the country for us. We used them for our fifth child, too and then for the grand kids. That's the kind of man that Jimmie was. I'd always go see him when the Angels would play the Orioles.

I got in good straits with Lefty (O'Doul). It was a tight game and he puts on the squeeze. I picked up the sign and laid down a good bunt. He said, 'Hot damn, Johnny, that was great' and he'd always say how I picked up that sign. Old Lefty was great.

He hated it if the pitchers would throw a strike when they were ahead. He'd fine the pitchers if they put it in

Jack Merson

John Merson

too close to hit on an oh-two. When you were batting and you got a good pitch, he didn't care what the count was. He wanted you hitting and if you made an out, he wouldn't get mad. He was the best manager I ever had.

Another thing I remember about Lefty was when he'd hit during batting practice. He was in his fifties, but he'd pick up a bat and hit the ball to the fence. He could hit the ball anywhere and your job was to get out of the way.

Ed Erautt and I were good friends. People didn't think Ed liked to talk, but he did. He's a real straight shooter. Now if Bill Wight was standing next to a light pole, you'd hear more from that light bulb than you would from Bill. He was really quiet! Ed and I liked old Theolic (Smith) and convinced him to go to dinner with us. We just asked him, 'Are you hungry? Then let's go.' He played in Mexico before African-Americans could play in the U.S.. He was a nice guy, a laid-back guy, very humorous and he laughed a lot. He liked to win and was a good pitcher. We had a lot of camaraderie back then. There were cliques, but everybody got along.

We had a good ball club in '54 and had that championship game with Hollywood. Everybody was wondering who the devil is gonna pitch this game? Then Lefty asks Bob (Kerrigan) how he feels. Bob said he wasn't feeling good, but he'd try. Lefty said, 'You're my pitcher' and Bob said, 'I'll get 'em!' It was quite a shock. He pitched a great game and old Bob Elliott hit a couple of home runs. It was great. I have my ring, but don't wear it very much, because I'm not a ring kind of guy.

Dick Faber was a good guy. He lived in Ocean Beach and he'd pick me up for the game and take me home. We'd talk about the game when we were driving. We had so much fun in those days. We were close to the fans and the kids. We signed autographs and talked with the kids. Everything starts with the kids. They'd save cards and we'd sign them. If they don't start treating the kids proper, they'll lose them and that's what's wrong with baseball today. You've got to be good to the kids.

I remember when my boys were in Little League. The manager of another team used to be the bullpen catcher for the Orioles. Not the major league Orioles, but back in the International League days. You know how you always put the worst kid in right field. One day, a ball went out to his right fielder. The kid missed the ball and threw it to the wrong base. Three runs scored and the manager came out of the dugout heading for right field. The kid was trying to hold it in, but he could keep it any longer after the manager was screaming at him and be broke into tears in the dugout. That manager ruined baseball for that kid by treating him that way and he was a ballplayer himself. He should have known you don't treat kids like that.

When I was a kid, all I ever wanted to be was a baseball player. I practiced and practiced. I'd throw a tennis ball against the side of our home for hours. When it would start getting dark, I'd throw it up in the air and keep catching it until it was too dark to see. My teacher said, 'Jack Merson, you could be an A student if you'd study, but all you want to do is play baseball.' It was my dream to be a major leaguer and I made it.

My best day was in 1951 when I went up with the Pirates. I had 4-for-6 and drove in 6 runs. It was against Brooklyn and it was their last trip into Pittsburgh. We beat 'em 11-4 or 11-6 and that was the year Bobby Thompson hit 'the shot heard round the world' when the Giants beat the Dodgers in that playoff game. I felt I had a little something to do with them ending up in a tie. In fact, I led the National League in hitting that year, but I didn't have enough plate appearances (.360 BA, 18 hits in 50 ABs).

I've got a scrapbook from every year I played. My father would subscribe to the paper from the town and cut out every article and put it in an envelope. When we'd get home at the end of the year, we'd put them in scrapbooks. I started in 1940 with Newport in the Appalachian League. I was with Uniontown, PA in '47 and hit .388. I went to York, PA and then Indianapolis and hit .390. I hit .290 at New Orleans and I was in Nashville when Del Ballinger went into that flooded dugout and came out with the ball. He was a very funny guy. I remember when (manager Hal) Luby wanted him to pinch hit, but he couldn't find him in the dugout. A little while later, we hear these spikes coming down the cement and it was Del. He had cobwebs on his cap. He'd been under the stands looking up women's dresses. Players liked to do that.

I remember some advice from old Doc Jurgenson, the trainer at Pittsburgh. He used to say. 'You gotta be good to the people you meet on the way up, because you'll meet them on your way down.' In my day, we'd almost pay them (the owners) to play baseball. I played with great guys. I can't say that I met more than half a dozen guys I didn't like.

I never forgot something that happened in my first game in the big leagues. We were playing in Boston. You remember old Earl Torgeson, the first baseman. I got a base hit and I'm standing on first. He says, 'Hey, kid. Move over, I gotta to straighten the bag.' I said, 'Kiss my ass. Throw the ball back.' He grinned and threw it back to the pitcher. I'll never forget how he tried to show me up. The next time we played them and I got on first, I said, 'Hey, Torgey, got the ball in your glove?'

Old Campanella used to spit on your shoes. He was a nice guy, but he'd do anything to try to get your mind off hitting. Funny how you remember those things...

JOHN ROMONOSKY, pitcher.
BORN: 7-7-29   PADRES: 1954

John Romonosky pitched for San Diego during the first half of the 1954 championship season. The previous year he was with the St. Louis Cardinals and he later returned to the major leagues with the Washington Senators in 1958 and 1959. Some of his most vivid memories are playing "beisbol" in Latin America.

"I went out to San Diego with Dick Sisler and Bob Elliott. We were optioned out by St. Louis. I was only there for half the season. I was just there for two or two and a half months and I went back to Columbus (Redbirds, Cardinal farm team in the American Association). I enjoyed playing for Lefty O'Doul who was one of the greatest managers in baseball. He was a great hitter! He hit three ninety-something in the big leagues. (.398 for the Phillies in 1929) And Jimmie Reese. Everybody says he was the greatest fungo hitter in baseball. He'd work out with the pitchers. He'd start you running and you'd never break stride. You'd just run full speed and the ball was there. He was still coaching for the Angels when he was in his nineties! He'd be at home plate and hit line drives to the guy covering second base. Can you imagine being able to do that?

I started in Fresno and made $150 a month... $35 a week! That was 1949 and I won 18 games and was named Rookie of the Year. I got a 100% pay raise... $300 a month and said 'I'm on my way.'

I played in the bad times in the South. The black players couldn't stay or eat with us. We'd have to take them their box lunches and they'd catch a cab to the games. I ended up in Nashville and they never had a black player and that was 1961. There weren't any black players in the Southern Association.

John Romonosky

I was playing in Cuba when Castro took over. He stopped us from playing baseball for a week. After five days, he figured he had things under control. He came to some of games. There were soldiers in the bullpens and in the dugout. You were always looking down the barrel of an M-1, but if an American hit a home run, they'd carry him around the field on their shoulders. They loved baseball. We played all our games in Havana and won the league.

We went to the Caribbean World Series. We had Tommy Lasorda, Mike Cuellar, Camilo Pascual, Bob Allison, Sandy Amoros, Tony Taylor, Jim Baxes and Dick Brown. We could take two or three players from the other teams, so we took Minnie Minoso. Camilo Pascual beat Juan Marichal, 1-0 and we went to Caracas. 35,000 people would watch the games. When we beat Caracas, we had difficulty getting to the airport. They threw bricks and smashed the back window of our limousine. They were throwing rocks, but Castro gave us a nice parade when we got to Cuba.

I went to spring training with Memo Luna in 1954. He was a pretty good left-handed pitcher with good control. I also played for Guadalajara in '54. Charlie Lau, Whitey Herzog, Gene Bearden and Jungle Jim Rivera were on that team. I remember playing in Los Mochis. That ball park never had a blade of grass. They took a water truck and sprayed it every night. They sprayed the streets, too. Roland LeBlanc was our manager and I enjoyed hunting and fishing with him on our days off."

DICK AYLWARD, catcher.
BORN: 6-4-25   DIED: 6-11-83   PADRES: 1954-56

Throughout baseball, base runners were reluctant to try to pilfer a base on the man known as "The Arm." If only Dick Aylward could have hit a little better, he surely would have been a fixture behind the plate for some major league team. He appeared briefly

Dick Aylward

with the Cleveland Indians in 1953 and they optioned him to San Diego. Aylward hit .189, .227 and .262 in his three seasons with the Padres, but his fielding average in 1954 was a perfect 1.000. Dick's teammates from the '54 PCL Championship Padres, Bob Kerrigan, Ed Erautt and Buddy Pe-

terson discussed Aylward's value when they visited together on July 11, 1995.

[Peterson] "Aylward kept the pitchers on track; he had a knack. He was the greatest catcher and the worst hitter I ever saw! There's no way he shouldn't have been a second-string defensive catcher in the major leagues. When he threw, the ball was on the bag. He was a good friend and we had some good times together."

[Kerrigan] "If I had my druthers, I'd rather have Dick behind the plate than anybody else. He was the best catcher I ever had!"

[Erautt] "What an arm! When you were on the mound and there was a runner on first, you'd better be ready to duck when Dick threw to second. The ball was coming right at you! One time, Carlos Bernier of Hollywood was stealing and Aylward's throw hit him in the helmet. That's when Hollywood was starting to wear helmets. The throw was so hard it split the helmet! We called him 'The Arm.' Dick could really throw."

ED ERAUTT, pitcher.
BORN: 9-26-24   PADRES: 1954-57

Young Eddie Erautt was pitching for Hollywood and Salem (Western International League) in 1942. He served in the Infantry with the Army from 1943 to 1945 and saw action in the Pacific. Ed blossomed with the Stars in 1946 by leading the PCL with 234 strikeouts and posting a 20-14 record. He spent most of the next five seasons with the Cincinnati Reds and led the American Association by going 21-5 for the Kansas City Blues in 1952. Erautt was later traded to the Cardinals and came to San Diego as part of the Memo Luna deal in 1954. He was 16-12 (3.12 ERA) during that championship season and 18-10 (2.76 ERA) for the Padres the next year.

Eddie Erautt, Jr. checks his Dad's muscle as John Merson looks on.

Ed Erautt pitching.

"Johnny Pesky was the clubhouse boy in Portland, then my brother and then me. They didn't sign any of us. Six bucks a week is what they paid. Do you know who was the visiting clubhouse boy? Mickey Lolich. I pitched in a semi-pro game when I was twelve-years old and we won, 4-1. Legion Ball was very important. You had to play Legion Ball. One year we couldn't get any sponsors, so every kid put up five dollars and we called ourselves 'The Kamm Kids,' because we played at Kamm Field. We made it all the way to the Western Finals and seven guys off that team went on to play professional ball. A lot of people wished they had been our sponsors after we went that far... but hockey is what we loved.

When I was a kid, there was an old guy who came to watch us play. He gave me a first baseman's glove from the Black Sox. He was a utility player and his name was Joe Berger. He introduced the curve ball to the West Coast. He said they'd didn't believe him that a ball could curve like that, so he threw one and ripped the buttons off their shirts. He taught me a pitch. It was like a knuckle-curve. It would just float. He knew a lot about baseball. He had some high-top spikes with long steel spikes. If they got you, they'd have torn you in half. He'd come and watch us play and sit out in right field. Sometimes he'd talk and sometimes he wouldn't, but I'd like to talk to him every day.

When I went to the Hollywood Stars in 1942, I was seventeen-years-old. They had a bunch of old-timers like Charlie Root. The pitchers take batting practice first, but they wouldn't let me bat. I was in the outfield shagging. I didn't get batting practice that whole first year. They were rough on young guys. They'd walk past you and spit tobacco on your shoes. It was an initiation.

Old Billy Schuster... he was intelligent, but what a nut! He'd ground out to the pitcher and run to third base. Other times, when he'd ground out, he'd take a wide turn at first and run through the opponents dugout. He'd kick guys and throw gloves. There were guys who just hated him, but he did a lot to bring excitement to the fans. He knew what he was doin'. He'd be a monkey and climb

the backstop. But I saw him get decked one night in Hollywood. He tried to beat out a bunt. They were way behind and it was the end of the game. Our pitcher, Ray Joiner, threw him out. Schuster came running to the mound and probably said something. Joiner just decked him. The game was over and everybody walked off the field and left Schuster laying there.

Johnny Pesky would break in a new glove by putting a couple of balls in it and then wrapping it up. He'd put it in a bucket of water for a week and when he took it out, it had a perfect pocket. He was the first one I ever saw punch holes in the fingers and lace it together in about '37 or '38. And Eddie Miller, who was our shortstop in Cincinnati, would just cut the first layer of leather out of the pocket and then just one piece of leather was all he had. He could really use that glove.

First base and catching are lost arts. They're always stepping out of the box nowadays. I hate that! It makes the game last twenty minutes longer. A two hour game was a long game. Even if Ted Williams would step out, he always kept the back foot in the box. But now those players just dig in. You didn't dig in back then.

Jackie Robinson - I really admire him. We both came up in '47. He'd get thrown at three times a game and go down, but he'd never say anything. He'd just get back up and get his hits. We had a pitcher at Cincinnati who was from Alabama. He bragged how he'd get him if he pitched and sure enough, he got the call. Who was the first batter? Jackie Robinson. We all knew something was going to happen. The first pitch was inside and the second pitch went over the center field wall. We teased him about how he pitched Robinson all year. They didn't want players' wives to attend the games when Brooklyn came to town because fights would break out in the stands. The Blacks would come out to cheer for Jackie Robinson. They'd cheer foul balls he'd hit. They were just so glad to see him.

Another player had it written in his contract that he'd be traded if a Black was on our team. His 'Daddy' had it written in. That's what he called him. He was from Texas and he called him 'Daddy.'

Charlie Grimm was a funny guy and he kept everybody loose. One time he was told, 'Hey, Charlie, I've got a great pitcher for you. He pitched a no-hitter in the minors and only one guy hit a foul ball.' Charlie said, 'I don't want the pitcher. I want the guy who hit the foul!' Another time, the whole team fouled up a play and nobody could hold on to the ball. It was booted all around. Charlie just dug a hole and buried it. Then he was covering it and everybody in the ballpark was laughing.

The best hitter was Stan Musial and what a nice guy. He worked hard. When he was in a slump in '53, he'd take batting practice until he had blisters. But he got his swing back and hit .330. I remember once Musial had the flu. He didn't play in the first game of the series and in the second game, he was sitting in the dugout with his jacket on and a towel around his neck. St. Louis was losing, three to one, and it was the first of the eighth. The manager went over and talked to Musial. He took off the towel and drug the bat to the plate. Smitty (Frank Smith) was pitching for us and he was thinking, 'This is my chance to get Musial out.' The first pitch was a strike and the second was fouled to the screen. Frank thought he had him - oh-and-two. The next pitch he hit over the 390 foot sign and it bounced off a three-story building across the street. His teammates carried him off the field.

In the majors, we got $6.00 a day for meals. So when the Padres offered me the same as the Cardinals, I was glad. I told them to send me as far away from St. Louis as possible and I got it. This (the PCL) was the league! We'd spend a week in each town and play a double header on Sundays. Mondays were off for travel and you'd get so tired of playing cards, but all the guys liked this league. The American Association and International League were for the young guys. This was for older, more experienced players.

George McDonald was so smooth at first base, but the best was Eddie Shokes at Syracuse. I saw him miss a ball once and it just fell out of his glove. Nobody could believe it. He never made it to the big leagues, because he had trouble hitting.

When I was with the Padres, two guys came down from Philadelphia: Charlie Bishop and Joe Astroth. Chris Pelekoudas was the umpire and he had a big nose. One day, Charlie said, 'If you had a nose on the back of your head, you'd look like a pick.' He got tossed, but it sure made everybody laugh.

When I came to the Padres, we only had six pitchers. I'd have one or two days rest and volunteer to pitch the second game of the double header which was seven

innings. My arm just went dead. We were in Oakland and I was shagging. I threw a ball in and my arm went dead. I threw and it just went limp. Nothing had ever happened like that to me before.

And, old Jimmie Reese, he was tremendous. I never saw him mad. He'd work for hours with that fungo helping ballplayers. He loved broken bats, because he knew just how to break them for his fungo bats. He'd use half a bat. I used to put on the catcher's glove and he'd hit strikes to me from the mound. Remember how they used to leave their gloves on the field? Jimmie Reese would always roll his up and put a rubber band around it and toss it on the field. In all the years I played ball, I saw a glove get hit only once.

Lefty O'Doul was a great hitting instructor. He'd tie ropes on guys and nail their shoes to the ground with a big spike to keep them in the box.

I think it was up in Oakland, John Merson and I asked Theolic Smith to come eat with us at a restaurant. He was Black and didn't want to go. He was real quiet, but we insisted and took him. 'Come on, 'T', you're goin' with us' and we dared anyone to say anything. After that, he'd go eat with us and felt comfortable.

My glove with the Padres cost me $5.00 from a guy who came down from Detroit. He got a new one and was going to throw it away. I said, 'I'll give you five bucks for it.' I used it for two years until it fell apart. We had to buy all our own equipment back then.

Now they've got weight rooms and all that medical attention. Weights cause too many injuries and make them muscle-bound. You've got to be flexible. When we'd get a sore arm, they'd just spit tobacco on it and say, 'Go get 'em!' Teams had just one trainer. Like hockey players, he'd just sew up their cuts on the bench. He'd rub guys down and pack all the equipment. He did it all and look at all the people they have now. It's a business now; it's not a sport anymore. When I played, you'd start looking for a job during the last week of the season. You had to work to support your family."

DICK SISLER, first base, outfield.
BORN: 11-2-20 DIED: 11-20-98   PADRES: 1954-56

Dick Sisler led the Pennsylvania State League with 16 home runs while batting .319 in 1939. He worked his way up through the minors and served three years in the military before making it to the St. Louis Cardinals in 1946. Most of his eight years in the majors were spent with the Philadelphia Phillies. Sisler hit .296 for the 1950 NL Champion "Whiz Kids." His home run in the tenth inning of the final game of the season against the Dodgers

Dick Sisler

Bill Wight

won the first pennant for lowly Philadelphia in 35 years. He finished his big league career back with the Cardinals in 1953 after a stopover in Cincinnati. His contributions to the 1954 Padres Championship included 99 RBIs, 19 home runs and a .318 batting average while sharing first base with Luke Easter. Dick slipped to .255 in 1955, but rebounded with .329 in 1956. He managed the Cincinnati Reds in 1964 and 1965. His father, George Sisler, was inducted into Baseball's Hall of Fame in 1939. Dick is afflicted with Alzheimer's disease, but his wife urged this interview, "because he still remembers baseball and loves to talk about it."

"Those bring back good memories. Bob Elliott was a good guy. I haven't seen any of the old gang in a long time. I really don't remember a lot about it, but I sure did enjoy playing with those guys. Lefty O'Doul was a good manager. He knew baseball real well and understood the players. He was a real nice fella. Mike Sandlock was the catcher.

These are good memories. I have so darn many memories. I just enjoyed my whole career. I enjoyed the playing, the coaching and the managing. I played first base and the outfield. Those are good memories... a bunch of good guys and a good manager. This brings back good memories. I don't remember them all, but I remember some of the players.

My father was a great man and a great father. He just let us grow up on our own. If we wanted to know anything,

of course, all we had to do was go ask him. He knew all about baseball and he is a Hall of Famer. These are such good memories. Thank you for calling, sir...

BILL WIGHT, pitcher.
BORN: 4-12-22   PADRES: 1954

Bill Wight's combined record after his first three years in minor league ball was 16-19. He served three years in the military and returned to baseball as a member of the 1946 New York Yankees. Traded to the lowly White Sox in 1948, "Lefty" was the ace of their staff, winning 15 games in 1949. He went to the Red Sox in 1951, Detroit in 1952 and Cleveland in 1953. Wight then came to San Diego and dominated the PCL with a 17-5 record (.773 winning percentage) and 1.93 ERA. These numbers represent the all-time best performance by a Lane Field Padre pitcher. He was again with Cleveland for 1955 and remained in the majors until 1958, pitching for the Baltimore Orioles, Chicago Cubs and St. Louis Cardinals. His lifetime statistics for twelve big league seasons include 77 wins, 99 loses and a 3.95 earned run average. His pick off move to first was legendary.

"Everything went very well in San Diego. I started the year in Cleveland, but they had all those Hall of Fame pitchers (Bob Feller, Early Wynn, Bob Lemon), and I didn't even get to San Diego until June. Lefty O'Doul was a great guy and such a great hitting instructor. I learned a lot about pitching just listening to him talk to the hitters. He was underrated, probably because he was so easy going, but he could really handle people and that's what's needed today.

Even though I'm from California, that was the only time I played in the PCL. When I was growing up, I was a Bay Area fan - Oakland and the Seals - but it was wonderful in San Diego. We lived out near La Jolla and almost bought a home. It was a good year for the team. I'd pitched against the Angels the day before and it came down to one game with Hollywood and we won it. Bob Kerrigan with those curves. He got a lot of ground balls and I'm a sinker ball pitcher. I always tell Buddy (Peterson) that I made him a star. He and Al Federoff set a PCL record for double plays that still exists, I think. They got a lot of ground balls when I was pitching, too.

After '54, Cleveland approached (Bill) Starr about my contract. Starr was a good businessman and he treated me well. He was a catcher on the Padres and ended up owning the team. That doesn't happen very often. Bill Starr tried to get me to buy my own contract. Now that doesn't happen! It would have been $25,000 which, of course, I didn't have. Starr would loan me the money, then he'd sell me to Milwaukee for about $40,000 and give me 10% or about $4,000. I'd pay back the loan and he'd make about $11,000 on it, but Cleveland wouldn't do it. They said that players can't buy their own contracts. All I wanted was to get back in the majors."

MIKE SANDLOCK, catcher.
BORN: 10-17-15   PADRES: 1954

Mike played eighteen years of professional baseball and was known as a student of the game. He was catching for the Montreal Royals in 1947 when Roy Campanella joined the Brooklyn Dodgers organization from the Negro Leagues. Campy credited Sandlock with teaching him how to quickly release his throws with runners on base. Sandlock was also considered to be one of the premier "sign stealers" in baseball. During his five year National League career, he played with Boston, Brooklyn and Pittsburgh. Lefty O'Doul used to tease that Mike should hit baseballs as well as he hit golf balls.

"I have some fond memories of the Coast League. I ended up beating my old team. I played four years with Fred Haney up in Hollywood and then the Padres played Hollywood in sudden-death at Lane Field. It was Lefty O'Doul as our manager and the great Jimmie Reese as our coach. That was some game. It was the last game of my career and I went out a winner with San Diego. It was a great finish!

I came up with the Boston Bees with Warren Spahn and Ducky Detweiler from the Three-Eye League. I started as a catcher in Class D in 1938 and who did I run into but Stan Musial who was a pitcher back then. They ran out of infielders on our team, so they put me there and I went up as an infielder. After the war, I knew PeeWee Reese was coming back, so I went back to catching. I was hitting .316 at the All-Star game, but my hitting fell off when I was catching. (Mike ended up at .282 for 1945.)

You take a beating as catcher. (Enos) Slaughter hit me once in Brooklyn. I mentioned it to him sometime later to see if he remembered. Know what he said? 'If you can't play the goddamn game, then get out!' That's how I ended up coming to San Diego. I'd played for Hollywood and returned to Pittsburgh. John Lindell and I were traded to the Phillies. Some kid plowed right into me. Christ, my knee swelled right up and I had to have it drained every other day. To keep getting your major league pay, you went where they sent you and I came to San Diego.

Well, Bob Elliott and Dick Sisler and Buddy Rapp were here. It was just wonderful. That was a good league and I thought it was as good as the majors. The ballplayers knew what to do at the right time. They knew where to hit. I still remember right at the end, we were playing L.A. in L.A.. We had to win and Hollywood had to lose. Who was that kid who was the Minnesota manager? Gene Mauch! We were coming to the last innings and he came up to bat. I'd talk to hitters and I was thinking, 'Boy, if we win this, who the hell do we have to pitch tomorrow?' Mauch said, 'Pitch Kerrigan.'

Mike Sandlock

There was a coin flip and we won it, so the game was to be played in San Diego. Everybody was celebrating, but who would pitch? Then O'Doul said, 'Here you are, Kerrigan' and he gave him the ball. He (Kerrigan) threw nothing but what we used to call 'crap!' I knew the guys from Hollywood and he drove them nuts with his stuff. He'd toss it in real slow, then slower, then a little faster and they just went nuts!

The bases got loaded and (Frank) Kelleher loved that change-up. We had a little centerfielder and the bases were loaded, but he caught the ball somehow for the final out and we won it! Bob Elliott hit two out of the park. Sisler hit one and I even got two hits myself and I was pulling the ball. It was wonderful and they were wonderful guys.

Something else I remember about that was we lived out by Mission Bay. My kids would get up in the morning and they couldn't wait to go swimming. Well, we were having this cookout the night before the game at the beach. It was Bob Elliott and his family and mine. There were people, about twenty yards away, and they were complaining about the ballplayers. They didn't know we were there. They were saying how we were going to lose and we couldn't do anything right. Their voices could really carry and they'd had a few 'popsicles,' I'd guess. My wife got mad listening to them doubt us and wanted

us to go over and tell them they were wrong. I told her not to and when we won, I thought to myself, 'I wonder what those people are saying now?'

You remember Frank Lovejoy, the actor? I used to call him 'Lover boy,' because he was always kissing the girls in the movies. Well, I knew him from when I played for Hollywood. The stars would come out to Gilmore Field and we got to know them. I went up to Hollywood after we beat them and I guess they were playing for second place, no, it was in the playoffs, and Frank Lovejoy's wife started cussing at me. I didn't know she could talk like that! 'You're the goddamn reason they (Hollywood) lost, because you knew all of their weaknesses.' She was an ardent fan and she was going on and on. I told her that all I did was catch and it was Kerrigan who threw all the pitches. She wouldn't stop and I got out of there.

I saw Bob, years and years later, at his liquor store when I was visiting out in California. He said right away, 'I know who you are by the way you walk.' Old catchers walk funny. I've had my hip replaced and my knee was just done five weeks ago. I might have to send away for more parts so they can do the other knee, too. But I'd do it all over again... I loved playing baseball."

ED BAILEY, catcher .
BORN: 4-15-31   PADRES: 1955

Ed Bailey was an all-star catcher during his fourteen years in the big leagues with Cincinnati, San Francisco, Milwaukee, the Chicago Cubs and California. He compiled a lifetime .256 batting average and hit over twenty home runs in three seasons. In 1959, Ed caught for his brother Jim in one of those rare moments when siblings are battery mates in the major leagues. He hit .282 in 108 games for the Padres in 1955.

"I thought San Diego had a pretty little ballpark, because I was a left-handed hitter. I was only there for about three months. The Reds bought a guy named Milt Smith from San Diego, so they loaned (Ray) Jablonski and myself out to the Padres. Cleveland had a deal with San Diego then, so it was unusual. Bob Elliott was the manager and Bill Starr owned the team. I had a lot of respect for the guys I played with in San Diego... Eddie Kazak, Dick Sisler, Earl Rapp. Although I liked the guys and the town, I wasn't too happy to be out there, because I wanted to stay with the Reds. But, since they sent me, I though I'd get to play, but there was some kind of agreement for Dick Aylward to play all the time. I pinch hit for Dick a couple of times and hit home runs, but they wouldn't let me stay in the game. I never could understand that. I always wanted to play. I went back to Cincinnati and did pretty good."
[Playing for Cincinnati in 1956, Ed Bailey hit 28 home runs and batted an even three hundred in 118 games. -Ed.]

Ed Bailey

JULIO BECQUER, first base.
BORN: 12-20-31   PADRES: 1955

During the Fifties, the Washington Senators signed many fine Cuban ballplayers. Julio Becquer was one of the best. An excellent left-handed first sacker, he even played some third base in the lower minors before coming to San Diego. Based on his fine performance with the Padres (.291 batting average), Becquer won promotion to the majors and twice led the American League in pinch hits (1957 and 1959). Most of his seven years in the big leagues were with the Washington franchise which later moved to Minnesota. He even pitched in a couple of games for the Senators and Twins. Julio was also an original member of the expansion Los Angeles Angels in 1961.

"The league (Pacific Coast League) was an extraordinary league. The following year, most of the players on the Padres were in the big leagues. We had a fantastic ball club - an outstanding ball club - and we weren't even the best in the league! Bilko had 56 home runs for L.A.. [37 in 1955; 55 in 1956. -Ed.]

They were big league players playing in the Pacific Coast League. We had Buddy Peterson, Al Federoff, Milton Smith, Eddie Erautt, all big leaguers. Buddy and Federoff were one of the best double play combinations I ever played with. They were definitely the best in the Pacific Coast League and maybe in all of baseball. I've seen Nellie Fox and Luis Aparicio, but Peterson and Federoff were unbelievable. Federoff could put the ball on second with his eyes closed. He was one of the best second basemen I've ever seen.

And Ray Jablonski at third. What a stick! Good stick man. Cal McLish was one of our pitchers and he went to the big leagues. I alternated at first base with Dick Sisler. He was such a gentleman and he played in Cuba, too. Bob Elliott was our manager. He was a great player, too. What a wonderful team it was.

After that year, I went to the big leagues. There weren't very many big league teams back then and Triple A was very good. The leagues were different. There were more younger players in the American Association and the International League. They were all pretty close to big league caliber. Look at Denver - 90% of that team went up to the Yankees and they weren't even the best team in the American Association. It was good baseball.

Minnie Minoso and I, we played together in Cuba for ten years and he was an old man then, but he always played with the same intensity. He played at San Diego, too and he is a good friend. We played for Marianao in Havana and then I was with the Havana Sugar Kings in 1953. We were in the Florida International League and it

was Class B. The next year, with the same guys, we were in the International League. We finished third or fourth that first year and they were in the Little World Series the next year.

The Florida International League was a very good league - much better than Class B. Our team was a combination of Americans and Cubans. We had a working agreement with the Washington Senators. Joe Cambria signed all the Cubans. He probably signed more major leaguers than any other scout in history. Even when Castro took over, he would still roam Havana. He was like a son or best friend to (Washington owner) Calvin Griffith and so many Cubans played for the Senators.

We were still able to play winter ball in Cuba until 1961. In March 1961, we all came back to play baseball in the United States, but we had to go to Mexico first. Twenty-one guys came through Mexico then and we didn't get to return to Cuba. Everything, all of my baseball things, are in Cuba. My pictures and uniforms and balls. I have a ball signed by President Eisenhower. I caught the first pitch he threw out and he signed it for me. I have my picture with Ted Williams. I have pictures of all the baseball players in the Fifties and they are all in Cuba.

I know they say that Castro was a good prospect, but if he was, don't you think that the Cuban players in 1951,

Julio Becquer

52 and 53 would have known about him? He was never on any teams we played with or against. He might have been an amateur pitcher or college, but he wasn't that good a pitcher or we would have known him. I met him once; it had nothing to do with baseball. They love baseball in Cuba!

When I came to San Diego, I didn't speak very good English, but the Black players could talk Spanish, because they played in Mexico. Milton Smith was married to a Mexican lady and he spoke fluent Spanish. I went to Mexican restaurants, so I felt right at home. I stayed at the San Diego Hotel and walked to Lane Field. I remember the Plaza and a clothing store by it and a lot of sailors. We got hundreds of sailors at every game.

I played in the Mexican League for two years in '62 and '63 and I played there in '64, too. I played for the Mexico Reds and Vera Cruz. It was an outstanding league and I don't know why more Mexican players didn't make it to the big leagues. They are very good and I played hard there. They were making good money in Mexico. The league drew pretty good. Twenty-thousand a game and the Diablos, the Mexico City Reds, they would get forty-fifty-thousand a game. The fans really supported their teams. They love baseball."

John Gray

JOHN GRAY, pitcher.
BORN: 12-11-27   PADRES: 1955,57

Big John Gray pitched for the Athletics in Philadelphia and Kansas City before he joined the Padres. In 1957 he went 5 and 4 for San Diego while posting a microscopic 1.84 earned run average. This performance earned a promotion to the Cleveland Indians and the following season Gray was with the Philadelphia Phillies. John played in the PCL, the American Association and the International League.

"I came down (to San Diego) from Cleveland, because I was always in some kind of squawk with (general manager Hank) Greenberg. I was having a good year in San Diego, about a point-fifty earned run average, and Herb Score got hit, so I was called back up. Greenberg said, 'Jump the first plane and leave.' I told him that I had my car here, but he said I could come back and get it. Now when would I be able to come back to get it? I was staying at the La Jollan at that time. Well, I packed up and drove back to Cleveland and I took my time. I never did like the way he treated me and I think he was always mad that I signed with the Yankees instead of the Indians.

It seemed like every time we played in L.A. that George Raft, the actor, was always there. And the Rifleman (Chuck Connors) would be at the ball games, too. He was on radio and TV back then. Steve Bilko was their big hitter, but he never got a hit off me on the West Coast. But when I was later pitching for Phila (sic), I hung a curve to him and he hit it four miles over the wall.

We had 'Mudcat' Grant in San Diego and he went on to the big leagues. Bud Daley and I played together at Cleveland. We ran the club for Kirby Farrell, because he couldn't make a decision. He'd always say, 'Don't talk to the press. Don't talk to the press.'

My roommate at Indianapolis was Roger Maris. I told everyone that he was going to be a great ballplayer. He was built like a tank and he could run like Mantle. He had a great attitude and he played baseball like he was going to work. He played with everything he had! Our team at Indianapolis was about sixteen games out, but we really put it together and won the American Association. I even married a girl from Indianapolis who was Miss Universe. Mr. Bush was the owner of the Indianapolis Indians and he was a real gentleman. Greenberg said he'd trade me if I did well at Indianapolis, but you couldn't believe anything he said. I remember Early Wynn had a good year and he wouldn't even give him a raise.

What else do I remember about San Diego? I remember that I caught about a million grunion. I'd never seen them before and I come from a fishing family. My father used to take a lot of ex-presidents out fishing here in Florida."

EDDIE KAZAK, third base, outfield.
BORN: 7-18-20   PADRES: 1955-58

Albany won the Georgia-Florida League pennant in 1941 with Eddie Kazak's league leading 221 hits, a .378 batting average and 133 runs scored. On April 23, 1946, after being hospitalized for 16 months from wounds received during the Normandy Invasion, Kazak hit 2 home runs, a single and double in his first game back for Columbus in the old "Sally" league. In his rookie year with the St. Louis Cardinals (1949), he hit .304 and was named to the National League All-Star team. Eddie would play five years in the major leagues with the Cardinals, Reds and Tigers. He had the most pinch hitting appearances for the National League in 1950. While a member of the Padres, he belted a team high 18 home runs in 1956 and led the club in runs batted in and sacrifice flies. Kazak was a steady and versatile ballplayer.

"Ah, hell, I don't have any memories. I'm a 75 year old man! I did enjoy the Pacific Coast League. I liked the schedule with Mondays off and we flew. I enjoyed playing at Lane Field. It was cool every night and you had to wear a sweatshirt or a jacket. All the fellows liked to play in the PCL, especially in San Diego. That's the best weather anywhere to play baseball. It was a good league to play it out. I was getting up in years. I was 35 years old when I went and I stayed until I was 38. San Diego was the best.

We had a good hitting team. Guys like Earl Rapp. I led the team in home runs? Is that right? It couldn't have been very many. I wasn't a long ball hitter. When I hit, the spin would do down and the ball would sink. Ralph Kiner would hit and the spin was going up. His balls would just keep climbing and go out of the ballpark.

That was the year (1949) that I started out great! But I got hurt in Brooklyn right after the All-Star game. I broke my ankle where it pivots. It took a long time for them to figure out what was wrong. It would just give out and I was never the same after that. Finally, they operated and took out four pieces. They put them in a jar and gave them to me.

AL ZARILLA, outfield.
BORN: 5-1-19   DIED: 8-28-96   PADRES: 1955

The St. Louis Browns won their only American League pennant in 1944 and Al Zarilla was their right fielder. Zeke hit .299 that memorable year and twice he hit over .300 while compiling a lifetime .276 average in ten seasons with the Brownies, Red Sox and White Sox. Al established the AL record by hitting two triples in the fourth inning of a game on July 13, 1946 and tied the major league record with four doubles in a single game on June 8, 1950. He was very briefly a member of the Padres in '55.

Ed Kazak

Al Zarilla

"I was on my way out when I came to San Diego. It was my last year in baseball. I was just there a couple of months and I don't have any memories of playing there. After that, I got into scouting and coaching. When I did finally retire from baseball, I'd put in 53 years. I was happy to play baseball. It was fun and it was an honor to play baseball. Where else can you play something you love and get paid on top of it?

Baseball was baseball; it was our national pastime back then. The competition was tough, but we all got along instead of moaning and groaning. If you didn't produce, it was bye-bye. If you moaned and groaned, bye-bye.

I was born in Los Angeles and grew up there. I remember old Wrigley Field and I signed just out of high school with the St. Louis Browns. I have great memories of those days. I took Tony Criscola's place with the Browns and we went to the World Series that year. That was a thrill and an honor. Johnny Berardino was an actor even back then. He'd put on skits for us. I hear from the Browns fan club, but I've never made their reunions. It would be great to see the guys. Great bunch of guys. I'm very sorry, but I just don't remember that much about San Diego, but I liked it there."

CALVIN COOLIDGE JULIUS CAESAR TUSKAHOMA McLISH, Pitcher.
BORN: 12-1-25 PADRES: 1955

Cal McLish pitched 15 seasons in the major leagues and enjoyed his best years with the Cleveland Indians in 1958 and 1959 when he went 16-8 and 19-8 respectively. His .704 winning percentage in 1959 was second highest in the American League. He was also a winning pitcher for the Padres (17-12) when they tried to repeat as PCL Champions in 1955. That performance earned Cal a return ticket to the big leagues.

"It was a long time ago that I was in San Diego, but I always liked the area and I always said it has the best climate in the U.S.. I liked old Lane Field, too. I never played in their new park (Westgate Park), wait, I did in an exhibition game when I was with the Indians a few years later. Nice park. I remember the guys I played with in San Diego: Ed Bailey from Strawberry Plains, Tennessee, Dick Sisler, Al Federoff, Buddy Peterson, Clarence Maddern, he's dead now. We had a good team.

Bob Elliott was my manager. I pitched on Saturday at the end of the season and Elliott asked me if I could pitch on Sunday if he needed me. We were playing a double header with Hollywood. I said I could do it and I came in in the second inning of the second game. We were ahead in the last inning and Hollywood had the bases loaded. I got Carlos Bernier to hit into a double play.

Pitcher to home to first. He was a tough out and that was the only way we ever could have doubled him up. The ball came right to me, I threw home and the catcher threw to first. It was the only time I'd ever done that in all my years playing baseball. It was the only way we'd have got him.

I left high school to go to the Dodgers. They had 4Fs, old men and young kids. President Roosevelt wanted there to be baseball. Tom Greenway was a scout with the Dodgers and he said I'd have a real good chance to make the club. [Cal was 18 years old when he pitched for Brooklyn in 1944. -Ed.] He also said that if you went into the service with a big league contract, you'd go back to the big leagues after the War and you wouldn't get lost in all the confusion. It was good advice because they'd have to keep you on that contract for a year after you got back.

Well, when they decided to drop the bomb, they also decided to start up Divisional baseball. I hadn't thrown and I went out without any real warm-up or spring training and started pitching. I hurt my arm and I didn't know if I'd ever be able to play again. I went back to the Dodgers in '46, but mostly pitched batting practice. Then I was traded to Pittsburgh and I pitched batting practice there. My year would have been up around June or July of '47, so I went to Kansas City (American Association) for Mel Queen. What a team we had in Kansas City! Hank

Cal McLish

Bauer, Jerry Coleman, Steve Souchock, Ed Stewart, Bill Wight, Tommy Byrne. Then I pitched up in Wrigley Field in L.A. I spent 4 1/2 years there before San Diego bought me."

I really do remember the guys I played with. I've got 'half-heimers,' but not about baseball. I remember guys I pitched with in San Diego like Lloyd Dickey, Bob Kerrigan, Eddie Erautt. I remember guys from Cleveland who played for the Padres like Rudy Regalado and Gene Leek. They were infielders. I really remember names.

Yes, I've been told by a lot of people that Dizzy Dean used to talk a lot about me when he'd do games on TV. There was always a focal point about my name. My Dad named me. I was one of the few kids he got to name. I was seven out of eight kids and I was the first one he named. He tried to catch up on me. He was probably sniffing the bottle when he did it. He named me for a president, a Roman emperor and an Indian chief. Tuskahoma was a chief and there's a town here in Oklahoma named after him. People do like my name."

BOB USHER, outfield & first base.
BORN: 3-1-25   PADRES: 1955-56

Bob Usher is another local boy who did well in baseball. He starred for Post 6 when they won the American Legion National Championship in 1941. After serving in the Navy during World War II, Bob was with Cincinnati from 1946 through 1951. He was traded to the Cubs in 1952 and farmed out to the Angels until he was bought by San Diego in 1955. Usher responded with an outstanding season as he led the Padres in several offensive categories including a .350 batting average. He returned to the majors with Cleveland and Washington in 1957 and retired from baseball after playing an additional year with the Miami Marlins.

"I had two bad years in L.A. and I caught Jimmie Reese in the outfield one day and asked if (General Manager Ralph) Kiner could buy my contract. I wanted to come home and I had my best year in pro ball!

We had spring training in Palm Springs. There was loose turf and I got shin splints. I thought my career was ended, but I got two hydro-cortisone shots in my heels and I was fine. We had a good team with Earl Rapp, Dick Sisler, Harry Elliott, Eddie Kazak, Al Federoff and Pete Mesa. They were all nice guys and it was a memorable year to come home and have that kind of a season.

I remember hitting an opposite field home run at Lane Field. There was a donut above the fence and if you could hit a ball through it, you'd get a million bucks. I came within two feet of it, but I don't know if anyone could

have put a ball through it at that angle. We'd try to throw a ball through it when we were in the outfield, but we could never do it. It was probably impossible.

As a kid, I remember watching the Padres play. Steve Mesner, Hal Patchett and George McDonald are players who stick out. Mesner was a good hitter and so was Dominic Dallessandro. He hit .368 in 1939.

As a Padre fan, it was wonderful to play back at home. Cleveland bought my contract and I went on to the Washington Senators on the strength of my season in 1956.

We won the Legion Championship at Lane Field in 1941. We would have probably won in 1940, too, if they would have let John Ritchey and Nelson Manual play down in Albemarle, North Carolina. I had to catch instead of them. We had never seen prejudice like that before.

One time when John was playing for Sacramento (Solons) and I was with L.A. (Angels), he hit a ball to right that I caught at my knees. It was one of the few times I was ever thrown out of a game. He (John) knew I caught it. I was arguing with the umpire and I'd look at him on first base and he was laughing. He knew I caught it! Everybody in the ballpark knew it!

One time, I played all of the positions with Birmingham.

Bob Usher

I threw a change-up to a guy from Knoxville and he hit it downtown. I even played first base a few games for the Padres.

When I retired from baseball from the Miami Marlins in 1958 and came back to San Diego, Kent Parker got me my first two jobs. One was as collection manager at 1st National Bank downtown and the other was doing private detective work for Sterling Security. That led to the job with Navy Intelligence and Frank Kern (former curator at the San Diego Hall of Champions) was the commanding officer. Coming home to San Diego was always a good thing."

RALPH KINER, general manager.
BORN: 10-27-22   PADRES: 1956-60

Ralph Kiner played for Albany in the Eastern League in 1941 and 1942. He hit .279 with 11 home runs in his first season and .257 with 14 round trippers the next year. After military service from 1943 to 1945, Kiner went to the Pittsburgh Pirates and led the National League in home runs for seven consecutive years from 1946 through 1952. During his ten year career he hit 369 home runs and twice hit over fifty home runs in a season (51 in 1947 and 54 in 1949). His home run percentage (7.1 home runs per 100 at bats) is second only to Babe Ruth. He was elected to Baseball's Hall of Fame in 1975. After his playing days with the Cleveland Indians were over in 1955, Ralph became general manager of the San Diego Padres. It was during his tenure that major league baseball came to the West Coast and the Padres moved to Westgate Park (1958).

"Bill Starr had just sold the ball club to C. Arnholt Smith and that's why I was hired, because he didn't know baseball. Starr was brilliant and he helped me tremendously. When I ran into a problem, he helped me a lot. He was behind the whole thing to make the Coast League an Open Classification. It was his idea. Because

L-R: Jack Murphy, Ralph Kiner, Pete Coscarart, and Bob Elliott

major league teams couldn't get their players in the draft, they could keep them or sell them. It was a great operation, but drafting and options took the money out of the minor leagues. We used to call the PCL the 'Old Folks League' and Bill Starr made his money selling players to the majors. It was a tremendous league.

When I took over, the Padres had spring training in Ontario (California). It was the first time I met Luke Easter and Bill Starr. I moved the team to Palm Springs, because I lived there. They had a nice park that the Angels took over. It was too expensive. Indio had a small park and I convinced them to give us $5,000 to practice there. Our accommodations cost less there, too. In our first game, I got Bing Crosby to throw the first pitch. I knew him, because he was a part-owner of the Pittsburgh Pirates.

I had Dick Sisler and Earl Rapp making well over what many major leaguers were making. I paid both of them fifteen-twenty thousand a year and there were only about fifteen or twenty in the majors making more than that then. Back in '52, I made $90,000 and Branch Rickey, Sr. wanted me to take a 25% cut. The punch line was during my hold-out and Rickey said, 'Son, where did we finish last year?' I said, 'Last.' He said, 'Well, we can finish there again without you.' Back then, you either took it or you didn't play.

I had a promotion between a doubleheader. It was a throwing contest between Rocky Colavito and some jai alai players. They had their cestas (baskets) and pelotas (balls). Rocky threw it over the center field fence and it was about four-twenty-five. That's a long way! I played an exhibition game at Lane Field in '47 and hit the back fence in center and they said not many hit 'em that far, but Rocky could throw a baseball that far! The jai alai players really had to give it all they had and they could throw their pelotas farther. When I told (Cleveland general manager Hank) Greenberg, he wanted to kill me. He didn't want Rocky's arm hurt.

I fired Bob Elliott and he was very popular in San Diego. Jack Murphy and Bob were good friends and so was Phil Collier. I liked Bob. When I joined Pittsburgh for spring training in '41, Bob let me hit in front of him in batting practice. That was back when young guys couldn't even get a chance. Nobody said anything, because Bob was a big player. He was good to me and I knew him well. It got so bad, he wouldn't come to the game until after it started. Jimmie Reese was doing everything. It was hard and I replaced him with my friend, George Metkovich, and then, a couple years later, I had to fire him, too. They were good men.

I did a study when I was general manager of the Padres. Between 1946 and 1956, Seattle averaged over 400,000 fans a year. That was back when major league teams weren't getting a million. Seattle out drew L.A. and San Francisco. They wanted to make the PCL another major league and they could have. It was a real attraction and a tremendous league.

Starr had tried to build a ballpark in Balboa Park. He eventually sold the team to C. Arnholt Smith who was great to work for. Of course, Smith owned everything in San Diego! Starr got his start when he took an option on property where Convair was and he exercised his option to sell. He was a good businessman and his brother, Dave Starr, ran concessions at Westgate. They had 'Tunies' (hot dogs made from tuna). They worked and worked on them and they weren't a bad product, but hot dogs are hot dogs and that's what people want at the ballpark.

I was involved in the building of Westgate Park. There were no dugouts. I talked to the architect, I believe he was named Frank. I said, 'This is high class baseball.' He said he'd seen pictures of baseball players sitting on benches. We had them put in the dugouts.

I sold Floyd Robinson to the White Sox for $50,000. Floyd might have been the last player sold. It was hard to make money in the minors after that. I thought I had Deron Johnson signed, but the Yankees got him and I tried to sign Larry Elliot, but some major league team got him.

Did Bob Lemon tell you about me releasing him? His arm was hurt, so he came down to play outfield for the Padres. He was the property of the Cleveland Indians and he got his release. We are friends and he likes to tell that story. When I was in high school, I played for Alhambra like Max West did. We had quite a league with Long Beach Wilson, Poly, Glendale and the two San Diego high schools. The highlight was going to San Diego and playing at Russ behind San Diego High School. It was a thrill to travel to San Diego and to know Ted Williams played there.

ROCKY COLAVITO, outfield.
BORN: 8-10-33   PADRES: 1956

From 1956 through 1966, Rocky Colavito averaged over 32 home runs a year for the Cleveland Indians, Detroit Tigers and Kansas City Athletics. Always among league leaders in power hitting, he topped the AL with 42 home runs in 1959 and 108 RBIs in 1965. Rocky was beloved by the Cleveland fans and he returned their affection. He remains one of the most popular men to ever play for the Tribe. In just 33 games for the Padres in 1956 he hit .368 with 12 home runs before moving on to Cleveland. Perhaps Colavito is best remembered in San Diego for attempting to break Don Grate's baseball distance throwing record of 443 feet, 3-1/2 inches established on August 23, 1953.

Rocky Colavito

"In an attempt to set the record straight, my memory is vivid! The wind at Lane Field almost always blew from left to right field and that's how they had me set up to throw. But that Sunday, it blew the opposite. The first throw, which I felt was one of my best, traveled 404 feet against the wind. Realizing this, they turned it around a bit and I threw from home plate to the center field wall which was 425 feet. I threw three in a row over the wall against a cross wind. The furthest hit the top of the batting cage which was stationed there and couldn't be measured. The other two were measured at 439 feet." [On July 2, 1956, the San Diego Union, reported that Rocky's throw went "435-foot, 10-inch." He also hit two home runs in the doubleheader against the San Francisco Seals. -Ed.]

JOE ASTROTH, catcher.
BORN: 9-1-22   PADRES: 1956

After ten years behind the plate for the Athletics, Joe Astroth came to San Diego. He was Bobby Shantz's catcher when the little left-hander was named the American League's most valuable player in 1952. A lifetime .254 hitter, Astroth enjoyed his best season when he averaged .327 in 1950. Joe tied a major league record on September 23, 1950 by knocking in six runs in a single inning. He is one of the few players who did not play in the minor leagues until his major league career was over.

"I came out there in '56. I was on loan from the A's to the Indians as part of a deal and Cleveland had a working agreement with San Diego. When your time is up, you wanted to play in the Coast League. That was my first time on the Coast; I'm from the East. But things were already changing by then. I know people out there think the Coast League was as good as the big leagues, but when they started seeing big league ball on TV, they wanted to see big leaguers. The people liked to see us. They'd heard of us, but they knew we were beyond our prime and they wanted to see young big leaguers. They wanted the real thing and I said, 'You'll have big league ball in '58.'

I still remember going up to L.A. for a weekend series and 800 people came to the game. You could see that people wouldn't settle for old-timers. It was like going to an alumni game. They were saying, 'We want big league ball.' People thought I was nuts saying that, but baseball is a business and you can't make money without a good product to sell. The PCL was very relaxing and they had great ballplayers, but they were past their prime. It was where old elephants went to die.

Joe Astroth

Ebba St. Claire was the catcher in San Diego when I came. He was a switch-hitter. Bob Elliott is the manager. Ebba wants to get back to the big leagues and he's hitting over three-hundred, but when they'd pitch a left-hander, I play. He's about three-forty-five, three-forty and he's provoked. I'd read the morning paper and if it was a right-hander, I'd play golf before the game. If it's a left-handed pitcher, I knew I'd play.

97% of baseball players are great guys. All they are trying to do is get to the big leagues. We'd play against each other and later be teammates. You get along, but baseball is a business. When you start playing for money, you're paid for your performance. (Barry) Bonds will be the first to tell you he ain't worth forty-four million - nobody is! They laugh at it, but you take what they give. Rumor was that the A's were cheap, but as I got older, I realized that Mr. (Connie) Mack was a very intelligent man. A reporter asked him, 'I understand you're trying to get Ted Williams?' Mr. Mack said, 'Young man, Mr. Williams would pay his way and fifteen other guys.' They bring people into the ballpark. They are merchandising ballplayers. Look at pitchers who bring in ten-fifteen thousand more people every time they pitch. Baseball is a business.

Vic Lombardi was pitching for us in San Diego. He's down from the Pirates and Dodgers. He needs another pitch to get back. Pitchers are always experimenting... spitters, oil on the cap... we'd work out on the sidelines, working on the spitter. It's not an easy pitch and a lot of them leave the ballpark. People don't even know when a spitball turns into a home run. I was chewing behind the plate and wetting around the plate. In a tough situation in a ball game, we loaded one up. The guy hit it and, running to first, he was yelling, 'Spitter! Spitter! Spitter!' He was thrown out and by the time it (the ball) went around the infield, it was all rubbed off. It was thrown out of the game and the umpire hands me another ball. I said, 'I can't believe it. That's terrible when pitchers do that. I don't believe in that.' All the while, I'm loading it up and I throw it back to Vic. He realized I'd loaded it, but the next guy hit it and they beat us by one run. Cheaters never win...

The secret of pitching is anything you can do with that ball to upset the hitter will make you successful. The secret of hitting is timing and rhythm. The secret of pitching is breaking up the hitter's timing and rhythm.

In 1945, I came out of the service and started with the A's. I'm glad that I played there (in San Diego) and I played in Toronto, Memphis, Savannah and Buffalo. I retired three times before they let me stay retired, but I also got to play for Buffalo in the Little World Series in '58 against Denver. They (Denver) had (Ryne) Duren, (Tony) Kubek and (Bobbie) Richardson. It would have

Al Gettell

"Two Gun" Al Gettel

Pete Mesa

been great for me to stay in baseball, but it's not fair to your wife and family. Bobby Shantz and I went into business together.

They wanted me to manage, but I gave them the reasons why I wouldn't: I can't play anymore. You'll second-guess me. There's no longevity. No money. And, if you don't have the horses, you can't win."

AL GETTEL, pitcher.
BORN: 9-17-17   PADRES: 1956

In 1938, Al Gettel was 16-7 for Snow Hill in the Coastal Plain League. He led the Piedmont League with 17 wins and 232 strikeouts for Norfolk in 1944. In the major leagues, Gettel went 38 and 45 for the Yankees, Indians, White Sox and Senators from 1945 through 1949. Over the next five seasons with the Oaks, "Two Gun" was one of the top guns in the Coast League. While compiling a 104-71 lifetime record in the PCL, he also led the league with 24 victories in 1953. He returned briefly to the Giants and Cardinals during the years he played for Oakland. Al was happiest pitching on the west coast where he also appeared on the silver screen. San Diego would be the final stop on his baseball journey.

"Ballplayers back in those days loved to play ball. They didn't play for the money. People liked ballplayers back then. I never charged for an autograph. If I had a dollar for every autograph I signed, I'd be a multi-millionaire now. They've ruined baseball. People don't want to see the major leagues anymore. We've got a pretty good team here in Norfolk (Virginia) and those boys play hard. People like to see that. I enjoy watchin' it. I started here in Norfolk with the Tars in 1936. They were part of the Yankee organization.

I was only there (San Diego) in '56. Old Ralph Kiner was the business manager. The little time that I was there, Ralph treated me real good. Most of my time was with Oakland. I enjoyed being out there on the Coast. I had a lot of fans and friends up in Oakland and in the PCL. Charlie Dressen was the manager up there. They sold the club in '55 and they wanted me to go up to (Vancouver) Canada, but I said, 'No way.' Ralph asked if I would like to come play for him and I said I would. I don't even remember what my cotton-pickin' record was that year. I liked it in San Diego, but I just don't remember that much. It was my last year in baseball. It was a long time ago.

You know I was in some movies when I was out there. This picture is me on a palomino in my Oaks uniform wearin' an old cowboy hat with my two guns, but you can only see one of them. I was in *The Tin Star* with Henry Fonda.

The biggest memory I have of the Coast was when I won 27 and lost 7 with Oakland in '52 or '53 [23-7, 1950 -Ed.] . Another thing I remember was pitchin' a 21 inning game against Hollywood in '52 or '53. [May 12, 1954 -Ed.] We pitched longer in those days. You wanted to win your game. Nowadays, ballplayers are just playin' for the money. They are money crazy. The ballplayers of today don't realize the fans are the ones that pay the salaries. They're not playin' for the love of the game like we did. Of course, the money we made was plenty then."

PETE MESA, Pitcher.
DOB: 8-29-29   PADRES: 1956-57

Pete Mesa posted the best won-lost record for the Padres in 1956 with 13 victories and 12 defeats. He registered a 10-11 record the following season while fanning over 130 batsmen each year. Pete went into education following baseball and is currently with the National Science Foundation.

"San Diego was very friendly. We enjoyed the hell out of it. It was great! Harry Douglas was a great guy. We rented one of his apartments in Mission Beach and he gave my wife a shower for our first child. I belonged to the Cleveland Indians and I was fortunate to play for San Diego. I guess my best memory is the caliber of the ballplayers and the caliber of the people. They were fair minded.

I remember getting hooked up with Elmer Singleton. I think he was with Portland. He had a helluva slider. He was a good pitcher and we had some duels. I had a lot of innings that first year. [246 -Ed.] They don't pitch that many innings anymore. John Carmichael pitched a lot of innings, too. I remember Eddie Erautt and Vic Lombardi.

We (the Padres) got into a fight. Al Federoff knocked a guy over tea kettles at second. It's a typical baseball fight - a lot of pushing and shoving. It was against San Francisco, because I remember Sal Yvars running in. Lombardi rushes out and I asked, 'What would you have done, you little shit?' He said, 'I'd bite 'em in the balls!'

Earl Rapp couldn't catch a ball ten feet on either side of him, but he could hit like hell! We had some good players: Floyd Robinson, Earl Averill, Bob Usher, Rudy Regalado, Rocky Colavito and 'Gator Gut' Bob Lennon. Rocky, Hank Aguirre, Rod Graber, they all married girls from Reading (Pennsylvania). Reading had the prettiest girls in the Eastern League, so a lot of players married them.

I grew up in the Bay Area in Sunnyvale, so I remember the old-timers. I was a Seals fan. My brother-in-law used to follow baseball. Fans really do remember the old PCL. When I was in college (San Jose State), Jackie Jensen and I worked out with the Oaks and I remember Billy Martin.

I feel I played in a great period of baseball. I got to see a lot of the Negro League players.

VIC LOMBARDI, pitcher.
BORN: 9-20-22   DIED: 12-3-97   PADRES: 1956-58

Vic Lombardi was a crafty left-hander who won 45 games for the Brooklyn Dodgers from 1945 through 1947. He spent the next three seasons with Pittsburgh before coming to the Pacific Coast League. Lombardi was 15-16 for the Padres during his three years in San Diego. He was also known to throw a spitball or two. Following baseball, Lombardi became a golf pro in Fresno and remained active on the links until his death.

"I played for Bob Elliott when I first got there (San Diego). Then, (George) Metkovich took over, because he was (General Manager Ralph) Kiner's friend. Metkovich didn't know what was going on. Of course, Jimmie Reese was a great guy. We stayed at the San Diego Hotel and the owner took the whole ball club out deep sea fishing one night. I got seasick and said, 'God Damn, can't you take me ashore?' He said he'd do it for a cap. I said, 'I'll get you a whole damn uniform!' When I finally did get off that boat, I was fine.

We had Eddie Kazak who played third, (Ebba) St. Claire and (Joe) Astroth were the catchers. Joe didn't have to load it up for me. I used to do it myself, but Joe would like to help. I didn't even know how to throw a spitter in the majors. I couldn't throw as hard as I used to because I had a rotator cuff (injury). I worked on other pitches. And, Rocky Colavito was there, too. When he was throwing the ball out of the park, I threw him the ball before he threw it. We had Al Federoff at second. Cal McLish turned out to be a great pitcher for Cleveland. I liked Cal; he was a decent guy. Eddie Erautt, he really had good stuff. Dave Pope, Billy Harrell and Floyd Robinson... they were all good, young players. We had Earl Averill and Rudy Regalado. We had a pretty good ball team. A good bunch of guys, but, then there was

Vic Lombardi

Rudy Regalado

Floyd Robinson shakes hands with Rudy Regalado following home run at Lane Field.

Harry Elliott. He wanted his four hits and didn't care about the team.

The game I remember most was when I had a no-hitter going into the seventh inning of a doubleheader which was a seven inning game and there were two outs and I had two strikes on Luis Marquez, the left fielder for Portland. He was a big guy and a good guy from Cuba. He got a hit!

I broke into baseball in '41 with Santa Barbara, Class D ball in the Dodger organization. I got up to the big leagues and then Pittsburgh sent me to Hollywood. Then I went to Toronto, Seattle, San Diego and Portland. When people get out of baseball, they don't work out like they used to. I work out six times a week, 30 minutes in the morning and thirty minutes in the afternoon and sometimes at night, too. I'm the same weight as when I played ball. I feel like I'm 35 years old.

It's tough when guys get traded. When they don't tell you about it, it's worse. There is no compassion. When you get rid of a guy, you pull the world out from him. I don't think it will ever change.

Look at what is going on now with (Darryl) Strawberry going to the Yankees. How many chances do these guys get? Steve Howe? Look at George Steinbrenner! Mickey Mantle was a womanizer and a boozer, but he was Mickey Mantle. If they judged everybody in the Hall of Fame by the same rules, there would be some guys they'd have to kick out.

But Pete Rose can't get in. Pete Rose loved to play baseball. I hated to pitch to guys like Pete who spray it all around. It seems they have rules for some people and another set of rules for others. I don't get it. Right is right and wrong is wrong!"

◆◆◆

RUDY REGALADO, third base.
BORN: 5-21-30   PADRES: 1957-59

Rudy Regalado grew up in Los Angeles and remembers his father taking him to watch the Angels at Wrigley Field. Rudy played baseball for Rod Dedeaux at the University of Southern California and is still a proud Trojan. From 1954 through 1956, Regalado was with the Cleveland Indians. He appeared in all four World Series games in 1954 and compiled a .333 Series batting average. Rudy also played for Indianapolis during 1955 where he hit .316. He appeared on The Ed Sullivan Show in 1957 as the third baseman on the All-Minor League All-Star Team. That season, he led the Padres with a .306 batting average. Rudy hit .277 the following year for the Westgate Padres and was traded at mid-season in 1959 to the Seattle Rainers for Dee Fondy.

"When I came to San Diego, I was appreciative of the friendliness of those connected with the Padres. We came to town on the Cabrillo Freeway through Balboa Park and I didn't realize how beautiful San Diego was. The single ballplayers and a lot of the coaches lived at the San Diego Hotel on Broadway. We would walk to Lane Field. All the sailors in their white uniforms and locker clubs and uniform shops along the way are still fresh in my memory. The charm was the closeness of the people in those days. We had a short right field fence, too. I wish I had been a left-handed hitter.

During the 1957 season, the Padres were battling with San Francisco for first place in the PCL. Joe Gordon was the Seals manager and it was raining hard at Lane Field. Gordon wanted the doubleheader called, but the umpires wouldn't budge. Joe tried to convince them that the field was unplayable. When that didn't work, he went to third base. Running full speed, he did a Pete Rose head first slide into home and splattered mud all over the umpires. They called the game off!

In 1958, (Padre manager) 'Mudcat' Metkovich wanted Howie Rodemoyer to come in from the bullpen to pitch in a tight spot. He kept signaling for Rodemoyer, but he didn't appear. Finally, Jimmie Reese ran out to the bullpen and asked, 'Where is he?' The response was, 'He's in Mobile.' Apparently Howie had one more option left to go to the lower minors, so (general manager Ralph) Kiner shipped him off that morning, but forgot to tell his manager.

One time, I went in to pinch hit late in a tight game. I missed the squeeze sign from Catfish who was coaching at third. I was swinging as Earl Averill, Jr. was coming to the plate and I almost hit him. Metkovich was very angry and he fined me $100, which was a lot of money in 1957. A year later, in a game against Seattle, with an oh-two count and trailing by a run in the late innings, I jumped on a curve and hit a home run to win the game. To my surprise, Ralph gave me a check for $100 exactly. He remembered.

San Diego was a great place to play ball. It's got the climate, good fans and it's a great place to raise kids. A final memory I have of old Lane Field was that every time someone flushed the clubhouse toilets, the showers went cold!"

BILLY HARRELL, infield.
BORN: 7-18-28   PADRES: 1957

Billy Harrell hit .307 for the Indianapolis Indians as they ran away with the American Association championship in 1954. As a member of the big Tribe in 1955, he smoked a .421 batting average in 13 games for Cleveland. Two years later, Billy batted .276 for the San Diego Padres. This earned him an encore with the major league Indians. A very versatile player, Harrell played every infield position and the outfield during a four year major league career which ended in 1961 with the Boston Red Sox. Then, as a veteran and coach, he provided stability and encouragement for the younger players coming up through the minors. He is a retired probation officer in New York.

"I enjoyed that town. I had so much fun with the guys: Preston Ward, Rudy Regalado, Floyd Robinson - he knew my family and helped us get a home. I told Mr. Greenberg that I couldn't afford to bring my family all the way to San Diego, so they paid the expenses. I remember going to the zoo. My wife and kids really enjoyed it. The kids were little then. It was great being in San Diego. All the guys were great. It didn't matter if you played with 'em or against 'em. They were all great. It was just great being part of the sport.

Bill Harrell

You know who I think I remember the most was Dick Stuart when they came down to play us. They called him 'Clank Clank,' but he was so big. Now they work out, but he was all muscles and he could hit that ball damn far. I thought that the Pacific Coast League was a great league. Back then, it was tougher to get to the big leagues. Oh, it was so hard to break in, but now they have a youth movement. And it involves money, too. We'd get the minimum six-thousand when we'd go up. I remember a big star like (Larry) Doby couldn't even get $45,000 and he was great. You just existed back then, but there was always a chance of making it to the Big Show.

I spent most of my time in Triple A ball, but age caught up and I was there to help the kids. You'd set a good example and keep them calm. You love the game. You'd love to make the big dough, but you love the game. You say to the young guys, 'You'll make it. You'll make it.' and you pitch them batting practice until your arm hurts, but you feel so good when they do make it. Reggie Smith and the volcano man, George Scott, were on Toronto when I was there. Scotty and Reggie both wanted to hit the most home runs and they were in competition with each other. George would go off like a volcano and I'd calm 'em both down. I'd tell 'em we're all part of the same team and it would help. They had so much talent and I felt good for both of them. I got them to talking to each other.

I started in Albany (New York), then to Reading (Pennsylvania) and Cedar Rapids (Iowa) and back to Reading. We were with Cleveland and we had so many good players coming up like Bud Daley, Rocky Colavito, Rudy (Regalado), Hank Aguirre, Rod Graber and then most of us went to Indianapolis and that's when we went crazy in '54 with Herb Score and all those great young pitchers.

Herb Score pitching for the Padres in 1961,

Cleveland had so many guys like (Bob) Lemon, (Bob) Feller and (Early) Wynn, it was tough for the pitchers to get to the Show. Sam Jones was a good pitcher. He'd come back so slow and then he'd really fire that ball. (Howie) Rodemoyer is a guy who should have gone up, but Cleveland just had too many fine pitchers.

I would have liked to have been a coach, but there are cliques. They tell you they want you, but then they bring in somebody else. I liked helping the young ballplayers and I became a probation officer. I like helping kids. It makes you feel good when you can straighten some of them out, but you know how it goes. You can't straighten them all out and some get into more trouble when they grow up, but at least you tried. I loved it all. I have so many good memories and my life has been blessed.

I was so excited after '55, then George Strickland went crazy in spring training the next year and he was hitting over three-hundred, so I never really got a chance to play as much as I wanted. But I did get a chance. There are so many good, really good players, who never even had a chance to play in the big leagues. It was wonderful to play baseball."

BUD DALEY, pitcher.
BORN: 10-7-32   PADRES: 1957

Bud Daley had a solid ten-year career in the major leagues with Cleveland, Kansas City and the New York Yankees. He appeared in two World Series and earned the win in the final game of the 1961 Series between the Yankees and the Cincinnati Reds. Bud's best season in the big leagues was 1959 with Kansas City when he went 16-13 and batted .295. Daley was a perfect 3-0 with a 0.83 ERA for the '57 Padres.

"I remember playing against the Padres more than playing for them. I spent two years at Sacramento and about two weeks with San Diego, but I remember coming down and pitching at Lane Field. I remember the short right field fence and San Diego was always loaded with left-handed power hitters. I liked pitching there, because I was a left-handed pitcher. I liked the park, because it was right next to the water and I thought that was neat.

I was raised in Harbison Canyon until I was seven. I remember that there was a nudist colony out there and the first school I went to had all eight classes in one room. It was at the bottom of the canyon. Then I moved up to Long Beach. Jack Graham and I were real good friends. He was involved in youth baseball and he is a good man.

The first year that I came out of high school, I signed with the Indians and went to spring training with the Padres in Yuma. Red Embree was pitching for them. I weighed 198# and I don't remember who the manager was, but he said, 'I want you to run with Embree.' Well, Embree could run all day and at the end of spring training, I weighed 172#. I had lost twenty-six pounds! I got to pitch against Cleveland in an exhibition game for one inning and then I got sent to Bakersfield.

I really enjoyed the Coast League. When I was in high school, I don't think I could name all of the major league teams. If I could make a Coast League team, I thought that would be as good as making any big league team. It was a good blend of former big leaguers and young guys going up. I think my favorite town to play in was Sacramento. It was a small town back then."

Bud Daley

STAN PAWLOSKI, infield.
BORN: 9-6-31   PADRES: 1957

Stan Pawloski chose baseball over football and the coal mines when he graduated from high school in Pennsylvania. He realized his biggest thrill by playing for the 1955 Cleveland Indians. Stan enjoyed several successful seasons within the Cleveland organization with stops at Wilkes-Barre, Reading, Indianapolis, San Diego and Mobile.

"I was offered scholarships to play football at Pittsburgh and Georgia. Someone told me they'd guaranteed I'd graduate if I went to Georgia, but all you'll do is practice football ten months a year.

I signed with Cleveland out of high school and they sent me to Wilkes-Barre. I played with good teams at Reading and Indianapolis. I spent three years with Indianapolis. We had Rocky Colavito, Roger Maris, Rudy Regalado. I went up with Cleveland for 30 days at the end of the '54 season. I didn't get in any games that year, but it was great just to be there. They should have won the series against New York. I got a check for about $175. It must have been about 1/100th of a (world series) share. I hadn't done anything for the team, but they voted me a share. I got one hit for them in 1955 and it will always be in *The Baseball Encyclopedia*.

In the short time I was in San Diego, I got to know George 'Catfish' Metkovich and we became friends. He owned some liquor stores. He said, 'I'll give you $100 a week to work for me in the off-season.' Ralph Kiner was the general manager. Big Ralph spent more time taking batting practice at Lane Field than anything else. Cleveland got him to pinch hit in '55. I remember sitting next to him on the bench and we became friends. He became the GM of the Padres and wanted to cut my salary!

We stayed at the San Diego Hotel. Lane Field was cozy and the sailors got a little nasty if you didn't put out. It's like here in Philly. If you don't give it all you've got, the fans will get on you. If a player puts out, the fans appreciate that."

GARY BELL, pitcher.
BORN: 11-17-36   PADRES: 1957-58

Young Gary Bell had difficulties in his first season at Lane Field and finished the year with a disappointing 1-5 record. After a 6-2 start in 1958, Bell was promptly promoted to Cleveland in mid-season where he won 12 games and lost 10. During a twelve year major league career, he compiled a record of 121-117. Gary remained with the Tribe until 1967 when they traded him to the "Impossible Dream" Boston Red Sox.

Stan Pawloski   *Gary Bell*

He lost the third game of the World Series, but came back in the sixth game to earn a save which forced the seventh game against the St. Louis Cardinals. Bell went to the expansion Seattle SeaPilots in 1969, who traded him to the Chicago White Sox. His best year in the majors was in 1959 with the Indians when he posted a 16-11 season. Gary has fond memories of San Diego because of the confidence he gained from his experience here.

"I went out there in 1957. It was a Cleveland Indians farm club and I was in the Southern Association with Mobile. I remember that I flew up to Vancouver to meet the team and I don't even remember my first game, I was so scared. I got beat up pretty good that first year. I was nineteen-years-old, but in '58, everything came together and I started winning. But that first year, I know one damn thing, I was scared!

You saw some big names in the Coast League - big leaguers who were experienced veterans. Probably half of those guys were making more than guys in the big leagues were. Guys like Steve Bilko and Jim Marshall and, I remember Bobby Balcena and Joe Frazier, because I'd seen them play for the San Antonio team when I was a kid. I knew they were ex-major leaguers.

I played at old Lane Field and we opened in Westgate the next year and I thought it was a gorgeous park. I can remember that Ralph Kiner was the GM and he didn't want to give me an extra $150 a month even though I'd come up from Mobile. I think that would have only given me about $750 a month, but he said it just wasn't there.

What I remember are the old ballparks in L.A., San Francisco and Hollywood. They had Carlos Bernier and Paul Pettit. Pettit was the bonus baby who started as a pitcher with Pittsburgh and he was a good hitter with Hollywood. Ken Aspromonte led the league in hitting (.334 in 1957) with San Francisco.

The fence in right field at Lane Field ran along Pacific Highway. I remember that fence and I know I didn't like it! They used to stop traffic out there when I pitched, because they didn't want to cause too many accidents from the balls flying over the fence.

Do you see Phil Collier, the sportswriter? Ask him if he knows where Goose Creek, Texas is? He's from Goose Creek. It's by Houston and they call it Baytown, Texas now.

I remember those guys from San Diego: Rudy (Regalado), Rod Graber, Bill Glynn, Allen Jones from Cleveland, Tennessee. Gene Leek played football at Arizona. He was such a nice guy. We tried to corrupt him, but I don't think we succeeded. Julio Becquer, I just saw him yesterday at a benefit up in Minneapolis. You ought to set up an old-

timers game and fly the guys in. When you're in baseball, you never get over it. I think what you're doing is wonderful and it means a lot to the old-timers.

Let me know if there is anything I can do to help. I'll go through my old scrapbooks. I loved San Diego and my time there."

FLOYD ROBINSON, outfield.
BORN: 5-9-36   PADRES: 1954-57,60

Floyd Robinson signed with the Padres after graduation from San Diego High School where he starred both on the diamond and the gridiron. He enjoyed three fine seasons that were interrupted by a stint in the Marine Corps where he played ball for the Recruit Depot in San Diego. After hitting .318 for the Padres in 1960, Floyd was called up by the White Sox. During a nine year major league career, Robinson had a .283 lifetime batting average and in 1962 led the American League with 45 doubles. From 1961 through 1964, he averaged over .300 and placed in the American League's top five hitters for three of those seasons. In 1962 only batting champion Pete Runnels (.326) hit for a higher average than Floyd (.312).

"Two men who were always good to me were Kent Parker and Fido Murphy. Fido wanted me to play football at Arizona. Then he went to the Bears. He always stayed in

Floyd Robinson

touch with me and wanted me to play for the Bears. That was a friendship. Mr. Parker is a fine gentleman and he followed me very closely. He really made it easier for you. He'd talk to you. Things were different back then. They took advantage of you when they signed you. Bill Starr liked to sign Mexican and Black players cheap and sell them for a lot of money. He gave them a break, but they made him a lot of money in the process. I think Kent was instrumental in recruiting from the Negro Leagues. He was good friends with Theolic Smith and Milt Smith. Rudy Regalado was playing winter ball in Culican (Mexico) and he wanted to come home for the Holidays. Kent Parker called me and I went down to take Rudy's place. Kent did things like that for me.

When I signed with the Padres, there were old-timers that I idolized. I didn't mingle that much. I remember when John Ritchey signed with the Padres - he was a heck of a third baseman. They made him into a catcher and that's hard to learn how to handle the pitchers. John could sure hit and he could run. Dick Sisler was a friend. My son signed with the Cardinals and Dick was one of their minor league batting instructors. Dick was one of the guys who brought me out of my shell. He was one of the veterans and that was in the days when rookies respected veterans. He is a very classy man - he really stood out.

I don't know of a better ballplayer than Milt Smith! He got a bad rap, because he was so aggressive. The guy who taught me the most about baseball was Milt Smith. In those days, they played by the numbers. Milt said if you can run, take advantage of it. I remember how Rocky Colavito loved to throw from center field to home. He'd say, 'See that? I love that.' I remembered it and realized I could take an extra base. You didn't do that in those days. If you got thrown out, you're a bonehead, but I was always grateful for Milt's advice: 'Take advantage of it!'

Dave Pope was a gentleman and a scholar. He was one of the best players and family men I have ever known. He couldn't hit until June when school would get out, because his wife was a teacher and she'd join him then. He was a ballplayer and a student of the game. He got a bad rap, because he was seen once driving with Luke Easter. Luke hit the ball as well as any of the big home run hitters. I was so thrilled to meet him, because he'd played for the Padres when I was young. I'd go to Lane Field every Sunday. He said, 'Hey, young blood.' He was a fun loving guy. He was dynamic with confidence written all over him. Harry Simpson was quiet and I was quiet, too. I was more of a homebody and didn't go out a lot with the guys.

In 1961, Orestes Minoso came up to me. He used to call me 'Bob.' He said, 'Hey, kid, don't be disappointed if you don't make Rookie of the Year.' I listened to him very

carefully. In 1951, he hit .326, but they gave it to Gil McDougal instead. He said, 'Bob, don't give up!' My friend, Luis Aparicio, told me the same thing. It meant a lot coming from them. [Boston pitcher Don Schwall (15-7) won American League Rookie of the Year honors in 1961. Robinson hit .310 in 432 plate appearances. -Ed.]

I was a team ballplayer. You'd give yourself up for the team. Today, you play for yourself and the money. You didn't play for money in those days. We played for the love of the game."

EARL AVERILL, all positions.
BORN: 9-9-31   PADRES: 1957-58

On July 7, 1955, Earl Averill hit 3 consecutive home runs and a double to establish a Southern Association record with 16 total bases. After hitting a respectable .273 with 19 home runs in the Padres final season at Lane Field, Earl was the Most Valuable Player in the PCL for 1958. He hit .347 that season and led the team with 24 home runs. His totals would probably have been higher, but for a mid-season "call-up" by the Indians. Such moves, appreciated by the players, caused havoc with the minor league pennant races as the Padres finished their first season at Westgate Park 4-1/2 games behind the league leading Phoenix Giants. Earl went on to a seven year major league career with the Indians, Cubs, White Sox, Angels and Phillies. He played all of the field positions except pitcher. He is the son of Hall of Famer, Earl Averill, who was also an outstanding PCL player in the Twenties.

"I think I had about 80 runs batted in by July 1st (1958) and Dave Pope was right behind me. I got called up by Cleveland, but got hurt and came back to San Diego. It wasn't supposed to happen when they bought you and the Commissioner even talked to me. I agreed to go back if they would trade me. It ended up costing me on my pension, but I didn't think of it back then.

I had played several years with the guys on the Padres. Quite a few of them were on the Reading (Pennsylvania) team and then we went to Indianapolis and had a great team. Rudy (Regalado) and Rod (Graber) were on those teams. I played two years in San Diego. I got to close out Lane Field and open Westgate Park. In fact, I think I also played in the last game in L.A. and Hollywood parks, since the Dodgers came the next year. The PCL changed a lot then, but it was a good league.

Some crazy things happened down there (in San Diego). Hollywood started one season in San Diego and that was when Dick Stuart was hitting all of those home runs. He'd jump up and click his heels running out a home run. We had a big, blond centerfielder and he hit a high fly that didn't even get out of the infield. The shortstop and

Earl Averill

second baseman collided - Dick Smith and Spider Jorgensen for Hollywood. One had a concussion and the other was out cold. The ball didn't reach the outfield grass and our guy was standing on second base with a double. That was the only time I ever saw that happen in baseball... an infield double.

(General Manager Ralph) Kiner used to tell this story. We were behind in a couple games with Sacramento, but Harry Bright booted a couple of balls at third to let us win. They had a round little bald headed manager. I can't think of his name, but he went into the dugout and started drinking. After the game, he said, 'Does anyone want a third baseman? I'll sell him for a pencil.'

I remember one time, our first two hitters each got a hit on the first pitch and they were on first and second. On the first pitch, I hit a bullet down the third base line and the third baseman caught it. The ball then went second to first and it was a triple play. Three pitches and the inning was over!

I remember Opening Day and Joe E. Brown was there to speak. A worker was using a hammer up in the press box area and everybody could hear it. Brown said, 'Get a paint brush' and everybody laughed. Up in Hollywood, there was a sign that said if you hit a home run over that spot, you'd get a hundred dollars. I hit a home run, but it didn't come within a hundred feet of the sign. A guy told them it did and we split the money.

Whitey Wietelmann and Del Ballinger, the Blue Boy... they were friends of Bob Elliott, our manager. They were the groundskeepers and they'd pitch batting practice. I can just hear Ballinger's voice and that accent. He told great stories. Did Whitey tell you about Roy Helser? Ballinger said he could never hit Helser. Not only did he always step in the bucket, but he'd also throw his bat. So he decided to tape his bat to his hand and that was the only hit he said he ever got off him, but he had to run to first with the bat taped to his hand. Blue Boy was great to listen to. Helser pitched for years for Portland. He was athletic director at McMinnville College outside Portland and he'd only pitch on Sundays when Portland was home. Chet Johnson did the same thing for Seattle on Sundays.

You know something I remember about '58 in San Diego is that Hal Woodeshick and I both left for Cleveland together and it was on the front page of the San Diego paper. That was the only time I was ever on the front page of a newspaper.

In '58, Phoenix came into the league. I remember it was one hundred and eight degrees at night in the stands... a hundred and eight degrees at night! George Metkovich was our manager then and I started the season on the bench, but I went in to pinch hit in Phoenix and got a long home run and never returned to the bench. He played me everywhere including a lot of second base. I'd never played second before. Davey Pope and I would switch hitting third and fourth. I just hit everything they threw and it was a wonderful year.

Do you remember Carroll Hardy? He was an outfielder for us that year and he was a defensive back for the 49ers. He's the answer to a great trivia question: who is the only guy to pinch hit for Ted Williams? Ted had fouled a pitch off and got hurt, so Carroll Hardy came in to hit for him.

My dad was part of that great San Francisco outfield that hit 120 home runs. My dad had 36 homers, Smead Jolley had 40 and Roy Johnson had 44. [Averill 36, Jolley 45, Johnson 20 -Ed.] My dad was the first big money transaction between the Coast League and the big leagues. He wasn't young when he got to San Francisco. Dad was born in ought-two and went to San Francisco when he was twenty-five years old. He wasn't a kid. Then he went to Cleveland where he replaced Tris Speaker. That first year, his number was originally number five, because that is where he was in the batting order, but they changed it to number three and that is the number they retired for him.

I was back in Cleveland last year when they opened Jacobs Field and President Clinton was there. I got locked in the stadium with Mel Harder and Bob Feller, because security was so tight. It took us 45 minutes just to get to our seats.

When dad was playing for San Francisco, they would play one of their Sunday games at Recreation Park and the other one at Mission Field. My mother told me, 'Your dad was really interested in airplanes.' There was a carnival and they had wing walkers and airplane rides for twenty-five bucks. He saved up his money and that was his first airplane ride. I remember when I was playing in the (American) Association and we used to fly in DC-3s. There were many times when we'd have to all go to the front of the plane just so it could take off, because there was too much weight in the back. We didn't even think anything of it back then. Yes, those were the days when you carried your own bags. We were just glad to be flying.

My wife and I had 39 homes in our first thirteen years of marriage. I don't think many couples can match that, but that's how it was for baseball players, because we were always moving around.

I remember Bob Lennon in San Diego. We moved out to Mission Beach and we lived in the same place. Before that, we lived at Buena Vista (Apartments in Clairemont). Rudy and Rod and Stu Locklin lived there, too. All a good bunch of guys, but I really remember Bob Lennon as an interesting and unique guy. We used to call him 'Gator Gut.' There wasn't anything he couldn't eat! And he never made a sound when he laughed. He was an interesting guy. There were a lot of good guys on that team and I'd sure like to see them again."

BOB LENNON, Outfield.
BORN: 9-15-28   PADRES: 1957

Playing for Nashville in 1954, Bob Lennon won the Southern Association Triple Crown by hitting .345, knocking in 161 runs and smashing an incredible 64 home runs! The following season, he "slumped" to 31 homers for Minneapolis, but added four more as the Millers defeated the Rochester Red Wings in the Junior World Series. After brief appearances with the Giants in '54 and '56, Lennon was traded to the Cubs in 1957. During that season, he was optioned to the Padres. In 102 games, the Alligator put up good numbers in San Diego, hitting at a .308 clip with 12 home runs and 53 RBIs.

"Where did you ever get the name 'Gator Gut?' Did you get it from Bob DiPietro? He was the one who gave me that name. I hit a home run - I think it was in Portland. Bobby put up a sign on the hill that said, 'Alligator hit one here.' I'll try anything. My theory was if you never tried it, you don't know if you'll like it. (Les) Cook brought

Bob Lennon

in some frog legs and I guess that was how I got the name. Almost everybody else knew me as Archie.

Do you remember the radio show, Duffy's Tavern? I came from Brooklyn. When I went down south to play ball, everybody used to think I sounded like the guy who'd answer the phone. He'd say, 'Duffy's Tavern. Duffy ain't here. This is Archie the waiter.'

My first memory of San Diego was getting there and a doubleheader was rained out. Preston Ward and I arrived and (Ralph) Kiner wanted to fine us for being late! I'd been driving 750 miles a day to get there! George Metkovich said it would be OK. At the end of the year, Billy Glynn drove my car home all the way to New York. He lived in New Jersey. I flew to New York because I was sold to Detroit. I got a uniform and walked around Yankee Stadium. They sent me back to the Cubs, so that was my American League career, walking around Yankee Stadium in a Tigers uniform.

I remember the last day of the season was a doubleheader in L.A.. I was hitting about .303. I went oh-for-three in the first game. George asked if I wanted to sit out the second game to keep my average at .300. I said I wanted to play. I think I got four or five hits and ended up at .308. I didn't hit as many home runs as I should have in San Diego. In '56, I was up to the Giants, back to Minneapolis, up to the Giants and back to Minneapolis. I was hittin' good, but Chub Feeney said, 'We brought you up to hit home runs and you're not.' I told him if I could hit a home run every time I wanted to, I'd be worth a million bucks! Ballplayers today don't have to hit home runs and they get a million! Of course, back then, a million dollars seemed impossible.

When I was a kid, we'd go Ebbets Field and you'd fantasize about hitting a home run. When I was with the Cubs, there I was at Ebbets Field. (Sal) Maglie was

Bill Glynn

Bill Glynn, Rudy Regalado and Vic Lombardi limber up in spring training.

pitching. I hit one off the top of the screen I thought was out. The next time up, I hit a three run home run. I was lucky to get a chance to play there. I remember it so clear. I remember going to Ebbets Field as a kid and watching Max West. He was a great home run hitter.

Rotator cuff problems ended my baseball. I just woke up one morning and I couldn't throw. They used to shoot it up with cortisone in San Diego. You know, there was a trainer in New Orleans that reminded me of (Les) Cookie. I was playing for Nashville and I had a charlie horse. The old trainer took a baseball bat and rubbed the heck out of the charlie horse and I was OK. Another thing I remember about Cookie - he had his Early Times and water. Jimmie Reese was amazing to me. He'd hit strikes to me with his fungo bat. He could get 'em in there.

I started when I was 16 in the Dodger chain. I still remember my father and my uncle - they were New York cops - they were sitting at the table having a few beers. They were telling me that I would be picking tomatoes and corn all day on the farm and playin' baseball all night in Thomasville, North Carolina. I didn't know they were kiddin' me. I never played in a ballpark with fences. I shied away from the fence. The coach would hit balls high off the fence and I learned how to play it. It was quite an experience for a young kid. I used to try to hit like Mel Ott and they tried to change me. The best advice I ever got was 'keep your eye on the ball!' I was there three weeks or a month. When I got older, I picked up speed.

I played with (Roberto) Clemente and (Orlando) Cepeda in Puerto Rico. We had a good team. When I took my hat off for the National Anthem, the fans would call me 'poco pelo'. I asked what it meant? Little hair! It meant I was bald. I'm still bald!

I played with Jack Harshman at Nashville. He turned out to be a good pitcher and he had a good stroke. He could

hit with power. I hit three (home runs) in the last day of the season (Nashville 1954). I left and went to the Giants for a few games. That was the year they beat Cleveland in the World Series. That was exciting. They had a day for the Polo Grounds Giants at Belmont (race track) here and I was invited - Willie Mays, Monte Irvin, Don Mueller, Jim Hearn. The people couldn't get over what nice guys they were signing autographs and talking to the fans. That was a big thrill for me. They knew me and I hardly played with 'em. They'd say, 'Hi, Arch!'

◆◆◆

BILL GLYNN, first base.
BORN: 1-30-25   PADRES: 1957-58

Bill Glynn hit .328 for Americus to lead the Georgia-Florida League in 1946. In 1949, he hit two home runs in the first minor league game ever played at Doubleday Field in Cooperstown, New York. Later, with Cleveland, he shared first base with former Padre legend Luke Easter. Glynn likes to joke that he played in 111 games during the 1954 season and the Indians won every one of them which remains a major league record for the 154 game season. In reality, he enjoyed his greatest day on July 5, 1954 when he hit 3 consecutive home runs against Detroit. Bill joined the Padres late in '57 and was the starting first sacker when they opened Westgate Park. He hit .270 in Mission Valley that season and duplicated his 3 consecutive home run feat over two games for the '58 Padres.

"I broke in in 1946 with Americus, Georgia. I had a pretty good year and went up to Utica with a bunch of kids who became 'The Whiz Kids' with the Phillies in 1950. In '49, I was up with the Phillies and my main memory was the umpiring. The first pitch was high; I mean high! I said it was high and Al Barlick said, 'Get back in there, rookie.' That's how umpires were then. After the game, (Philadelphia manager Eddie) Sawyer pushed me into Barlick. I was glad he knew Sawyer did it as a joke. [On

September 18, 1949, in his first major league plate appearance, Bill was called out on strikes. He was ejected from the game for arguing with the umpire.]

I was in Toronto with the Maple Leafs for two years and Baltimore for a year and then I was sold to Sacramento. If you couldn't play in the big leagues, the league everybody wanted to play in was the PCL. They had good fans and it was as close to the big leagues as you could get. Joe Gordon was my manager. I was a great ice cream eater and I loved malts. Joe took off my belt and put a notch in it and said to get to that size which was quite a few notches. I weighed two-ten and went down to 187. I was already in good shape, but he made me faster. I loved to run. He got me to bunt. He'd say, 'Bill, chop down on that ball. Aim for the pitcher like you're gonna hit him in the head.' I was hitting two-seventy, two-eighty and in July, I was up to .310 with 14 or 15 home runs."

We were in 'Frisco. Gordon called me to his room. He said he had some good news and some bad news. I said I wanted the good news first, so he told me, 'We just sold you to Cleveland.' Then he gave me the bad news: 'They want you tomorrow.' My wife sold everything we had and the following day, we got on a flight for New York and there was a twilight doubleheader. They sure don't have doubleheaders like they used to. Well, I was in the lineup and who was pitching? Allie Reynolds and Vic Raschi! I went two-for-nine, but the next day I got my first home run in Boston.

Something I'll never forget that happened in Boston was Ted Williams hitting a home run. It was late in a game and, of course, we wanted to win. He had just come back from Korea. He hit a home run to beat us and as he rounded first, all I could say was, 'Nice hit.'

The fans could really get on you. Bob Feller was at the end of his career and he was always getting letters. One he got said, 'I'm a mechanic and if I fixed cars like you pitched, I'd be out of business.' I told a sportswriter in Cleveland that I wished I was as good as Ferris Fain. He wrote that I thought I was another Ferris Fain. The sportswriter said he knew I didn't say that after I asked him about it. He said it made the story more interesting. I got a letter from a fan and it said, 'Ferris Fain, my ass! You couldn't hit an elephant in the ass with an oar paddle.' It was a funny letter, but I never said I was as good as Ferris Fain.

There was a writer who was timing runners from home to first and Mickey Mantle was the fastest in the baseball [3.1 seconds- Ed.] (Jim) Busby was second in the American League and, to my surprise, I was tied for third. I guess I could run pretty good and that made me pretty proud.

There was only one thing I didn't like about baseball -

public speaking. I don't like to get up in front of large groups and talk. I don't remember how many whisk brooms I signed those two days, but it wasn't as bad as banquets and public speaking engagements. I would worry about it for weeks before I had to go.

Luke Easter - what a wonderful, nice guy. It was Luke and me at first base, but we were friends. Look at him here in a wheelchair when he got injured and he's telling me to 'take good care of it, son.' We thought of Blacks as ballplayers and not by the color of their skin. We thought it was terrible they couldn't stay in the same hotels with us in the South. I remember being in South Carolina when I was with Americus. A siren went off about five o'clock and I didn't know if it was an ambulance or a fire. Then someone told us it was to tell the Blacks to get off the streets in a half hour. I'm from New Jersey and I'd never heard of anything like that.

Here's another column I like [August 30, 1986]. See where it shows Joe Carter hitting three home runs in one game. Look, here it shows that I was the last Indian to do it: 'Joe Carter hit three home runs for the first time since Bill Glynn did it on July 5, 1954.' A funny thing happened when I hit those home runs. My teammates greeted me after the first and second home runs, but I was surprised when I came into the dugout after the third. Everyone was just sitting there like nothing happened. I was stunned. Then, about 30 seconds later, they all jumped up and cheered. They were all in on it and, you know, ballplayers have a sense of humor.

Rudy (Regalado) tells me how lucky we were to play in a World Series and he's right. I had the greatest opportunity in the first game of the (1954) World Series. The score was tied in the eighth and the bases were loaded with one out. I was sent in to pinch hit. Lopez asked if I could hit good against (Marv) Grissom and I said I did. He told me to look out for his screwball. All I needed was a long fly to score a run and we'd win. Instead, I struck out on a screwball that was high and outside! I though, 'Oh, my God! What a golden moment and I blew it!' I kept saying to myself, 'What did Gordon teach you to do? What did Gordon teach you to do? What did Gordon tell you to do instead of looking at that short fence 250 feet down the line?' The guys didn't hold it against me, but I felt terrible. [Willie Mays made his famous back-to-the-plate catch of Vic Wertz's 440 foot fly to end the eighth inning in the Polo Grounds. The Giants swept Cleveland, but Bill got a hit in his other Series appearance. -Ed.]

I went to an old-timers game up in Candlestick a few years ago and I hadn't seen Tommy Lasorda in thirty years. Tommy looked right at me and said, 'Bill, how are you?' We played together years ago. He's such a good guy. Hal Naragon was talking with him and Tommy said he could remember winning this game. I was a wise guy and said, 'If you won as few games as Tommy did, you'd remember every one, too.' He laughed. That's the kind of a guy he is.

The only thing that I remember about San Diego was that I got suspended from baseball. I went to spring training in '59 and (General Manager Ralph) Kiner said he sold me to Birmingham. I called Eddie Glennon and asked if I could stay in San Diego a little longer, because my in-laws were coming in. I hadn't played in a couple of days, because I hurt my back horsing around in the pool with the other guys. It wasn't anything serious. Eddie said, 'You tell Kiner the deal is off!' Kiner was mad and said, 'You queered the deal.' But I didn't and I was willing to go. He suspended me from baseball!

So I bought my milk route and never thought about baseball again. I made more money in the milk business than I ever did in baseball. I would run through my route and my competitors would complain that I'd talk baseball and people would buy my milk. I went to an old-timers game and Kiner saw me in a suit. He commented on my outfit and I told him I was making more now compared to what you used to pay me. We became friends and he became one of my customers."

BILL WERLE, pitcher.
BORN: 12-21-20   PADRES: 1957-60

Bill Werle broke into organized baseball with San Francisco in 1943. He went 56-48 over the next four seasons, losing 1945 to military service. After going 17-7 for the Seals in 1948, Bill was promoted to Pittsburgh in 1949 and spent the next six years in the major leagues. Playing for the Pirates, Cardinals and Red Sox, he posted a lifetime 29-39 record with his rookie season (12-13) being his best effort. In four years with the Padres, Bill won 31 while losing 32 and his 3.11 ERA in 1958 was lowest on the staff. He managed several years in the minor leagues and is still an active scout for the Cleveland Indians.

"We had outstanding ball clubs when I was in San Diego. We should have done better than we did. George Metkovich was a good guy, but over his head as a manager. Look at who we had: Billy Moran at second, Preston Ward and Bill Glynn at first, Eddie Kazak at third and Rudy Regalado. Floyd Robinson was becoming a great outfielder and Dave Pope. Earl Averill was catching and playing the outfield. Allen Jones was a good catcher, too, but he didn't hit like Earl. Then Ken McBride when they switched working agreements from Cleveland to the White Sox.

I came over when (Ralph) Kiner was the GM. He fired poor Bob Elliott and brought in his friend, George Metkovich. I remember one time, Metkovich was

swinging a bat in the dugout and he got mad at the umpire, so he went out with a bat in one hand and a cigar in the other. He was so embarrassed he went back in the dugout. Another time, he sent in a pinch hitter for the pitcher, but he didn't have anybody warming up. So he gave Bob Alexander five or six warm-ups and brought him in. He wasn't ready and didn't do well. Bob complained that he wasn't properly warmed up, so the next time, Metkovich had him warm-up in the first, the second, the third, the sixth and the seventh. For Chrissake, it just wasn't right to treat him like that. The Padres had outstanding people, but lousy management.

I have very little use for today's players. Back then, each team had fourteen-fifteen farm clubs. Look at the Dodgers; they had three triple-A teams in Montreal and St. Paul and Spokane. Look at all the shortstops they put in the big leagues on other clubs because nobody could replace PeeWee Reese.

The first games I saw as a kid were in Oakland and Sacramento. I remember when Sacramento would play Sunday doubleheaders and the first game would be in the morning down in Stockton and the afternoon game was up in Sacramento. During the war, I remember that Tom Seats worked in the shipyard and he'd pitch on Sundays. In my career I played against six fathers and sons: Jo-Jo White and his son, the Averills, the Pillettes, Gabrielsons, Camillis... who was the other one? I can't think of them, but I played with or against all of them. I spanned the generations.

Bill Werle

I pitched the first game in Multnomah (Stadium in Portland) and the last game at Vaughn Street (Ballpark, also in Portland). You know, the biggest thing I remember about Lane Field was actually when I was with Lefty O'Doul and the Seals. It was the last day of the season and all we had to do was win to win the pennant. I think it was (Dino) Restelli on third (with the bases loaded) and he broke for home. It was three and two on the hitter and the pitch was almost like a pitch-out and if he (the umpire) calls it a ball, the run scores. He called it a strike! O'Doul was furious and he fell down right at home plate. They fired the umpire afterwards, but it was too late. I think it was Max West who hit a home run in the tenth or eleventh to beat us and we lost the title.

Lefty was one of those guys who'd pick up derelicts and all he said was, 'Give me 100% on the field.' He had no rules; no curfews. That was real unusual back then. He'd pick up the problem children, but they were good players and played hard for him. But he had little use for left-handed hitters who couldn't pull. Frank Shofner was a left-handed hitter and he went to the opposite field and it drove Lefty nuts! He made Gene Woodling into a good hitter. You remember those years with the Yankees. Lefty put a bat behind him so he couldn't step back and he tied a rope on him. Frank got him to pull. He got seventeen hits and twenty-one RBIs in one series or was it twenty-one hits and seventeen RBIs? It was in Portland's Vaughn Street and he was rainin' em on the foundry (beyond the outfield fence). It was all through the efforts of Lefty.

Ferris Fain was a real competitor. I won't tell you the name of the centerfielder who didn't hustle on a play. When he came in to the dugout, Fain chewed him out and said he'd kick his ass if he ever did that again. You respect a competitor like that. And he was clever, too. With a runner on first and in a bunt situation, if he rubbed his leg one time with his bare hand, you'd throw once. On the second pitch, he'd be breaking for home and you knew not to throw. If he rubbed twice, that meant to throw twice before he'd break. We'd pick off more guys that way and he'd throw guys out at third on sacrifices, too. He hustled and played hard and you like that. You know he could hit. Twice led the American League. [.344 in 1951 and .327 in 1952 -Ed.]

I played in San Francisco, Pittsburgh, St. Louis, Boston, Portland, Tacoma and ended up my playing, I believe it was in '61, in Hawaii. They were a Kansas City farm team, but (Charlie) Finley didn't like sending his players that far out in the Pacific so he was sending them to Birmingham which was double-A in the Southern Association. The PCL didn't like that and they couldn't allow that imbalance to exist, so every team had to send two or three guys to Hawaii. Poor Tommy Heath... He had all the malcontents, over-the-hills and guys nobody wanted: Ray Jablonski, Jim McManus, Bobby Balcena, Bud Podbelian, Blackie Schwamb... poor Tommy Heath.

I was manager in Fresno, Aberdeen, Stockton and Phoenix. I still scout and watch games at Candlestick and Oakland."

BOB DiPIETRO, 1b, 3b, of.
BORN: 9-1-27   PADRES: 1957

Most of Bob DiPietro's PCL career was spent with his hometown San Francisco Seals. He was up with the Boston Red Sox in 1951 and then returned to Portland in the Coast League. While a member of the Padres during their final season at Lane Field, Bob was selected to the Pacific Coast League All-Star Team. He finished the season with a .274 batting average. San Diego Union Hall of Fame columnist Phil Collier remembers Bob as one of the PCL's more colorful ballplayers.

"It was such a short period of time (in San Diego). Ralph Kiner was the manager. No, maybe he was the general manager. Tommy Heath was the manager of Portland. He and Kiner made an agreement for me to go back to Portland. They got into it big time. That would lead me to believe he (Kiner) must have been part of management.

San Diego was a great place to play. One thing that sticks in my memory - we were in the All-Star game and to have some fun with me, the guys put Frank Howard's pants in my locker. Frank was 6'8" so when I put on his pants, they came up to my ears. They were taking pictures and it was kind of funny. Since I was on the team, it must have been a slow year for all-stars.

We had a good ball club. There was Mudcat Grant, Floyd Robinson, Earl Rapp, Earl Averill. I just talked to him. He's quite a guy. He puts on golf tournaments. And, Rudy Regalado - he's related to Vic Regalado, the golfer, I think. Maybe that's his son. You don't think about those names for years, but they pop into your head, like (Leo) Righetti

Bob DiPietro

Bud Hardin

Jim "Mudcat" Grant

who played for San Francisco. His son (Dave) was a pitcher. Do you know I watched Frank Dasso pitch for San Diego when I was a kid and I'd go watch the ball games in San Francisco.

We played in a good time. It was before the era of the agent. When he was managing in Portland, Larry Jansen said, 'The hardest thing for me is that you can't talk to these guys. You have to go through their agent.' Baseball sure has changed."

BUD HARDIN, second base.
BORN: 6-14-22   DIED: 7-28-97   PADRES: 1957

Gifted gloveman Bud Hardin was the last Lane Field Padre to be acquired in the 1957 season. The following year, he retired from baseball and Lane Field was replaced by Westgate Park. Bud played briefly with the Cubs in 1952. They sent him back to Los Angeles where he remained with the Angels until being dealt to San Diego. Hardin played fifteen years of professional baseball.

"I was only with the Padres for the end of the season. They needed a utility fielder, so I filled in. Ralph Kiner called me and asked me to come down. I always liked Rudy Regalado. I liked to see him play and I thought he should have stayed up in the majors. We had some other good players on that team like Mudcat Grant and Dave Pope. George (Metkovich) was managin'.

I signed in '42 for $100 in the North Carolina State League

with the Giants organization. I was makin' $85 a month. We played good ball in the South. We had a good Legion team when I was growin' up. It was the best ball club around, but our third baseman got hurt. The fella who took his place had a hard time catchin' the ball. When I was at Rochester, my second baseman was Lou Ortiz and he was from San Diego. He told me how his Legion team came to the South to play for the National Championship. They had two colored boys who weren't allowed to play. He said they'd have won it if those boys had played, because he said they were that good. He was probably right.

Lou was the best second baseman I ever played with. I'll tell you how great he was. If Lou could have hit better, he would have been the same caliber as Red Schoendienst. He was never knocked down once makin' the double play.

Al Rosen started in the North Carolina State League. One day, he was jabberin' a lot and our manager told Sal Frederico to quiet him. Sal went over to third and decked him with a short punch. Years later, we (Cubs) were in Mesa (Arizona) playin' the Indians. I said, 'Al, can that Frederico hit?' He said, 'You're damn right, Bud!' Both of them were Golden Gloves. That Sal - he was really built.

Talkin' 'bout gettin' decked, you remember Charlie Fox who was the manager for the Giants? I was with Charlie playin' up in Manchester, New Hampshire. Charlie was catchin' and one of our pitchers kept crossin' him up.

This pitcher was a big left-hander whose name I do not recall. Charlie just walked out to the mound, decked him and said 'Don't cross me up anymore.' I was standing at shortstop watchin'.

I set a record for not makin' any errors in 52 games playin' second, third and short when I was with L.A.. I was just fillin' in. I was a good fielder, but only about a .250 hitter. It was a wonderful time."

◆◆◆

JIM MULVANEY, President.
BORN: 11-2-22   PADRES: 1956-1968

Growing up in Chicago, Jim Mulvaney was a loyal Cubs fan. Never in the wildest dreams of his youth did he imagine he would someday become president of a ball club. In his capacity as President of the Pacific Coast League Padres, Mulvaney provided vision and leadership as the Padres moved from their beginnings at Lane Field to Westgate Park and, ultimately, to the Stadium and major league status.

"Mr. Smith (C. Arnholt Smith) bought the Padres in 1955. He bought them, ostensibly, because he owned KSDO, the station that carried the Padre broadcasts for many, many years. He and Jim Copley had purchased KSDO in 1950 and moved the studio to the U.S. National Bank Building. Because Arnholt was the type of person that worked late many nights, he often passed through the studios during the out-of-town recreated broadcasts of Padre game that Al Schuss was doing.

The ownership of the Padres was placed in one of Smith's corporations, Breast-O-Chicken Tuna, with Jim Lane (no relation to Bill Lane), president of that organization. Mr. Smith and Jim (Lane) brought me into the organization

as an attorney in late 1955. He said to me at that time, 'Mulvaney, you probably know the most about baseball. I'm putting you in charge.'

One of my early recollections of Mr. Smith was his politeness and humility. He and I had been traveling somewhere in his car. As we came back to the bank garage, I started to get out of the car to press the button to open the door, but Arnholt beat me to it. He was older and he was the boss, but that's the way he was. He made people feel like they were working with him, not for him.

When we acquired the Padres from Bill Starr, we immediately saw the need for a general manager. Bill was a very bright baseball man as well as a wonderful individual. He was smart, not just about baseball, but also business. A truly outstanding person, Bill helped us a lot in the early days.

I was aware that Ralph (Kiner) was getting out of baseball, so I contacted him. The next day, I got a real heated call from Hank Greenberg. Hank turned out to be a great, good friend, but he reminded me, nonetheless, that I had no right to call one of his baseball players without first clearing it with him. This is called the tampering rule.

Ralph came to us in January of 1956 and brought a whole new dimension to the city. Ralph was New York, Hollywood, Palm Springs. He and Bill Starr became quite good friends and I know he credits Bill for helping him.

The firing of Bob Elliott, which came about early in the next season, was very difficult for Ralph. People said he fired Bob in order to bring in George (Catfish) Metkovich, an old friend of his, but that's not true. He told me that he had to do it and I was well aware of how Ralph felt about Bob. He held Bob in the greatest esteem since Bob

Jim Mulvaney

RIGHT: Imperial Beach Baseball Team. Back, third from left: C. Arnholt Smith.

had been very helpful to him, but in Ralph's estimation, Bob was 'just not performing.' As a result, we went forward and hired Metkovich.

I remember the first time I went to the baseball meetings with Ralph. It was exciting. I'm at a cocktail party and a guy walks in. He says, 'I'd like you to meet Paul Waner?' Paul was the 'Big Poison' of the Waner brothers. Lloyd was 'Little Poison.' I was amazed to see that 'Big Poison' wasn't much taller than my shoulder. Yet he had roughed up the Cubs on many, many occasions. Both brothers were incredibly good ballplayers.

I suppose a lot of us almost worship ballplayers, certainly without knowing a great deal about them. Almost without exception, however, I've found that the great ballplayers were also very nice people. When you see how unimpressed most of them are with their very impressive statistics, you recognize that baseball is really a great game.

In 1957, we realized we had to get out of Lane Field. Arnholt owned Valley Lane Farm in Mission Valley where his daughter, Carol Shannon, trained horses. She was quite an equestrian. Pappy Hazard was a big name in San Diego in those days and owned a diner at what is now the corner of Friars Road and Ulric Street. Smith arranged to buy property from Pappy, Charlie Brown (Town & Country Hotel) and several other people in the Valley and put together the site for Westgate Park (which is now Fashion Valley Shopping Center).

Unfortunately, the University of San Diego was close by on the hill and somebody got to Bishop Buddy. They convinced him that the new park would be an eyesore, bring undesirable people to the area and that the light would interfere with the view from Alcala Park at night. The bishop convinced the Planning Commission that he was right and we were turned down on our application for a ballpark. We appealed to the City Council and won on a 5-2 vote that allowed the park to be built. Smith had to make a lot of concessions like expanding Friars Road and installing a sewer system all the way to Morena Boulevard and that increased the cost of Westgate Park considerably.

Westgate Park was one of the most beautiful ballparks in the country - all of the roofs were cantilever so there were no poles to obstruct any view. The outfield banks were planted in grass and the fans were quite close to the play because the distance between the foul lines and the stands was very short.

The construction of Westgate Park was a real experience. Arnholt had several designers that he used for his bank buildings and he hired them to design the ballpark. Unfortunately, neither knew anything about baseball and,

as a result, we had a number of change orders. In fact, they forgot to add dugouts in the original design, thinking that the ballplayers sat on a bench along the wall.

From the time Westgate Park opened, attendance soared. I can remember one Sunday when Bob Lemon pitched and we had double the capacity of the ballpark attending.

Did Ralph tell you about the problem with Herb Score? You remember what a great pitcher he was. He had to break into the Cleveland line-up that consisted of Early Wynn, Bob Feller, Bob Lemon and Mike Garcia. While he was still a youngster, Gil McDougal of the Yankees hit a line drive that struck Score in the head and broke his eye socket. From that time on, he was very gun-shy and was sent to San Diego for rehab. We noted that Herb would start a game and cruise along for a few innings only to fade rather quickly. He'd start out great and fade quickly. We found out he had been warming up for an hour before the game. Bob Lemon changed his warmup procedure and Score was successful again.

In 1961, Ralph decided that he would have a better future in broadcasting than in general managing and he, with help from Hank Greenberg, became the Mets' broadcaster He worked with Jack Murphy's brother and still does.

One of the smartest things I ever did in my life was hiring Eddie Leishman. He was the consummate baseball man. He knew the front office. He was stadium man and a groundskeeper. He knew baseball talent and we always did well with Eddie in charge. I recently reread a letter I got years ago from Eddie. I start to cry when I think about him. He was a good man.

We had a couple of rough years when we had a working agreement with the Chicago White Sox- Billy Veeck and Hank Greenberg. I worked for Veeck with the Chicago Cubs when I was young as an Andy Frain usher. Veeck was in charge of the ushers at that time.

Eddie Leishman came to us and brought a working agreement with the Cincinnati Reds and Bill DeWitt. The Big Red Machine was just being put together. I remember one night in July when our manager, Dave Bristol, said he was bringing up a young man from the (Class) A league he had formerly managed in. The man's name was Tony Perez and Dave said he would be sensational.

Tony arrived too late to get into uniform one night, so he sat in the bullpen. He could speak little English, but was such a nice guy and great ballplayer that everybody loved him. Of course, he became a great player and I hope he will get into the Hall of Fame.

Chico Ruiz was one of the finest individuals you'd ever want to meet. He was killed in a traffic accident when

Mira Mesa was first going in. I think Camino Ruiz was named after Chico. He was such a spark plug. When we won the pennant in 1962, Chico didn't even have a top batting average (.283), but he sure put a lot of fire in the ball club. I recall the time my wife and I went to Hawaii with the team to play the Islanders. We stayed at the same hotel on Waikiki and I really got to know the ballplayers. They were a great bunch, but Chico was the nicest of them all.

We had been working very hard to get a major league team from the time I came to San Diego. San Francisco columnist Herb Caen called me a knight on a white charger without a horse for my efforts. Al Anderson, Al Hartunian, Bud Porter, Jack Murphy and Gene Gregson - they all worked extremely hard to bring a major league baseball team to San Diego. Murphy came to me at one point and said Buzzie Bavasi might have some interest in coming down to San Diego. I knew he'd be a perfect fit for San Diego. I knew too that we'd have to give him an ownership interest and when I talked to Mr. Smith, he bought the idea.

Chub Feeney and Buzzie were friends, so we had (Giants owner Horace) Stoneham and (Dodgers owner Walter) O'Malley on our side. John Gabrielsen of Pittsburgh and Mrs. Payson in New York were also with us. The toughest major league owner to convince was Roy Hofheinz.

Buzzie, Doug Giddings and I went down to Houston to meet with Judge Hofheinz. On the day of our meeting, an exhibition game was scheduled as part of spring training. Martin Luther King had been killed the day before and, as a result, the games were all canceled. When we arrived at the Astrodome, Judge Hofheinz, without looking at us, snarled, 'Come in and sit down. You're watching the only game in major league history that has been played for one person... me!' On second thought, the reason that Judge Hofheinz didn't get out of his chair

to greet us was probably the fact that he couldn't - he must have weighed 350 pounds.

The Astrodome was really a fancy place. It had a presidential suite for Lyndon B. Johnson complete with an oval office and gold telephone.

Buzzie was the primary reason we got the franchise and Jack Murphy was extremely helpful, too. I stayed with the club as a vice president until Ray (Kroc) bought the club. I stayed on with Ray as the club attorney.

I recall that Arnholt Smith liked everything brown. He painted his bank buildings, his shipyards, his tuna cannery and other buildings brown. He wore brown suits all the time and his letterhead was on brown tinted paper. Because he was the boss, everybody went along with brown for the Padres. It seemed appropriate, because the team is the Padres, but I don't think Buzzie ever really liked the color.

Becoming a major league city was very important to San Diego and Buzzie thought we would damage ourselves from a public relations standpoint if we didn't break completely with the PCL Padres. As time has passed, however, I think that we more and more realize that looking back on our antecedents gives us a great basis upon which to go forward. I'm particularly pleased that the new owners of the Padres, who really know baseball and are doing such a great job, seem to agree."

◆◆◆

LARRY ELLIOT, outfield.
BORN: 3-5-38   PADRES: 1965

Larry Elliott was a star pitcher and outfielder for San Diego American Legion Post 492 when they won the National Championship in 1954. After graduating from Hoover High

Tony Perez

Larry Elliot

Bob Shumake and Casey Stengel

School and playing a year for Rod Dedeaux's USC Trojans, Larry signed with the Pittsburgh organization. He hit .300 for the Pirates in '62 and was briefly back with the Bucs in 1963 before being sold to the Mets in 1964. The following year, Larry enrolled at San Diego State College intending to secure his degree, but the Padres coaxed him into leaving school to play for them. His 14 home runs earned a return ticket to the Big Apple in 1966. Larry became a teacher and coach after his playing days.

"It was sort of a bittersweet feeling (to play in San Diego). Minor league baseball is a lot of fun and I had been a Padre fan since I was a boy. I was making $7,000 in New York. We opened Shea Stadium in 1964. I signed the contract in front of the fans. If you were a Met, they really loved you. They'd literally tear your clothes off. I was from San Diego and had never experienced anything like that! The next year, they only offered $7,000. I said, 'I can't go back and play for $7,000.'

I was going to San Diego State. Eddie Leishman (Padre GM) called and said, 'Larry, you'd better get down here. They can't find you.' They knew I was going to college. Eddie asked, 'Larry, how would you like to play for the Padres?' I said, 'I can't. I'm with the Mets and I'm going to school.' Eddie got me from New York. We had a five day trip to Hawaii, but I worked it out with my professors. I was living with my grandfather in Pt. Loma. I'd go to my 8:00 class and come home. My grandfather made me take a nap. I was 27 years old, but I was taught to respect age, so I would take a nap. I had a lot of fun playing with the Padres and I went back to New York in '66.

We played at Lane Field in the Lions Tournament when I was in high school. Gene Leek hit a home run over the center field fence. Gene was one of the best fielding third basemen I ever saw. After I graduated, I went with Deron Johnson and Jimmie Gilchrist to Lane Field. Ralph Kiner was the Padre general manager and he'd pitch to us. He'd lay it in there and I hit some on Pacific Highway. I was a skinny kid. Kiner really wanted to sign Deron.

I started following baseball with the Padres. San Diego was a different town then. It was twenty cents in the bleachers. Dain Clay was number eight. I remember Luke Easter playing first base. I copied my style after him. Years later, we were both playing in the International League. Luke was about 52 at the time. I used to tease him and said I watched him when I was in the fourth grade. In every town, people would tell stories about how far Luke Easter's home runs went. He was so strong!

We had a lot of talent on that '65 team. Tommy Helms had a good season (.319) and Lee Maye, who is now the hitting instructor for the Baltimore Orioles, had the shortest swing, but he could hit them out! (34 home runs in 1965). It was wonderful and they should have kept

Westgate. It was a nice ballpark. Jim Coates would be the nicest guy, but he was a different guy on the mound. He'd knock people down! Don Rudolph was my friend, but I remember him pitching against me and he knocked me down several times. Afterwards, we were still friends and he didn't think anything of it.

Mel Queen was on that team. He was good enough to make it in the big leagues as an outfielder and a pitcher. His dad, Mel Queen, was a big league pitcher, too. One time, he was playing center field and I was in right. We both go back for a ball. He stuck his glove up and it popped out. I asked, 'What's going on?' (He said) 'It got in the lights.' The next inning, the same thing. He said, 'It got in the moon!'

I don't have a lot of things up in my home. A lot of players are like that. We weren't that successful. We didn't reach the top. The high expectations put a lot of pressure on you. I signed in '57 and I'd never seen a lot of major leaguers before. I was in awe of them. Being a young kid from San Diego, I was in awe of everything. It was something to be playing with Roberto Clemente, Bill Virdon and Bob Skinner. I was trying to get Bob's position with the ball club - It's him or me. They were evaluating me and thought I could hang in on left-handers. I thought they (pitchers) had such good control in the big leagues that they wouldn't hit you. Topps Bubble Gum gave me three suits. That was a big deal for me.

I started in 'D' ball and worked my way up. Every town that I played in, my mother subscribed to the newspaper and kept a scrapbook. They were able to option me down three times. In those days, you had three major league options and three minor league options. They owned you for life until Curt Flood challenged them. They'd sign South American players for $175 a month and those ballplayers weren't even getting enough to eat. There was a legendary minor league pitcher named Steve Dalkowski. He was fast and wild. They left the holes in the screen made by some of his pitches.

I had some good years in Columbus and they had to give me a major league contract, but I couldn't break in. They sold me to New York where I played for Casey Stengel. Casey Stengel was the greatest! He was a great teacher. Good coaches don't yell; they teach. We had good coaches here in San Diego like Les Cassie and Fulton Vickery. Casey knew everything that was going on. If you came in at 2:00 a.m., that was OK. If you came in at 4:00 a.m., you ran into Casey. He'd never say anything. He'd be up at 7:00 a.m. and he would talk to the sportswriters. They couldn't figure out how he did it, but he'd go back in the clubhouse and take a nap. Casey would snooze a little in the dugout, too. I wanted to get a picture of Shea Stadium and I had one of those little spy cameras, so I didn't look too obvious using it in the outfield. I got a picture of Casey sleeping in the dugout, but I had my finger over the lens, so they didn't turn out.

Even Mickey Mantle said that you'd get a fast ball down the middle on a 3-1 count when he broke in, but it's not like that anymore. You don't get to see the same pitcher several times in a game. There are all kinds of relief specialists. That is a big change in baseball. When you're in the outfield, you can tell when the pitcher is losing it. You should catch balls with both hands. You're able to immediately take the ball out of the glove to throw it. When you catch one handed, it takes two steps to get the ball out of your glove. Today's players are bigger, stronger and faster, but they make mental mistakes that you'd never see when I played. I walked out of the last game when I saw Darryl Strawberry walking to the outfield.

I remember going down to Ensenada to play exhibition games in the off-season. They would give you fifty bucks and all you could eat and drink. Don Larsen would fill up his trunk. I haven't talked this much about baseball for a long time. It's wonderful to talk baseball with people who love the game. I remember being rained out in Vancouver. Bob Shaw was the pitching instructor and he talked mechanics. We ate breakfast in a restaurant and we were still there at lunch time, so we ordered lunch, too."

GENE LEEK, third base.
BORN: 7-15-36   PADRES: 1959

Gene Leek was a football and baseball standout at Hoover High School and the University of Arizona. While still in college, Cleveland Indians General Manager Frank Lane signed him to a major league contract and Gene responded with a home run in his first professional game against Detroit on April 22, 1959. Later that season, he was sent to San Diego to gain experience with his hometown Padres. Leek returned to the majors with the expansion Los Angeles Angels in 1961 and 1962. He also played with Portland, Spokane, Mobile (AL) and Reading (PA).

"I started on top and worked my way down, but I loved playing the game and being with the guys. When I went to spring training with Cleveland, right there in Tucson, they gave me Billy Hunter's uniform. I said, 'What's this?' The front was all stained. It was Billy's tobacco. He didn't spit - he just let it run out of his mouth, down his chin and all over his uniform. It wouldn't come out!

I really wasn't in San Diego that long, but it was wonderful to play for the Padres. My dad used to take me all the time when I was a kid. When I was with Cleveland, I was playing with Minnie Minoso. My grandmother used to cheer for Minnie at Lane Field. And

Gene Leek

Ted Williams even said 'Hi' to me. I think he knew I was from Hoover. It was a thrill for me just to be with these guys!

I chewed Beechnut at Arizona. Bud Podbelian gave me Copenhagen when I came to San Diego. It's dynamite! it makes you dizzy, almost drunk, the first time you try it. The skipper sent me to pinch hit. He said, 'Geno, get up there.' The main thing I was trying to do was walk to the plate without staggering. I think I grounded out.

Billy Hunter was out here in San Diego. We'd finish off all the beer together after the game in the clubhouse. Allen Jones had a bat he called 'Big Bertha.' It was about 40 ounces. I couldn't even pick the thing up. They were good guys like Rudy Regalado, Mitch June, he was a Black guy, Kenny Retzer. I played with Kenny at Mobile, too.

John Briggs was a little right-hander. He was a good pitcher. They called him 'The Chinaman.' He had high cheekbones. Dick Smith was an older player. He said, 'Hey, Geno, you're the best third baseman I've heard of since Pie Traynor.' Funny how you remember things like that. The older guys were nice guys. I was just a young guy. Rod Graber was a young guy, too. He could really stroke that ball. Time after time, he'd just hit ropes like Tony Gwynn. He was a pure hitter. He ran good. He could go get 'em with the best of 'em in center field. He just didn't hit with power. Rod was a good guy. He'd drink coke, but he was fun, too. He should have been in the big leagues.

Rod and I played together up in Spokane, too. Preston Gomez was our manager. He was great. He'd pitch you batting practice until your hands would bleed. He'd really work with you. One day, I was practicing my swing in front of the full length mirror in my hotel room and I broke it. When I went to pay for it at the front desk, they told me that Preston had already taken care of it. He felt that I was practicing what he was teaching me, so I shouldn't have to pay. That's the kind of man that Preston Gomez was.

When I was at Reading, my roommate and I had three girls in our room. Our manager, Bob Wellman, knocked on the door for room check. We told the girls to hide under the bed. He came in and talked to us for a while. When he started cussin', the girls started gigglin' and I started coughing to cover it up. He never found out we had those girls in our room. He was a big guy.

Maybe my biggest thrill in baseball was wearing a real uniform for the first time. I was on the Post 201 midget team. We had T-shirts and caps. I think we were eleven or twelve years old. We won in San Diego and got to go up to L.A. to play their champions in Echo Park. They gave us real uniforms. They were too big, but we didn't care. Deron Johnson and Joel Mogy were on that team, too. We won and we didn't even realize the significance of beating the best team in L.A.. That was probably a bigger thrill than even hitting a home run in my first professional game. You know how it is when you're a kid. Getting to wear a real uniform is what you dream about. You know, Bill, I think my best memories are being

Billy Hunter

a kid and going down to watch the Padres play at Lane Field. You'd get there early and chase down home runs in the bleachers with the other kids. Sometimes the players would toss you a ball. They were good. Better than I ever was...

HARRISMEN SET SAIL ON PERILOUS JOURNE
Bound for the first division, it hopes, the Padre Rocket Ship of 1949 take the first time tonight at Lane Field against the Hollywood Stars. Stanley Harris will be at the controls for the first time. Riding the Rocket Ship are t who will start against the Stars, from the left, Center Fielder Dain Clay, Cat Ritchey, Third Baseman Lee Handley, First Baseman Luke Easter, Second Right Fielder Max West, Left Fielder Buster Adams, Shorts

1937. *Right photo with players wearing caps is rarely seen. Back, 2nd from right: Ted Williams.*

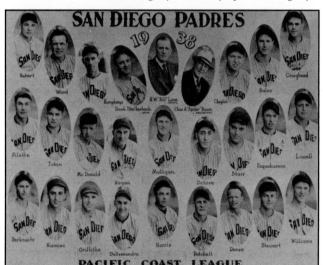

1938

1939

1940

1941

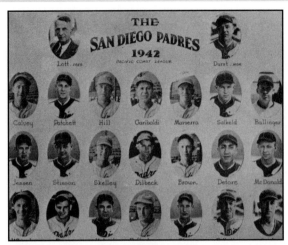

1942

1943

1944

1945

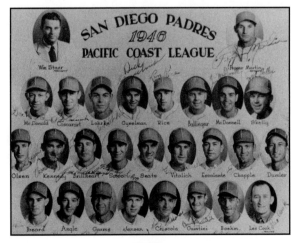

1946

1947

1948

1949

1950

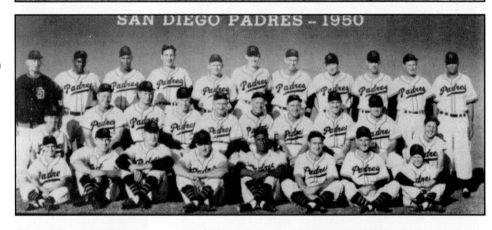

Back Row: LES COOK HENRY MILLER JACK GRAHAM CHARLIE HARRIS SAM JONES NEILL SHERIDAN HARRY MALMBERG JOE ROWELL HARVEY STOREY BILL STARR
Middle Row: RED EMBREE CLARENCE MADDERN AL OLSEN JIMMIE REESE DEL BAKER JACK TOBIN HAL MARAGON BOB WILSON GUY FLETCHER
PAUL GAUGHEN BOB MALLOY CHARLES SIPPLE TONY YORK WHITEY WIETELMANN BOB KERRIGAN JIM TABOR THURMAN TUCKER LLOYD PORTER

1951

SAN DIEGO PADRES--1952

THEOLIC SMITH JOHN DAVIS GUY FLETCHER JACK TOBIN FRANK KERR RON FLOWERS JACK SALVESON ART DOLLAGHAN ALLEN RICHTER LOU STRINGER
AL BENTON JACK GRAHAM LOU KLEIN JIMMIE REESE FRANK "Lefty" O'DOUL BILL STARR MURRAY FRANKLIN MEMO LUNA LONN
DAVID JORDAN AL OLSEN BOB MALLOY THURMAN TUCKER WHITEY WIETELMANN DICK FABER DAIN CLAY HERB GORMAN

1952

1953

1954

1955

1956

1957

A History of the San Diego Padres (1936-1957)

SAN DIEGO PADRE STATISTICS
1936-1957

Byron Humphreys

*RIGHT:
Rocky Colavito's
attempt to break Don
Grate's baseball
distance throwing
record. (7-1-56)*

*BELOW:
Dismantling
Lane Field*

◆1936

NAME	GAMES	AB	R	H	2B	3B	HR	RBI	PCT
Berkowitz, Joseph	45	97	15	24	2	2		6	.247
Campbell, Archie	48	42	3	10	2		1	3	.238
Cook, Lester	7	7							.000
Craghead, Howard *	40	72	2	3				4	.042
Desautels, Eugene	148	480	68	153	18	5	3	69	.319
Doerr, Hal	10	27	1	4					.148
Doerr, Robert	175	695	100	238	37	12	2	77	.342
DiMaggio, Vince	176	641	109	188	43	14	19	102	.293
Durst, Cedric	159	621	71	190	32	3	1	81	.306
Evert, Elmer *	6	14	1	2					.143
Hebert, Wallace	37	91	8	18	3		1	11	.198
Hockette, George	11	9	1	2					.222
Holman, Ernie	174	627	92	197	29	7	6	108	.314
Horne, Berly	40	47	4	10	1			2	.213
Jacobs, Ray	106	332	42	93	23	1	5	46	.280
Joerndt, Ashley	12	19	3	5					.263
Kerr, James	52	124	9	32	4	2	1	17	.258
McDonald, George	103	334	36	106	11	5		52	.317
Monohan, Joe	5	5	2	2					.400
Mulligan, Ed	39	12	6	1					.083
Myatt, George	162	652	117	180	16	12	1	50	.276
Pillette, Herman	31	66	6	13	1			7	.197
Salvo, Manuel	45	82	8	14				2	.171
Shellenback, Frank	31	57	8	20	2			8	.351
Shiver, Ivey, Jr.	54	191	27	59	9	6	7	41	.309
Ward, Dick *	38	64	4	12				9	.188
Wells, Edwin *	43	82	6	17	2	3		6	.207
Williams, Ted	42	107	18	29	8	2		11	.271
Wirthman, Vance	132	428	58	123	20	6	1	49	.287

NAME	GAMES	IP	W	L	PCT	SO	BB	ERA
Campbell, Archie	48	129	6	9	.400	45	73	4.95
Craghead, Howard *	40	235	16	12	.571	109	83	3.60
Hebert, Wallace	35	229	18	12	.600	87	51	3.03
Hill, Jack	2	9		1	.000			
Hockette, George	8	33		3	.000			
Horne, Berly	38	164	7	14	.333	76	78	4.39
Pillette, Herman	31	191	11	8	.579	63	37	3.16
Salvo, Manuel	45	239	15	12	.556	145	74	3.31
Shellenback, Frank	15	102	6	7	.462	38	13	3.53
Ward, Dick *	37	184	15	7	.682	83	100	3.42
Wells, Edwin *	30	196	9	13	.409	62	60	4.32

(* Craghead: Sea-SD, Evert: SD-Sac, Ward: Sac-SD, Wells: SD-Sea)

◆1937

NAME	GAMES	AB	R	H	2B	3B	HR	RBI	PCT
Berkowitz, Joe	126	422	49	107	23	2		35	.254
Chaplin, James	56	124	13	30	5	1	2	18	.242
Craghead, Howard	42	80	4	11	2			7	.138

1937-Con't.	GAMES	AB	R	H	2B	3B	HR	RBI	PCT
Detore, George	133	434	70	145	22	8	3	72	.3341
Durst, Cedric	137	458	52	134	25	2	2	57	.293
Gonzales, Joe	10	12	1	2					.167
Hebert, Wally	40	89	3	17	2	1		7	.191
Holman, Ernie	94	305	38	68	6	3	1	28	.223
McDonald, George	163	632	95	197	22	7	4	102	.312
Mulligan, Ed	35	86	13	22	4			5	.256
Myatt, George	155	565	102	159	17	6	6	51	.281
Patchett, Hal	169	689	105	211	38	8	8	66	.306
Pillette, Herman	35	41	8	2				5	.195
Reese, Jimmie	138	506	59	159	23	7	2	78	.314
Salvo, Manuel	46	96	12	16	3			4	.167
Shellenback, Frank	10	9	1	2					.222
Skelley, Bill	10	9							.000
Starr, Bill	92	278	17	61	13	1		34	.219
Stewart, Ed	9	8	2						.000
Thompson, Rupert	169	647	111	211	31	5	16	92	.326
Walters, John	14	18		3					.167
Ward, Dick	42	112	11	22	1			9	.196
Williams, Ted	138	454	66	132	24	2	23	98	.291

NAME	GAMES	IP	W	L	PCT	SO	BB	ERA
Chaplin, James	43	318	23	15	.605	151	114	2.72
Craghead, Howard	42	245	16	13	.552	119	74	3.27
Gonzales, Joe	6	26		2	.000			
Hebert, Wallace	39	244	17	14	.549	90	42	3.02
Pillette, Herman	36	126	4	5	.444	38	29	3.78
Salvo, Manuel	46	278	19	13	.594	196	107	3.08
Shellenback, Frank	6	16		1	.000			
Ward, Dick	42	284	18	18	.500	92	116	4.44

◆1938

NAME	GAMES	AB	R	H	2B	3B	HR	RBI	PCT
Berkowitz, Joe	129	443	72	132	23	6	1	52	.298
Chaplin, James	54	116	12	28	3		1	16	.241
Craghead, Howard	47	95	4	8		1		2	.084
Dallessandro, Dom	155	541	108	167	29	8	22	91	.309
Detore, George	109	296	48	77	12	4	3	40	.260
Durst, Cedric*	134	474	54	146	17	5	4	46	.308
Griffiths, John	169	613	78	173	27			69	.282
Harris, Spencer	163	545	86	164	39	4	7	92	.301
Hebert, Wallace	40	94	10	27	2			17	.287
Hogan, Francis	109	331	27	85	11		1	42	.257
Holman, Ernie	8	17		2					.118
Humphreys, Byron	28	53	4	8	1			3	.151
McDonald, George	143	549	49	147	26	4		61	.268
Mulligan, Ed	8	12	3	3					.250
Niemiec, Al	130	461	60	140	18	2	2	66	.304
Patchett, Hal	166	668	98	202	38	12	3	57	.302
Pillette, Herman	26	26	2	2	1				.077
Reese, Jimmie	108	349	41	81	11	1		28	.232

1938-Con't.	GAMES	AB	R	H	2B	3B	HR	RBI	PCT
Rhodes, Gordon	11	8	1	2					.250
Salvo, Manuel	42	89	6	15	1	2		10	.168
Starr, Bill	10	26	1	7					.269
Stewart, Ed	94	230	33	62	8	2		15	.270
Tobin, Marion	10	10	2	3					.300
Ward, Dick	32	70	5	15	1	1		5	.214
Williams, John	43	116	10	24	2	1	1	9	.207

NAME	GAMES	IP	W	L	PCT	SO	BB	ERA
Chaplin, James	45	285	20	16	.556	137	85	3.57
Craghead, Howard	47	271	18	18	.500	138	79	2.86
Hebert, Wallace	37	243	12	16	.429	102	58	3.11
Humphreys, Byron	28	166	9	12	.429	50	35	2.33
Pillette, Herman	26	78	2	2	.500	29	18	2.65
Salvo, Manuel	40	239	22	9	.710	191	82	2.60
Ward, Dick	30	174	9	12	.429	55	65	5.02

(Forty-five innings or more)
(* Durst: SD-Holly)

◆1939

NAME	GAMES	AB	R	H	2B	3B	HR	RBI	PCT
Berkowitz, Joe	132	402	61	105	17	8		43	.261
Berger, Fred	13	39	3	8					.205
Carlyle, Cleo	77	258	30	70	12	3	2	31	.271
Craghead, Howard	34	66	2	6				3	.091
Dallessandro, Dom	157	541	101	199	50	9	18	98	.368
Dedeaux, Raoul *	30	79	9	13	1			5	.165
Detore, George	129	411	59	146	28	5	4	72	.355
Durst, Cedric	73	155	12	41	6			18	.265
Farquharson, Bill	6	6		2					.333
Gonzales, Joe	29	49	2	12	1			2	.245
Gray, Bill	6	13		2					.154
Griffiths, John	119	384	34	87	12	1		25	.227
Hare, Joe	14	7	1	1					.143
Haslin, Mickey	151	537	85	185	29	5	11	79	.345
Hebert, Wallace	39	117	12	30	5	1		12	.256
Humphreys, Byron	35	74	2	10	2	2		6	.135
Jensen, John	68	153	19	37	3	4	4	24	.242
McDonald, George	134	490	53	112	17	6	1	50	.229
Newsome, Heber *	38	62	1	15	1	1		6	.242
Niemiec, Al	155	531	54	148	20	6		63	.279
Olsen, Al	34	51	7	11			1	5	.216
Patchett, Hal	160	610	83	177	24	7		32	.290
Pillette, Herman	25	29	3	6				1	.207
Starr, Bill	86	248	15	56	5	1	1	21	.226
Stewart, Ed	61	186	33	57	10	3	4	17	.306
Tobin, Marion	46	71	5	21	5	1		4	.296
Ward, Dick *	7	8							.000
Weldon, Lawrence	7	13	2	3+					.154
Williams, John	95	289	33	81	10	2	2	30	.280

NAME	GAMES	IP	W	L	PCT	SO	BB	ERA
Craghead, Howard	34	203	11	16	.407	94	56	4.75
Gonzales, Joe	22	138	11	7	.611	42	46	3.52
Hare, Joe	14	31	1	2	.333			
Hebert, Wallace	39	299	20	10	.667	104	64	3.13
Humphreys, Byron	36	208	9	15	.375	54	55	4.07
Link, Edward	4	19	1	2	.333			
Newsome, Heber *	38	178	6	14	.300	60	61	5.26
Olsen, Al	34	164	7	12	.368	76	94	4.72
Pillette, Herman	25	89	8	6	.571	22	21	2.32
Tobin, Marion	45	186	7	15	.318	124	119	3.92
Ward, Dick *	7	25	1	3	.250			
Weldon, Lawrence	7	29	3	1	.750			

(* Dedeaux: SD-Holly, Newsome: Port-SD, Ward: SD-LA) [+ Weldon: 2 hits?]

◆1940

NAME	GAMES	AB	R	H	2B	3B	HR	RBI	PCT
Berkowitz, Joe	53	100	11	21	6			5	.210
Charowhas, Pete	1	2							.000
Craghead, Howard	38	56	3	6				2	.107
Detore, George	90	265	45	85	18	5	2	35	.321
DeVolder, Ed	5	3							.000
Dumler, Carl	5	4							.000
Durst, Cedric	47	67	10	19	2	1	1	13	.284
Garibaldi, Art *	165	582	83	146	31	4	5	70	.251
Haslin, Mickey	164	616	98	198	43	2	9	103	.321
Hebert, Wallace	45	116	6	30	5	2		16	.259
Humphreys, Byron	40	76	10	17	4	2		7	.224
Jeli, Anton	1	1		1					1.000
Jensen, John	140	481	50	146	18	3	1	64	.304
McDonald, George	141	537	56	155	20	5	2	63	.289
Mesner, Steve	179	680	114	232	40	12		97	.341
Millard, Jack	9	11		2					.182
Morris, James	35	36	3	6				3	.167
Newsome, Heber	39	121	9	23	4			13	.190
Olsen, Al	20	49	1	7				4	.143
Patchett, Hal	166	686	109	195	28	5		51	.284
Pillette, Herman	21	25	2	5				3	.200
Salkeld, Bill	127	431	70	124	20	4	20	81	.288
Shores, Bill	8	5		1					.200
Sperry, Stan	158	551	72	167	27	3		76	.303
Stewart, Ed	179	723	107	231	32	12	6	71	.320
Stinson, Frank	34	106	11	21				14	.198
Tobin, Marion	22	11	1	2				2	.182
Thomas, Bill *	50	115	8	20		1		4	.174
Tubb, Julian	3								.000
Williams, John	35	77	10	19	3	1		12	.247

NAME	GAMES	IP	W	L	PCT	SO	BB	ERA
Craghead, Howard	38	175	8	14	.364	66	74	4.88
Dumler, Carl	5	12		1	.000			

1940-Con't.	GAMES	IP	W	L	PCT	SO	BB	ERA
Hebert, Wallace	38	280	15	18	.455	106	100	3.91
Humphreys, Byron	40	216	13	14	.481	48	55	3.71
Morris, James	35	100	4	1	.800	34	50	4.14
Newsome, Heber	39	315	23	11	.676	128	74	2.62
Olson, Al	20	118	7	7	.500	47	39	4.11
Pillette, Herman	22	89	7	2	.778	31	18	2.82
Shores, Bill	8	16	2	3	.400			
Thomas, Bill *	44	294	16	20	.444	96	70	3.91
Tobin, Marion	21	45	3	5	.375	26	37	7.39

(* Garibaldi: Sac-SD, Thomas: Port-SD)

◆1941

NAMES	GAMES	AB	R	H	2B	3B	HR	RBI	PCT
Ballinger, Del	46	102	9	30	5	1		9	.294
Brewer, Bernard	18	11	1	1	1				.091
Detore, George	118	378	61	121	26	6	5	61	.320
Devincenzi, Jack	12	28		3					.107
Dilbeck, Rex	32	32	3	3				2	.094
Durst, Cedric	30	53	4	13	2			2	.245
Garibaldi, Art	107	329	46	94	14	2	5	49	.286
Hallbourg, Darwin	4	1		1					1.000
Haslin, Mickey	125	458	65	138	27	3	5	75	.301
Hebert, Wallace	41	113	9	33	1	2		9	.292
Humphreys, Byron *	34	42	3	11	1			2	.262
Jensen, John	148	509	69	155	17	6	7	55	.305
Kirby, Jordan	15	55	7	15	1	3	1	6	.273
Lanifero, Fred	17	60	8	18	2			7	.300
Malman, Joseph	16	10	2	1					.100
Mazzera, Melvin	171	626	87	168	33	11	16	104	.268
McDonald, George	157	611	80	173	23	3	1	58	.283
Morris, James	3	2							.000
Oliver, Dell	4	3							.000
Olsen, Al	39	78	2	8				6	.103
Patchett, Hal	168	622	78	184	21	8		60	.296
Peel, Homer *	29	71	8	17	1			9	.239
Pellagrini, Eddie	173	659	107	180	39	10	8	70	.273
Pillette, Herman	15	4							.000
Powell, Larry	5	6		1					.167
Rich, Woodrow	23	50	4	12	1			6	.240
Salkeld, Bill	116	324	39	73	12	3	7	51	.225
Sperry, Stanley	148	523	60	140	25	6	2	60	.268
Terry, Yank	41	111	8	19	1	1		9	.171
Thomas, Bill	54	94	8	22	2			8	.234

NAME	GAMES	IP	W	L	PCT	SO	BB	ERA
Brewer, Bernard	18	39	1		1.000			
Dilbeck, Rex	33	95	6	4	.600	43	32	2.65
Hebert, Wallace	39	279	22	10	.688	102	58	3.00
Humphreys, Byron *	33	128	5	12	.294	35	41	5.06
Malman, Joseph	16	37	2	3	.400			
Olsen, Al	38	247	14	16	.467	107	90	3.72

1941 Con't.	GAMES	IP	W	L	PCT	SO	BB	ERA
Pillette, Herman	15	20	1	2	.333			
Powell, Larry	5	19	2		1.000			
Rich, Woodrow	23	139	9	9	.500	66	60	3.50
Terry, Yank	40	315	26	8	.765	172	74	2.31
Thomas, Bill	44	272	15	17	.469	78	61	3.31

(* Humphreys: SD-LA, Peel: Oak-SD)

◆1942

NAME	GAMES	AB	R	H	2B	3B	HR	RBI	PCT
Brown, Norman	47	68	6	15	2			6	.221
Calvey, Jack	149	545	61	153	16	6	4	66	.281
Dasso, Frank	43	102	4	23	4	1	1	12	.225
Detore, George	106	303	37	76	12	3	2	38	.251
Dilbeck, Rex	31	39	3	10				3	.256
Garibaldi, Art	100	298	27	67	14			25	.225
Hebert, Wallace	41	123	9	27	1	1		9	.220
Hill, John	146	544	60	154	21	6	2	62	.283
Jensen, John	164	578	75	159	23	5	11	64	.275
Lohrke, Jack	7	17		2	1			2	.118
Mazzera, Melvin	158	575	77	177	30	13	14	90	.308
McDonald, George	70	272	25	73	10	4		19	.268
Patchett, Hal	172	663	83	191	23	5		43	.288
Poffenberger, Cletus	39	67	6	23	1	2	1	14	.343
Salkeld, Bill	121	354	59	101	20	2	7	60	.285
Skelley, Melvin	148	489	60	123	21	4	2	49	.252
Sperry, Stanley	36	96	10	28	4	1		1	.292
Stinson, Frank	78	259	26	68	6	3	1	18	.263
Thomas, Bill *	52	53	4	11				3	.208
Whipple, Jack	85	259	31	65	11	1	3	20	.251

(Fifteen or More Games)

NAME	GAMES	IP	W	L	PCT	SO	BB	ERA
Brown, Norman	41	197	13	12	.520	76	80	3.58
Dasso, Frank	42	284	15	18	.454	155	127	2.88
Dilbeck, Rex	30	123	11	6	.647	48	23	3.29
Hebert, Wallace	40	319	22	15	.594	125	78	2.37
Olsen, Al	45	293	18	16	.529	94	93	2.76
Pillette, Herman	11	41	1	1	.500	7	9	
Poffenberger, Cletus	38	168	9	10	.474	40	80	3.86
Thomas, Bill *	44	163	9	13	.409	57	35	2.65

(Forty-five or More Innings)
(* Thomas: SD-Holly)

◆1943

NAME	GAMES	AB	R	H	2B	3B	HR	RBI	PCT
Abbott, Morrison	85	247	14	60	9		1	27	.243
Ballinger, Del	59	135	12	38	5	1	2	15	.281
Brillheart, James	35	70	7	17	2			5	.243
Cailteaux, Al	67	185	22	42	2			13	.227
Calvey, Jack	149	534	69	145	16	5		54	.272

1943 Con't.	GAMES	AB	R	H	2B	3B	HR	RBI	PCT
Cecil, Rex	22	46	3	9				4	.196
Chapple, Earl	15	10		1				1	.100
Dasso, Frank	33	67	7	19	3		1	6	.284
Detore, George	73	187	26	60	12	1	1	29	.321
Dilbeck, Rex	21	41	1	6					.146
Durst, Cedric	10	7							.000
Estes, Lou	53	115	9	24	3	1		11	.209
Gudat, Marvin *	128	407	47	104	14	1		26	.256
Jensen, John	49	153	26	39	10		3	21	.255
Johnson, Chet	36	85	8	11	3			6	.129
Lamanski, Frank	8	4		1					.250
Lowe, Walter	144	499	54	132	17	3	2	55	.265
Martin, Joe	13	13		2					.154
McCarty, Jack	1	2		2					1.000
McDonald, George	112	391	42	129	24	10		50	.330
Merkle, Warren	23	11	1	1				1	.091
Morgan, George	71	152	13	41	6	2		16	.270
Olsen, Al	9	16		1					.063
Patchett, Hal	141	522	63	148	12	15	1	49	.284
Salkeld, Bill	111	309	32	85	18	4	2	47	.275
Schanz, Charley	47	105	10	19	5		1	6	.181
Steiner, Mel	36	90	8	18	2			10	.200
Wheeler, Eddie	133	493	83	150	18	7	3	32	.304
Whipple, Jack	64	225	22	49	5	3	1	25	.218

NAME	GAMES	IP	W	L	PCT	SO	BB	ERA
Brillheart, James	33	213	9	14	.391	53	99	3.51
Cecil, Rex	20	137	8	10	.444	81	51	2.89
Chapple, Earl	19	41		3	.000			
Dasso, Frank	27	177	12	8	.600	154	93	2.75
Dilbeck, Rex	21	118	7	9	.438	37	24	3.51
Lamanski, Frank	8	20	1	1	.500			
Olsen, Al	9	50	2	4	.333	7	8	4.14
Johnson, Chet	35	242	14	16	.467	106	97	3.27
Merkle, Warren	23	49		2	.000	16	19	6.06
Schanz, Charley	44	276	17	18	.486	137	130	3.23

(* Gudat: Holly-SD)

◆1944

NAME	GAMES	AB	R	H	2B	3B	HR	RBI	PCT
Abbott, Morrison	87	197	17	50	7		5	25	.254
Ballinger, Del	99	278	17	67	3	1		26	.241
Bauer, Keith	6	4		1					.250
Brillheart, James	28	61	2	8	2			2	.131
Cailteaux, Al	46	119	14	21	5	1		7	.176
Calvey, Jack	138	514	54	128	10	6	1	44	.249
Cecil, Rex	36	90	8	23	2	1	1	8	.256
Dasso, Frank	46	94	10	17	3		1	11	.181
Detore, George	32	48	8	14	3	1		4	.292
Dilbeck, Rex	9	6		1					.167
Dumler, Carl	22	21	1	4					.190

1944 Con't.	GAMES	AB	R	H	2B	3B	HR	RBI	PCT
Estes, Lou	5	9		2					.222
Filippo, Anthony	4								.000
Gudat, Marvin	113	369	38	104	14	2		31	.282
Hanski, Donald	15	25		2	2			2	.080
Hernandez, Manuel	30	82	9	17	2	2		5	.207
Johnson, Chet	28	63	2	4				3	.063
Kleinke, Norbert *	32	43	2	5					.116
Lane, Omar	3	3							.000
Lazor, John	35	124	17	38	3	1	1	7	.306
Lowe, Walter	46	148	19	41	7	2		27	.277
Lucier, Louis	9	15		5					.333
MacFaden, James *	4	1		1					1.000
Martin, Joseph	8	13		2					.154
Mazzera, Melvin	14	40		8					.200
McDonald, George	85	313	32	97	18	2		34	.310
Merkle, Warren	15	10	1	3	1				.300
Morgan, George	86	224	21	52	5	2		15	.232
Patchett, Hal	128	426	49	117	10	5	1	56	.275
Paynich, Rudy	3	1							.000
Ortiz, Vidal	1	3							.000
Reynolds, Vernon	120	371	46	99	11	7		39	.267
Salkeld, Bill	115	340	49	82	16		3	49	.241
Sciarra, Hank	16	19	2	3	1				.158
Steiner, Melvin *	110	345	37	92	12		1	36	.267
Thompson, Rupert	39	127	14	27	2			8	.213
Valenzuela, Joe	36	49	5	11	3	1		4	.224
Vezelich, Lou	79	265	28	73	16	2	1	31	.275
Wheeler, Eddie	163	655	97	175	36	9	2	56	.267
Whipple, Jack	43	152	19	37	10	1		12	.243
Wood, Joe Jr.	10	29	7						.241

NAME	GAMES	IP	W	L	PCT	SO	BB	ERA
Bauer, Keith	8	13		1	.000			
Brillheart, James	27	190	8	14	.364	43	65	3.38+
Cecil, Rex	36	246	19	11	.633	186	103	2.16
Dasso, Frank	40	298	20	19	.513	253	131	2.81
Dilbeck, Rex	9	24	1	1	.500			
Dumler, Carl	22	74	3	6	.333	32	45	3.28
Hanski, Donald	15	73	2	7	.222	21	22	4.07
Johnson, Chet	29	186	12	11	.522	138	94	3.53
Kleinke, Norbert *	30	138	5	10	.333	45	57	3.91
Lowe, Walter	4	18		2	.000			
Lucier, Louis	8	46	1	5	.167	19	7	4.50
MacFaden, James *	4	7		1	.000			
Merkle, Warren	15	38	1	3	.250			
Valenzuela, Joe	36	137	3	10	.231	58	98	4.66
Wood, Joe Jr.	10	79	5	4	.556	35	37	2.50

(* Kleinke: Oak-SD, MacFaden: Sac-SD, Steiner SD-Oak) [+Brillheart 3.05?]

NAME	GAMES	AB	R	H	2B	3B	HR	RBI	PCT
Abbott, Morrison	111	268	21	75	14		5	42	.280
Amaro, Jesus	6	10		1					.100
Bailey, Robert	7	5							.000
Ballinger, Del	171	562	46	168	27	3	2	82	.299
Bey, Herman	1	1							.000
Boken, Robert	68	233	38	77	14	1	8	57	.330
Brillheart, James	46	70	9	11	1			5	.157
Campbell. Donald	3	1							.000
Crimele, Frank	23	37	5	5				2	.135
Criscola, Tony	180	689	134	214	27	8	1	58	.311
Dumler, Carl	41	94	9	15	1			3	.159
Dunphy, Jack	98	283	37	61	6	4		12	.216
Eaves, Vallie	52	106	5	14	3		1	13	.132
Ferguson, Robert	39	68	1	7					.103
Gira, Frank	77	225	13	46	3			16	.204
Greene, John	2	2							.000
Grigg, Donald *	43	81	4	12	2			5	.148
Gudat, Marvin	102	238	21	63	11	2		25	.265
Gyselman, Dick	154	576	102	185	31	4	2	74	.321
Harshman, Jack	21	67	2	17				11	.254
Jones, Earl	3								.000
Justice, William	9	15		2					.133
Katnich, Joe	5	2		1					.500
Knowles, Giles *	26	56	4	13	2			11	.232
Kreevich, John	71	294	33	74	10	4	1	25	.252
Kubiak, Louis	16	52	4	8	2			6	.154
Martin, John	53	97	27	30	6	4	1	15	.309
McClure, Jack	3								.000
McNamara, Robert	14	42		9					.214
Miller, John	10	11		1					.091
Monzo, Carl *	21	10							.000
Morales, William	7	2		1					.500
Nelson, Gerry	12	13		1					.077
Pacheco, Frank	24	35	1	8	2			2	.229
Prout, William *	110	356	31	104	19	2		59	.292
Reynolds, Vern *	143	473	70	110	17	7		42	.233
Savin, Henry	11	31		7					.226
Sciarra, Hank	38	79	17	12	2	1		3	.152
Solano, Claudio	7	13		2					.154
Stockman, Bruce	5	13		2					.154
Sweeney, Henry	26	91	12	19	3			8	.209
Thompson, Rupert	126	344	65	119	16	2	1	26	.346
Tincup, Frank	19	13	1	1				2	.077
Trahd. Victor	53	31	9	9	2	1		3	.290
Valenzuela, Joe	10	4		2					.500
Vezelich, Louis	175	628	97	193	38	6	6	110	.307
Watson, Ralph *	23	42	10	12	1			4	.286
Willis, Dick	2	2							.000
Wensloff, Charles	10	22		4					.182

1954 Con't.	GAMES	AB	R	H	2B	3B	HR	RBI	PCT
Wetmore, Ray *	17	2		42	1	12		3	.286
Wolfe, Donald	3	1		1					1.000
Womack, Jerry	13	20		5					.250

NAME	GAMES	IP	W	L	PCT	SO	BB	ERA
Bailey, Robert	6	18		2	.000			
Brillheart, James	45	236	15	13	.536	87	101	4.50
Dumler, Carl	42	282	21	16	.568	143	104	2.42
Eaves, Vallie	52	312	21	15	.583	187	127	3.00
Ferguson, Robert	39	211	5	21	.192	108	114	3.54
Jones, Earl	3	4		1	.000			
Knowles, Giles *	26	153	8	7	.533	43	83	4.29
Martin, John	1	5	1		1.000			
Monzo, Carl *	21	48	3	3	.500	25	29	5.06
Morales, William	7	13	1		1.000			
Nelson, Gerry	12	42	1	2	.333			
Tincup, Frank	16	46		3	.000	18	36	7.82
Trahd, Victor	39	121	5	10	.333	41	75	5.21
Valenzuela, Joe	9	17		4	.000			
Wensloff, Charles	10	73	3	4	.429	40	24	3.82
Womack, Jerry	10	27		1	.000			

(* Grigg: LA-SD, Knowles: Sac-SD, Monzo: Oak-SD, Prout: Sac-SD, Reynolds: SD-Holly, Watson: SF-SD, Wetmore: Sac-SD)

◆1946

NAME	GAMES	AB	R	H	2B	3B	HR	RBI	PCT
Angle, Jack	121	368	47	92	7	6	2	24	.250
Ballinger, Del*	92	276	19	76	11	2	1	32	.275
Boehm, Edward	62	206	29	42	6	1	4	17	.204
Bowman, Joseph	16	14		1	1			2	.077
Breard, Stanislaus	96	318	18	69	11	4	1	32	.217
Brillheart, James	19	6	1	2	1				.333
Chapetta, Anthony	4								.000
Chapple, Earl	36	28	3	4	1				.143
Coscarart, Pete	76	251	23	54	10	1	4	24	.215
Criscola, Tony	163	603	81	165	29	6	2	56	.274
Dejan, Mike	18	38	4	4				1	.105
Dumler, Carl	40	30	1	4				3	.133
Eaves, Vallie	4	9		1					.111
Eisenmann, Charles	18	20		4					.200
Escalante, Earl *	19	16	1	4				1	.250
Estes, Louis	3	2							.000
Faria, Joseph	1								.000
Garms, Debs	142	466	48	126	14	3	1	44	.270
Gedzius, Joseph	18	46	4	6	3			3	.130
Guintini, Ben*	72	257	29	66	13	3	4	24	.257
Gyselman, Dick	171	619	77	174	22	8		58	.281
Hackett, Jack	4	3							.000
Harshmann, Jack	3	13		2					.154
Hill, John	10	11		1					.091
Ignasiak, Edwin	9	32		4					.125

1946 Con't.	GAMES	AB	R	H	2B	3B	HR	RBI	PCT
Jensen, John	155	496	60	149	27	6	4	53	.300
Jordan, Kirby	5	3							.000
Kennedy, Vern	34	85	6	17	3	2		4	.200
Knowles, Giles	5	1		1					1.000
Konopka, Bruce	25	69	9	14	2	1	2	11	.203
Lanifero, Fred	73	224	21	48	5			19	.214
Lohrke, Jack	92	350	41	106	19	4	8	48	.303
Lund, Donald	12	33		5					.152
Martin, John	11	15		3					.200
Martin, L.L.	5	11		4					.364
McDonald, George*	142	506	55	140	21	5	1	56	.277
McDonnell, James	69	189	14	45	4			13	.238
Olsen, Al	45	91	5	10	2			7	.110
Poffenberger, Cletus	17	25	2	5				1	.200
Rice, Leonard	108	286	32	70	9	2		26	.245
Salvo, Manuel	13	30		5					.167
Seats, Thomas	36	68	4	8	1			4	.118
Skelley, Melvin	40	72	8	13	2			6	.181
Thompson, Rupert	3	3							.000
Treichel, Albert	13	14		2					.143
Trusky, Victor	7	17		2					.118
Vezelich, Louis	24	67	6	17	3		1	2	.254
Vitalich, Edward	38	60	3	6				3	.100

NAME	GAMES	IP	W	L	PCT	SO	BB	ERA
Bowman, Joseph	15	40	1	2	.333			
Brillheart, James	20	37	1	1	.500			
Chapple, Earl	35	108	2	6	.250	50	74	4.33
Dumler, Carl	40	114	1	11	.083	48	43	4.18
Eaves, Vallie	4	29	1	3	.250			
Eisenmann, Charles	17	72	3	6	.333	62	51	3.62
Escalante, Earl *	19	58	3	5	.375	19	27	3.57
Kennedy, Vern	34	225	18	13	.581	95	103	2.92
Knowles, Giles	5	6	1	1	.500			
Olsen, Al	45	288	17	15	.531	104	68	2.91
Poffenberger, Cletus	16	70	5	6	.455	19	32	3.86
Salvo, Manuel	13	92	3	6	.333	20	20	3.33
Seats, Thomas	36	236	11	18	.379	96	52	3.13
Treichel, Albert	13	48	3	3	.500	43	30	4.87
Vitalich, Edward	38	213	11	16	.407	78	82	3.42

(* Ballinger: SD-Port, Escalante: Holly-SD, Guintini: Holly-SD, McDonald: Sea-SD)

◆1947

NAME	GAMES	AB	R	H	2B	3B	HR	RBI	AVE
Barrett, John	158	524	78	145	33	7	9	70	.277
Caster, George *	23	4							.000
Clay, Dain	168	668	107	209	36	9	10	62	.313
Coscarart, Peter	142	545	72	139	29	2	6	55	.255
Criscola, Anthony *	50	94	14	17	2		1	5	.181
Gyselman, Dick *	133	446	54	113	16	3	1	36	.253
Hamilton, Robert	87	186	22	42	9	3		13	.226
Jensen, John	137	462	63	142	31	4	5	59	.307

1947 Con't.	GAMES	AB	R	H	2B	3B	HR	RBI	AVE
Kennedy, Lloyd V.	36	72	8	15			1	5	.208
Kerr, Frank	143	433	66	130	30	3	11	60	.300
Kerrigan, Robert	40	59	6	10	2			2	.169
Lee, Larry	108	343	24	84	7	3	1	13	.245
McDonnell, James	33	62	9	15	2	1		6	.242
Nance, L. Eugene	19	52	6	13	2	1	2	11	.250
Olsen, Albert	46	44	4	5	1	1		2	.114
Rice, Leonard	87	237	20	56	10		1	18	.236
Salvo, Manuel	34	63	6	10	1	1		3	.159
Seats, Thomas	46	110	11	23	5	1	2	13	.209
Shupe, Vincent	175	669	74	175	42	9	9	97	.262
Tran, Ray	152	531	51	113	17	6		44	.213
Treichel, Albert	36	98	9	25	3	1	2	10	.255
Vitalich, Edward	44	49		7	2			1	.143
West, Max	167	562	103	172	26	6	43	124	.306
Winters, Mickey+	25	52	6	13	1			3	.250

(Fifteen or more games)
[+Winters, Mickey AKA: Weintraub, Mickey]

NAME	GAMES	IP	W	L	PCT	SO	BB	ERA
Kennedy, Lloyd V.	36	195	9	15	.375	102	82	4.11
Kerrigan, Robert	40	185	9	12	.429	61	64	4.67
Olsen, Albert	46	162	6	13	.316	48	41	4.72
Salvo, Manuel	34	200	14	13	.519	77	44	3.83
Seats, Thomas	45	306	17	17	.500	130	39	3.65
Treichel, Albert	35	249	14	15	.483	147	151	4.12
Vitalich, Edward	44	181	7	15	.318	60	67	3.78

(Forty-five or More Innings)
(* Caster: Holly-SD, Criscola: SD-Sea, Gyselman: SD-Sea)

◆1948

NAME	GAMES	AB	R	H	2B	3B	HR	RBI	AVE
Adams, Elvin	102	273	31	69	13	1	8	34	.253
Barrett, John	154	513	105	174	33	12	14	90	.339
Budnick, Michael	28	26	2	9				4	.346
Camelli, Henry	79	202	18	54	12		4	22	.267
Caulfield, John	10	13	1	4				1	.308
Clay, Dain	186	756	133	220	36	5	15	77	.291
Coscarart, Peter	114	309	34	64	4		3	25	.207
DeVito, Vito	36	72	14	16	2			4	.222
Flores, Jesse	41	74	4	10	2			1	.135
Graham, Jack	138	473	111	141	23	6	48	136	.298
Greco, Richard	26	78	12	19	4		4	17	.244
Handley, Lee	181	703	94	211	40	3	5	65	.300
Jensen, John	97	251	28	70	16		6	34	.279
Jurisich, Albert	38	57	4	6				3	.105
Kerrigan, Robert	44	31	1	2					.065
Kuper, Earl	36	37	1	10	1		1	8	.270
Lee, Larry	22	68	9	16	3		1	6	.235
Lillard, William	31	66	5	12	2		1	7	.182
Mesner, Stephen *	172	586	75	174	35	1	8	76	.297

1948 Con't.	GAMES	AB	R	H	2B	3B	HR	RBI	AVE
Nicholas, George	13	13	3	5	1			1	.385
Olsen, Albert	35	51	2	10	1			1	.196
Perlmutter, Daniel	12	12	5	6				1	.500
Rescigno, Xavier	41	66	15	15	8		1	12	.227
Rice, Leonard	108	305	31	85	9	1		34	.279
Ritchey, John	103	217	35	70	10	2	4	44	.323
Salvo, Manuel *	36	39	3	5	1			2	.128
Seats, Thomas	43	84	7	22	1	1	1	12	.262
Shupe, Vincent	135	469	48	115	18	4	6	60	.245
Thompson, Gene	32	15		1				1	.067
Tran, Ray	25	48	7	12	3	1		5	.250
Venturelli, Angelo	10	4		1					.250
Wade, Jacob	13	14		1				3	.071
Walden, Phillip	52	26	1	3					.115
Wells, Leo *	151	474	47	127	26	2	3	61	.268

(Ten or More Games)

NAME	GAMES	IP	W	L	PCT	SO	BB	ERA
Budnick, Michael	28	104	4	8	.333	53	46	4.67
Flores, Jesse	41	225	11	19	.367	111	81	4.36
Jurisich, Albert	38	189	11	12	.478	124	73	5.62
Kerrigan, Robert	46	131	3	6	.333	31	58	4.74
Nicholas, George	13	47	2	4	.333	19	23	6.89
Olsen, Albert	34	159	10	14	.417	76	52	4.81
Rescigno, Xavier	38	221	18	14	.563	87	70	4.64
Salvo, Manuel *	36	121	5	7	.417	59	46	4.39
Seats, Thomas	43	258	12	14	.462	114	39	4.15
Thompson, Gene	32	72	8	3	.727	31	40	2.00
Wade, Jacob	12	47		4	.000	18	33	7.08
Walden, Phillip	52	113	3	4	.429	31	48	5.65

(Forty-five or More Innings)
(* Mesner: Sac-SD, Salvo: SD-Sac, Wells: Sac-SD)

◆1949

NAME	GAMES	AB	R	H	2B	3B	HR	RBI	AVE
Adams, C.D."Red" *	30	63	6	10	1			6	.159
Adams, Elvin	144	514	78	140	23	5	21	69	.272
Barr, Edward *	26	31	5	6	3			1	.194
Barrett, John *	37	126	12	27	2		2	14	.214
Barrett, Richard *	26	42	2	9				4	.214
Clark, Allie	42	149	19	44	6	1	11	39	.295
Clay, Dain	165	605	101	178	23	4	11	43	.294
Coscarart, Peter *	148	481	55	131	27	2	5	65	.272
Easter, Luke	80	273	56	99	23		25	92	.363
Flores, Jesse	37	100	9	19	2	1		7	.190
Hafey, Wilbert	27	33	6	9	2		1	6	.273
Handley, Lee *	52	202	34	57	9		1	24	.282
Jensen, John	13	13	1	1				1	.077
Jurisich, Alvin	35	65	8	9				1	.138
Kipp, Thomas	40	33	1	3					.091
Linde, Lyman	36	74	8	11	3			3	.149

1949 Con't.	GAMES	AB	R	H	2B	3B	HR	RBI	AVE
Mesner, Stephen	114	343	49	102	17	1		40	.297
Minoso, Minnie	137	532	99	158	19	7	22	75	.297
Moore, Dee *	121	383	50	119	21	2	11	54	.311
Mooty, Jacob *	42	25	1	3					.120
Rescigno, Xavier	33	51	6	3	1			4	.059
Ritchey, John	112	327	29	84	10	1	3	35	.257
Rosen, Al	83	273	49	87	12	1	14	51	.319
Savage, J. Robert	28	39	2	4				1	.103
Seats, Tom *	29	10	1	2					.200
Shupe, Vincent *	161	627	71	173	39	1	8	81	.275
Storey, Harvey *	146	491	61	148	22	4	17	97	.301
Thompson, Gene	46	21	1	3	1			2	.143
West, Max	189	619	166	180	41	2	48	166	.291
Wietelmann, W. *	149	496	67	119	24	2	4	37	.240
Wilson, Artie *	165	607	129	211	19	9		37	.348
Wilson, Robert	173	683	82	183	17	8	1	67	.268
Zak, Frank *	52	140	12	31	4			12	.221

(Ten or More Games)

NAME	GAMES	IP	W	L	PCT	SO	BB	ERA
Adams, Red *	24	161	8	7	.533	73	58	3.86
Barrett, Richard *	26	135	12	6	.667	62	68	3.73
Flores, Jesse	36	279	21	10	.677	139	74	3.03
Jurisich, Alvin	35	191	13	11	.542	104	59	4.85
Kipp, Tom	40	126	7	5	.583	53	51	4.86
Linde, Lyman	35	226	14	15	.483	105	100	4.42
Mooty, Jacob *	42	114	3	8	.273	38	44	5.37
Rescigno, Xavier	32	178	10	15	.400	74	59	5.61
Savage, Bob	29	117	4	10	.286	46	39	4.23
Seats, Tom *	29	66	2	2	.500	25	29	4.64
Thompson, Gene	46	91	7	8	.467	65	50	5.64

(Forty-five and More Innings)

(* Adams: 5LA-25SD, Barr: 19Port-7SD, Barrett, J: 8SD-29Port,
Barrett, R: 11Sea-15SD, Coscarart: 8SD-140Sac, Handley: 19SD-33LA,
Moore: 7Sac-114SD, Mooty: 10Port-32SD, Seats: 5SD-12Oak-12Holly,
Shupe: 21SD-140Port, Storey: 12Port-134SD, Wietelmann: 51Sac-98SD,
Wilson, A: 31SD-134Oak, Zak: 40Port-12SD)

◆1950

NAME	GAMES	AB	R	H	2B	3B	HR	RBI	AVE
Adams, Elvin	123	340	53	108	26	3	15	62	.318
Bache, Jose	12	18	2	1					.056
Barrett, Richard *	31	34	3	6				2	.176
Berardino, John *	57	197	18	45	8		3	15	.228
Bevans, Floyd *	30	20	1	3	1				.150
Clay, Dain *	84	168	29	41	7	2	1	20	.244
Combs, Merrill	50	173	22	49	8	1	3	23	.283
Conyers, Herbert	66	220	20	49	11	1	1	24	.223
Embree, Charles	40	86	4	10				6	.116
Graham, Jack	185	663	98	194	23	8	33	136	.293
Jurisich, Alvin	36	30		3					.100

1950 Con't.	GAMES	AB	R	H	2B	3B	HR	RBI	AVE
Kerr, Frank *	52	144	21	39	8	1	7	26	.271
Kraus, Jack *	41	43	1	7	3			3	.163
Minoso, Minnie	169	599	130	203	40	10	20	115	.339
Moore, Dee	127	370	40	104	16		1	35	.281
Nielsen, Milton	126	429	86	128	21	4	8	41	.298
Olsen, Albert	40	88	8	14	2	1		2	.159
Rowe, Lynwood	17	11	2	1				2	.091
Saltzman, Harold	37	63	5	6				1	.095
Savage, Robert	51	35	4	6				2	.171
Simpson, Harry	178	697	121	225	41	19	33	156	.323
Smith, Alphonse	104	326	73	81	13	4	10	50	.248
Storey, Harvey	123	297	39	79	23	2	6	54	.266
Tresh, Michael	55	158	16	35	2	2	1	17	.222
Welmaker, Roy	47	74	10	16		1	1	9	.216
West, Max	162	520	92	148	30	1	30	109	.285
Wietelmann, W.	138	418	65	109	18		2	35	.261
Wilson, Robert	182	710	103	182	24	6	2	55	.256
Zuverink, George	47	93	16	16	1			4	.172

(Ten or More Games)

NAME	GAMES	IP	W	L	PCT	SO	BB	ERA
Barrett, Richard *	31	111	9	5	.643	34	58	5.76
Bevans, Floyd *	30	77	3	8	.273	16	71	7.48
Embree, Charles	38	255	18	12	.600	113	99	3.32
Jurisich, Alvin	36	97	8	2	.800	60	39	2.69
Kraus, Jack *	41	141	6	8	.429	78	55	4.72
Olsen, Albert	39	272	20	15	.571	96	56	3.71
Saltzman, Harold	37	179	11	10	.524	62	79	4.93
Savage, Robert	51	122	6	8	.429	68	59	4.65
Welmaker, Roy	47	213	16	10	.615	143	107	4.27
Zuverink, George	45	279	20	14	.588	116	116	3.71

(Forty-five or More Innings)
(* Barrett: 16SD-15Holly, Berardino: 17SD-40Sac, Bevans: 10Sac-20SD,
  Clay: 13SD-71Port, Kerr: 6Oak-46SD, Kraus: 5LA-36SD)

◆1951

NAME	GAMES	AB	R	H	2B	3B	HR	RBI	AVE
Adams, Elvin *	103	232	31	58	11		8	42	.250
Benton, J. Alton *	43	32		2					.063
Conyers, Herbert	35	122	15	27	8	3		17	.221
Dropo, Walter	33	126	17	36	4		5	13	.286
Embree, Charles	34	58	3	7	2			1	.121
Fletcher, Guy *	28	59	2	6				1	.102
Graham, Jack *	108	387	67	108	23		22	70	.279
Harris, Charles	15	10		1					.100
Jennings, William *	92	350	72	87	7	2	9	37	.249
Jones, Samuel	40	85	7	16	2		1	8	.188
Jurisich, Alvin	12	3							.000
Kerr, Frank	94	261	29	68	11		6	29	.261
Kerrigan, Robert	44	53		4	1			6	.075
Locklin, Stuart	71	277	42	74	9	3	5	21	.267
Maddern, Clarence	99	373	57	116	22	4	14	76	.311

1951 Con't.	GAMES	AB	R	H	2B	3B	HR	RBI	AVE
Malloy, Robert	40	19	2	3				4	.158
Malmberg, Harry	82	259	20	64	8	3		27	.247
Olsen, Albert	25	44	3	8				1	.182
Naragon, Harold	91	278	23	70	5		2	22	.252
Nielsen, Milton	41	138	23	38	3	2	4	20	.275
Rowell, Joseph	82	271	35	72	11	1	8	39	.266
Santiago, Jose	12	8	1	1				1	.125
Sauer, Edward *	136	459	70	121	22	1	16	61	.264
Sheridan, Neill *	56	137	13	28	3	1	3	14	.204
Sipple, Charles	40	62	2	12	3		1	7	.194
Smith, Alphonse	25	89	16	25	5	2	3	10	.281
Storey, Harvey	104	352	34	89	20		14	54	.253
Tabor, Jim *	112	366	39	110	19	1	7	57	.301
Tobin, John	87	246	42	62	9	2		18	.252
Tucker, Thurman	88	234	35	52	8	2		4	.222
Welmaker, Roy *	29	22	1	3	2			1	.136
White, Donald *	99	242	34	64	7		5	26	.264
Wietelmann, W.	125	390	53	102	12	5	8	44	.262
Wilson, Robert	160	628	63	168	18	3		48	.268
York, Anthony	68	89	7	23	7	1	1	7	.258

(Ten or More Games)

NAME	GAMES	IP	W	L	PCT	SO	BB	ERA
Benton, J. Alton *	43	130	5	7	.417	48	43	4.02
Embree, Charles	33	176	11	15	.423	70	65	4.70
Fletcher, Guy *	28	170	9	12	.429	91	62	3.44
Jones, Samuel	40	267	16	13	.552	246	175	2.76
Kerrigan, Robert	44	182	14	8	.636	52	51	3.12
Malloy, Robert	40	87	3	6	.333	31	28	2.79
Olsen, Albert	25	138	7	10	.412	47	33	4.70
Sipple, Charles	40	201	11	14	.440	75	88	4.25
Welmaker, Roy *	29	87	3	4	.429	50	47	4.76

(Forty-five or More Innings)

(*Adams: SD-SF, Benton: Sac-SD, Fletcher: SF-SD, Graham: SF-SD, Jennings: Oak-SD, Sauer: Holly-SD-SF, Sheridan: SF-SD, Tabor: Sac-SD, Welmaker: SD-Holly, White: SD-Port)

◆1952

NAME	GAMES	AB	R	H	2B	3B	HR	RBI	PCT
Alston, Tom	78	258	29	63	10	1	2	26	.244
Benton, J. Alton	21	16		1				1	.063
Bowman, Keith	11	4						2	.000
Clay, Dain	96	239	34	67	12	5		27	.280
Davis, John	61	167	26	44	9	1	6	36	.263
Dollaghan, Arthur	19	11	1	1	1				.091
Faber, Dick	143	438	50	101	12	3	8	35	.231
Fletcher, Guy	36	65	2	3				2	.046
Flowers, Bennett	26	55	3	6			1	4	.109
Franklin, Murray	144	458	56	104	16		6	45	.227
Gorman, Herbert	108	352	41	92	19	1	8	39	.261
Graham, Jack	167	552	87	151	31	7	22	88	.274
Henry, Bill	20	46	2	9				2	.196

1952 Con't.	GAMES	AB	R	H	2B	3B	HR	RBI	PCT
Hisner, Harley	25	13	1	1	1				.077
Jacobs, Eugene	23	70	4	17	3			7	.243
Kerr, Frank	59	174	16	37	3		3	19	.213
Klein, Lou	122	418	55	117	23	2	4	44	.280
Luna, Memo	38	86	8	9	1			1	.105
Malloy, Bob	38	19	3	3	1				.158
Okrie, Leonard	40	102	11	18	2			9	.176
Olsen, Al	30	44	3	8	1			3	.182
Perry, Raymond	12	27	1	3			1	1	.111
Peterson, Buddy	22	74	9	19	2			8	.257
Richter, Allen	152	516	49	128	21	4	1	61	.248
Salveson, Jack	26	57	1	10	2			8	.175
Smith, Theolic	36	45	2	7	2			3	.156
Stringer, Lou *	163	538	78	148	26	6	17	85	.275
Storey, Harvey	15	12	1					1	.000
Summers, Lonnie	125	340	31	82	21	2	7	57	.241
Tobin, John	166	599	89	172	16	4	3	33	.287
Tucker, Thurman	47	89	7	20	3			5	.225
Wietelmann, Whitey	23	24	3	5					.208
Workman, Hank	10	9	3	3			2	5	.333

(Ten or More Games)

NAME	GAMES	IP	W	L	PCT	SO	BB	ERA
Benton, J. Alton	21	56	6	1	.857	32	19	1.29
Fletcher, Guy	36	232	14	16	.467	108	87	3.76
Flowers, Bennett	26	167	11	10	.524	114	62	3.18
Henry, Bill	17	123	7	9	.438	85	55	3.59
Hisner, Harley	24	61	2	4	.333	33	28	4.72
Luna, Memo	38	260	15	16	.484	138	96	2.94
Malloy, Bob	38	94	4	2	.667	27	39	3.26
Olsen, Al	30	147	6	13	.316	67	26	3.67
Salveson, Jack	26	168	10	10	.500	57	34	3.80
Smith, Theolic	35	147	9	10	.474	75	60	3.24

(Forty-five or More Innings)
(* Stringer: 45Holly-118SD)

◆1953

NAME	GAMES	AB	R	H	2B	3B	HR	RBI	AVE
Alston, Thomas	180	697	101	207	25	5	23	101	.297
Benton, J. Alton	50	17		2				2	.118
Brucker, Earle	3								.500
Clay, Dain	16	38	3	6	2			3	.158
Dahle, David	15	7							.000
Dickey, Lloyd	31	44	5	7	2			3	.159
Faber, Richard	175	634	89	161	23	9	19	92	.254
Fannin, Clifford	37	87	8	23				4	.264
Federoff, Alfred	136	531	66	147	22			30	.277
Franklin, Murray *	94	274	27	71	6	1	2	27	.259
Grace, Joseph*	76	221	14	51	13	1	1	20	.231
Gorman, Herbert	4								.750
Hall, Everett	9								.250
Herrera, Tomas	7								.000

1953 Con't.	GAMES	AB	R	H	2B	3B	HR	RBI	AVE
Kerrigan, Robert	38	78	4	7				4	.090
LeBlanc, Remy	30	49	4	7	2	1	1	5	.143
Luna, Memo	40	77	8	8				3	.104
Malloy, Robert	51	25	3	4				1	.160
Mathis, Willie	136	407	37	91	21	5	6	47	.224
Merson, John	104	327	28	75	15		4	44	.229
Murray, Frank	105	275	34	60	8	2	1	19	.218
Nicolosi, Christopher	2								.000
Peterson, Buddy	179	666	76	186	31	5	5	60	.279
Pocekay, Walter	133	401	55	112	20	1	14	58	.279
Rapp, Earl	180	630	104	196	32	7	24	108	.311
Rayle, Jose	5								.286
Salveson, John *	12	17	3	3			1	4	.176
Shulte, Robert	5								.000
Smith, Milton	55	144	20	39	5	1	3	10	.271
Smith, Theolic	41	55	6	14		1	1	7	.255
Stringer, Louis *	127	396	57	102	24	4	2	30	.258
Summers, Lonnie	43	85	6	14	2		1	7	.165
Thomason, William	38	61	3	7				6	.115
Van Eman, Robert	43	101	6	21	1		2	11	.208

NAME	GAMES	IP	W	L	PCT	SO	BB	ERA
Benton, J. Alton	50	82	6	6	.500	24	28	2.85
Dahle, David			0	2				.000
Dickey, Lloyd	25	132	7	9	.438	50	41	3.01
Fannin, Clifford	31	214	14	12	.538	137	70	3.24
Herrera, Tomas			0	2				.000
Kerrigan, Robert	38	259	16	16	.500	103	79	3.19
Luna, Memo	39	263	17	12	.586	90	98	2.67
Malloy, Robert	51	105	4	3	.571	31	41	4.47
Rayle, Jose			0	2				.000
Nicolosi, Christopher			0	2				.000
Salveson, Jack *	12	60	1	7	.125	16	22	5.85
Schulte, Robert			0	1				.000
Smith, Theolic	39	185	13	16	.448	80	84	4.52
Thomason, William	37	194	11	10	.524	104	101	3.99

(*Franklin: 49SD-45LA, Grace: 21SF-55SD, Salveson: 4SD-8Oak, Stringer: 26SD-101SF)

◆1954

NAMES	GAMES	AB	R	H	2B	3B	HR	RBI	PCT
Aylward, Richard	47	159	6	30	3			10	.189
Chambers, Cliff	25	23	3	4	1		1	4	.174
Dickey, Lloyd	49	86	6	14	2			9	.163
Easter, Luke	56	198	43	55	8	1	13	42	.278
Elliott, Harry	168	640	93	224	42	4	15	110	.350
Elliott, Robert	81	203	28	52	6	1	12	39	.256
Erautt, Edward	41	89	4	13	5			8	.146
Faber, Dick	114	243	29	51	7	3	6	28	.210
Fannin, Cliff	22	50	2	6				4	.120
Federoff, Al	168	630	110	175	19	1		29	.278

1954 Con't.	GAMES	AB	R	H	2B	3B	HR	RBI	PCT
Hall, Everett	2								.000
Herrera, Tomas	18	13	2	1					.077
Kerrigan, Bob	37	73	4	2				1	.027
Lyons, Albert *	108	264	37	70	14		10	42	.265
Mathis, Willie	12	15	3	4	1				.267
Merson. John	82	207	16	47	4	1	2	20	.227
Murray, Frank	5	3							.000
Nicolosi, Christopher	2								.000
Peterson, Buddy	157	591	91	171	19	1	10	61	.289
Pocekay, Walter	87	199	20	56	6		1	13	.281
Romonosky. John	12	8		1					.125
Rapp, Earl	162	566	102	191	37	7	24	111	.337
Rayle, Jose	1								.000
Robinson, Floyd	3	6							.000
Sandlock, Mike	80	229	10	42	7	1		22	.183
Sisler, Dick	155	591	83	188	29	3	19	99	.318
Smith, Milton	131	388	61	114	22	5	9	51	.294
Smith, Theolic	26	30	3	3	1			1	.100
Thomason, Willie	34	41	6	9	1			2	.220
Van Eman, Robert	8	7		2					.286
Wight, Bill	28	71	10	16	2		1	9	.225

NAME	GAMES	IP	W	L	PCT	SO	BB	ERA
Chambers, Cliff	25	75	6	4	.600	27	45	5.30
Dickey, Lloyd	37	218	14	11	.560	86	68	2.69
Erautt, Edward	41	274	16	12	.571	115	85	3.12
Fannin, Cliff	21	131	8	5	.615	99	60	2.54
Herrera, Tomas	18	41	1	4	.200	15	31	5.41
Kerrigan, Robert	37	240	17	11	.607	104	60	2.77
Lyons, Albert *	21	43	8	2	.800	30	13	2.30
Nicolosi, Christopher	2							
Rayle, Jose	1	1						1.000
Romonosky, John	11	31	1	2	.333	15	17	6.16
Smith, Theolic	24	83	3	2	.600	36	32	4.03
Thomason, Willie	34	138	10	9	.526	65	92	4.37
Wight, Bill	28	210	17	5	.773	87	72	1.93

(* Lyons: 48SF-60SD)

◆1955

NAME	GAMES	AB	R	H	2B	3B	HR	RBI	AVE
Aylward, Richard	75	216	10	49	6			17	.227
Bailey, L. Edgar	108	344	52	97	16		16	60	.282
Becquer, Julio	124	392	34	114	13	3	7	54	.291
Bishop, Charles	23	32	2	3					.094
Bollweg, Donald	11	37	1	7	2		1	4	.189
Carmichael, John	35	74	4	15	3			5	.203
Davidson, Billy Joe	1	0							.000
Dickey, Lloyd	44	47	8	11			1	0+	.234
Erautt, Edward	37	87	5	11	2			4	.126
Faber, Richard	155	422	30	90	11	1	4	30	.213
Fannin, Clifford	2	2							.000

1955 Con't.	GAMES	AB	R	H	2B	3B	HR	RBI	AVE
Federoff, Alfred	149	587	68	161	14			25	.274
Gladd, James	19	44	4	10	1		1	8	.227
Gray, John	4	6		1					.167
Herrera, Tomas	39	35	1	5				1	.143
Hogan, Richard	9	11		3					.273
Jablonski, Raymond	62	213	32	60	8		13	40	.282
Kazak, Edward	129	421	50	127	11	1	12	67	.302
Kerrigan, Robert	30	44	1	0					.000
Lyons, Albert *	79	102	7	11	2		1	5	.108
Maddern,Clarence*	88	223	22	60	15	1	4	39	.269
McLish, Calvin *	37	86	6	11	4		1	4	.128
Melton, James *	19	16		1				1	.063
Merson, John	96	298	41	84	14		6	31	.282
Peterson, Buddy	154	576	105	176	34	3	2	38	.306
Rapp, Earl	169	582	109	176	25	6	30	133	.302
Ridzik, Stephen	16	22		5					.227
Robinson, Floyd	4	2							.000
Smith, Theolic	7	4							.000
Sisler, Richard	136	427	46	109	19		11	52	.255
Smith, Milton	108	414	89	140	35	9	9	65	.338
Thomason, William	29	25	2	2					.080
Usher, Robert *	129	395	37	89	12	2	10	46	.225
Wortham, John	1								.000
Zarilla, Allen *	42	90	6	18	4		2	14	.200

NAME	GAMES	IP	W	L	PCT	SO	BB	ERA
Carmichael, John	35	224	13	10	.565	77	72	3.46
Bishop, Charles	23	107	7	8	.467	38	42	3.87
Davidson, Billy Joe	1							
Dickey, Lloyd	30	145	7	11	.389	36	41	4.21
Erautt, Edward	37	241	18	10	.643	94	64	2.76
Fannin, Clifford	2		0	1	.000			
Gray, John	4		0	2	.000			
Herrera, Tomas	39	122	5	8	.385	39	39	3.60
Kerrigan, Robert	30	159	7	9	.438	79	47	3.62
Lyons, Albert *	44	74	10	5	.667	36	30	5.81
McLish, Calvin *	35	233	17	12	.586	116	69	3.09
Melton, James *	19	57	3	4	.429	19	13	5.65
Ridzik, Stephen	15	61	2	1	.667	41	30	3.71
Smith, Theolic	7		2	1	.667			
Thomason, William	29	109	5	5	.500	58	43	3.48
Wortham, John	1							

(* Lyons: 57SD-22Holly, Maddern: 18SF-21Port-49SD, McLish: 5LA-32SD, Melton: 10SD-9SF, Usher: 128LA-1SD, Zarilla: 19SD-23Holly) [+Dickey: 1 HR, but 0 RBI?]

◆1956

NAME	GAMES	AB	R	H	2B	3B	HR	RBI	AVE
Astroth, Joseph	96	284	29	70	14	1	6	45	.246
Atkins, Arnold *	35	48	4	6				3	.125
Aylward, Richard *	80	206	17	54	6	2	1	27	.262
Caffie, Joe	19	47	5	11	3			2	.234

1956 Con't.	GAMES	AB	R	H	2B	3B	HR	RBI	AVE
Carmichael, John	35	82	5	10	1		1	4	.122
Colavito, Rocco	35	133	31	49	10	1	12	32	.368
Dickey, Lloyd *	24	15	1	2	1				.133
Elliott, Harry	142	474	61	138	20	4	9	52	.291
Erautt, Edward	37	62	6	12	2		1	3	.194
Federoff, Alfred	153	617	101	179	18	2		47	.290
Gettel, Allen	26	15	2	3	1		1	2	.200
Greenwood, Robert	18	17	3	4			1	2	.235
Hall, Robert *	24	21	1	5	1			1	.238
Hansen, Douglas	2	1							.000
Harrington, Billy	3	2							.000
Herrera, Tomas	28	14	3	7					.500
Hogan, Richard	2	1							.000
Hoskins, David	55	67	6	16	3		1	7	.239
Jones, Allen	12	23	2	8				1	.348
Kazak, Edward	138	505	80	154	19	4	18	83	.305
Kerrigan, Robert	22	14		2				1	.143
Lombardi, Victor *	45	62	12	14	2			5	.226
Macko, Joseph	21	43	3	10	1		1	4	.233
Merson, John	116	332	24	84	14	3	2	29	.253
Mesa, R. Peter	40	84	5	15				4	.179
Moore, Clarence	136	462	52	119	19	5	5	46	.258
Peete, James	16	7		1					.143
Peterson, Kent	6	6							.000
Rapp, Earl	122	414	59	124	14	5	9	65	.300
Robinson, Floyd	133	406	60	110	11	4	11	39	.271
Ross, Clifford *	8	5							.000
Sisler, Richard	145	504	55	166	27	5	11	82	.329
Spencer, Leverette	11	9	1	1					.111
St. Claire, Edward	76	217	29	57	8	1	7	25	.263
Tanselli, Gene	28	72	9	17	3			12	.236
Usher, Robert	157	595	84	208	37	5	12	74	.350

NAME	GAMES	IP	W	L	PCT	SO	BB	ERA
Atkins, Arnold *	35	161	12	6	.667	121	87	4.46
Carmichael, John	35	233	10	16	.385	122	52	3.82
Dickey, Lloyd *	21	57	2	1	.667	13	20	4.92
Erautt, Edward	37	189	9	19	.321	91	60	4.71
Gettel, Allen	26	58	2	4	.333	32	23	5.46
Greenwood, Robert	18	60	3	5	.375	24	30	5.52
Hall, Robert *	23	70	4	7	.364	31	38	5.81
Harrington, Billy	3							
Herrera, Tomas	28	67	6	6	.500	43	21	4.99
Hoskins, David	46	158	7	11	.389	87	63	4.60
Kerrigan, Robert	22	57	3	4	.429	26	21	4.26
Lombardi, Victor *	28	157	9	10	.474	81	50	3.61
Mesa, R. Peter	40	246	13	12	.520	141	137	3.85
Peete, James	16	33	1	0	1.000	21	26	4.96
Peterson, Kent	6		1	0	1.000			
Ross, Clifford*	8							
Spencer, Leverette	11	35	1	2	.333	13	13	4.63

(* Atkins: Sea14-SD21, Aylward: SD17-Sea63, Dickey: SD4-Sea20,
  Hall: Port9-SD15, Lombardi: Sea15-SD30, Ross: SD2-Sac1-Van5)

A History of the San Diego Padres (1936-1957)

NAME	GAMES	AB	R	H	2B	3B	HR	RBI	AVE
Aguirre, Henry	24	39	1	3				1	.077
Averill, Earl	119	381	58	104	19	4	19	67	.273
Bell, Gary	10	19		4					.211
Brodowski, Richard	32	63	3	16	3			6	.254
Carmichael, John *	38	44	4	7	2		1	4	.159
Dailey, William	16	19							.000
Daley, Buddy	5	11		4					.364
Davidson, Crawford	9	30		8					.267
DiPietro, Robert *	81	208	28	57	9		5	21	.274
Erautt, Edward *	22	20	2	4	1			2	.200
Federoff, Alfred *	102	359	32	81	12			21	.226
Gasque, Edwin	34	44	3	7	5		1	3	.159
Glynn, William *	143	468	53	120	15	2	8	41	.256
Grant, James	41	85	7	20	4	1	1	8	.235
Gray, John	13	24		4				1	.167
Hardin, William	17	30	4	5	1			1	.167
Harrell, William	117	467	56	129	18		6	42	.276
Jones, Allen	104	340	27	83	10	1	8	40	.244
Kazak, Edward	104	339	35	98	9	2	4	50	.289
Kinder, Ellis	2								.000
Lary, Gene	21	30	5	7	1	1			.233
Lennon, Robert	102	325	49	100	17	5	12	53	.308
Locklin, Stuart	44	142	17	44	5		3	24	.310
Lombardi, Victor	29	35	6	11	1			3	.314
Mesa, R. Peter	34	55	7	10	2			6	.182
Metkovich, George	24	90	13	24	4	1	1	8	.267
Moran, William	158	513	40	108	25	1	4	45	.211
Murszewski, Marion	1								.000
Nichols, Dolan *	46	30	2	4	2				.133
Pawloski, Stanley	18	31	4	6	1			1	.194
Pinckard, William	3	3							.000
Pope, David	129	460	74	144	21	6	18	83	.313
Rapp, Earl *	83	205	27	57	7	2	3	19	.278
Regalado, Rudolph	134	480	78	147	19	2	8	50	.306
Robinson, Floyd	140	498	93	139	11	5	11	41	.279
Rodemoyer, Howard	3	2		1					.500
Ward, Preston	100	327	49	108	15	1	22	70	.330
Werle, William *	40	74	5	13	1			3	.176
Young, Robert	25	85	8	21	4			1	.247

NAME	GAMES	IP	W	L	PCT	SO	BB	ERA
Aguirre, Henry	24	132	6	13	.316	100	69	3.75
Bell, Gary	10	56	1	5	.167	54	33	4.95
Brodowski, Richard	30	169	13	6	.684	107	59	2.93
Carmichael, John *	37	164	8	18	.308	91	55	5.20
Dailey, William	16	64	3	6	.333	32	26	3.78
Daley, Buddy	5	33	3	0	1.000	35	6	0.83

1957 Con't.	GAMES	IP	W	L	PCT	SO	BB	ERA
Erautt, Edward *	22	83	5	5	.500	39	20	2.39
Gasque, Edwin	34	136	9	7	.563	107	80	4.71
Grant, James	34	218	18	7	.720	178	102	2.32
Gray, John	13	73	4	3	.571	52	37	1.84
Kinder, Ellis	2							
Lary, Gene	18	94	3	5	.375	39	36	4.80
Lombardi, Victor	24	106	6	6	.500	61	20	3.32
Mesa, R. Peter	34	171	10	11	.476	130	96	4.06
Murszewski, Marion	1							
Nichols, Dolan*	46	106	8	5	.615	51	34	4.08
Rodemoyer, Howard	3							
Werle, William *	26	174	9	8	.529	58	17	3.88

(* Carmichael: 4SD-34Port, DiPietro: 6SF-75SD, Erautt: 3SD-19Van,
    Federoff: 64SD-38Sea, Glynn: 117Sea-26SD, Nichols: 41SD-5Port,
    Rapp: 12SD-71Port, Werle: 32Port-8SD)

The Old Padres shaved each other's heads. New Padre Rex Dilbeck cuts Fred Lanifero's hair as Dell Oliver, Jack Devincenzi and Gus Hallbourg wait their turn, 1941.

COMPOSITE BATTING STATISTICS (1936-1957)

NAME	YRS	G	AB	R	H	HR	RBI	AVE
Abbott, Morrison, of	3	283	712	52	185	11	94	.260
Adams, Buster, of *	4	472	1359	193	375	52	207	.276
Alston, Tom, 1b	2	258	955	130	270	25	127	.283
Angle, Jack, inf	1	121	368	47	92	2	24	.250
Astroth, Joe, c	1	96	284	29	70	6	45	.246
Averill, Earl,c	1	119	381	58	104	19	67	.273
Aylward, Dick, c	3	202	581	33	133	1	54	.229
Bache, Jose, ss	1	12	18	2	1			.056
Bailey, Ed, c	1	108	344	52	97	16	60	.282
Ballinger, Del, c *	6	479	1353	103	379	5	164	.280
Barr, Ed, of *	1	26	31	5	6		1	.194
Barrett, John, of *	3	349	1163	195	346	25	174	.298
Becquer, Julio, 1b	1	124	392	34	114	7	54	.291
Berardino, John, ss *	1	57	197	18	45	3	15	.228
Berger, Fred, of	1	13	39	3	8			.205
Berkowitz, Joe, inf	5	485	1464	208	389	1	141	.266
Bey, Herman	1	1	1					.000
Boehm, Ed, of	1	62	206	29	42	4	17	.204
Boken, Bob, 2b	1	68	233	38	77	8	57	.330
Bollweg, Don, 1b	1	11	37	1	7	1	4	.189
Bowman, Keith, p	1	11	4				2	.000
Breard, Stan, inf	1	96	318	18	69	1	32	.217
Brucker, Earle, c	1	3	2		1			.500
Caffie, Joe	1	19	47	5	11		2	.234
Cailteaux, Al, inf	2	113	304	36	63		20	.207
Calvey, Jack, ss	3	436	1593	184	426	5	164	.267
Camelli, Hank, c	1	79	202	18	54	4	22	.267
Campbell, Don	1	3	1					.000
Carlyle, Cleo, of	1	77	258	30	70	2	31	.271
Caster, George	1	23	4					.000
Caulfield, John	1	10	13	1	4		1	.308
Chapetta, Tony	1	4						.000
Charowhas, Pete, c	1	1	1	2				.000
Cirimele, Frank, 2b	1	23	37	5	5		2	.135
Clay, Dain, of-3b *	6	715	2474	407	721	31	254	.291
Clark, Allie, of	1	42	149	19	44	11	39	.295
Colavito, Rocky, of	1	35	133	31	49	12	32	.368
Combs, Merrill, ss	1	50	173	22	49	3	23	.283
Conyers, Herb, 1b	2	101	342	35	76	1	41	.222
Cook, Les	1	7	7					.000
Coscarart, Pete,2b-ss *	4	480	1586	184	388	24	169	.245
Criscola, Tony, of *	3	396	1386	229	396	4	119	.286
Dallessandro, Dominic, of	2	312	1082	209	366	26	189	.338
Davidson, Crawford	1	9	30		8			.267
Davis, John	1	61	167	26	44	6	36	.263
Dedeaux, Rod, inf *	1	30	79	9	13		5	.165
Dejan, Mike	1	18	38	4	4		1	.105
Desautels, Gene, c	1	148	480	68	153	3	69	.319
Detore, George, c-mgr	8	790	2322	354	724	20	351	.312
DeVincenzi, Jack, of	1	12	28		3			.107

NAME	YRS	G	AB	R	H	HR	RBI	AVE
DeVito, Vito, 2b	1	36	72	14	16		4	.222
DeVolder, Bus	1	5	3					.000
DiMaggio, Vince, of	1	176	641	109	188	19	102	.293
DiPietro, Bob, 1b-of *	1	81	208	28	57	5	21	.274
Doerr, Bobby, 2b	1	175	695	100	238	2	77	.342
Doerr, Hal, c	1	10	27	1	4			.148
Dollaghan, Art, p	1	19	11	1	1			.091
Dropo, Walt, 1b	1	33	126	17	36	5	13	.286
Dunphy, Jack, inf	1	98	283	37	61		12	.216
Durst, Cedric, of-1b-mgr *	6	580	1828	203	543	8	217	.297
Easter, Luke, 1b	2	136	471	99	154	28	134	.327
Elliott, Harry, of	2	310	1114	154	362	24	162	.325
Elliott, Bob, 3b	1	81	203	28	52	12	39	.256
Estes, Lou, 3b	3	61	126	9	26		11	.206
Evert, Elmer *	1	6	14	1	2			.143
Faber, Dick, of	4	587	1737	198	403	37	185	.232
Faria, Joe	1	1	1					.000
Farquharson, William	1	6	6		2			.333
Federoff, Al, 2b *	5	708	2724	377	743		152	.273
Filippo, Anthony	1	4						.000
Franklin, Murray *	2	238	732	83	175	8	72	.239
Garibaldi, Art *	3	372	1209	156	307	9	144	.254
Garms, Debs, of	1	142	466	48	126	1	44	.270
Gedzius, Joe, ss	1	18	46	4	6		3	.130
Gira, Frank, ss	1	77	225	13	46		16	.204
Gladd, Jim, c	1	19	44	4	10	1	8	.227
Glynn, Bill, 1b *	1	143	468	53	120	8	41	.256
Gorman, Herb, of	2	112	360	41	98	8	39	.272
Grace, Joe *	1	76	221	14	51	1	20	.231
Graham, Jack, of-1b *	4	642	2224	387	631	133	465	.284
Gray, Bill	1	6	13		2			.154
Greco, Dick, of	1	26	78	12	19	4	17	.244
Greene, John	1	2	2					.000
Griffiths, Bunny, ss	2	288	997	112	260		94	.261
Grigg, Donald, c *	1	43	81	4	12		5	.148
Gudat, Marv, of *	3	343	1014	106	271		82	.267
Guintini, Ben, of *	1	72	257	29	66	4	24	.257
Gyselman, Dick, 3b *	3	458	1641	233	472	3	168	.288
Hafey, Wil, p	1	27	33	6	9	1	6	.273
Hallbourg, Gus, p	1	1	1		1			1.000
Hatchett, Jack	1	4	3					.000
Hall, Everett	2	11						.250
Hamilton, Bob, 2b-of	1	87	186	22	42		13	.226
Handley, Jeep, 3b *	2	233	905	128	268	7	89	.296
Hansen, Doug	1	2	1					.000
Hardin, Bud, 2b	1	17	30	4	5		1	.167
Harrell, Billy, 3b-ss	1	117	467	56	129	6	42	.276
Harris, Charles, p	1	15	10		1			.100
Harris, Spencer, 1b-of	1	163	545	86	164	7	92	.301
Harshman, Jack, 1b	2	24	80	2	19		11	.238
Haslin, Mickey, 2b-3b	3	440	1611	248	521	25	257	.323
Hernandez, Manuel, of	1	30	82	9	17		5	.207
Hill, John, 3b	2	156	555	60	155	2	62	.279

NAME	YRS	G	AB	R	H	HR	RBI	AVE
Hogan, Shanty, c	1	109	331	27	85	1	42	.257
Hogan, Dick	2	11	12		3			.250
Holman, Ernie, 3b	3	276	949	130	267	7	136	.281
Ignasiak, Edwin	1	9	32		4			.125
Jablonski, Ray, 3b	1	62	213	32	60	13	40	.282
Jacobs, Eugene, of	1	23	70	4	17		7	.243
Jacobs, Ray, 1b	1	106	332	42	93	5	46	.280
Jeli, Anton, p	1	1	1		1			1.000
Jennings, Bill, ss *	1	92	350	72	87	9	37	.249
Jensen, Swede, of	9	971	3096	391	898	41	375	.290
Joerndt, Ashley, of	1	12	19	3	5			.263
Jones, Allen, c	2	116	363	29	91	8	41	.251
Jordan, Kirby	1	5	3					.000
Justice, Bill	1	9	15		2			.133
Katnich, Joe	1	5	2		1			.500
Kazak, Ed, 3b-of	3	371	1265	165	379	34	200	.300
Kerr, Frank, c *	4	348	1012	132	274	27	134	.271
Kerr, James, c	1	52	124	9	32	1	17	.258
Klein, Lou, 2b-3b	1	122	418	55	117	4	44	.280
Konopka, Bruno, of	1	25	69	9	14	2	11	.203
Kreevich, John, 2b-of	1	71	294	33	74	1	25	.252
Kubiak, Lou, ss	1	16	52	4	8		6	.154
Kuper, Earl	1	36	37	1	10	1	8	.270
Lane, Omar	1	3	3					.000
Lanifero, Fred, 2b	2	90	284	29	66		26	.232
Lazor, Johnny, of	1	35	124	17	38	1	7	.306
LeBlanc, Rey, of	1	30	49	4	7	1	5	.143
Lee, Larry, 2b-3b	2	130	411	33	100	2	19	.243
Lennon, Bob, of	1	102	325	49	100	12	53	.308
Lillard, Bill, ss	1	31	66	5	12	1	7	.182
Locklin, Stu, of	2	115	419	59	118	8	45	.282
Lohrke, Jack, ss	1	92	350	41	106	8	48	.303
Lowe, Walter, 1b	2	190	647	73	173	2	83	.267
Lund, Don, of	1	12	33		5			.152
Lyons, Al, of-p *	2	187	366	44	81	11	47	.221
Macko, Joe, 1b	1	21	43	3	10	1	4	.233
Maddern, Clarence, of-1b *	2	187	596	79	176	18	115	.295
Malmberg, Harry, ss	1	82	259	20	64		27	.247
Martin, Pepper, mgr-2b-p	1	53	97	27	30	1	15	.309
Martin, L.L.	1	5	11	4				.364
Martin, Joe, 1b-3b	2	21	26		4			.154
Mathis, Willie, c	2	148	422	40	95	6	47	.225
Mazzera, Mel. of-1b	3	343	1241	164	353	30	194	.284
McCarty, Jack	1	1	2		2			1.000
McClure, Jack	1	3						.000
McDonald, George, 1b *	10	1165	4635	578	1329	9	545	.287
McDonnell, Jim, c	2	69	189	14	45		13	.238
McNamara, Bob, ss	1	14	42		9			.214
Merson, John, inf	4	398	1164	109	290	14	124	.249
Mesner, Steve, inf *	3	465	1609	238	508	40	213	.316
Metkovich, George, mgr	1	24	90	13	24	1	8	.267
Millard, Jack	1	9	11		2			.182

NAME	YRS	G	AB	R	H	HR	RBI	AVE
Miller, John	1	10	11		1			.091
Minoso, Minnie, of-3b-ss	2	306	1131	229	361	42	190	.319
Monohan, Joe	1	5	5	2	2			.400
Moore, Clarence, ss	1	136	462	52	119	5	46	.258
Moore, Dee, c *	2	248	753	90	223	12	89	.296
Morgan, George, inf	2	157	376	34	93		31	.247
Mulligan, Eddie, 3b	3	82	110	22	26		5	.236
Murray, Franklin, 2b-3b	2	110	278	34	60	1	19	.216
Myatt, George, ss-3b	2	317	1217	219	339	7	101	.279
Nance, Eugene, 3b	1	19	52	6	13	2	11	.250
Naragon, Hal, c	1	91	278	23	70	2	22	.252
Nielsen, Milt, of	2	167	567	109	166	12	61	.293
Niemiec, Al, 2b-3b	2	285	992	114	288	2	129	.290
Okrie, Len, c	1	40	102	11	18		9	.176
Oliver, Dell, p	1	4	3					.000
Ortiz, Vidal	1	1	3					.000
Pacheco, Frank, 2b	1	24	35	1	8		2	.229
Patchett, Hal, of	8	1270	4886	668	1425	13	414	.292
Pawloski, Stan	1	18	31	4	6		1	.194
Paynick, Rudy	1	3	1					.000
Peel, Homer, of *	1	29	71	8	17		9	.239
Pellagrini, Eddie, ss	1	173	659	107	180	8	70	.273
Perlmutter, Daniel	1	12	12	5	6			.500
Perry, Ray, of	1	12	27	1	3	1	1	.111
Peterson, Buddy, ss	4	512	1907	281	552	17	167	.289
Pinckard, William	1	3	3					.000
Pocekay, Walt, of-c	2	220	600	75	168	15	71	.280
Pope, Dave, of	1	129	460	74	144	18	83	.313
Prout, William, 1b *	1	110	356	31	104		59	.292
Rapp, Earl "Buddy", of *	5	716	2397	401	744	90	436	.310
Reese, Jimmie, 2b	2	246	855	100	240	2	106	.281
Regalado, Rudy, 3b-of	1	134	480	78	147	8	50	.306
Reynolds, Vern, 2b-3b-ss	2	263	844	116	209		81	.248
Rhodes, Gordon, p	1	11	8	1	2			.250
Rice, Len, c	3	303	828	83	211	1	78	.255
Richter, Allen, ss	1	152	516	49	128	1	61	.248
Ritchey, John, c	2	215	544	64	154	7	79	.283
Robinson, Floyd, of	4	280	912	153	249	22	80	.273
Rosen, Al, 3b-1b	1	83	273	49	87	14	51	.319
Rowe, Lynwood "Schoolboy"	1	17	11	2	1			.091
Rowell, Joe, 1b-of	1	82	271	35	72	8	39	.266
St. Claire, Ebba, c	1	76	217	29	57	7	25	.263
Salkeld, Bill, c	5	590	1758	249	465	39	288	.265
Sandlock, Mike, c	1	80	229	10	42		22	.183
Savin, Henry, ss	1	11	31		7			.226
Santiago, Jose, p	1	12	8	1	1		1	.125
Sauer, Ed, of *	1	136	459	70	121	16	61	.264
Sciarra, Hank, ss	2	54	98	19	15		3	.153
Sheridan, Neill, of *	1	56	137	13	28	3	14	.204
Shiver, Ivey, of	1	54	191	27	59	7	41	.309
Shupe, Vince, 1b *	3	471	1765	193	463	23	238	.262
Simpson, Harry "Suitcase", of	1	178	697	121	225	33	156	.323

A History of the San Diego Padres (1936-1957)

NAME	YRS	G	AB	R	H	HR	RBI	AVE
Sisler Dick, 1b-of	3	436	1522	184	463	41	233	.304
Skelley, Bill	1	10	9					.000
Skelley, Mel, 2b	2	188	561	68	136	2	55	.242
Smith, Al, of	2	129	415	89	106	13	60	.255
Smith, Milt, 3b-of	3	294	946	170	293	21	126	.310
Solano, Claudio, of	1	7	13		2			.154
Sperry, Stan, 2b	3	342	1170	142	335	2	137	.286
Starr, Bill, c-owner	3	188	552	33	124	1	70	.225
Steiner, Mel *	2	110	345	37	92	1	36	.267
Stewart, Ed, of-3b	4	343	1147	175	350	10	103	.305
Stinson, Frank, 1b	2	112	365	37	89	1	32	.244
Stockman, Bruce	1	5	13		2			.154
Storey, Harvey, 3b *	4	388	1152	145	316	37	156	.274
Stringer, Lou, 2b-3b-of *	2	290	934	135	250	19	115	.268
Summers, Lonnie, c	2	168	425	37	96	8	64	.226
Sweeney, Henry, 1b	1	26	91	12	19		8	.209
Tabor, Jim, 3b-1b *	1	112	366	39	110	7	57	.301
Tanselli, Gene, 3b	1	28	72	9	17		12	.236
Thompson, Rupert, of-1b-3b	4	337	1121	190	357	17	126	.318
Tobin, John, of-3b	2	253	845	131	234	3	51	.277
Tran, Ray, ss	2	177	579	58	125		49	.216
Tresh, Mike, c	1	55	158	16	35	1	17	.222
Trusky, Victor	1	7	17		2			.118
Tubb, Julian	1	3						.000
Tucker, Thurman, of	2	88	234	35	52		4	.222
Usher, Bob, of-1b *	2	286	990	121	297	22	120	.300
Van Eman, Robert, of	2	51	108	6	23	2	11	.213
Venturelli, Angelo, p	1	10	4		1			.250
Vezilich, Lou, 1b-of	3	278	960	131	283	8	143	.295
Walters, John	1	14	18		3			.167
Ward, Preston, 1b	1	100	327	49	108	22	70	.330
Watson, Ralph *	1	23	42	10	12		4	.286
Weintraub(Winters), Mickey, 2b	1	25	52	6	13		3	.250
Wells, Leo, ss *	1	151	474	47	127	3	61	.268
West, Max, of-1b	3	518	1701	361	500	121	399	.294
Wetmore, Ray, 1b *	1	17	42	1	12		3	.286
Wheeler, Eddie, 2b-3b	2	296	1148	180	325	5	88	.283
Whipple, Jack, of	3	192	636	72	151	4	57	.237
White, Don, of *	1	99	242	34	64	5	26	.264
Wietelmann, Whitey, all *	4	435	1328	188	335	14	116	.252
Williams, John, of	3	173	482	53	124	3	51	.257
Williams, Ted, of	2	180	561	84	161	23	109	.287
Willis, Richard	1	2	2					.000
Wilson, Artie, ss *	1	165	607	129	211		37	.348
Wilson, Bobbie	3	515	2021	248	533	3	170	.264
Wirthman, Vance	1	132	428	58	123	1	49	.287
Wolfe, Donald	1	3	1		1			1.000
Workman, Hank	1	10	9	3	3	2	5	.333
York, Tony, 2b-3b	1	68	89	7	23	1	7	.258
Young, Bob, 2b	1	25	85	8	21		1	.247
Zak, Frank, ss	1	52	140	12	31		12	.221

NAME	YRS	G	AB	R	H	HR	RBI	AVE
Zarilla, Al, of *	1	42	90	6	18	2	14	.200

* Numbers include statistics from other PCL teams when players were traded that year
Bold print: denotes players whose interviews appear in this book.

COMPOSITE PITCHING STATISTICS (1936-1957)

NAME	YRS	G	IP	W	L	PCT	SO	ERA
Adams, Red *	1	24	161	8	7	.533	73	3.86
Aguirre, Hank	1	24	132	6	13	.316	100	3.75
Atkins, Dewey *	1	35	161	12	6	.667	121	4.46
Bailey, Bob	1	6	18		2	.000		
Barrett, "Kewpie" Dick *	2	57	246	21	11	.656	96	4.65
Bauer, Keith	1	8	13		1	.000		
Bell, Gary	1	10	56	1	5	.167	54	4.95
Benton, Al	3	114	268	17	14	.548	104	3.09
Bevens, Floyd *	1	30	77	3	8	.273	71	7.48
Bishop, Charlie	1	23	107	7	8	.467	38	3.87
Bowman, Joe	1	15	40	1	2	.333		
Brewer, Bernard	1	18	39	1		1.000		
Brillheart, Jim	4	125	639	33	42	.440	183	3.77
Brodowski, Dick	1	30	169	13	6	.684	107	2.93
Brown, Norm	1	41	197	13	12	.520	76	3.58
Budnick, Mike	1	28	104	4	8	.333	53	4.67
Campbell, Archie	1	48	129	6	9	.400	45	4.95
Carmichael, John	3	107	621	31	44	.413	290	4.06
Cecil, Rex	2	56	383	27	21	.563	267	2.42
Chambers, Cliff	1	25	75	6	4	.600	27	5.30
Chaplin, Jim "Tiny"	2	48	603	43	31	.581	288	3.12
Chapple, Earl	2	54	149	2	9	.182	50	4.33
Craghead, Howard *	5	201	1129	69	73	.486	526	3.75
Dahle, David	1				2	.000		
Dailey, William	1	16	64	3	6	.333	32	3.78
Daley, Bud	1	5	33	3		1.000	35	0.83
Dasso, Frank	3	109	759	44	45	.494	562	2.82
Davidson, Billy Joe	1	1						
Dickey, Lloyd *	4	113	552	30	32	.484	185	3.39
Dilbeck, Rex	4	93	360	25	20	.556	128	3.19
Dumler, Carl	5	109	482	25	34	.424	223	2.99
Eaves, Vallie	2	56	341	22	18	.550	187	3.00
Eisenmann, Charles	2	17	72	3	6	.333	62	3.62
Embree, Charles "Red"	2	71	431	29	27	.518	183	3.88
Erautt, Ed *	4	137	787	48	46	.511	339	3.32
Escalante, Earl *	1	19	58	3	5	.375	19	3.57
Fannin, Cliff	3	54	345	22	18	.550	236	2.97
Ferguson, Bob	1	39	211	5	21	.192	108	3.54
Fletcher, Guy *	2	64	402	23	28	.451	199	3.56
Flores, Jesse	2	77	504	32	29	.525	250	3.62
Flowers, Bennett	1	26	167	11	10	.524	114	3.18
Gasque, Edwin	1	34	136	9	7	.563	107	4.71

NAME	YRS	G	IP	W	L	PCT	SO	ERA
Gettel, Al	1	26	58	2	4	.333	32	5.46
Gleason, Jim	1	11						
Gonzales, Joe	2	28	164	11	9	.550	42	3.52
Grant, Jim "Mudcat"	1	34	218	18	7	.720	178	2.32
Gray, John	2	17	73	4	5	.444	52	1.84
Hanski, Donald	1	15	73	2	7	.222	21	4.07
Hare, Joe	1	14	31	1	2	.333		
Harrington, Billy	1	3						
Hebert, Wally "Preacher"	7	267	1893	104	80	.565	716	3.07
Henry, Bill	1	17	123	7	9	.438	85	3.59
Herrera, Tomas	4	85	230	12	18	.400	97	4.34
Hill, Jack	1	2	9		1	.000		
Hisner, Jim	1	24	61	2	4	.333	33	4.72
Hockette, George	1	8	33		3	.000		
Horne, Berlyn	1	38	164	7	14	.333	76	4.39
Hoskins, Dave	1	46	158	7	11	.389	87	4.60
Humphreys, Byron *	4	137	718	36	53	.396	295	3.74
Johnson, Chet	2	64	428	26	27	.491	244	3.39
Jones, Earl	1	3	4		1	.000		
Jones, "Toothpick" Sam	1	40	267	16	13	.552	246	2.76
Jurisich, Al	4	109	477	32	25	.561	288	4.72
Kennedy, Vern	2	70	420	27	28	.491	197	3.32
Kerrigan, Bob	7	257	1213	69	66	.511	456	3.60
Kinder, Ellis	1	2						
Kipp, Tom	1	40	126	7	5	.583	53	4.86
Kleinke, Norbert	1	30	138	5	10	.333	45	3.91
Knowles, Giles *	2	31	153	9	8	.529	43	4.29
Kraus, Jack	1	41	141	6	8	.429	78	4.72
Lamanske, Frank	1	8	20	1	1	.500		
Lary, Gene	1	18	94	3	5	.375	39	4.80
Linde, Lyman	1	35	226	14	15	.483	105	4.42
Linke, Edward	1	4	19	1	2	.333		
Lombardi, Vic *	2	52	263	15	16	.484	142	3.49
Lucier, Lou	1	8	46	1	5	.167	19	4.50
Luna, Memo	2	77	523	32	28	.533	228	2.80
Lyons, Al *	2	65	117	18	7	.720	66	4.54
MacFadden, Jim *	1	4	7		1	.000		
Malloy, Bob	3	129	286	11	11	.500	89	3.56
Malman, Joe	1	16	37	2	3	.400		
McLish, Cal *	1	35	233	17	12	.586	116	3.09
Melton, Jim *	1	19	57	3	4	.429	19	5.65
Merkle, Warren	2	38	87	1	5	.167	16	6.06
Mesa, Pete	2	74	417	23	23	.500	271	3.88
Monzo, Carl *	1	21	48	3	3	.500	25	5.06
Mooty, Jacob	1	42	114	3	8	.273	38	5.37
Morales, William	1	7	13	1		1.000		
Morris, Jim	2	38	100	4	1	.800	34	4.14
Murszewski, Marion	1	1						
Nelson, Gerry	1	12	42	1	2	.333		
Newsome, Heber *	2	77	493	29	25	.537	188	3.58
Nicholas, George	1	13	47	2	4	.333	19	6.89

NAME	YRS	G	IP	W	L	PCT	SO	ERA
Nichols, Dolan *	1	46	106	8	5	.615	51	4.08
Nicolosi, Christopher	2	4			2	.000		
Olsen, Al	11	365	2038	114	135	.458	769	3.81
Peete, James	1	16	33	1		1.000	21	4.96
Peterson, Kent	1	6		1		1.000		
Pillette, Herm "Old Folks"	7	166	617	34	26	.567	190	3.05
Poffenberger, "Boots"	2	54	238	14	16	.467	59	3.86
Powell, Larry	1	5	19	2		1.000		
Rayle, Jose	2			1	2	.333		
Rescigno, Xavier "Mr.X"	2	70	399	28	29	.491	161	5.08
Rich, Woodrow	1	23	139	9	9	.500	66	3.50
Ridzik, Steve	1	15	61	2	1	.667	41	3.71
Rodemoyer, Howie	1	3						
Romonosky, John	1	11	31	1	2	.333	15	6.16
Ross, Cliff	1	8						
Saltzman, Hal	1	37	179	11	10	.524	62	4.93
Salveson, Jack *	2	38	228	11	17	.407	73	4.34
Salvo, Manuel	6	214	1169	78	60	.565	688	3.31
Savage, Bob	3	100	239	10	18	.357	114	4.44
Schanz, Charlie	1	44	276	17	18	.486	137	3.23
Schulte, Bob	1	1			1	.000		
Seats, Tom	4	153	866	42	51	.452	365	3.73
Shellenback, Frank, mgr	2	21	118	6	8	.429	38	3.53
Shores, Bill	1	8	16	2	3	.400		
Sipple, Charles	1	40	201	11	14	.440	75	4.25
Smith, Theolic	4	105	415	27	29	.482	191	3.97
Spencer, Leverette	1	11	35	1	2	.333	13	4.63
Terry, Yank	1	40	315	26	8	.705	172	2.31
Thomas, Bill *	3	132	729	40	50	.444	231	3.41
Thomason, Willie	3	100	441	26	24	.520	227	3.98
Thompson, Gene "Junior"	2	88	163	15	11	.577	96	4.03
Tincup, Frank	1	16	46		3	.000	18	7.82
Tobin, Marion	3	89	116	10	20	.333	150	4.60
Trahd, Victor	1	39	121	5	10	.333	41	5.21
Treichel, Al	1	35	249	14	15	.483	147	4.12
Valenzuela, Joe	2	35	154	3	14	.176	58	4.66
Vitalich, Ed	3	82	394	18	31	.367	138	3.59
Wade, Jacob	1	12	47		4	.000	18	7.08
Walden, Gordon	1	52	113	3	4	.429	31	5.65
Ward, Dick *	4	116	667	43	40	.512	230	4.14
Weldon, Lawrence	1	7	29	3	1	.750		
Wells, Edwin	1	30	196	9	13	.409	62	4.32
Welmaker, Roy *	2	76	300	19	14	.576	157	4.41
Wensloff, Charles "Butch"	1	10	73	3	4	.429	40	3.82
Werle, Bill	1	26	174	9	8	.529	58	3.88
Wight, Bill	1	28	210	17	5	.773	87	1.93
Womack, Jerry	1	10	27		1	.000		
Wood, Joe	1	10	79	5	4	.556	35	2.50
Wortham, John	1	1						
Zuverink, George	1	45	279	20	14	.588	116	3.71

LANE FIELD PADRES

INDIVIDUAL ALL-TIME BATTING LEADERS

BATTING AVERAGE

Single Season				Career (two or more seasons)		
Name	Year	AB	Ave	Name	Seasons	Ave
Dominic Dallessandro	1939	(541)	.368	Dominic Dallessandro	2	.338
George Detore	1939	(411)	.355	Luke Easter	2	.327
Harry Elliott	1954	(640)	.350	Harry Elliott	2	.325
Bob Usher	1956	(595)	.350	Mickey Haslin	3	.323
Mickey Haslin	1939	(537)	.345	Minnie Minoso	2	.319
Bobby Doerr	1936	(695)	.342	Rupert Thompson	3	.318
Steve Mesner	1940	(680)	.341	Steve Mesner	3	.316
Johnny Barrett	1948	(513)	.339	George Detore	8	.312
Minnie Minoso	1950	(599)	.339	Earl Rapp	5 *	.310
Milt Smith	1955	(414)	.338	Milt Smith	3	.310

HOME RUNS

Single Season			Career (two or more seasons)		
Name	Year	HR	Name	Seasons	HR
Jack Graham	1948	48	Jack Graham	4 *	133
Max West	1949	48	Max West	3	121
Max West	1947	43	Earl Rapp	5 *	90
Jack Graham	1950	33	Buster Adams	4 *	52
Harry Simpson	1950	33	Minnie Minoso	2	42
Max West	1950	30	Dick Sisler	3	41
Jack Graham	1951	30	Swede Jensen	9	41
Earl Rapp	1955	30	Steve Mesner	3	40
Luke Easter	1949	25	Bill Salkeld	5	39
Earl Rapp	1953	24	Dick Faber	4	37
Earl Rapp	1954	24	Harvey Storey	4 *	37

RUNS BATTED IN

Single Season			Career (two or more seasons)		
Name	Year	RBI	Name	Seasons	RBI
Max West	1949	166	George McDonald	10	545
Harry Simpson	1950	156	Jack Graham	4 *	465
Jack Graham	1948	136	Earl Rapp	5 *	436
Jack Graham	1950	136	Hal Patchett	8	414
Earl Rapp	1955	133	Max West	3	399
Max West	1947	124	Swede Jensen	9	375
Earl Rapp	1954	111	George Detore	8	351
Lou Vezilich	1945	110	Bill Salkeld	5	288
Harry Elliott	1954	110	Mickey Haslin	3	257
Max West	1947	109	Dain Clay	6 *	254

* part of season with another Pacific Coast League team

LANE FIELD PADRES

INDIVIDUAL ALL-TIME PITCHING LEADERS

WON-LOST RECORD   (20+ decisions)

Name	Year	Record	PCT
Bill Wight	1954	17-5	.773
Yank Terry	1941	26-8	.765
Jim Grant	1957	18-7	.720
Manuel Salvo	1938	22-9	.710
Wally Hebert	1941	22-10	.688
Jesse Flores	1949	21-10	.677
Heber Newsome	1940	23-11	.676
Wally Hebert	1939	20-10	.667
Ed Erautt	1955	18-10	.643
Bob Kerrigan	1951	14-8	.636

Career Wins (two or more seasons)

Name	Seasons	Wins
Wally "Preacher" Hebert	7	126
Al Olsen	11	114
Manuel Salvo	6	78
Howard Craghead	5 *	69
Bob Kerrigan	7	69
Ed Erautt	4	48
Frank Dasso	3	44
Jim "Tiny" Chaplin	2	43
Dick Ward	4 *	43
Tom Seats	4	42

EARNED RUN AVERAGE Single Season

Name	Year	IP	ERA
Bill Wight	1954	210	1.93
Rex Cecil	1944	246	2.16
Yank Terry	1940	315	2.31
Jim "Mudcat" Grant	1957	218	2.32
Byron Humphreys	1938	166	2.33
Wally Hebert	1942	319	2.37
Carl Dumler	1945	282	2.42
Manuel Salvo	1938	239	2.60
Heber Newsome	1940	315	2.62
Memo Luna	1953	263	2.67

Career (two or more seasons)

Name	Seasons	IP	Ave
Rex Cecil	2	383	2.42
Memo Luna	2	523	2.80
Frank Dasso	3	759	2.82
Cliff Fannin	3	345	2.97
Carl Dumler	5	482	2.99
Vallie Eaves	2	341	3.00
Herm "Old Folks" Pillette	5	617	3.05
Wally "Preacher" Hebert	7	1893	3.07
Al Benton	3	268	3.09
Jim "Tiny" Chaplin	2	603	3.12

STRIKEOUTS   Single Season

Name	Year	Strikeouts
Frank Dasso	1944	253
"Sad" Sam Jones	1951	246
Manuel Salvo	1937	196
Manuel Salvo	1938	191
Vallie Eaves	1945	187
Jim "Mudcat" Grant	1957	178
Yank Terry	1941	172
Frank Dasso	1942	155
Frank Dasso	1943	154
Jim "Tiny" Chaplin	1937	151

Career (two or more seasons)

Name	Seasons	Strikeouts
Al Olsen	11	769
Wally "Preacher" Hebert	7	716
Manuel Salvo	6	688
Frank Dasso	3	562
Howard Craghead	5 *	526
Bob Kerrigan	7	456
Tom Seats	4	365
Ed Erautt	4	339
Byron Humphreys	4 *	295
John Carmichael	3	290

* part of season with another Pacific Coast League team

LANE FIELD MODEL

*I*n 1997, I built a scale model of Lane Field from the WPA blueprints. This was the brainchild of San Diego Hall of Champions Historian Don King. The original ballpark was built in less than two months by the Works Progress Administration following the Hollywood Stars move to San Diego in 1936. It took me almost five months to recreate this 48" by 54" basswood replica which went on display at the Hall of Champions in July 1997. It was removed in June 1998 to make room for the San Diego Padres old ballparks exhibition. The model is currently waiting for a permanent home where it can again be enjoyed by old-time fans who loved the Lane Field Padres and newer fans with an appreciation for baseball's golden history in San Diego.

The Lane Field model is as complete and accurate as possible. Even the distance from home plate to first base is scaled to 87 feet just as embarrassed groundskeepers discovered after 17 years at the "real" Lane Field. The only things missing from the model are the players, the fans and the termites.

Special thanks are extended to former Padres concessions and advertising manager Al Hogan who provided extensive information about Lane Field including photographs of the exact billboards used during the 1948 season. Graphic artist Tim Wayne reproduced colorized miniatures of the outfield signs and the center field scoreboard. The entire model was sprayed forest green by Jim Johnson of U. S. Painting Company and the plexiglass cover and stand were built by Chuck and Keith Bruso. Baseball scout Bob Dreher served as the sidewalk superintendent and Attorney Chuck Primeau provided legal advice for the project.

People have said that while looking at the model, they were able to hear echoes from the past...

Bill Swank, building Lane Field model.

BIBLIOGRAPHY

BOOKS:

Brandes, Ray and Swank, Bill, *The Pacific Coast League Padres, Lane Field: The Early Years, 1936-1946, Volume I*, San Diego Padres and San Diego Baseball Historical Society, 1997

Brandes, Ray and Swank, Bill, *The Pacific Coast League Padres, Lane Field: The Later Years, 1947-1957, Volume II*, San Diego Padres and San Diego Baseball Historical Society, 1997

Carter, Craig, *The Complete Baseball Record Book*, The Sporting News, 1989

Dobbins, Dick and Twichell, Jon, *Nuggets on the Diamond: Professional Baseball in the Bay Area from the Gold Rush to the Present*, Woodford Press, 1994

Gough, David, *They've Stolen Our Team!: A Chronology and Recollection of the 1960 Washington Senators*, Maverick Publications, 1998

Howard, Stacie Lee, *A Biography of Jack Graham*, University of San Diego, 1996

King, Donald R., *Caver Conquest: An Athletic History of San Diego High School*, San Diego High School Foundation, Inc., 1994

Lange, Fred W., *History of Baseball in California and Pacific Coast Leagues, 1847-1938*, 1938

Leutzinger, Richard, *Lefty O'Doul: The Legend That Baseball Nearly Forgot*, Carmel Bay Publishing Group, 1997

Mack, Connie, *My 66 Years in the Big Leagues*, John C. Winston Company, 1950

Marazzi, Rich and Fiorito, Len, *Aaron to Zuverink*, Avon Books, 1984

Mead, William B., *Even the Browns*, Contemporary Books, Inc., 1978

Okrent, Daniel and Lewine, Harris, *The Ultimate Baseball Book*, Houghton Mifflin Co., 1979

O'Neal, Bill, *The Pacific Coast League, 1903-1988*, Eakin Publications, Inc., 1990

Reichler, Joseph L., *The Baseball Encyclopedia*, Macmillan Publishing Company, 1988

Ritter, Lawrence S., *The Glory of Their Times*, William Morrow and Company, 1984

Society for American Baseball Research, *Minor League Baseball Stars*, Revised Edition, Ag Press, 1984

Society for American Baseball Research, *Minor League Baseball Stars, Volume II*, Ag Press, 1985

Spalding, John E., *Pacific Coast League Date Book*, Second Printing, 1997

Spalding, John E., *Pacific Coast League Stars: One Hundred of the Best, 1903 to 1957*, Ag Press, 1994

Spalding, John E., *Pacific Coast League Stars: Ninety Who Made It In The Majors, 1903 to 1957*, Ag Press, 1997

Spalding, John E., *Pacific Coast League Trivia Book*, 1997

Spalding, John E., *Sacramento Senators and Solons: Baseball in California's Capital, 1886 to 1976*, Ag Press, 1995

Starr, Bill, *Clearing the Bases: Baseball Then and Now*, Michael Kesend Publishing, Ltd., 1989

Stein, Fred, *Under Coogan's Bluff*, Chapter and Cask, 1981

Turner, Frederick, *When the Boys Came Back: Baseball and 1946*, Henry Holt, 1996

Zingg, Paul J. and Medeiros, Mark D., *Runs, Hits, and an Era*, University of Illinois Press, 1994

YEARBOOKS, MAGAZINES, NEWSLETTERS:

Baseball Guide and Record Book, Charles C. Spink & Son, 1943, 1944, 1945, 1946, 1947, 1948, 1949, 1950, 1951, 1952, 1953, 1954, 1955, 1956, 1957, 1958

Ebbets Field Flannels, Catalog No. 8, "El Beisbol," Fall 1994

Official Baseball Record Book, 1942, Charles C. Spink & Son, 1942

Pacific Coast Baseball League, 1903 to 1947, Pacific Coast Baseball League, 1947

Pacific Coast League News, various articles, 1946-49

Padre Parade, 1949, Padre Parade, 1949

Padre Parade, 1950, Padre Parade, 1950

Padre Parade, 1951, Padre Parade, 1951

Player Sketches and Lifetime Records,1950 Season, San Diego Baseball Club, 1950

Potpourri, Pacific Coast League Historical Society, various issues, 1994-1998

Records of San Diego Padres, 1936-1965, San Diego Evening Tribune, 1965

San Diego Magazine, "The All-Time Padre Team," Bojens, Ken, April-May 1952

Spaulding's Official Base Ball Guide, American Sports Publishing Co., 1937, 1938, 1939

Spaulding-Reach Official Base Ball Guide, American Sports Publishing Co., 1940, 1941

The Journal of San Diego History, "This was Paradise," Swank, William G. and Smith, James D. III, Winter 1995

The Museum of California, "Baseball Memories: The Pacific Coast League," Santiago, Chiori, Spring 1994

NEWSPAPERS:

San Diego Evening Tribune, various issues, 1950-58

San Diego Daily Journal, various issues, 1948-49

San Diego Reader, "Double-A Dago: When the Padres Played the Bush Leagues," Maracin, Paul R., July 11, 1991

San Diego Tribune-Sun, various issues, 1936-47

San Diego Union, various issues, 1936-58

San Diego Union-Tribune, various issues, 1993-1998

INDEX

Surnames in ALL CAPS indicate beginning of interview.